PIML

33

BEHIND THE BATTLE

Ralph Bennett was a leading producer of Ultra at
Bletchley Park during the war, and over the last
twenty years his many publications – notably his
books *Ultra in the West* and *Ultra and Mediterranean
Strategy* – have established his high reputation as an
intelligence historian.

Originally a medievalist, he was elected a Fellow
of Magdalene College, Cambridge in 1938, and
taught medieval history in college and university
before and after the war. He retired as President of
Magdalene in 1982 and now lives in Teddington.

BEHIND THE BATTLE

Intelligence in the War with Germany, 1939–1945

NEW AND ENLARGED EDITION

———

RALPH BENNETT

PIMLICO

Published by Pimlico 1999

2 4 6 8 10 9 7 5 3 1

First published in Great Britain by
Sinclair-Stevenson 1994
Pimlico edition 1999

Pimlico
Random House, 20 Vauxhall Bridge Road,
London SW1V 2SA

Random House Australia (Pty) Limited
20 Alfred Street, Milsons Point, Sydney,
New South Wales 2061, Australia

Random House New Zealand Limited
18 Poland Road, Glenfield,
Auckland 10, New Zealand

Random House South Africa (Pty) Limited
Endulini, 5A Jubilee Road, Parktown 2193, South Africa

Random House UK Limited Reg. No. 954009

A CIP catalogue record for this book
is available from the British Library

ISBN 0-7126-6521-8

Papers used by Random House UK Limited are natural,
recyclable products made from wood grown in sustainable forests.
The manufacturing processes conform to the environmental
regulations of the country of origin

Typeset by Deltatype Ltd, Birkenhead, Merseyside
Printed and bound in Great Britain by
Mackays of Chatham PLC

For
DAPHNE
in loving memory

Contents

List of Maps

Preface to the Pimlico Edition

This edition differs from that of 1994 in four main ways: several of the friends named on page xi, and one or two other readers, unknown to me, kindly pointed out accidental errors which had escaped my notice when reading the proofs. I am most grateful to them and have embodied their suggestions.

Fresh material, from newly-released documents and from recently-published books, has come to hand from time to time during the last few years. I have incorporated it where appropriate.

Appendices V, VI, and VII provide additional information, reprinted from my earlier books, illustrating both the way in which Ultra was produced and, in particular, the nature and effectiveness of its contribution in greater detail than was possible within the structure of the original text.

A very great deal of new information has been released to the Public Record Office in the last year or two. The bulk is so great that many months would be needed to examine it thoroughly. I have therefore attempted only to survey and sample it, incorporating such new evidence as fleshed out points I had made already. This seemed a safe procedure for two reasons. The new material appears to add much fresh detail but not to alter the broad shape of what is already known; the part played by high-grade intelligence in the Second World War is already well-established. There is one exception: decrypted Abwehr signals. Long promised, these are still embargoed. It seems likely that they will reveal more than is already known about how deception assisted in the formulation of Allied military plans.

Acknowledgments

Many people have helped me in many ways during the writing of this book, particularly by giving me information within their own special fields. Among them, I wish to thank the following with special warmth: Sir John Adye, Lord Annan, Professor Christine Brooke-Rose, Robert Cecil, Tony Clayton, Geoffrey Cowell, Noël Currer-Briggs, the late Rodney Dennys, Professor David Dilks, Hugh Dovey, Nicholas Elliott, Lord Ezra, the late Lord Freyberg, M. R. D. Foot, Sir Alexander Glen, the late Lord Harding of Petherton, the Reverend Nigel Hancock, Mrs Jean Howard, Sir David Hunt, Professor R. V. Jones, Hilary King, David Long, Andrew Lownie, Dr James Mark, Sir Stuart Milner-Barry, Mrs Mary Noble, Sir Patrick Reilly, Sir Brooks Richards, Ken Robertson, Mrs Annette Street, Alan Stripp, Dr Derek Taunt, Edward Thomas, Sir Peter Thorne, Dr Mark Wheeler, Sir Peter Wilkinson, Sir Edgar Williams.

I am grateful to Messrs Hamish Hamilton for permission to reuse maps drawn for *Ultra and Mediterranean Strategy, 1941–1945* (first published in 1989), to Mr David Charles who drew them, and to Mr Neil Hyslop who has drawn those which illustrate Chapter 7. Messrs Hodder & Stoughton and the author have kindly permitted the reproduction of a map from Mr Correlli Barnett's *Engage the Enemy More Closely* (first published in 1991).

Taking time off from her primary occupations, Mrs Jo Wallace-Hadrill converted successive instalments of my clumsy typescript, with its half-legible manuscript alterations, into a perfectly clean text, and this eased the labours of my editor, Miss Penelope Hoare, to whom I am also very grateful. My friend and publisher, Christopher Sinclair-Stevenson, has been a welcome guide and support throughout.

Finally, I want to thank my wife for her forbearance in tolerating my moods of abstraction and my sometimes one-track conversation over the last two or three years: I hope that, as an authoress herself, she will have understood the reason for my occasional absent-mindedness.

Ralph Bennett
London
November 1993

For the help in my attempt to survey the vast amount of new material which has come into the Public Records Office recently, I am extremely grateful for the guidance of Mrs Sarah Tyacke, Keeper of the Records, and Mr William Spencer, and for the assistance of Mrs Evelyn Nugent.

Ralph Bennett
July 1998

Europe and the Mediterranean
1939

Axis Powers and dependencies

Introduction

Behind the battle stands the admiral, general or air marshal in command of operations, and behind him the politician who appointed him and gave him his objective. But behind both lies intelligence about the enemy, without which the commander can only fumble blindly in the dark and must move towards his objective more by accident than design. Such at least is the position as we know it today. Intelligence has not always held so prominent a place, however, because in the past it was often so poor that commanders could afford to neglect it. The cardinal influence it now holds in military affairs was achieved only fifty years ago as it steadily improved in both quality and quantity. The ascent of intelligence to a secure place in the councils of military decision-makers may indeed in the future even be regarded as the chief legacy of the Second World War, perhaps ranking with the victory it did so much to win in the years between 1939 and 1945.

From 1941 or 1942, intelligence became sufficiently accurate and timely to light a commander's path towards victorious tactical action, and increasingly often to point his military and political superiors towards strategic decisions – but not, be it said at once, to deprive either of their freedom of initiative: if intelligence be allowed to shackle initiative, the advantage of possessing it is lost and the commander becomes no more than a puppet dancing to the enemy's tune.

Symbolically, the revolution in intelligence began on the day in December 1901 when Marconi showed that wireless communication over long distances was possible. If information could be exchanged between headquarters at home and ships at sea or armies in the field hundreds of miles away, and if orders issued by the former could take immediate effect, then agents (hitherto the usual gatherers and reporters of intelligence), with their unavoidably slower means of communication, were at once relegated to a secondary position. Nothing could prevent the other side from intercepting one's radio messages, reading them at once if in clear, or with some delay if in code or cipher* and if cryptographers could strip away the mask which hid their meaning. Both sides conducted the Battle of Jutland in 1916 with the aid of encoded radio messages, but the British had the advantage because the famous Room 40 had long been reading the High Seas Fleet's signals with the aid of the German naval codebook, captured by the Russians and handed over to the Admiralty in 1914. Marconi's demonstration was just twelve years old.

After years of neglect, the navy regained part of its former respect for intelligence before the outbreak of war in 1939, but the army and the RAF lagged sadly behind. Forgetting the radio and photographic intelligence which it had learned to exploit so profitably as early as 1916, the army began to rate intelligence as highly as it deserved only by the summer of 1942; progress to this end had taken several months longer than twenty-five years earlier. The RAF had far less use for it except in a narrowly tactical sense, and it played only a small part in Bomber Command's operations.[†]

Signals intelligence (Sigint) did not reach a dominant position until 1942, but it was unchallenged for the last three years of the war. Since I had been a producer of the special form of Sigint known as Ultra[‡] which fuelled its rise, when I began to write the present book I vowed not to let Ultra take all the limelight but to give fair treatment to all other sources of intelligence. My purpose has been much frustrated in a number of ways and for a number of reasons.

In the first place, Ultra practically monopolised strategic intelligence,

---

* Strictly, a *code* is based on a list of arbitrary number-groups the assigned meanings of which are known to both sender and receiver through a previously distributed codebook: a *cipher* replaces individual letters of the original plain text by some (usually mechanical) means according to a key which can be changed at intervals. The words 'code' and 'cipher', and derivatives like 'decode' and 'decipher' are, however, still sometimes used interchangeably. 'Cryptanalysis' is the process of recovering the plain text of the original message; when recovered, the original text becomes a 'decrypt'.

† The almost total (and irremediable) absence of the kind of intelligence Bomber Command most needed was only one of the reasons for this. See Chapter 4 below.

‡ See Appendix I, F. H. Hinsley and Alan Stripp, *Codebreakers* (Oxford University Press, 1993), 30–40, and *Oxford Companion to the Second World War* (Oxford University Press, 1995), s.v. 'Ultra'.

which is of more enduring value than short-term tactical or operational intelligence and therefore more worthy of record. Front-line patrols regularly took prisoners who, under interrogation, would reveal their units' present positions and occasionally also their likely future movements; the result was a constantly updated picture of the immediate opposition, its strength and its fighting quality. Intelligence officers in every theatre regularly followed the enemy order of battle 'with the piercing and almost affectionate scrutiny a Victorian Great Lady devoted to a legion of grandchildren'. Precise knowledge of it on all active fronts may be taken for granted from 1942 onwards, but it would have been tedious to repeat it over and over again here. On the other hand, the interrogation of prisoners, even of higher rank, or the bugging of their accommodation, seems to have contributed little strategic information except on a few occasions, some of which are described in the text.

The Y Service, which decoded just behind the front line the simpler codes used for instant communication between (for instance) tank squadron commanders and their headquarters, provided the same sort of tactical intelligence, but it varied widely in quantity and quality and in any case only scanty records appear to have survived. When, as frequently happened in the desert, Y gave access to tank repair-shop returns, valuable logistical results could be tabulated.

The interpretation of air photography was slow to receive proper recognition, but before long became an indispensable primary source, valued so highly that its headquarters at Medmenham in the Thames Valley saw the first full integration of British and United States intelligence staffs and produced the millions of photographs of the Normandy beaches from which scale models of its area were made for every assaulting unit before D-Day. Some of its most spectacular successes are recorded below, but this may scarcely have done justice to the repeated labours which, for instance, built up a complete record of the defences of the Gothic Line across Italy at all stages of its construction for comparison with Ultra reports of the same process.

Much ingenuity was expended on devising codes by which communication might be established with Allied servicemen in enemy hands, and useful information resulted in cases where speedy transmission of results was not essential – for example, prisoners in camps near enough to V1 and V2 research stations were able to report on test flights. But the escape of prisoners and their return to duty was the prime object of MI9, the section set up to handle this work: as Airey Neave observed, 'in the world of military intelligence we were extremely small beer'.

The records of the Secret Intelligence Service (SIS – otherwise known as MI6) and the Special Operations Executive (SOE) have hitherto been largely withheld from public scrutiny, but the more relaxed policy announced in 1993 is already bearing fruit, though too late for more than a few scraps to be used here. It must in any case be borne in mind that MI6's network of agents across the face of Europe was destroyed in 1940 and could not be rebuilt during the years of Nazi occupation. SOE was designed for subversion, not the gathering of intelligence, though the two could not always be kept separate – for example, in the Balkans. When information could be smuggled out of occupied Europe by Resistance organisations quickly enough for it to retain operational value it sometimes proved very useful; several examples are recorded below. As D-Day approached, such intelligence became more frequent and still more operational, like the information about the state of the railways provided by French and Belgian railway employees.

The Joint Intelligence Committee (JIC) – and the Joint Intelligence Staff (JIS) which served it with appreciations of enemy capabilities and intentions – was, in the reorganised form imposed upon it by Churchill in May 1940, theoretically the pinnacle of the intelligence pyramid, the point where digested and well-considered intelligence was prepared for the guidance of the Prime Minister and the Chiefs of Staff. But how far did they in fact fulfil the purpose for which they were founded? And to what extent did the JIC manage to reconcile the conflicting views of the service ministries which had so bedevilled pre-war intelligence and planning? It has usually been assumed that they were highly successful in both respects, at any rate once intelligence reliable enough to warrant reasonably confident forecasts became available. The only broad outline survey of the JIC and JIS regards them as 'truly effective' and as having incorporated 'the principle of the search for truth', while the official history of British Intelligence cites several JIC predictions approvingly without attempting a general verdict.*

It seems inherently unlikely, on the other hand, that the service ministries' and the Foreign Office's long-standing habit of nurturing their own predilections and avoiding discussion with others who were really partners in a joint enterprise could have been corrected so quickly while successive emergencies pressed on government and country and critical

---

* No up-to-date assessment of the JIC has been published, although some of the necessary material is already in the Public Record Office. See also Michael Herman, *Intelligence Power in Peace and War* (Cambridge University Press, 1996) and Peter Hennessy, *Muddling Through* (Gollancz, 1996).

decisions had to be taken in haste. Indeed, there were manifestly cases where divergent views were never harmonised – between the War Office and Air Ministry over bombing policy, for instance, or between Admiralty and Air Ministry about aircraft for Coastal Command. Again, the failure of the JIC to recognise the need, in the late autumn of 1944, to institute an in-depth re-examination of accumulated past intelligence to see whether it could yield a clue to the purpose of German preparations in the Ardennes has never been explained. It is to be hoped that the imminent release of the relevant JIC papers may throw light on these and similar matters and on the degree to which the question of a unified Ministry of Defence has prevented a recurrence.[*]

'Military intelligence is always out of date,' Sir Edgar Williams, Montgomery's Chief Intelligence Officer from November 1942 onwards, reminds us; 'there is a built-in time-lag. Better the best half-truth on time than the whole truth too late.' ('Too late', of course, in the sense that action must often be taken without waiting for complete and perfect intelligence.) 'In battle,' continues Sir Edgar, 'we deal not with the true but with the likely. Speed is therefore of the essence of the matter,' because it was so intimately associated with action.[†] Ultra was therefore his primary material. For a parallel reason the closeness of the intelligence/action relationship has usually been the basis of selection in what follows, and Ultra has predominated. In battle, most other sources were ancillary, although they contributed indispensable information in a number of cases, but usually with a time-lag.

---

[*] Apart from what is said in *British Intelligence* (but this is rather superficial and platitudinous) and the article by Edward Thomas in Andrew and Noares, *Intelligence and International Relations* (Exeter 1987) – but the author was also one of the authors of *British Intelligence* – there has been no investigation into the effectiveness of the JIC. Grave doubts about the extent to which it reconciled conflicting evidence were suggested by Lord Annan (who was a member of the JIS) in *Changing Enemies* (HarperCollins 1995).

In retrospect it is clear that it was a serious defect that it was never made the duty of the JIC, GC&CS or any other body to engage in long-range research and to produce reports and forecasts based upon it.

[†] Army and air Ultra signals could occasionally reach their destination in little more than three hours from the time at which the German message underlying them was sent, though the average delay was perhaps twice as much; at the height of the U-boat war in the Atlantic, the time-lag for naval signals was sometimes less than an hour.

When Thomas Hobbes wrote *Leviathan* in 1651 his famous dictum 'Force and fraud are in war the two cardinal virtues' was not a reflection upon the civil war which had just ended so much as a restatement of a practice at least as old as the Trojan Horse of Homeric legend or the Israelites' siege of Ai nearly 2,000 years ago.* The modern reinventor of the use of deception as a 'force-multiplier', Colonel Dudley Clarke, had a historical pedigree of more recent origin. In October 1917, Allenby had used deception (a briefcase containing false plans was 'lost' in no-man's land†) to mask his intention to take the practically impregnable Gaza entrenchments on the coast not by direct assault but by an outflanking attack through Beersheba, some thirty miles inland. Wavell, Commander-in-Chief Middle East in 1940, had served under Allenby, whom he greatly admired and whose biographer he became. It was Wavell who summoned Dudley Clarke to engineer deception first in Abyssinia and later in the whole Mediterranean theatre. From Clarke and the 'A' force he organised, there stemmed over the next three years schemes which, by planting 'notional' British divisions in Egypt and Palestine, allegedly waiting ready to pounce on Greece and the Balkans, utterly confused German strategy. Dudley Clarke's aims and methods were transferred westwards in time to shape the FORTITUDE deception which held German armour away from Normandy during the tricky period just after the D-Day landing by suggesting that Calais was the Allies' main objective and Normandy only a diversionary attack. An exact knowledge of the enemy's order of battle was essential, Clarke always insisted, and he looked to intelligence of all kinds to supply it. But Sigint, particularly Ultra, could give him two advantages that previous deception planners had lacked: first, an insight into enemy intentions and into their fears of what the Allies might do (he knew, for instance, that Hitler believed that the Balkans were the prime Allied objective in the Mediterranean and Italy only a convenient approach-route thither), for another of his principles was that deception could only be successful to the extent to which it played on existing hopes and fears; and secondly, a clear indication of the degree to which the enemy was being deceived, without which there was no way of knowing whether a particular deception plan was worth persisting in or not.

---

* Joshua hid 5,000 men in ambush to the west of the town before attacking frontally from the north, feigning flight with his main body and so luring the defenders away in vain pursuit. The ambushing force then captured and burned the town (Joshua. c. 9).
† An almost identical ploy was used in the desert in August 1942, with debatable results.

In sum: as the anaesthetist to the surgeon about to perform an operation, so the deception planner to his general; but the anaesthetic was intelligence.

Did intelligence, particularly Ultra intelligence, win the war? it may be asked. Did it measurably shorten it? The brief answers are 'No, but it greatly helped' and 'Not measurably.' A reasoned and responsible answer has many facets, and most of its conclusions can be only tentative.

First, however, an obvious point has to be emphasised: intelligence is useless unless there is sufficient force to exploit it. Ultra revealed German plans in detail before the Battle of Crete in May 1941 and again before the Battle of Medenine in March 1943: Crete was lost because there were too few men, guns and tanks to hold it; Medenine was won, clearing the way for Mongomery's advance into Tunisia, because there were plenty.

This limitation granted, in a number of specific cases intelligence may be credited with victory. Radar enabled the Few to defeat the larger numbers ranged against them in the Battle of Britain. Skilled interpretation of air photographs, stimulated by French and Polish Resistance reports, provided enough material for distinguished scientists to deduce the likely size and range of the V1s and V2s and to identify the factories which made them and the purpose of the sites being built to launch them; the bombing raids that followed so impaired construction that Hitler's secret weapon did not destroy London and win the war against all the odds in the autumn of 1944.

But as soon as the inquiry moves from the specific to the general, complex questions of historical method arise. To pretend for a moment that a particular piece of intelligence had not existed, in the hope of illuminating its value by observing the consequences does not help in the slightest, and may actually mislead. To remove, notionally, a single feature does not leave the rest of the situation unchanged. It merely takes away the bridle of reason which would otherwise restrain unlimited conjecture and opens the way to so many avenues of speculation that the mental horizon soon becomes clouded by fantasy. Other elements would probably have entered, for attempts would surely have been made to reach the same end by a different route from that which the absent intelligence offered. What these new elements would have been can only be guessed. Thus the imagined removal of one element in the real situation, undertaken with a view to deepening understanding of the whole, ends by so confusing it that history risks being turned into fiction.

Consider, for example, the Battle of the Atlantic, and suppose that the Allies had not been able to read Dönitz's instructions to his U-boat commanders. Convoys could not then have been re-routed round the U-boat packs, and the nearly disastrous ten-month intelligence black-out of 1942 would have been perpetuated. It would at first seem that in consequence so many ships would have been sunk that Great Britain would have been starved out and too few United States soldiers ferried across the Atlantic to make an invasion of Nazi Europe possible. But had the Admiralty been faced with such a situation without hope of relief (during the 1942 black-out, be it remembered, they always optimistically believed that the new U-boat key would yield to the cryptographers sooner or later), then who can tell whether 'Bomber' Harris might not have been forced against his will to surrender dozens of long-range Liberator aircraft to close the Atlantic air-gap and to scour the ocean for their prey (U-boats did not have *Schnorkels** at the critical time – though of course their development might have been accelerated)? Would not more money have been put into hastening the readiness of Hedgehog depth-charges, ship-borne radar, high-frequency direction-finding, more escort vessels and hunter-killer groups? What would have followed? Could a combination of these have made up for the loss of Ultra? How avoid recourse to guesswork when composing a reply to that question? The Hydra has grown new heads, one question has in no time become many, each more difficult to answer than the original. If we follow this route, purposeful historical analysis soon gives way to uncontrolled imaginings which lead nowhere.

Starting from scratch in 1939, British and American intelligence made up the lost ground in three years, and improved out of all knowledge in scope, incisiveness and penetration, while the German declined. Its contribution to naval and military operations was enormous, and by helping to win battles it also helped to raise morale – but to attempt to measure the exact size of that contribution or count the number of months by which it shortened the war is futile. Sound criteria of historical investigation repudiate any such attempt, and calculations of quantity cannot assist appreciation of quality. It is enough to wonder, with retrospective trepidation, how victory could have been won without Ultra.

But here there lurks an even more insidious danger, and one which no historian can wholly escape. 'Hindsight contributes powerfully to wisdom,' wrote Webster and Frankland in the last paragraph of their monumental study of the strategic air offensive. No one can avoid all the

---

* Air intakes on the surface enabling them to use their diesel engines when submerged.

pitfalls of hindsight, especially he who attempts to assess the effects of so obviously great an influence as Ultra. I have constantly sought to avoid them, but I hardly dare hope that I have circumvented them all.

Two final points.

Ultra intelligence existed only because of the cryptographers' skill, and was in that sense totally dependent upon it. On the other hand, the raw decrypts would have been of little value without the work of the translators and intelligence officers who rendered them into militarily comprehensible language and acquired skills of their own in extracting maximum meaning from them.* Ultra was created by a partnership of equals, given always that one partner was *primus inter pares*.

But both partners owed more than is often remembered to the devoted labours of the thousands of intercept operators who spent hours straining their ears to record faint and fading radio transmissions. The cryptographers who discovered how to break the cipher they recorded derived satisfaction from triumphing over seemingly insuperable obstacles, and the intelligence officers knew that by penetrating the obscurities of telegraphic German they were promoting victory. The intercept operators had no such immediate reward. The gabble of arbitrary Morse letters in their headphones conveyed no meaning, and they were not allowed to know the purpose of their work, yet the two main partners depended entirely on its accuracy.†

Ever present though it still is to those who lived through it, the Second World War now belongs to the past. No one much under the age of seventy now can remember the events to which the intelligence discussed here relates.‡ It does no harm to remind ourselves how much has changed since the 1940s, for history is best appreciated in perspective. In 1945, when the war ended, Marconi's transatlantic experiment (see p. xv)

---

* At Bletchley Park, Hut 6 produced the army and air raw material which Hut 3 translated, annotated and signalled to commands abroad. Hut 8 produced the naval decrypts which Hut 4 translated and teleprinted to the Admiralty for action.
† I vividly recall one example. A decrypt contained obviously important information about the movement of German troops, yet the word or phrase upon which its meaning turned was hopelessly corrupt. We called for duplicates from other intercept stations. Six or seven were equally corrupt, until the last of all gave a beautifully clear text. Only the vigilance of a single operator at his or her listening-set had preserved an important piece of military intelligence.
‡ The list of main events printed on pp. 378–81 may be useful.

was forty-four years old; 1945 itself is already forty-nine years ago. Hundreds of passengers now fly the Atlantic every day in Boeing 747s at speeds higher than any Spitfire, with only one man aboard, could ever reach. Had the 'smart bombs' of the Gulf war existed over fifty years ago, there would have been no need for Harris's 'area bombing', and no long-lasting controversy surrounding his name. If it were necessary, a desk-top computer could probably be devised now to perform the same task of decrypting Enigma which was once done by roomfuls of 'bombes' and their attendant Wrens.

It may be useful to draw attention to a few other differences of a more general nature between Then and Now.

Radio (but we usually called it 'the wireless') and telephones (but they were far less common than today) were taken for granted, but not television (the first, experimental, station was closed down after only a year's service on the outbreak of war).

Non-conductors and microchips did not exist, so nor did computers. The ancestor of modern computers was invented at Bletchley Park half-way through the war to decrypt messages transmitted by the Germans' new *Geheimschreiber* machine: the fact that it was officially christened 'Colossus' and nicknamed 'Heath Robinson' (from the famous cartoonist) indicates its size and complexity. That both Colossus and the 'bombes' which decrypted Enigma were so large was due to the absence of microchips.

Because decrypts might help to win the war, they were highly secret. 'Leaks', however, were not then greatly to be feared. In the 1940s it was accepted that secrets would of course always be kept; nowadays leaks are common even at the highest level and are busily seized on by the media. This is one of the most striking changes in social manners during the twentieth century.

There were no motorways. The thousands of troops placed in position for D-Day were conveyed along roads which had never carried anything but horse traffic until little more than a generation previously and had surfaces in conformity. There were few cars about; petrol rationing was strict, for every gallon had to be imported in tankers which were appallingly vulnerable to U-boats.

Rutherford had split the atom in 1935, but it remained to be discovered whether a bomb of devastating explosive power could consequently be constructed.

Technical means of protecting the secrecy of radio communications, and, conversely, of defeating others' efforts towards the same end, have undoubtedly changed and will continue to do so. The guiding principles of intelligence work, on the other hand, remain constant. There may be only one difference between then and now, resulting from the arrival on the scene of a new element. During the hectic months before and after D-Day, the intelligence organisation was almost but never quite overwhelmed by the volume of material it had to deal with. Already by the autumn of 1942 overtime working had occasionally been necessary in Hut 3 to clear an accumulation of decodes, and a little later there was a call for brevity in the working of signals because our exclusive radio channels were becoming overloaded. Although a backlog still sometimes occurred temporarily, increases in staff and more bombes kept the problem under control thereafter until an unprecedented increase in the number of new recipient stations stretched capacity dangerously after D-Day and again during the 'Battle of the Bulge'. In today's more peaceful conditions, where deliberate disinformation pollutes so many sources, where human agents can operate more freely but deliver reports of widely varying degrees of reliability (there were few agents of any consequence in the Second World War), and where in consequence 'noise' drowns out 'signals' (to borrow the radio operators' jargon), it may well be that sheer bulk makes it difficult to distinguish truth from falsehood and that decision-making may be more liable to error. If so, then military intelligence may have reached heights between 1939 and 1945 which will never be scaled again.

* * * *

The last sentence was pure speculation when it was written in 1994, but it seems to have been prophetic – though for a very different reason than that which I then proposed.

Like most others, only a few years ago I took it for granted the decryption would remain considerable, though perhaps a diminishing, element in intelligence-gathering. This seems no longer to be true.

On page 984 of the new edition (1996) or his classic work *The Codebreakers*, David Kahn writes: 'The war of cryptographer against cryptanalyst has been won by the cryptographer. The only way properly encrypted messages can be read nowadays is by theft or betrayal . . . of course cipher clerks will always make mistakes . . . but massive solutions, as of Enigma, are becoming a thing of the past.'

Intelligence is therefore reverting to the situation which prevailed before 20 May 1940. Fifty years later, an era has closed for ever. Where Ultra once brought light, thick darkness broods again.

1

1939

Thick Darkness Brooding

The warrior heroes of Britain's past well understood how intelligence about the enemy could help them shape their own plans and confuse the opposition. 'No war can ever be conducted without early and good intelligence,' wrote the Duke of Marlborough. With this in mind he designed the daring strategy which fooled the French into thinking that from his base in Holland he intended to thrust either up the Moselle valley or into Alsace; instead, he led his army on a 500-mile march to the Danube (on the banks of which he had prepared dumps of food, clothing and boots in advance) to the victory of Blenheim and a check to Louis XIV's ambitions. On the way he received the reward of his boldness in striking deep into enemy-held territory: one of his agents discovered Marshal Tallard's whole plan of campaign.

Wellington went one better in the Peninsula. He founded the Corps of Guides to plan his route through unmapped country, to interrogate French, Spanish and Portuguese prisoners and to collect any intelligence which might help him fulfil his assigned task of diverting as much of Napoleon's army as possible away from the conquest of Europe (in doing so he was exactly foreshadowing the methods Eisenhower and Alexander, acting under identical instructions, would use in Italy in 1943–4). At sea, in a century when even the most urgent naval news could travel little faster than the battle fleets, Nelson nevertheless managed to locate the French ships in Aboukir Bay and off Cape Trafalgar and beat them soundly each time.

Sadly, their examples were forgotten in the hundred years of peace between Waterloo and Mons – the wars in the Crimea and South Africa abound with evidence – during which the ever-growing burden of Empire and an increasingly narrow profes-sionalism of military routine discouraged original thought. The trench warfare of 1914–18 so embedded in the military mind the conviction that intelligence (whether secured by air photography or by patrolling no-man's land) was purely tactical that for the next twenty years the army lost sight of all wider aims and scarcely concerned itself with intelligence at all. Though Allenby had briefly broken the constricting mould in Palestine, few paid heed except Wavell, who was himself to become Commander-in-Chief in the Middle East in 1940–1 and launch both the Long Range Desert Group for land reconnaissance and a hugely successful deception programme to convince the enemy that he had far more troops and resources than he disposed of in reality.

The navy adhered strictly to traditional practices dating back to the age of sail; promotion came only to men with a good record of sea service, and 'specialists' were looked down on. This attitude so shackled the first modern intelligence-gathering feat (the decoding of the German High Seas Fleet's radio communi-cations) that Jutland ended as a drawn battle instead of a victory of annihilation. The next twenty years saw little change in outlook; almost the sole concession to modernisation was Lord Louis Mountbatten's establishment in 1927 of the naval Y Service, to intercept, decode and exploit potential enemies' wireless telegraphy (W/T) signals in the Mediterranean.

So hampered by the parsimony of politicians and so overlaid with the mildew of the years were the thought-processes of the senior officers of the British armed services by the 1930s that it is small wonder that they were ill-prepared for the emergency of 1939. Scarce and obsolete equipment was a handicap, but so was their lack of the mental resilience required to counter the quicker reactions of Hitler's generals. If the army was out of date and the navy unready to face a recurrence of the U-boat threat it had overcome twenty-five years before, the RAF, whose traditions were no more than a generation old, was dominated by a misguided strategic theory – that wars could be won by bombs alone – which blinded it to the fact that it had no means of locating its targets accurately enough to cause significant damage, nor bombs large enough to cripple German industry, nor aircraft capable of carrying them.

Fifty years later it is astonishing that Britain was not overwhelmed in the weeks after the fall of France and the nightmare of Dunkirk in May and June 1940; still more surprising that Providence or Hitler's stupidity granted the two further years required to organise an adequate intelligence system as well as to manufacture new weapons; most remarkable of all, that within that period it was possible to develop and exploit a new and unprecedented intelligence source: the German Enigma cipher, which revealed the enemy's dispositions, his state of readiness for battle, and even his strategic intentions, thus giving the Allied commanders an advantage enjoyed by none of their predecessors.

The distinction between political and military intelligence is far harder to draw in time of peace than in time of war, since democratic states at any rate will only take military action when political pressure has failed, as in the Gulf crisis of 1990–1. In Britain in the 1930s, politicians and civil servants, admirals and generals, were far from clear about the nature of either, and were not in the habit of distinguishing between political and military intelligence. By itself, this accounts for much of pre-war Britain's failure to realise the danger into which it was drifting. The drift and the danger were exacerbated, moreover, by a lack of urgency at the top – it did not help the conduct of government business that Chamberlain did not like being disturbed after dinner in London or at weekends when he was at Chequers (where anyhow there was only one telephone, and that in the butler's pantry)* – by a too rigid demarcation between government departments, and by the mutual jealousies of their staffs. The Foreign Office regarded intelligence as its own province, but so did Admiralty, War Office and Air Ministry within their own spheres, with the result that there followed duplication or triplication of effort on the one hand and a refusal on the other to collaborate in drawing operational conclusions. Each service made separate submissions to the Chiefs of Staff without taking into account how others' needs could affect a situation which all knew made tight financial control unavoidable.

Public opinion must bear much of the blame for Britain's unreadiness for war. The England of the mid-1930s was strangely unconcerned with events beyond its shores and slow to note the signs of coming danger. In the carefree days of 1934, millions voted in the Peace Ballot for the total abolition of military aircraft. In both Abyssinia (when Italy invaded in 1935) and Spain (when Franco rebelled against the elected government in 1936 and overthrew it in 1939) there seemed to be 'a quarrel in a far-away country between people of whom we know nothing' – Chamberlain's infamous phrase of 1938 – even though in the latter case Englishmen had been recruited to fight in the International Brigade for the Spanish government. The discovery, at the time of Edward VIII's abdication in December 1936, that the press had kept the public ignorant of the King's disgraceful goings-on with Mrs Simpson caused little outcry against it; and few listened attentively to Winston Churchill's warnings about Hitler until it was almost too late. 'Neither Parliament nor public opinion seemed to have any idea of the vital need for urgency,' wrote Sir Hastings Ismay, then Deputy Secretary of the Committee of Imperial Defence, as late as 1937; 'in the years before the war we lived in a world of imagination.'†

---

* Similarly, the Prime Minister was not provided with a domestic staff, a car, or an official to deal with press and radio at this time. D. Dilks, *The Office of Prime Minister* (Hull U.P. 1993), p. 4.
† Noël Coward wrote *Present Laughter* and the patriotic *This Happy Breed*

The dreadful casualties on the western front between 1914 and 1918 engendered a faith in the League of Nations which even the League's failure to stop Italy's invasion of Abyssinia did not diminish. But an 'insular electorate whom none dared to educate', as Sir Robert Vansittart (Permanent Under-Secretary at the Foreign Office 1930–7) called the public, was firmly convinced that 'it could not happen again' because the whole world recognised that war was now unthinkable and could not envisage any other than a peaceful outcome to international tension.

Yet, paradoxically, the Japanese bombing of Nanking in 1938 and the film of H. G. Wells's *Shape of Things to Come* seized the public mind, and so did the popular broadcaster C. E. M. Joad's announcement that 'a bomb [he did not specify what size or weight] will flatten a square mile of a city'. In view of opinions like these it seemed vain to prepare a defence which could not possibly succeed; at least 200,000 casualties were expected in 1938 from the first raid on London but ony 6,000 hospital beds were set aside to receive them. Ignorance even infected the scientists: Professor J. B. S. Haldane convinced himself that the sound wave which a bomb creates is like the Last Trump, because those within its range will either be killed or disabled for life by burst eardrums. Government circles were not immune; in May 1938 the head of the Civil Service and the Secretary of the Committee of Imperial Defence, recommending the establishment of a Ministry of Home Security should war break out,

during the summer of 1939, and planned rehearsals to begin in August. Although he feared that they might get no further in the autumn (they were in fact first produced in 1942) he wrote 'bathed, as we all were at that time, in a glow of governmental optimism and complacency, it would have been churlish to take too gloomy a view and so I persevered, . . .' – Drawing on the menus for Stanley Baldwin's farewell dinner on 25 May 1937 and other grand occasions, the present Duchess of Devonshire pointed out in the *Spectator* of 12 February 1994 that London society in the 1930s was given to overeating as gross as that of Edwardian times.

registered their impression that 'the national will to resist might be broken' by mass bombing 'if the situation in the devastated areas cannot be got under control at once'.

Politicians and public alike in fact committed the cardinal sin against which the intelligence community has constantly to be on its guard: too often they read the objective facts of German rearmament and the deeply militaristic nature of even the Nazi Labour Service and other superficially Boy-Scout-like organisations in the light of their subjective presupposition that peace would endure. Baldwin was realistically right, though he may have been morally wrong, to keep the rearmament he knew was necessary out of his 1935 manifesto because it might lose him the General Election. Those of us who experienced life in Germany in the middle 1930s remember how impossible it was, two or three years before Munich, to convince even our most intelligent friends at home that appeasement could not avert war because Nazism was intrinsically warlike. When I returned to Cambridge in October 1936 after a year's study at Munich University, my views about Nazism were dismissed by my older colleagues as those of a too impressionable young man who would, of course, see sense as he grew in age and experience.

Hindsight makes the attitude of government and people almost incomprehensible today, but recognition of it is an indispensable preliminary to understanding British political and military intelligence failures in the 1930s, and to the avoidance of a too simplistic dismissal of them as the consequence of mere stupidity.

To avoid hindsight and so far as possible to interpret past records in the light of contemporary, not later, habits of mind is a fundamental lesson for every historian. Unless he learns this lesson he cannot present a fair and balanced picture of the past. On the whole, the nearer the events described are to the historian's own time, the truer his description will be; it will be easier to reconstruct the outlook of the infantry who manned the Flanders trenches in 1917 or even of the cavalry at Balaclava than that of the longbowmen at Agincourt or the *huscarles* at Hastings, or of the leaders under whom each fought. Unfortunately, however, during the last dozen or so years – that is, since the Ultra and other previously secret files were opened – several books about the Second World War have been published which display an almost complete disregard for the known risks of hindsight and distort the events of only forty or fifty years ago for a polemical purpose. One reason for this may be a thirst to be 'different', to gain prestige as the author of a 'historical revision' aimed at overthrowing accepted beliefs about leading figures like Churchill, or key strategic decisions like that to invade Italy in 1943. Another reason may be the Cold War, which gained almost universal acceptance for the need to prepare against sudden attack by a hostile power, and a desire to show that mistaken decisions were at least partly responsible for forty years' hostility to Russia, the former ally of Britain and America. Whether these be the reasons or no, such books make it necessary to emphasise firmly that many plausible but misleading interpretations of Second World War events, usually resting on half-truths, doubtful inferences and a biased selection of evidence, are in circulation today, and to warn against apportioning blame for actions which appear wrong or ill-advised only in the light of things which have happened since and which therefore can have had no influence on the decisions or policies that caused them.

Underlying the attitude of the government and the armed services in the 1930s lay the stark fact of financial stringency after 1918 and the Depression a decade later, with resultant Treasury control over defence expenditure. Ironically, it was Winston Churchill who, as Chancellor of the Exchequer, in 1919 imposed the Ten-Year Rule – the axiom that Britain would not be engaged in a major war for the next ten years and therefore need not prepare for it during the next twelve months – which was progressively extended until 1932, paralysing the armed services because, it has been said, they came to feel that they need never be ready for war. In the material sphere the Rule was responsible for shortages which proved nearly disastrous at the end of the decade. Examples are legion. As early as 1930 the Chiefs of Staff reported that Britain could defend neither itself nor its Empire against attack, and they repeated the warning annually; the fleet had only enough ammunition to fire its anti-aircraft guns for twenty minutes in the mid-1930s; only forty-four AA guns could be assembled to defend London at the time of Munich; the British army did not possess a single complete armoured division in 1939, and its tanks were inferior to the German throughout the war; our pre-war petrol tins leaked precious fuel into the sand throughout the desert campaign and even later, but German jerricans did not; during the 1930s SIS agents were not provided with the portable W/T sets needed to report their discoveries, even in 1941 the sets issued to British agents in the Balkans were too heavy for easy transport in the frequent emergencies of their users' lives (the first model was so heavy that it had to be carried on mule-back), and really light, compact and reliable sets were not designed until 1943.

Material signs of Britain's unpreparedness for war are sufficiently well known today. Less familiar is an equally disturbing unreadiness in the sphere of intelligence. It is a commonplace now that an efficient and productive intelligence service is even more valuable to the weaker party in a potential conflict than to the stronger, yet little thought was given to intelligence and its uses before 1939. It was ridiculous as well as disgraceful that the delegation sent to Moscow in August 1939 to negotiate a military convention was not given the political and military intelligence briefing (for instance, would Russian troops be allowed to cross Poland to fight against Germany?) it would need if humiliation of the kind it in fact received at Marshal Voroshilov's (Commissar for Defence) hands was to be avoided, and it was naive not to wonder whether Stalin, long distrusted as an arbitrary tyrant, might double-cross the delegation and prepare an agreement with Hitler (as the Soviet defector Krivitsky had predicted a year earlier) while the talks were still going on.

There was common agreement that Germany's rapid rearmament was rendering Britain relatively weaker almost by the day, yet no one in authority seems to have realised that greater attention to gathering intelligence (particularly to measure the real strengths of the German army and air force more accurately and analyse them more objectively, and to discover more about Hitler's intentions) might compensate in some degree for material weakness. Both Fuller and Liddell Hart, the two accredited military writers of the day, preached economy of force, but neither seems to have extended his thought in this apparently obvious direction. The warnings of a better-oriented and more highly regarded intelligence service would at least have enabled scarce resources to be disposed to the best advantage. No one at any level of authority in the 1930s, however, seems to have realised that a little more money and effort spent on gathering and analysing intelligence in a deliberately planned, rational and purposeful way might to some degree offset the inadequacy of the means available to undertake the country's worldwide responsibilities and to protect their nerve-centre in Britain.

The universal failure to recognise where help might be found distinguished the 1930s from the present, but no more than their lack of computer technology or satellite surveillance can it justify over-hasty or disdainful condemnation. What seems obvious to the 1990s simply had not dawned on the consciousness of the 1930s. However, although intelligence is collected today with incomparably greater assiduity than sixty years ago, this does not always bring greater enlightenment: the modern deluge of apparently irreconcilable detail can be great enough to hinder the process of analysis or even obstruct it altogether. An opposite situation, that is to say, may lead to a similar state of bewilderment: too much information, it has been felicitously said, 'would super-saturate the organisation that was trying to interpret it – the collation cat would be choked by cream and drowned in whey'.

Unawareness of the extent to which intelligence could resolve their uncertainties and relieve their tensions disfigured the thought of the Cabinet and permeated every level of authority. Vansittart, whose private sources enabled him to give repeated warnings of the German danger, called Neville Chamberlain 'an earnest and ignorant provincial who was bound to err if he plunged into diplomacy', ignorant of strategy (like the rest of his Cabinet) and 'with no idea what Germans were like'. But Vansittart made no allowance for the Foreign Office's own lack of any system for sifting the important from the unimportant in the intelligence with which it provided the Prime Minister. At the time of the Munich crisis, for instance, reliable reports from the British Military Attaché in Prague to the effect that the Czech army could hold out for two or three months were not accorded proper weight (they may, however, have been over-optimistic). In March 1939, when Hitler was occupying Prague and extinguishing the Czech state, Vansittart's successor, Cadogan, was 'daily inundated by all sorts of reports' which he had no means of evaluating. In spite of this, it was more than four months before the Foreign Office agreed to remedy this disastrous state of affairs by agreeing to participate in the work of the Joint Intelligence Committee (which it had shunned since its inception three years before), whose main duty was to assess and co-ordinate intelligence for the Chiefs of Staff.

Hore Belisha, Secretary of State for War 1937–40, was ignorant of military affairs when he was appointed, and for almost his first twelve months of office relied on the advice of Basil Liddell Hart, the prolific military writer, whose radical views on tank warfare and much else did not prevent him from backing the policy of appeasement.

Lord Halifax, Foreign Secretary 1938–40, long believed the Nazis open to rational persuasion; 'Hitler struck me as very sincere,' he reflected after meeting him in 1937. Detesting war, and paralysed by current overestimates of German strength, he was ill equipped to see through the reassuringly optimistic reports of Sir Nevile Henderson, the gullible British Ambassador in Berlin. Halifax acquiesced in the ascendancy which the arch-appeaser, Horace Wilson, gained over Chamberlain when that of Warren Fisher waned after Munich,* and, since he did not accompany the Prime Minister on any of his solo attempts to negotiate with Hitler, had no opportunity to restrain him.

The unconcern of the Cabinet and its senior officials with the looming Nazi danger, and their extraordinary incomprehension of its true nature, which nearly led to the destruction of their country, are easy to ridicule nowadays. But this at least can be said in their defence. They had agents' reports, but very little else, to rely on apart from their own personal observation and judgment. The Government Code and Cipher School could not read German diplomatic traffic (or Russian either) because it was transmitted in a code (the one-time pad) which is practically unbreakable. Agents' reports are not only often contradictory but are bound to include a measure of subjective impression the degree of which cannot be tested except by an equally fallible subjective judgment. Decrypts of official correspondence, on the other hand, escape this (from the eavesdropper's point of view) tremendous drawback because neither of the correspondents knows that he is being overheard. Provided they were properly understood, Enigma decrypts could safely be trusted to give an objective picture. If men like Halifax and Cadogan distrusted the reliability of agents, they deserve a degree of respect for their caution; and they can hardly be blamed for lacking decrypt experience they had no means of acquiring.

The War Office had a semblance of an excuse for unpreparedness. Although as early as 1934 the Chiefs of Staff had (more by

---

* Sir Warren Fisher, PUS Treasury 1919–39; Sir Horace Wilson, Adviser to Government 1923, confidant of Baldwin and Chamberlain, Head of Civil Service 1939–40.

luck than by judgment) set 1939 as the likely date for war against
Germany, it was not until 1937 that the Cabinet put the
hypothesis of a European war even as high as fourth on its list of
priorities (anti-aircraft for home defence was now at the top), and
although the Minister for the Co-ordination of Defence realised
that there would be severe criticism if in the end the country had
to defend France as it had done in 1914, there was in his opinion
no feasible financial alternative to restricting exenditure on the
army. With the annexation of Austria in March 1938 and the
approach of the crisis over Czechoslovakia it at last became clear
that an army might have to be committed to fighting on the
continent, but it was only after the occupation of Prague in
March 1939 that the army began to reap any benefit from this
welcome change of policy. At this stage, instead of earlier, it
became apparent that to expand the army in a hurry and to
improvise an intelligence service to suit the new political
direction would be even more difficult than anything which had
been attempted in 1914.

What makes this blindness to the probability of eventual war
with Germany so astonishing is that well-founded warnings had
been given in good time and fully appreciated by some in
Whitehall. Colonel (later General Sir Andrew) Thorne was the
author of one of the earliest and certainly one of the most
explicit. Thorne was Military Attaché in Berlin 1932–5. His
reports have not received the attention they deserve, although
they evidently formed the basis of War Office appreciations of
German army developments at the time. In 1934 Thorne
foretold the reorganisation and threefold expansion of the
Wehrmacht and revealed the (still illegal) build-up of an air
force. During the first half of 1935 his final reports noted that
mobility of armour, mechanisation and the choice of favourable
ground for attack were leading features of army training. In
addition, Thorne passed on an account which had been given
him by the Assistant Military Attaché of the development of
long-range rockets, and noted that the most promising way for

Germany to break the hostile ring it felt surrounding it was, according to German generals of his acquaintance, to reach an agreement with the USSR. Thorne's observation and logical analysis were appreciated at their true worth not only by Sir Eric Phipps, British Ambassador in Berlin, but by the Foreign Office (notably, but unsurprisingly, by Vansittart), which sent copies to the Admiralty and Air Ministry. Some thought, of course, that he had 'gone native'; Earl Stanhope, Parliamentary Under-Secretary for Foreign Affairs, minuted that after six months in command of the Guards Brigade at Aldershot (his next posting) 'his views will be much healthier ... than this effusion'.

Large sections of two 1935 War Office appreciations of German rearmament and of the future shape of the British army owe much to Thorne's reports. These papers, on the whole accurate in their estimate of present trends and future needs, make it clear that even in the unwelcoming atmosphere of the 1930s a diligent and critical observer could collect reliable evidence and by presenting it lucidly ensure that it made an impact on the appropriate professional authorities. The exception unfortunately proved the rule – that both the War Office and the Cabinet were unable or unwilling to draw the logical conclusions and take the necessary action. One of Thorne's successors, the later Major-General Kenneth Strong, who had also served in the German intelligence section of the War Office, later explained the reason: 'There was an extraordinary disinclination to listen to our reports, and much disbelief.' He goes on to say that, when he lectured on the German army, the senior officer present would always follow with a warning to the audience not to be too much influenced by what he had said about German military strength.

Numbers had fallen rapidly in the post-1919 army, under the impact of the Ten-Year Rule; the prospects of promotion were too limited to offer an attractive career to young men, and intake from the universities dropped from eighty in 1914 to twelve in

1924, for instance. Moreover, there was a return to nineteenth-century ways in the early inter-war years. Senior officers hoped to go back to the horse – 'that major obstacle to military development' – and at the Staff College, Camberley, where promising officers of middle rank were groomed for high command, snobbery was rife. Wing Commander Trafford Leigh-Mallory (who as an air chief marshal was to command the Allied air forces under Eisenhower in 1944) was looked down on in 1929 because he had no private income, and the drag hunt (participation in which twice a week was compulsory for many years) was as prominent a feature of life as military studies, and there was no instruction in strategic intelligence at all. A veteran of 1914–18 and a lieutenant-colonel at the age of twenty-two but now reduced in rank with the return of peace, Captain John Harding (later Field Marshal Lord Harding of Petherton, CIGS 1953–5) attended Staff College in 1928–30; he recalled Montgomery as a brilliant teacher of tactics but remembered no instruction in strategic intelligence. (However, many years later he warned me against supposing that 'in the course of instruction in tactics and battlefield leadership no attention was paid to the collection of information from all available sources, and to the collation and the use of [tactical] intelligence'.) The future Major-General Strong, who was to be Eisenhower's Chief of Intelligence 1943–5, recorded that when he was at Camberley in 1932–3 the teaching was based almost entirely on 1914–18 tactics, in spite of their manifest lack of success, that initiative was not encouraged, and that the participation of the RAF in the land battle was discounted. 'I remain astonished that the British army performed so well in the second world war,' he wrote in reference to the Harding case, 'in spite of its almost conscious efforts to delay the promotion of its best officers and its pre-war inadequacy of training.' Later on, he was forbidden to refer, in his lectures at the Imperial Defence College, to the possibility that the German air force might be employed in the land battle, although this was in fact its main function. The official War

Office report drawn up in 1940 after an examination of current shortcomings admitted that 'Little time is devoted to intelligence instruction at the Staff College.' Haig had set the pattern for the inter-war years when he wrote, 'Intelligence has a very small place in the army in peace time.'

During the 1914–18 war Major Alexander Scotland had become an ace interrogator of prisoners-of-war and an acknowledged expert on the German army. He returned to civilian life in 1919, but retained such close connexions with Germany that he was one of the first to sense the coming danger. In 1937, being nearly sixty years old and believing that British intelligence was in an even worse state than in 1914, he wrote to the War Office offering to lecture (without fee) on military intelligence at Sandhurst or elsewhere. He received a polite postcard in acknowledgment, but no more. Yet there was no one as well qualified as he in a field which would certainly be of vital importance if war broke out.[*]

The post of Director of Military Intelligence was suppressed in 1928 and its duties combined with those of the Director of Military Operations until the two were again separated in 1939. The Intelligence Corps suffered a similar period of eclipse, during which instruction in intelligence ceased altogether; there was no provision for training intelligence officers until after Munich, and fewer than 250 (mostly retired regular 'dug-outs' of First World War vintage) had been through even a short refresher course by the summer of 1939. Most of the intelligence officers sent to France with the British Expeditionary Force (BEF) were therefore either out of touch with recent developments or entirely untaught; there were none at all in the Middle East until spring 1940.

There was far too much dead wood in the higher command; few senior officers had much use for intelligence, particularly

[*] The error was corrected in 1940. Scotland rose to command the London interrogation centre and took a leading part in the war-crimes trials at Nuremburg.

anything that was not severely tactical. Montgomery later said that 'an extensive use of weed-killer' would have been the only remedy. Liddell Hart thought Montgomery-Massingberd 'the high priest of humbug' and 'only positive in stamping out originality', Cadogan that Ironside (who had been the model for John Buchan's Richard Hannay) was stupid, Grigg (Permanent Under-Secretary at the War Office) that he was 'the worst and most incompetent of men'; yet both held the office of Chief of the Imperial General Staff (for which Ironside is said to have had 'neither the clarity of mind nor the strength and articulacy to persuade politicians which the post demanded') in the years immediately before the war. A few months after Dunkirk, Dill (CIGS 1940–1, and a great improvement on his immediate predecessors) saw the army's main weakness as consisting in the fact that officers were 'admirably versed in weapon training but had little stimulus to use their imagination and look at military problems with a broad view'; Brooke, who succeeded to the same office in 1942 and held it with the greatest distinction until victory was won, lamented in 1942 that 'half our corps and division commanders are totally unfit for their appointments, and yet if I were to sack them I could find no better'. Probably their chief shortcomings were their total inability to comprehend the value or purpose of intelligence (in both senses of the word) and the intense conservatism which often made them ignore unpalatable information that ran contrary to their inherited beliefs.

Spellbound by the rise of the German army and mistakenly confident that German industry would be able to supply all its needs as soon as war came, the War Office took no steps to work out in advance what would be the best way to counter the threatened *Blitzkrieg*. Its technical branch refused to believe that anti-aircraft guns could be used against tanks (Thorne had already indicated increasing German reliance on anti-tank guns) and persisted in that belief not only when the later-famous 88s appeared in an anti-tank role in pre-war German manoeuvres and were used for the same purpose in France in 1940, but for many months after Rommel had repeatedly used them to cut British armoured formations to pieces in the desert two years later – a prime example of the opinionated obstinacy which prevented all the service departments from crediting any evidence which could not be reconciled with their established doctrines. Later, such warnings of the speed and extent of German rearmament as the military attachés in Berlin (hedged round as they were by international conventions which forbade spying) could gather fell victim to the same obstinacy. As psychologists conclude, 'the greater the impact of new information, the more strenuously will it be resisted'.

General Sir Hastings Ismay, Churchill's right-hand man at the Ministry of Defence, expressed a general truth in succinct terms when he wrote that on being posted to the War Office in 1933 he found it 'hidebound, unimaginative, impersonal and overpopulated', though he respected the ability of a few individuals.

In material terms, the navy suffered less than the army from the Ten-Year Rule – not that this meant that it was at all well off – because imperial defence might at any moment require the despatch of a considerable fleet to the Pacific, where Japanese ambitions were a constant source of anxiety in the 1920s and early 1930s. Warships were a more urgent need than tanks or guns, and took far longer to build, so they were given priority.

While this meant that naval officers were more actively engaged in time of peace than their army equivalents, it did not make them immune from similar diseases. They forgot until almost too late that a revived German navy might again threaten British trade routes and restore the need for convoys and convoy protection, misguidedly believed that an immediate return could be made to the hunter-killer groups that had harried U-boats in 1917, and grossly underestimated the number of ships that would be required to escort a convoy across the Atlantic. Yet in 1929 a German admiral, Wolfgang Wegener, had published a book (a copy of which lay, unread, in the Admiralty library until Vansittart drew the attention of the First Sea Lord to it ten years later) which advocated combined attacks on convoys by surface ships and submarines as a main feature of German naval strategy. Tradition reigned almost unchallenged and called for little innovative openness of mind. A conflict arose between the 'blue-water school', to whom experience at sea and acceptance of senior officers' superior wisdom represented all that was right and proper, and the so-called 'intellectuals', who endeavoured to move a little away from past practice in recruitment and training. Admiral Sir Herbert Richmond, a leader of the 'intellectuals' and later Professor of Naval History at Cambridge, issued a set of proposals in 1933, but the Admiralty turned them down. Richmond's *Naval Training*, based on his experiences as Director of Training in 1918 and on later reflection, makes the conflict of views plain but at the same time reveals the limitations of the apparently liberal and progressive case. 'It is not long since a highly placed Sea Lord informed the present writer that the accurate running of torpedoes in the battleships was a factor of greater importance to the efficiency of the Navy than a study of war,' he wrote, adding (evidently in reference to a recent controversy), 'We cannot afford again to waste our efforts . . . in attempting to deal with the danger of submarines by the utilisation of trained seals while rejecting the method of convoy.' Yet, while he cogently urged the beneficent influence of a broad education upon the character of naval officers and wrote wisely about strategy, he deprecated the need for a staff course or an exclusive staff branch and nowhere mentions intelligence as a component of that education or of sound strategical appreciations.

Hand in hand with this went a steady decline in the repute of intelligence in the navy of the 1920s and early 1930s: no steps were taken, for instance, in spite of continuing fears of Japan, to increase the number of naval officers who could understand Japanese. Outside the Mediterranean, signals intelligence was almost completely ignored: the naval W/T traffic of foreign powers was not studied before 1938, although it had been a prime source twenty years earlier. In June 1939, on the eve of war, the Admiralty did not even know, until the Prime Minister informed it, that Raeder, the head of the German navy, had announced in a public speech that Hitler had sanctioned a huge expansion of the fleet. It has been suggested that this lassitude represented both a reaction against the fame of Room 40 (where German naval signals had been decoded) and Admiral 'Blinker' Hall during the 1914–18 war and a completely mistaken belief that former skills could be instantly recreated should the need arise. Whatever the reason, the decline was not arrested until Admiral Godfrey was appointed Director of Naval Intelligence (DNI) in 1938, although his predecessor, Admiral Troup, had made some moves in the right direction, notably by founding the Operational Intelligence Centre (OIC) at the Admiralty, which was subsequently to become the focal point where intelligence and operations met.

Until Godfrey saw the need to create an organisation to analyse incoming news, little progress was made towards linking intelligence to action. But Godfrey himself knew little about intelligence when he took office. In 1939, he later wrote, 'none of the Assistant Chiefs of Staff or directors of operational divisions knew anything about intelligence. I myself knew precious little. There is no particular reason why we should have done, because the subject was swept out of sight during the twenty years of peace.' In the spring of 1939 the Abwehr (the German equivalent of SIS) planted a rumour on the British Embassy in Berlin to the effect that the Luftwaffe would make a surprise bombing attack on the Home Fleet during the Easter leave period. Without consulting the DNI, the Cabinet ordered the manning of the fleet's anti-aircraft guns,* and the First Lord

---

* This may have been a less useful precaution than it seemed. So strong was the prevalent belief that a future naval war would be a fight between surface ships that even the newest destroyers had been built with gun-

referred to the threat in a public speech. Startling newspaper headlines followed, and there was great embarrassment when it was discovered that there was no solid foundation for the rumour. Not only was *U-47*'s penetration of the Scapa Flow anchorage (where she sank the *Royal Oak*) in October 1939 completely undetected, but an Admiralty Board of Inquiry after the event concluded that she could not have entered Scapa Flow by the route she had in fact used!

Godfrey once said, 'War changes intelligence officers from Cinderella into Princess.' He himself promoted the change and saw it through, but it was largely the foresight of his predecessor in office twenty years earlier, Admiral James, who had been head of Room 40 in 1917–18, which ensured that by the autumn of 1939 the Admiralty was prepared to recognise the need for change.

As Deputy Chief of the Naval Staff from 1936, James saw that the Naval Intelligence Division (NID) had neither the manpower nor the experience to collate and analyse the various types of information it was receiving during the Abyssinian war and later the Spanish civil war. Conscious that far more advantage could have been taken of Room 40's cryptographic feats if its product had been better understood and better mediated to operational commands, he stimulated Troup, the DNI, to create a small specialist department, the Operational Intelligence Centre, to undertake the task. Two inspired choices set the OIC on its way: that of a regular officer, Paymaster Lieutenant-Commander Norman Denning RN as its head and, in January 1941, that of a civilian (soon commissioned), the barrister Rodger Winn, to lead what soon became its chief sub-department, the Submarine Tracking Room. Denning and Winn – a future vice-admiral and future lord justice of appeal respectively – were soon followed by wartime RNVR recruits who were later to earn fame in other

mountings which precluded elevation of their 4.7-inch guns above 40 degrees (Barnett, 44).

spheres: Patrick Beesly, Ian Fleming, Donald MacLachlan, Euan Montagu.

By the autumn of 1939 the OIC was ready and able to handle intelligence far more coherently than were the other armed services. All that was lacking was enough material worthy of its talents. Unhappily this was not forthcoming until the capture two years later of a weather vessel, the *München*, and of *U-110* yielded cipher lists which led to the first break into naval Enigma in May 1941.

Long before this stage was reached, however – indeed by the beginning of the war – the profession of intelligence was established and its practice appreciated in at least one corner of the Royal Navy, which was already showing greater tolerance towards the newly commissioned civilians who were to form its main strength in the next five years. The vast majority of naval officers retained the old-fashioned views already discussed, but in the OIC at any rate far more objective and lively thought was to be found than anywhere in either the army or the air force.

Nowhere was the neglect of intelligence more marked than at the Air Ministry. Lord Trenchard,[*] the first head of the RAF, was convinced that bombing alone could subdue an enemy, and his belief became a legacy which paralysed the service he had founded. Factual evidence which conflicted with it was disregarded, and no periodic checks were made to establish whether it still accorded with changing realities. Nourished on this 'Trenchard doctrine' and inheriting in full measure an almost contemptuous attitude towards intelligence, successive heads of Bomber Command distorted Britain's war effort in a vain attempt to subdue Germany by air power alone (see Chapter 4).

The same doctrine took a hold on Germany at the time when the Luftwaffe was being set up in the middle 1930s. The retrospectively ludicrous consequence was that the two future

---

[*] For Trenchard's curiously ambivalent attitude in 1914–18, see Nigel Steel and Peter Hart, *Tumult in the Clouds* (Hodder and Stoughton 1997).

enemies made equal but opposite errors – but with one almost
fatal difference. Confident that its bombers (faster and in all
respects better than the British, though capable of carrying only
a little over 200 tons between them) could destroy the enemy's
power to resist – a belief which was to be proved vain in the
winter of 1940–1 – Germany nevertheless forged a formidable
army co-operation force of bombers and fighters of whose
purpose Britain remained ignorant but which overwhelmed
France and might have overwhelmed Britain too had the
Channel not existed.

Scorning all other aspects of air power, on the other hand,
Britain depended in 1939 on obsolete bombers and built none
big enough or modern enough to carry out the strategy in which
the Air Ministry persisted in believing. 'There were three Air
Ministry officials for every aircraft in squadron service, and in
the 1920s one-fifth of the RAF's budget was spent on buildings'
rather than on research into the size, speed and structure of
aircraft (two- or four-engined planes), the weight of bombs and
methods of delivering them, for instance. Bombing indeed
demonstrated its value in pacifying the tribesmen on the North-
west Frontier of India, but this bore no relation to European
warfare, where noise would not compensate for an inaccuracy of
aim which did not matter much in open and mountainous
country, where no great weight of bombs was needed to achieve
the desired end.

Still worse: it did not follow from the Air Ministry's own faith
in bombing that the Germans shared it and would aim a knock-
out blow at London directly war was declared, and since no
reliable intelligence about German intentions had been discovered the only course was to seek enlightenment through
subjective but logical reasoning. Instead of this, however, the
Ministry fell into a trap which is familiar enough to intelligence
analysts today but seems to have passed unnoticed then: that of
crediting the enemy with one's own patterns of thought – 'That's
what we would do in like circumstances, so that's what they will

do next' is the negation of good sense, for 'they' may have patterns of thought quite different from ours. Ignorant of and much overestimating the true facts about German aircraft types, their speeds, armaments, range and bomb-load, the Air Ministry misled itself.* Behind this lay a gross failure to collect essential intelligence. The Germans in fact attempted the knock-out blow only after the Battle of Britain put an end to all hope of mounting a successful invasion and another triumph of army–air co-operation. Horrible though it was (I witnessed it myself from Droitwich across the valley, and the memory is still vivid), the bombing of Coventry represented the most that was technologically possible in November 1940. The vastly more destructive Hamburg and Dresden raids, three and four years later, depended for the far greater devastation they caused on scientific and technical advances made since Coventry and exploited not by the Luftwaffe, which never mass-produced heavy four-engined bombers, but by the RAF and the USAAF. Both the fears prevalent in 1939 and the early faith in bombing could have been avoided had the RAF consulted its own scientific advisers.

Unshakeable faith in bombing led to a failure to produce a new generation of fighters until almost too late.† Little was

---

* The Air Ministry had no monopoloy of error in this repect. (Horst Boog in INS 5.355–73.) German intelligence about the RAF was almost as defective. After the war a senior Abwehr officer admitted that many of his colleagues were still untrained in 1941 (H. J. Giskes, *London Calling North Pole* (Kimber, 1953), 20).
† A paralysis of independent thought, similar to that which guaranteed the continuing ascendancy of the Trenchard bombing doctrine, contributed towards the same end. It afflicted the Air Ministry's scientific staff, with only a small number of honourable exceptions, leading them to cold-shoulder Sir Frank Whittle's plans for jet-propelled aircraft throughout the 1930s. His first approaches in 1929 were rejected on the ground that they were impossible of realisation and, even after a further eight years' research and experimentation, were held to be uneconomic and suitable only for special purposes. The Air Ministry's conversion only began under the shadow of war. The first jet fighter flew on 15 May 1941, attaining a speed considerably higher than the fastest contemporary

known about German strategic intentions and little effort made to discover them (they may, of course, have been undiscoverable, so many of Hitler's actions being unpredictable even by himself), but until late in 1937 prudence does not seem to have suggested preparations either to defend the country against bombing or to support an army on the continent. Instead, the Air Ministry continued well into 1938 to 'dole out soothing syrup and incompetence in equal measure', in the words of Sir Warren Fisher, one of its severest critics and prominent among those who forced the change in policy which provided the Few with their Spitfires and Hurricanes. Tunnel vision even starved Coastal Command of the aircraft it would soon need in the hunt for U-boats.

Defects of foresight and logic on the part of the leaders of all three service ministries can in large part be traced to a failure to understand the importance of intelligence or to assess impartially such items as did come their way. Each collected evidence separately from the others, each assessed it in isolation without considering whether it overlapped the interests of others or admitting that (for instance) a land campaign would necessarily be a joint enterprise by army and air force working in concert for a common purpose. This fault was compounded by the absence of any machinery for comparative assessment at some central point, with the bizarre consequence that the Chiefs of Staff sometimes received irreconcilably differing recommendations from two services. A belated attempt was made to supply a remedy by the establishment of the Joint Intelligence Committee in 1936, but inherited traditions of exclusivity and mutual

Spitfires and Messerschmitts on its maiden flight. Jet-propelled aircraft did not enter squadron service with the RAF until April 1945. A more welcoming attitude towards what was of course a revolutionary innovation might have advanced this date by a year or two. German jet aircraft were operating over the front by June 1944, although their development had begun only in 1938 (F. Whittle, *Jet* (Muller, 1953), esp. chs 4, 11, 12, 13, 17, 18, 30).

jealousy restricted the influence of the Committee until the outbreak of war forced it into prominence.

Operating clandestinely out of the limelight (though their disguise as passport control officers at British embassies was wearing thin), the members of the Secret Intelligence Service had an advantage over the service attachés, whose opportunities to discover information which the host country preferred to conceal were restricted by the formal rules governing their appointment. The SIS was scarcely more successful, however, and did nothing during the inter-war years to sustain the quite groundless reputation for omniscience with which Europe had credited it since the previous century. One reason for this was the absence of firm direction from above. Neither Vansittart nor Cadogan saw to it that the SIS was given clearly defined tasks to perform; rather, they accepted its offerings without much discrimination. Carrying to extremes Woodrow Wilson's cry for 'open covenants openly arrived at', Henry Stimson closed down American cryptographic assaults on foreign countries' diplomatic ciphers when he became US Secretary of State in 1929 with the famous remark 'Gentlemen do not read each other's mail.' This was matched in Britain by Arthur Henderson, Foreign Secretary 1929–31, who (according to Vansittart) 'rated the Secret Service like hard liquor, because he knew, and wanted to know, nothing of it.'

The SIS reported its findings to the Foreign Office, whose lack of machinery for analysing and appraising intelligence[*] – until

---

[*] On 22 November 1934 Captain Malcolm Kennedy, a senior Japanese linguist at Broadway, recorded in his diary the opinion of an Air Ministry friend: 'our Army General Staff works out a line of policy, which is generally right, and sticks to it; the Air Ministry, though not always so correct in its judgement, does the same; the Admiralty inevitably has 3 or 4 policies, all running counter to one another; the F.O., on the other hand, never has any fixed policy at all, but just blunders on'. (Quoted in Ferris, *From Broadway House to Bletchley Park*, INS 4: 430.)

the Joint Intelligence Committee took over the task for it in 1939
– left it incapable of distinguishing the true from the false, fact
from the fictions planted by Goebbels's propaganda minions for
the express purpose of misleading it. 'Kell [head of MI5,
counter-espionage] came to raise my hair with tales of the
Germans going into Czechoslovakia in the next twenty-four
hours. Maybe,' Cadogan wrote in his diary for 11 March 1939.
'Told Halifax, but let him go off to Oxford. . . . Jebb [Foreign
Office official] rang to say SIS have some hair-raising tales of
Czecho for 14th. It can wait.' Lightly though Cadogan dismissed
them, the 'tales' were true: on 15 March Hitler occupied the
rump of Czechoslovakia which had been left after Munich. But
by no means all SIS reports were as worthy of credence as these;
no more than one in five was reliable, it was said. Repeated
suggestions that Hitler intended to invade Belgium and Holland
in the early weeks of 1939, for instance, were entirely without
foundation, although they did have the beneficial result of
turning the British government's mind further in the direction of
continental commitment for the army and led to the introduction of conscription.

At the age of twenty-four John Colville, a junior member of
the Foreign Office staff, was appointed Assistant Private Secretary to Winston Churchill in October 1939. He came to the job
with scant knowledge of intelligence, but even a slight acquaintance with it and its impact at the highest level soon showed him
its glaring defects. 'Our Intelligence Service seems very weak,'*

---

* A single document has somehow escaped the censorship which hides
SIS papers from public view (FO 371/4659). It is dated 18 September
1938 and appears to embody SIS's advice on foreign policy in the weeks
before Munich, although it is unusual to find SIS proffering advice
instead of simply acting as a channel for passing unedited snippets to
higher authority. The document recommends watchful acquiescence in
German demands and British rearmament, but otherwise conforms to the
familiar pattern of appeasement. It has been used to rebut the charge,
made at the time and since, that the Chamberlain government adopted a
policy of appeasement in spite of being in possession of intelligence
suggesting a different course of action (Dilks in Andrew and Dilks, *The*

he remarked in his diary for 5 November; '. . . we never seem to have certain information about German troop movements. . . .' On 10 May 1940 (the day the German armies crossed the Dutch and French frontiers) he wrote, 'Rab Butler tells me that the Secret Service told him yesterday that there was no chance of an invasion of the Netherlands: it was a feint. An attack on Hungary, on the other hand, was imminent. So much for our renowned foreign agents!' (R. A. Butler was at that time Under-Secretary of State, Foreign Office.)

There were several reasons for the unreliability of SIS reports. Low salaries (in part the consequence of the Ten-Year Rule) and uncertain career prospects did not attract men of lively mind or much ambition. SIS headquarters seemed 'a dusty, run-down and mediocre outfit' to Sir Alexander Glen, who saw something of it between 1936 and 1939 at the start of a career in naval intelligence which took him from Spitzbergen through Jugoslavia and Albania to service on the Danube with Marshal Tolbukhin's Third Ukrainian Army.

Only a few exceptions disturbed the generally poor standard of the SIS, among them dedicated professionals like Gibson in Prague and two unusually talented men of a different kind, both curiously enough from well-to-do merchant families in Odessa and both just old enough to have been commissioned in the British Black Sea Fleet in 1917.

As Passport Control Officer, Paris from 1924 to 1939, Wilfrid ('Biffy') Dunderdale transformed what had been a modest post far from the limelight into a focus of attention. His substantial private means enabled him to live in sumptuous style and to entertain lavishly. His links with the leaders of French social and political life were close, as were his contacts with the General Staff and with men like Colonel Bertrand, head of the French cryptographic service. It was he who brought to London the reconstructed Enigma machine which the Poles handed over to

Missing Dimension (Macmillan, 1984), 122, and letter 27 November 1991).

the British and French in July 1939. Forced out of Paris in June 1940, from London he played a prominent part in maintaining the French and Polish intelligence network throughout the war.

Vladimir Wolfson's early career was more orthodox. Though strictly a member of naval intelligence, he had a great influence on recruiting for SIS as well as for naval intelligence in the later 1930s, and on the outbreak of war took on a pivotal intelligence role in the eastern Mediterranean as Assistant Naval Attaché, Istanbul, where all the threads of Middle Eastern rumour and intelligence met and crossed on neutral Turkish territory and agents of the warring powers eyed each other with veiled hostility. Wolfson played a major part in damage-control after the Cicero incident (see p. 262) in spring 1944.

Prominent among the younger recruits to the SIS, and working in the same area as Wolfson, was Nicholas Elliott, who was appointed SIS Section V officer at Istanbul in July 1942. In receipt not only of the Abwehr and SD (Sicherheitsdienst – Security Service) hand-cipher traffic (ISOS) but also of the newly decrypted (since December 1941) Abwehr Enigma (ISK), he was in an excellent position both to keep track of German agents and to give material assistance to the plan of Colonel Dudley Clarke and 'A' Force (see pp. 71–2) to deceive the Germans into overestimating the British forces in the Middle East and into crediting them with designs which in reality they never contemplated.

Support to 'straight' intelligence on this scale was unusual. A further reason for the generally poor quality of SIS reports was that even the most energetic agent could hardly be expected to gain access to Hitler's inner circle and discover his intended strategy (in any case W/T sets to report their findings quickly were not provided) or to be able to assess the productive capacity of German industry from clandestine surveillance of a few factories; yet information about strategy and the rate at which aircraft, tanks and guns could be manufactured were the most urgent needs in the months before the outbreak of war.

A third partial explanation was uncertain leadership of the SIS, notably at a critical moment, the time of the so-called Venlo incident in early November 1939. Admiral 'Quex' Sinclair, Chief of the SIS since 1923, had been suffering from cancer for some time before he died on 4 November. A disputed succession was not resolved until the end of the month with the appointment of Major-General Stewart Menzies, Sinclair's deputy. Menzies's disappointed rivals, Dansey and Vivian (responsible respectively for espionage and counter-espionage), remained unsatisfied and, armed with the titles of Assistant Chief and Vice-Chief, often impeded Menzies's authority and were in turn excluded from his major decisions. Menzies himself was always a hard worker devoted to his job, but after Venlo the results the SIS was producing grew less and less commensurate with the needs of the situation.

It has been suggested that Menzies saved SIS from oblivion by managing to gain control of Ultra. Ultra (see p. xvi and note) had no connection with espionage, but for security reasons was initially disguised as the work of an agent when it suddenly became available in 1940, just as SIS's own power to provide military intelligence was on the wane. While this may underestimate the significance of SIS information, and may credit Menzies with more foresight than he could possibly have possessed, it is probaby true in essentials and cannot be decisively contradicted so long as all SIS records are closed to the public and plenty of Ultra is available.

The *Anschluss* of 1938 had already reduced the SIS's catchment area (Austria had been the base for its operations in Germany) before the Venlo incident carried the process an enormous step further. In the autumn of 1939, two senior SIS officers in Holland, Major Stevens and Captain Best, fell into a trap against which they had been expressly warned. Leading members of the SD deluded them into believing that they spoke for a group of German generals who were plotting to overthrow Hitler. They persuaded Stevens and Best of their *bona fides* sufficiently to ensure that their suggestions were reported back to Cadogan, and by him to Halifax and Chamberlain, who authorised further contacts; these in turn eventually led to the kidnapping of Stevens and Best at Venlo on the German–Dutch frontier on 9 November. Interrogation of Stevens and Best, and papers seized in SIS HQ at The Hague in May 1940, revealed the names of other British agents, who were of course quickly rounded up, with the consequence that SIS operations in Europe were severely curtailed. The occupation of France and the German domination of central Europe completed the process. At the time of Britain's greatest peril in 1940 and 1941, SIS could provide no information about the enemy's strength or intentions to give guidance to the defence of Britain.

Stevens and Best were too gullible. They had not been on their guard enough to sense that they were being tricked, although Cadogan had been sceptical at first and although they had been given, but had rejected, a plain warning by Captain (later Vice-Admiral) Schofield, Naval Attaché at The Hague, whom the omnipresence of Gestapo agents had swiftly convinced that to reside in Holland at that time was 'like living out a chapter in a melodramatic spy story'.

The Venlo incident illustrates what was probably the chief reason for the ineffectiveness of the SIS in the 1930s: the poor quality of most of its members (Menzies was well aware of this) and the casualness with which they were selected – 'that unique system of recruitment in London clubland by which SIS kept itself free from contamination by intellectuals and university men', in the words of a recent and highly perceptive study of the road to war, Professor Cameron Watt's *How War Came*. Competition for entry was entirely unknown, and anything resembling scrutiny of personal background and political allegiance was missing – hence the enrolment of some of the 'Cambridge Comintern'. Frederick Winterbotham, who later played an important role in the dissemination of Ultra, was recruited in 1930 and immediately appointed to set up a new Air Section of the SIS, after just half an hour's conversation with the Deputy Chief of Air Staff in the course of which they talked about India and mutual friends. Winterbotham had been a pilot in the 1914–18 war, had farmed without much success in England, Kenya and Rhodesia, and his only apparent qualification for the post was a rudimentary knowledge of German acquired in prisoner-of-war camp. Though he was in fact the first graduate recruit to the SIS, his published works are not marked by intellectual rigour.

While it would be thoroughly unjust to give the impression that none of the pre-war members of the security services were up to their job – some younger men, like Elliott and Dick White (who joined MI5 in 1936 and played a considerable part in ensuring the success of the 'Double Cross' system's (see p. 259) most famous success on D-Day before becoming head of MI5 and MI6 (SIS) in turn) were exceptions – the conclusion seems inescapable that the inadequate capacity of most pre-war members of SIS was the reason why its contribution to military intelligence was not greater. Some indication of the indifferent intellectual standard of many of the old hands in SIS is given by a story told me by Sir Patrick Reilly, a former Fellow of All Souls, who entered the Diplomatic Service in 1933 and was seconded to SIS as C's* Personal Assistant from May 1942 to October 1943. Finding that the heavy load which any Chief of SIS would have had to carry in wartime was being unnecessarily increased for Menzies by the often poor presentation of files submitted to him, early in his time at Broadway Reilly summarised the contents of a confusing file coherently and set out the points requiring urgent decision. Menzies read the paper with a puzzled frown and then, to Reilly's relief, said with an air of astonishment, 'But that is perfectly clear.'

It is plain that SIS did not sufficiently respond to the demands

---

* The Chief of the SIS was always known as 'C'.

made upon it by the political and military needs of the 1930s and
1940s, but the extent by which it fell short cannot be measured
with any accuracy while most of the evidence upon which
judgment could be based remains inaccessible. In the first two
decades of the twentieth century the game of espionage had been
played by a self-selected few according to thoroughly 'amateur'
rules, and even in the 1930s 'invisible inks and false beards were
still standard issue'. As the German danger mounted, more
professionalism and greater intellectual acuity were required. It
was provided in great measure from outside the ranks of the old-
style SIS by men and women recruited after the outbreak of war.
That mercifully this was not merely shutting the stable door
when the horse had bolted bears witness less to the merits of
improvisation under the stress of necessity, great though these
merits were, than to the defects of the pre-war system.

One evening in November 1939 a package landed on the desk of
Dr R. V. Jones, Scientific Officer at the Air Ministry. It proved
to contain vital information about Germany's progress in
weapons research and construction, but the degree of its
importance was not discernible for months or even years to come
and its origins as well as its contents were mysterious. It had been
delivered to the Naval Attaché at the British Embasssy in Oslo
(hence it was called the Oslo Report), but nothing more was
known about its provenance. Because of this, and because the
information in it went so far beyond anything reported by other
sources – whether because of effective German security measures
or because of the inadequacies of British agents must remain a
matter of speculation – it was dismissed as a German 'plant' by
the service ministries and soon forgotten by all save Dr Jones,
whom its air of authority and technical competence had
convinced of its genuineness.

The significance of the package's contents became gradually
apparent and increasingly menacing as the war proceeded; the
mystery of its origins – a deliberate warning about the

manufacture of secret weapons given by a local but deeply anti-Nazi German industrial scientist – was only solved, after a series of the most extraordinary coincidences, by Dr Jones himself in 1955.

The Oslo Report gave details of research being pursued in a dozen closely related fields, from acoustic and magnetic torpedoes (which latter had just been used for the first time to sink the *Royal Oak*) to the V1 and V2 rockets aimed at London in 1944. It said nothing about *Knickebein*, the equipment which lay behind the first wave of German bombing in 1940, but offered useful clues to the nature of the second (the single beam, as contrasted with *Knickebein*'s crossing beams) sufficient to hasten the improvisation of counter-measures which greatly reduced its effectiveness by 1941.

The Oslo Report's information proved to be of enormous value as in the course of time its hints became realities: sooner or later most of the weapons it predicted appeared on the battlefield, in the air above it or in the sea surrounding it. How much more useful it would have been had it not so far outranged British experimental knowledge and technical capability in 1939 can only be guessed. But it is beyond doubt that here, within a few weeks of the outbreak of war, was a body of intelligence of much greater potential, though unfortunately not of actual and current, importance than anything received hitherto. And it had not been obtained by any effort on our part, but had been offered, unsolicited, through the conscientious revulsion against Nazism of a German scientist.

In 1939, and even when they entered the war two years later, the American armed forces were in much the same state as the British were with respect to intelligence. Neither General Marshall (whose influence on the course of the war was second only to that of Roosevelt), who became Chief of Staff of the army in September 1939, nor his opposite number Admiral King,

Commander-in-Chief of the navy, nor current and later prominent figures like MacArthur, Eisenhower, Bradley and Patton,
appear to have laid any stress on intelligence before the war or to
have had any significant experience of it except at the lowest
tactical level. A recent study entitled 'The United States Views of
Germany and Japan in 1941' begins with the following sentence:
'Intelligence had little to do with American assessments of
Germany and Japan before December 1941.'

Forrest Pogue's biography of Marshall dwells more than once
on the store he set upon tactical intelligence and training
(according to Pogue, Marshall may well have been the first to use
wireless in a Staff College command exercise; but the first
message he received back from troops he had sent out to
reconnoitre presaged little enough of the future – it was from a
cavlary troop commander who reported, 'I am just west of the
manure pile'). The deep influence of a radically-minded instruc-
tor at Fort Leavenworth, John F. Morrison, who was 'the first to
apply thought to military problems in place of the traditional
language of regulations', does not seem to have extended beyond
tactics, and there is no trace of intelligence or strategy in
Marshall's Staff College studies. The formal *Report on the Army* for
1939–43, which he prepared for the Secretary of War, nowhere
mentions intelligence. Similarly with Admiral King: neither in
his autobiography nor in *The U.S. Navy at War*, his official report
on the war at sea between 1941 and 1945, is there a word about
intelligence. One draws a similar blank in General MacArthur's
Reminiscences, *The Patton Papers* and biographies of Patton,
Eisenhower and Bradley.

The United States had no secret agents abroad in 1939.
Together with its embassies in other countries, radio intercepts
(reintroduced after the Stimson black-out) were its main source
of information; but they came from Japan – where diplomatic
traffic (Purple) was first decrypted in August 1940 – not from
Germany, although Germany was regarded as the greater
danger. Diplomatic sources gave alarming news about German

rearmament, and so did Colonel Lindbergh, the famous solo
Atlantic flyer, after his well-publicised visits to Luftwaffe bases in
1936 and 1938. Stocktaking in 1941 revealed that the material
collected by US naval and military attachés was haphazard and
indiscriminate becasuse the attachés 'saw what was not there, did
not see what was there, and in general saw without appreciation
of significance'.

It was not shortage of material so much as other things which
impeded the proper use of intelligence by the US army (which in
those days included the air force) and navy before 1942. There
was even less realisation at the top than in Great Britain of the
strategic value of intelligence and as complete a lack of provision
for analysing it; analysis did not become a priority until the
appointment of Colonel Donovan as Co-ordinator of Information in July 1941. But whereas in Britain the service ministries
merely worked in isolation from each other, in America they
worked actively against each other. Army and navy ran separate
intelligence agencies and refused to share information for the
benefit of the state; it was said that they hated each other more
than either hated the Germans. The principal cause of the
disaster at Pearl Harbor on 7 December 1941 was a failure to
analyse and appreciate the meaning of the broad hints of it given
in advance by Japanese decrypts, but an important contributory
cause was the absurd nature of the compromise imposed upon
army and navy in a vain attempt to reduce their mutual hostility.
In turn, this hostility made still more difficult the tortuous and
protracted negotiations with Britain which preceded the Americans' full participation in the Ultra programme.

All in all, it is not surprising that Eisenhower could later write
that until 1941 'within the War Department a shocking
deficiency impeded all constructive planning in the field of
intelligence' – in 1940 there were only eighty-two officers in the
Military Intelligence Department, only one radio intelligence
company, and no central system for the dissemination of Sigint
material to field commanders – or that the historian of American

participation in the Ultra work at Bletchley Park (wartime home of the Government Code and Cipher School) should remark that since regular US naval officers (like their British counterparts) sought only sea commands 'here too the intelligence branch was an open city waiting to be occupied by civilian recruits'. Perhaps Roosevelt himself summed up a general American antipathy to anything but the plainest and simplest form of military activity when, angered by the introduction into Congress of a Bill to create a general staff for the navy in 1937, he encouraged the circulation of a rumour that any officer backing the Bill would be posted to Guam, the remote Pacific island base.

Britain and the United States were even more culpably unprepared for war in the field of intelligence than in material respects. As General Ismay, Churchill's Chief of Staff at the Ministry of Defence, recorded in his memoirs, 'In the years before the war we lived in a world of imagination, and the preparations on which our very existence might depend had to be based on forecasts which might prove to be entirely wrong.' Yet long before 1945 they were far ahead of Germany in every way. Most notably, military intelligence had been raised from the low estimation in which it had been held to become a primary element in strategic planning and a major determinant of operational discipline and battlefield tactics. No previous commander had ever had so complete a picture of his enemy's order of battle, logistics, dispositions and objectives as the Allied admirals, generals and air marshals in the last two years of the war. Progress towards this end had not come at a steady pace either over time or over the various fields of land, sea and air combat. The reasons why this progress was erratic are therefore best displayed chronologically, although this entails some fragmentation of individual topics, save where fragmentation would seriously blur the focus – for instance, in the development of central intelligence assessment and the presentation of agreed recommendations to the political decision-makers. Such a treatment will incidentally point the contrast with Germany, where intelligence-gathering was fragmented and intelligence remained inelastic until the fall of Canaris, head of the Abwehr in 1944, opened the way for a terminal decline.

1940–1941

First Rays of Light

It was perhaps fitting that the first British success of the war – the scuttling of the pocket-battleship *Graf Spee* off Montevideo by her own crew on 17 December 1939 – should have been the result of the ancient arts of naval warfare not of modern methods of intelligence-gathering. The *Graf Spee* had sailed on an Atlantic commerce-raiding expedition even before war was declared, but neither photo-reconnaissance (because long-range aircraft did not yet exist) nor radio direction-finding (because neither instruments nor skill were sufficient) managed to locate her. It was therefore nothing but his seamanly instincts for the enemy's probable movements which enabled Commodore Harwood, commanding the hunting squadron, to bring the *Graf Spee* to battle* in much the same way that Drake had located the Spanish treasure ships or Nelson the French fleet. His victory brought momentary relief to the Atlantic trade-routes, but this was not the way the war could be won.

Prime Minister Chamberlain's unfortunate phrase 'Hitler has missed the bus' in a House of Commons speech on 5 April 1940, just four days before the German invasion of Norway and Denmark, has fastened blame upon the politicians for the humiliations of the next few weeks; it has been reinforced by Ironside's branding of the Cabinet as 'a bewildered flock of

---

* The Admiralty had believed that it was hunting the *Admiral Scheer* and not the *Graf Spee*, until American radio broadcast the name after the pocket-battleship entered Montevideo harbour.

sheep' and Harold Macmillan's later strictures on the Cabinet's vacillation and repeated changes of front which, he said, illustrated Burke's aphorism about a 'proof of the irresistible operation of feeble counsel'.

This does not go to the heart of the matter, however. Chamberlain knew, when he spoke, that ever since January there had been an accelerating flow of reports, from a variety of sources, that Hitler had a mind to invade Scandinavia. (Nevertheless, the War Office is said to have had only one file on Norway, containing a single sheet of paper inscribed 'SFA'. But that story originates with a naval officer!) The reports were right (OKW – Supreme Command of the Armed Forces – began planning in January), but no one in authority was prepared to take them seriously, partly because they reached different Whitehall departments which seldom compared notes, so that no single mind had the chance to assess their cumulative impact, and partly because the Chiefs of Staff complacently felt that no one in his senses would take so foolhardy a risk in face of the Royal Navy's command of the sea. 'The whole thing is harebrained,' said Sir Cyril Newall, Chief of the Air Staff. In fact, of course, the Germans not only took the risk but won the race to Narvik, although the British had for some time been planning to occupy it in order to cut the Swedish iron-ore route to Germany. The Chiefs of Staff concluded on 4 April that a German descent on Norway was improbable, and even on the 6th, with only three days to go, the Foreign Office could not credit a warning from the British Minister in Copenhagen.

Too much should not be made of such things, absurd as hindsight makes them appear. Nearly five years later, in a far more alert and critical intelligence atmosphere, accumulating evidence that the Germans might attack in the Ardennes was disbelieved, and for a similar reason – that it seemed against reason and common sense. Nor must the gibe that the British had to use the 1912 Baedeker's *Scandinavia* and maps obtained from Cook's, because none had been prepared for the planned

seizure of Narvik, be allowed to colour judgment: the Germans
had to do the same.

A single incident well illustrates the imperfections of British
intelligence in these first contacts with the enemy, and its
inflexible refusal to credit deductions from new material which
did not conform to its presuppositions. The late Christopher
Morris, a distinguished young Cambridge historian and a Fellow
of King's College, was an early recruit to naval intelligence at
Bletchley Park. He was assigned to work on one of the many
German naval hand-ciphers which could be broken and read at
that time. During the first week of April 1940 he decrypted a
signal which ordered all ships bound for Bergen to report their
positions periodically to army HQ, Berlin. He was bluntly told
by his superiors that since ships report to naval, not military,
authorities his decryption must be wrong; he checked and found
it correct. As he wrote many years later, 'The ships were of
course troopships, and the signal would have given advance
warning of the invasion of Norway' had it been scrutinised more
carefully. A contemporary report from a neighbouring department drew attention to unusual German naval wireless activity
in the western Baltic on the night of 6/7 April;* Coastal
Command sightings and the Copenhagen warning pointed in
the same general direction. Proper collation of all these
indications, though none was conclusive in itself, could not have
failed, particularly in view of the repeated warnings in the
immediately preceding months, to promote watchfulness for an
immediate attack somewhere in Scandinavia. As it was, General
Hastings Ismay was startled from sleep in the early hours of 9
April by the news that the Germans were already in Copenhagen and Oslo.

But for this narrow-minded insensitivity, the brightest ray of light
in the nervous gloom of the Phoney War might have shone more
cheerfully in what quickly proved a lost campaign. The attack on

* For another, very similar example, see p. 54.

the Enigma enciphering machine, which both the French and the British had believed so doomed to failure that it was hardly worth making, took on new urgency when the more sanguine Poles handed over the secret of their surprising achievements in July 1939 (see Appendix I). Ultra (as the intelligence derived from Enigma decrypts was soon called) began to deliver its first operationally useful results in the spring of 1940. Until now, only a few days' traffic on the general Luftwaffe key (known at Bletchley Park as the Red, from the colour of the crayon used to number the intercepts) had been decrypted, in every case so late that the operational value of the messages had been negligible.

The Enigma machine* (machine encipherment was still a comparative novelty in 1939) was used by all three branches of the Wehrmacht, by the Abwehr, the state railways and one or two other authorities. Each was allotted several of the many variants of the basic cipher; security against decryption by an enemy depended on strict observance of the operating instructions. Because of the rapid expansion of the Luftwaffe in the years immediately before the outbreak of war, its signals personnel were more hastily trained and less well disciplined[†] than those of the army and navy; the result was that their habits allowed cryptographers a foothold into Enigma which cut at the root of the otherwise justified German belief in its inviolability.

Improvements upon the methods which had brought the Poles their astonishing successes – improvements made necessary to keep pace with successive new defensive complications introduced into Enigma procedures – had made possible a few

---

* See also Appendix I and Gilbert Bloch, *Enigma avant ultra (1939–1940)*, September 1988 (typescript).
† After the war, General Martini, head of the Luftwaffe signals service, explained the reason more fully to Professor R. V. Jones. (R. V. Jones, *Most Secret War*, 244). Martini was permitted only very low priority for recruiting, and had to make do with men graded unsuitable for other duties. There were no skilled radio amateurs in Germany for him to draw on, as there were in Britain, for Hitler had banned amateur radio before the war. Martini had to hope that the reliability of their equipment would make up for the operators' shortcomings. Fortunately, it did not.

scattered breaks in Red traffic early in 1940. But a cryptographer's *sine qua non* for breaking a cipher is a sufficiency of material
to work on. Since its operations were at a low level of intensity
(there being few emergencies) during the winter of 1939–40, the
Luftwaffe naturally preferred to use telephone and teleprinter,
with the result that radio traffic was scarce and intercepts rare.
Decryption consequently depended in large measure upon luck
and was accomplished only with a good deal of delay (each key
changed every day – three times a day later in the war – so that
each day's traffic had to be broken anew). The intelligence thus
derived seldom possessed much operational value, therefore,
much as it contributed towards filling out the Air Ministry's
woefully imperfect picture of the Luftwaffe's structure and
strength.

Then, suddenly, a new key, Yellow, devoted entirely to
army–air co-operation in Norway, appeared on 10 April; traffic
volume being high, it was decrypted as early as 15 April and
thereafter currently for the whole of its five or six weeks' life. For
the first time, therefore, intelligence capable of assisting operations was available from a most welcome but quite untested
source. This was something unprecedented in the history of
warfare. No spy had ever imagined in his wildest dreams that he
could discover so many of the enemy's secrets and deliver them
to his own side within a few hours, yet here there loomed a
future in which this might be done, not once or twice, but
regularly and as a matter of routine.

Could this new and exciting prospect be realised in practice?
Would the operational implications of a decrypted message be
self-evident, or would a new brand of intelligence officer be
needed to turn translated Enigma intercepts into forms consistent with English rather than German military usage and so
render them more readily acceptable by British commanders?
How would admirals, generals and air marshals, accustomed to
distrusting intelligence and paying little heed to it, react to a

flood of novel but undoubtedly reliable information? And would their utilisation of it have to be so tightly restricted by security measures to protect it from inadvertent revelation and the consequent possible loss of the source that their freedom of action would be reduced rather than extended?

These and similar questions, vaguely sensed by a few in 1940 but not yet precisely formulated by anyone, would need answers in the future. Looking back, it is a shock to recall that it took two years of trial and error to find them and to ensure the acceptance of Ultra as the primary source of operational intelligence.

Promising as the Yellow material may have been (neither decrypts nor translations are open to inspection), little use could be made of it. There were three main reasons. First, there was no sufficiently secure means of communication with the expedition commanders once they had landed. Second, no intelligence officers experienced in handling Ultra accompanied the expedition (for the good reason that none yet existed) and no provision had been made for intercepting lower-grade signals, which might have provided much-needed tactical detail – as the Y Service was so often to do in the future. Even without these handicaps, however, it is most unlikely that hard-pressed local commanders would have had time to benefit. Third, neither War Office nor Air Ministry showed much inclination to use Ultra; the novelty was too great, and minds were filled with the myriad emergencies of a confused campaign. The Admiralty, which already possessed secure means of communication with warships at sea, was more receptive, but found few occasions to use Ultra because so little of it referred to maritime matters. From the point of view of operations, the Norwegian campaign was from start to finish an example of the military incompetence which Professor Norman Dixon has so penetratingly analysed, but the intelligence aspect does not deserve quite so harsh a judgment.

Ultra's considerable part in the final victory is quite rightly taken for granted today, but it has often been misunderstood. In the first place, Enigma was not broken in a single dramatic moment like the instantaneous 'Big Bang' with which the universe is thought to have been created, nor in response to a magical 'Open Sesame'-style formula suddenly unlocking a treasure-house of priceless secrets ready and waiting to be plundered. A ceaseless and unrelenting war had to be waged day and night for five years to win, retain, enlarge and protect the access to the Germans' most confidential communications. What the Poles had done before the war was astonishing and beyond praise. But new German measures introduced when Poland was invaded had rendered much of it unhelpful within a few weeks of the revelations in the forest outside Warsaw, for they blocked the way for any further advance along the route the Poles had pioneered. All the subsequent discoveries which underlay fresh progress were made at GC&CS by the insights and industry of gifted mathematicians like Alan Turing, Gordon Welchman, Hugh Alexander, Dennis Babbage and Shaun Wylie. Their discoveries were of necessity made step by painful step over the years, in response to the new obstacles the Germans kept putting in their way. Cryptographic victory still hung in the balance in 1945; as Gordon Welchman wrote in *The Hut 6 Story*, 'we were lucky'.

Even the greatest mathematical skill could not turn a cipher text into a clear text alone and unaided; it could only point the way in what seemed promising directions and cut a myriad possible solutions down to a mere multitude. Machines had to be invented – they were the forerunners (but not the lineal ancestors) of modern computers – to undertake the laborious task of finding the needle in the haystack, testing the clues they had been given, distinguishing the correct solution from the rest, and thus restoring the original text. The machines (known as 'bombes') were immensely quicker than human brains and fingers, of course, but if the clues were a little vague (which sometimes was unavoidable) they might take a long time to come up with the solution.

Even when the original text had been recovered, however, there was still at first a long way to go and an unforeseen difficulty to overcome before the end-product became usable military intelligence. Because cryptography had meshed – though often unsatisfactorily – direct with operations in Room 40 twenty years earlier without the intervening lubricant of interpretation, no one in 1939 had realised the need to prepare in advance a staff of German linguists and teach them at least the elements of British military vocabulary and method. Although a few had understood, even before the Boer war, that an intelligence service cannot be improvised hurriedly in the hour of need, no one in the War Office or Air Ministry seems to have remembered this in the 1930s. The omission had to be repaired, but no serious steps to do so were taken for some time.

Because the supply of army/air Ultra – there was as yet no naval Ultra – declined substantially after the fall of France, little was done until late in 1940. Newly commissioned officers – civilians in uniform – who, like myself, were among the first to be recruited for the purpose, recall with a retrospective shudder how ill equipped we felt when, with nothing to guide us but our native wit and knowledge of strictly non-military German, backed by a very few weeks' experience of GC&CS, we were suddenly required to draft Ultra-based signals to Cairo (for army and air) and Alexandria (for the navy) when Greece, Crete and the Western Desert erupted into war in the spring of 1941.

Our inexperience proved in the event to be only one of several reasons why there was a delay of another twelve or eighteen months before Ultra was at last fully integrated into operations a few weeks before Alamein. The length of the delay presupposes a lack of foresight and advance preparation, and seems therefore to deserve censure. So it does, for it affected familiar forms of intelligence as well as Ultra, but two strands of thought commonly held in 1939 can fairly be pleaded in mitigation of the offence.

First, no one had seriously contemplated large-scale current decryption, so deeply rooted was the feeling that the Enigma machine cipher was as insoluble as its advocates proclaimed. The break of 22 May 1940 (see p. 47) was a shock; still more astonishing was it that the same key (the GAF – German Air Force – general key) turned out to be readable day after day – in the end daily throughout the war with scarcely a single intermission. It might even be urged that the rapidity with which the two ministries' pre-war omissions were repaired was at least as remarkable as the oversight which made the repair necessary.

Secondly, because high-grade Sigint had not been used for strategic communications during the 1914–18 war – trench warfare on a static front hardly required it – GC&CS (and therefore presumably also higher authority) believed that the outbreak of war would be followed rather by total wireless silence than by an increase in traffic. Both suppositions mercifully proved wrong, but it has to be conceded that both were reasonable deductions from the slender evidence available in the summer of 1939, and that together they explain, though they do not excuse, what now appears blameworthy negligence, the consequences of which were to impede British operations in Norway, France and (for the first year) the desert.

Nearly all the limiting factors which had applied in Norway still operated when the Battle of France began on 10 May 1940. Advance planning was better, and an intelligence component accompanied the BEF from the moment it went overseas in 1939. But this component consisted mainly of Field Security sections whose primary function was counter-intelligence not intelligence-gathering ('The area is thick with enemy agents . . . signallers are having their lines cut as soon as they're laid,' wrote Sir Basil Bartlett, a member of one such section, making no mention of intelligence in the usual sense of the word when describing his duties).

It might have been expected that the Y Service would have

been well prepared in advance to intercept *en clair* radio messages (much used during the *Blitzkrieg*) and to break lower-grade codes used for front-line communications. Several intercept detachments did indeed form part of the BEF, but there were more experienced radio operators on their strength than men fluent enough in German to understand the intelligence bearing (as distinct from the literal meaning) of what they intercepted, and more confusion than enlightenment seems to have resulted from the many abbreviations used for army and air units and formations, different types of weapon and similar military jargon which became so familiar in succeeding months and years. Such translations of Y and Enigma intercepts as survived the wholesale destruction of records before Dunkirk betray this by a clumsiness of phrasing and a lack of clarity which would have been shunned twelve months later.

The GAF Red key, hitherto readable only occasionally, was broken almost currently on 22 May (which has consequently been called 'the birthday of Ultra') and with minor exceptions regularly thereafter until the end of the war, usually by the middle of the day for which the particular setting was valid. This at last provided a trustworthy source of information, the lack of which had been so disabling a hindrance to preparations for meeting the German offensive which all had expected. Arriving in France on 1 May 1940, straight from a shortened course at Camberley, Major (later General Sir Charles) Richardson reflected on 'the intelligence that had *fortuitously* come to hand despite the rudimentary intelligence agencies of that time' pointing to a German thrust 'from *some* quarter' (my italics). The official history indeed concludes that there was no completely reliable source of intelligence at the beginning of May 1940.

Wonderful cryptographic triumph though it was, the advent of Red did not at once provide such a complete solution to the intelligence problem as might be thought, and for two reasons. The first was intrinsic to the material and therefore permanent. Red was a Luftwaffe cipher. It was composed of traffic between

GAF headquarters and stations and carried instructions for the transfer of squadrons from one airfield to another, returns of current fuel stocks, orders for bombing raids, and the like. Movements of aircraft were its business, not movements of tanks. When the two coincided, as they frequently did in France in May, the distinction mattered little. But when the main concerns of army and air force began to diverge with a slowing of the hectic pace of operations in June, how much the cipher did *not* reveal became more apparent. It carried little information about the German army (which had its own – as yet unreadable – key), yet this was badly needed. Except that captured documents revealed the German army order of battle before fighting began, and the widening gap between the British and Belgian forces on 25 May which led Gort (Commander-in-Chief BEF) to the decision to retreat which saved the BEF, the intelligence picture was in consequence very incomplete; Gort himself evinced little interest in it. The same situation prevailed in the desert in 1941, but the weakness of the foundations of purely military intelligence was sometimes forgotten in the heat of action – on a notorious occasion in January 1942, for instance, when the counter-attack by which Rommel regained Cyrenaica was greatly facilitated by the British lack of information (doubtless carried by an army key which was then unbreakable) about the arrival of twenty-five or more new tanks at Benghazi. The strategic consequences were disastrous.

The second reason was immediate but transient. The pressing emergencies of May and June 1940 created insuperable obstacles to the exploitation of Enigma and Y in operations. The advance into Belgium (itself the consequence of a failure to reflect that the capture of their invasion plan in December might have led the Germans to choose a different route now) and subsequent hurried withdrawal divided GHQ BEF and strained the communications network; security was more vital than ever. The battle was in effect already lost by 22 May,[*] so that there was in any

_____

[*] Or earlier? The French High Command refused to attach much

case little room for tactical or strategic adjustments based on intelligence (the paucity of surviving evidence makes it impossible to know, for instance, whether GHQ was even made aware of an *en clair* intercept timed 1142/24 May ordering the temporary suspension of pressure on the BEF – the order which made the Dunkirk evacuation possible). Over a thousand intercepts a day were being processed at Bletchley Park and passed, though with some delay, via the War Office to GHQ (the French were doing the same) but with no discernible effect on events). Commenting on his conclusion the Sigint was almost useless in France in 1940, the author of an official War Office handbook on intelligence organisation attributed it to the distances between HQs and to communications problems. The frustration in London is easy to imagine, but on the other hand, as the same War Office publication points out, attention had again been drawn to the potential value of Sigint and the lesson had been learned that signals and intelligence must work together. Of even greater long-term importance was the reassuring discovery that, in spite of the haste and confusion of the retreat, the Germans found no evidence that Enigma had been broken when they occupied France in June.* This is even more surprising in view of the casual and leisurely lifestyle which was so common in the army right up to 10 May ('The livers of my superior officers are sluggish'; 'One of my COs sits down after dinner almost every night to play bridge with three of his officers and four bottles of champagne,' wrote Sir Basil Bartlett.

weight to reports that the Germans might try to break through the Ardennes although there had been several reports to this effect, and took no steps to strengthen the defences there. German tanks were photographed massing in the Ardennes but were never bombed.
* Even more remarkable, and worthy of the highest praise, was the conduct of the Polish cipher staff after their country was overrun in 1939, and of the French and Poles (the latter had fled to France via Rumania and re-established their organisation there) after the occupation of Vichy France in 1942. Though most had to escape in conditions of great danger (some of them twice) and some were captured and tortured, none betrayed their priceless secret.

A curious sidelight on the sluggishness of the official mind in
face of the unforeseen collapse of France and the possibility of
invasion is thrown by a memorandum on Home Defence
prepared on 27 May 1940 by Lord Hankey, Chancellor of the
Duchy of Lancaster. (As Sir Maurice Hankey, he had been
Secretary of the Cabinet, 1916–38, the first to hold the new
office, and concurrently Secretary of the Committee of Imperial
Defence; Chamberlain brought him into the government on his
retirement, and Churchill retained him. He was sixty-three in
1940.) His twenty years' exposure to political and defence
matters meant that there were few men with more experience of
either on the outbreak of war. In spite of this, however, an air of
naivety hangs over his memorandum: 'Air reconnaissance should
be employed to check and supplement secret intelligence,' he
wrote, but he did not draw attention either to the shortage of
aircraft and cameras for the former or to the proven insufficien-
cies of the latter, nor did he notice that even at best this could
provide only a limited range of purely tactical intelligence. All
intelligence, he urged, should be 'carefully examined and
brought to the notice (insistently if need be) of those responsible
for action' and a 'small group of alert staff officers should be
entrusted with this task' – as if the JIC had not been set up for
this very purpose two years previously. A section on resistance to
a landing in a port consists mainly of warnings against deception
and camouflage (which he called 'treachery'), plus the after-
thought that 'it would be interesting to know whether the 9.2-
inch guns which defend the major ports have modern mountings
and modern shells'.

The memorandum was plainly composed in great haste (it is
in manuscript, with frequent erasures and corrections), but this is
hardly a sufficient explanation of its inadequacy as a response to
the sudden emergency on the day Belgium surrendered and the
evacuation of Dunkirk began.

Among the brightest of the fitful shafts of light which shone in the intelligence gloom during the summer of 1940 was aerial photography. Like other military arts widely practised during the First World War, it had languished for the next twenty years, partly because up to 1918 its use had been purely tactical and the need for trench photographs would not recur if, as became the prevailing assumption, the British army did not fight another continental war, and partly because the current state of lens technology demanded low-level flights with their attendant high casualty risks. So retrograde had the general attitude become by 1939 that there was only one fully qualified photo-interpretation (PI) officer at the War Office, which still retained control of the subject but refused to spend money on buying modern stereo-scopes. Only two PI officers accompanied the first contingents of the BEF, though more were hastily trained to follow them (the US army had none at all two years later).

Like so many other developments in the British war effort, from the theory and practice of deception to the 'private armies' which became so popular in the Middle East, the promotion of air photography to the position demanded by both established bombing doctrine and a war of movement over a wide area began with the initiative of one or two individuals, not as a matter of deliberate policy. Frederick Winterbotham, the SIS's senior air officer, had been a pioneer of air photography during the First World War. Working at first through the French intelligence authorities, who showed more interest than the British, he arranged a few photo-reconnaissance (PR) flights over Germany in the first months of 1939 by Sidney Cotton, a swashbuckling Australian aeronautical entrepreneur of his own generation. Until then, only a few sorties had been made in recent years, mainly in the Middle East, using oblique photogra-phy, which enabled an aircraft to remain at a safe distance from its target but produced less than satisfactorily informative results. It was plain, now, that the need to escape detection would oblige peacetime flights for military intelligence purposes to be carried out at the highest possible altitude and by the fastest possible aircraft, and that this in turn called for the latest planes (which were, of course, in short supply), improved lenses and some way of preventing these lenses from becoming frosted over by the cold. All these problems were solved, at least temporarily, and parts of Germany and most of Italy's Mediterranean territories had been covered under SIS auspices by the autumn of 1939. By this time the Air Ministry's interest had been sufficiently aroused for it to take the enterprise into its own control. All air photography was henceforth performed by the RAF, but on behalf of all three services – the first substantial departure from the stultifying departmentalism of the 1930s.

Faced by the urgent need to keep track of the construction of the new battleships *Tirpitz* and *Bismarck*, the new DNI, Admiral Godfrey, encouraged the development of PR from the moment of his appointment in December 1939, and was quickly rewarded by the discovery that *Tirpitz*, the more forward of the two, was still not ready for sea in February. When the fitting of extra fuel tanks gave a Spitfire the additional range required, the first PR of Kiel on 7 April 1940 heralded better coverage of the German navy in the future but failed to yield its full intelligence potential simply because it was the first of its kind. The harbour was full of ships and the airfield of transport aircraft; this was assumed to be normal, but in fact it indicated the final preparations for the Norwegian expedition: a reminder that, as had been discovered over the trenches twenty-five years earlier, what *is* can only be properly understood in the context of what *was*.

The usefulness of air photography came into sudden prominence with the virtual disappearance of all other intelligence sources after the fall of France. In some important respects at least PR could supply what was lacking: PR evidence was factually incontestable[*] (though the Kiel case showed that interpretation was required to make its meaning clear), and its collection could be controlled entirely within Great Britain. Its

[*] But see p. 54!

good qualities were abundantly demonstrated during the months of threatened invasion in the summer and autumn of 1940, when the concentration of barges in the Channel ports was the primary clue to the enemy's intentions. From this time on, widespread recognition of its potential led to gradually accelerating progress in the use of PR by all three services, to improvements in cameras and lenses and refinements in the skills of those who interpreted the photographs. Before long the OIC was combining Sigint with PR of German dockyards to monitor the rate of U-boat construction, essential for foreseeing the next stage in the Battle of the Atlantic. The brilliant success of the Fleet Air Arm attack on Taranto harbour on 11 November showed all and sundry not only the extraordinary bravery of the pilots of the obsolescent aircraft they had to fly, but also what PR could do to assist operations. A series of photographs, taken right up to a few hours before the torpedo aircraft took off, ensured that every pilot knew the exact positions of the battleships and of the defences that protected them. Twenty planes, facing fierce anti-aircraft fire in order to come down to sea level and aim their torpedoes with maximum accuracy, put half the Italian battle fleet out of action for six months; one of the ships took no further part in the war. By the early months of the New Year, PR and Sigint were once more combining to harass the cross-Mediterranean shipping which carried supplies and reinforcements to the Italian and (by this time) the German army in Libya.

In April 1941 PR was centralised under RAF Coastal Command, but on an inter-service basis, at Medmenham on the Thames. A year later, Medmenham assimilated an American contingent, and thus became the first fully integrated Allied headquarters. In this and other respects it paralleled or narrowly anticipated the development of army–air Ultra at Bletchley Park. In each case British and Americans worked together for a common purpose irrespective of their different national chains of command, and the pooling of service needs opened up new and highly profitable areas of research – call-signs and code words, bomb damage, shipping routes and a host of others, each requiring specialised knowledge to draw out every ounce of meaning from the material. Even the speed at which urgent needs could be met by photography and decryption proved similar – about three hours in each case. Finally, subsequent reflection suggests that each centre overcame initial obstacles and grew to maturity about the same time – spring 1942.

One serious blemish disfigured the face of the intelligence-operations complex affecting aerial warfare, and it persisted throughout the war. Air photography was slowly forcing Bomber Command towards the reluctant admission that most of its bombs were falling wide of their targets, some very wide indeed. Göring and OKW knew how little damage the only offensive weapon Britain possessed in 1940 and for most of 1941 was doing, and so did neutral observers like William Shirer, the United States newspaper correspondent and broadcaster. Shirer saw only negligible damage in the Ruhr in May 1940 after a raid which the BBC had reported as very successful, and again in Berlin after the first big attacks in August and September. But, in the absence of conclusive evidence to the contrary, Bomber Command clung obstinately to its belief in the accuracy of its aim and the explosive power of its bombs, tiny though the bombs were by the standards of later years. Its misplaced confidence could affect official announcements and the BBC news, thus letting the Germans know how inaccurate British intelligence still was. Chamberlain told the House of Commons, for instance, that the Hornum seaplane base on the Heligoland Bight had been destroyed in a raid on 30 March 1940, whereas all the bombs had fallen on a Danish island. How to explain the discrepancy between claim and reality? As the RAF official history says, photographic reconnaissance 'came as a great shock, and at first was taken to throw doubt on the efficiency of the photographic interpretation rather than on the accuracy of the visual reports' of the bomber crews, who were understandably convinced that they had done great damage. Blind conviction sometimes completely blotted out awkward facts: one Group intelligence officer abruptly dismissed photographs proving beyond doubt that an attack had missed its mark with the curt comment, 'I do not accept this report.' Bomber Command's handling of unwelcome intelligence is a subject so large that it demands separate treatment later (see Chapter 4).

So much has been written about the Battle of Britain that it is not easy to find anything new to say. Yet a closer look reveals unexpected areas of uncertainty and disconcerting gaps in the primary material which make the precise part played by intelligence difficult to ascertain.

Nothing can diminish the glory of the Few; their skill and daring won the victory without which Britain might not have survived. Nor must it be forgotten that all their bravery would have availed little if they had not had better planes to fly than their opponents and, by the autumn, more of them to supply battle wastage; the Spitfire always had the beating of the Me 109.

But the attacker has the initiative and can dictate the shape of the battle. Unless the RAF could get its fighters into the air and ready to meet an incoming raid and its protective escort, the dice would be loaded against it and the bombers would get through, so short was the interval between take-off from airfields just across the Channel and arrival over target in Kent, Sussex or Surrey. Radar was the saviour, and radar was the chief source of the intelligence which made victory possible. 'From the primitive beginnings in 1935, radar had developed by 1940 into a sufficiently effective instrument of war to transform air defence,' wrote John Terraine. In the short space of five years Sir Robert (as he later became) Watson-Watt's demonstration that an aircraft re-radiated a radio beam directed at it led to the construction of more than fifty radar stations round the coast of south-east England to detect approaching aircraft. Without the radar chain, wrote the official historian, 'it is as certain as such hypotheses can ever be that the Battle of Britain, and perhaps the whole war, would have been lost'.

Science and intelligence were here married more closely than ever before to assist military operations by giving a few minutes' warning of an imminent raid, its height and its approximate strength. It was the gift of foreseeing a raid before it could develop which discharged Air Chief Marshal Hugh Dowding, Air Officer Commanding (AOC), Fighter Command, and his staff from the obligation to keep patrols continuously in the air to guard against surprise, so making possible an immense saving in their scarcest commodity, pilots, and their capacity to endure the unremitting strain. Without radar, five or six times as many men and aircraft – more than were available at the time – would have been needed to give as good a guarantee. Economy of effort and tight command control, exercised through the display tables in the purpose-built control rooms at Fighter Command and 11 Group, were the distinctive features of the British victory. They contrasted sharply with the looser structure, variable direction and mistaken trust in the mere weight of numbers on the German side.

As soon as a raid was in the air over its French base, radar could pick it up; the Observer Corps could provide confirmatory detail as the planes passed overhead. By showing which airfields housed most bombers, PR – its sorties often guided by Ultra – might suggest which bases were the most likely source of raids, but neither radar nor PR could predict when a raid would take place nor where it would start from. The Y Service could extend the precious warning time by decrypting orders transmitted in lower-grade codes and could even assist fighter pilots after they were airborne by eavesdropping on conversations between their German enemies. By the late summer means had been found of passing this latter type of information to 11 Group within a minute of the conversation being heard, and by this time the tension of what they were coming to realise was a lost battle was so shortening German tempers that 'our knowledge of German swear words increased considerably,' according to one of the senior WAAF intercept officers (her phrase gives a glimpse of the change in women's sensibilities in the last fifty years).

By identifying call-signs with particular units and studying the WIT networks within which the call-signs were used, Y – with some assistance from Ultra – made possible the compilation of an almost complete Luftwaffe order of battle in the west, to the great benefit of the Air Ministry, which had hitherto been unable to discover it. This in turn led to a more accurate estimate of total Luftwaffe numbers than before; lack of a proper evidential basis had forced the Air Ministry to proceed largely by abstract reasoning, and this was now shown to have been the cause of wild fluctuations in former estimates and sometimes of unduly pessimistic conclusions.

Given the short range, the plain objective and the fact that the fighter and bomber stations which mounted the raids acted on the orders of higher authority – ultimately that of Göring, who personally directed the assault – it was unlikely that Y would reveal much about German strategy: high-level communications would be carried in securer ciphers or by telephone. Did Enigma fill the gap? How useful was it in the Battle of Britain? Surprising obscurity clouds the answer. Pieces may always have been missing from the intelligence jigsaw (only on rare occasions could Ultra ever supply them all), or never written down when operational decisions had to be made in haste, but in any case the primary evidence is still withheld from public view: neither decrypts nor translations of this period can be consulted. Lastly, the staff at Bletchley Park was still mainly civilian and mainly cryptographic, and it included few men with experience of military requirements. Moreover, the kind of information needed to direct war in the air has a very short useful life: an order for a bombing raid has no more operational value than William the Conqueror's battle orders for Hastings unless it reaches the intended victims in time for them to take steps to repel the raid – that is to say, perhaps within an hour or less from the moment the order was decrypted. Ultra could seldom manage this, and there was no staff at the Air Ministry capable of taking full advantage of the little it did provide; but Y (because it could be decrypted quickly) and PR in combination might do it. The official historians, whose judgment there is no ground to question, conclude that in general Enigma had little influence on the Battle of Britain, and they found only a few examples to the contrary.

Did Air Chief Marshal Dowding of Fighter Command receive Ultra? The official history does not say so, but may be read as implying it. The natural assumption, of course, is to take it for granted that he was given every possible assistance in his difficult task, but a curious uncertainty surrounds the matter. The only explicit statement that he did receive Ultra appears to be that of Winterbotham, who claimed to have established a direct link between Bletchley Park and Fighter Command in early August. In view of the many proven errors of an author who had no access to official records after the war and wrote entirely from memory thirty years later, this cannot be regarded as proof unless corroborated. There appears to be no other positive evidence that Dowding received Ultra except for a minute of Churchill's dated 16 October, long after the Battle of Britain was over, which asked for Dowding's name to be added to the Ultra list.[*]

---

[*] Even this cannot be regarded as conclusive, however. Churchill also asked for Eden's name to be added, yet this seems not to have been done: only the Permanent Under-Secretary and the Foreign Office representative on the JIC knew even that Ultra existed in the summer of 1943. Ultra was never sent direct from GC&CS to the FO, but by September 1943 it was being sent thither daily by 'C' (BI ii.5n., iii/1.139, iii/1.121n). This suggests that Eden was not in the secret until late in 1943, which is improbable on the face of it; Gilbert (vii. 255 n2) shows him receiving Ultra in November 1942.

Churchill's minute also asked for the inclusion of A. V. Alexander, the First Lord of the Admiralty, because he 'must know everything known to his subordinates', yet there is ample evidence that this was never done

Repugnant as arguments of the 'must have been' variety always are, we can probably do no better in this case than conclude that Dowding must have been given Ultra in some form at an early stage in the Battle of Britain. Very likely he was indoctrinated orally, and in haste, like Wavell later, and no record was ever kept.

That there is so little sign that Dowding used Ultra need occasion no surprise. Ultra did not wear its heart on its sleeve, and more than most sources needed both intuitive and rational examination before it could yield its best. Was there anyone with sufficient experience of military intelligence to adapt swiftly enough to an entirely new source of information, particularly under conditions which demanded almost instantaneous decisions? Or was part of the price for the neglect of intelligence during the inter-war years already being paid in the summer of 1940?

As the summer turned gradually into autumn, preoccupation with the possibility of invasion replaced that with the air battles over southern England which had clearly been its intended forerunner.

Photo-reconnaissance of the Channel ports showed which of them would probably be the chief embarkation ports and how fast the assembling of invasion craft was proceeding. It must be

and that Alexander was hustled out of the OIC's secret map room even when Ultra was playing a vital part in the Battle of the Atlantic (Beesly, *Very Special Intelligence*, 99).

Churchill also wanted the inclusion of Peirse, then Commander-in-Chief Bomber Command. No indication of what happened has survived, but it is clear that his successor, Harris, was excluded for the first two years of his tenure of power (see pp. 166–9).

The probable solution of the mystery is that Ismay, to whom Churchill's minute was addressed, consulted the supreme guardian of security, 'C', Sir Stewart Menzies (who had no doubt drawn up the original list on his own sole responsibility as soon as Ultra came on stream in May), and that on this occasion he did not sanction the inclusion of Eden and Peirse.

remembered, however, that Hitler had expected that Britain would either collapse or negotiate after Dunkirk, and that there was no precedent for a landing on the scale which would be needed for the conquest even of a half-defeated country. Invader and invaded alike had to improvise ways and means as best they could in the few weeks during which the weather would remain favourable. Specialised invasion craft after the 1944 patterns and in 1944 numbers were unknown. A miscellaneous collection of shipping was brought together; barges built for the calm waters of the Rhine were pressed into service, although they carried too little freeboard to guarantee their safety in the choppy waters of the Straits of Dover. Nevertheless, the threat of invasion was taken with every seriousness throughout Britain: the Home Guard ('Dad's Army') was founded, and the code-word CROM-WELL (meaning 'invasion imminent') was promulgated on 7 September.

If PR, now used on a massive scale, could predict the approximate size of the invasion fleet and indicate that it might start from anywhere between Le Havre and Rotterdam, this was hardly enough. Radar could help once the fleet sailed but could do nothing until then. The balance of intelligence changed, and for the first time Ultra gave really useful guidance of a kind which, though erratic and much scantier than could have been desired, was sufficient to prevent the complete surprise which would otherwise have been unavoidable.

Before the end of July Ultra gave positive proof that an invasion was being planned: an order not to bomb the Channel ports clearly implied that the Germans intended to use them. Thereafter details accumulated, but none did more than show that preparations were continuing; nothing definite emerged. A disaffected German, Hans-Thilo Schmidt, provided SIS with a great deal of valuable technical information about the working of the Enigma machine, and another indicated that there might be two landing places, one in Kent or Sussex and the other north of the Thames. With the main questions – timing and the weight of the first assault wave – still unanswered, the defence remained very much in the dark; several decrypts referring to *Seeloewe* ('sealion', subsequently known to have been the cover-name of the invasion plan) were too cryptic to convey much useful meaning. The way in which the limitations of the available intelligence were then recognised is for the historian the most arresting feature of a War Office appreciation dated 18 October. This ends by pointing out that everything that was known came from the area of Luftflotte 2 (the Low Countries) and that this was 'only about a quarter of the picture' – an early realisation that the true worth of Ultra could be assessed only by recognising its necessary limitations: northern France was under the command of Luftflotte 3, for instance, and no army or navy Enigma had yet been decrypted, besides which all high-level orders would be conveyed by telephone or teleprinter and thus be inaccessible to Ultra.

A month before this War Office appreciation was written the invasion had in fact been put off. Hitler postponed it and ordered the dispersal of the sea transport in mid-September, and in mid-October formally shelved it until 1941. Intelligence did no more than suggest that this might have been the case. During September PR showed some thinning out of the presumed invasion shipping, and Ultra gave belated support to the obvious deduction when it revealed that a small administrative unit with known invasion duties was being disbanded; an SIS report of undetermined reliability suggested postponement until 1941, but there was never any positive evidence that the threat of invasion had been lifted.

When it failed either to subdue the RAF by attacking its airfields or to paralyse Britain by bombing London in daylight, the Luftwaffe turned to raiding the capital and major industrial centres at night, when darkness would of course impede its aim but would also give the defence a far smaller chance of shooting its aircraft down. This change of tactics enabled it to do damage

almost with impunity: searchlights had greater difficulty in
finding the bombers and illuminating them continuously, anti-
aircraft guns (pitifully few at first) were inaccurate until predictors could forecast an aircraft's course and aim shells to meet it,
and night-fighting, an unknown art hitherto, was ineffectual. But
if in 1940 the Germans exploited what was for the moment an
exclusively British handicap (they were afflicted by it in turn
themselves when the balance of war shifted) they were not well
equipped to attack targets of a kind they had not seriously
envisaged.

Like the RAF, the Luftwaffe was restricted in its offensive
capabilities by what today's jargon would call 'the state of the
art'. Astro-navigation was useless for precise target identification,
especially in the heat of battle, and the primitive bomb-sights of
the day precluded accurate bomb-dropping. But partly because
the Luftwaffe was primarily designed for army co-operation in
daylight and needed to destroy relatively small targets like
command headquarters speedily, and partly because it nurtured
an intention eventually to attack more distant targets in order to
destroy military supplies and manufacturing centres (hence the
pre-war experiments with four-engined bombers, later cancelled
on Hitler's orders), German science had advanced much further
than British in target identification. Novel electronic means of
directing the bomber to its target and enabling it to drop its
bombs to maximum effect were already under development in
the 1930s, and at least one of them was foreseen in the Oslo
Report.

The bomber got through because the attack had outrun the
defence technologically. There is a curious reverse parallel here
with the land warfare of 1914–18. *Then*, the defence – barbed
wire, trenches and machine guns – possessed a lethal advantage
because the only means of attack was to launch wave after wave
of fragile human bodies against them; men died in their
thousands to gain only a few yards of ground without advancing
victory one whit. *Now*, the air defences were no match for the

bombers under cover of darkness. In each case the reason was technological, and the remedy scientific and technical: an armoured vehicle which could beat down the wire and cross trenches in the first, airborne radar, predictors and proximity fuses – none of which had been invented by 1940 – in the second. Unfortunately it was far easier to identify the disease than to discover and manufacture the cure, and the interval between the two was painfully long in both cases. (On the other hand, recent experience in the Gulf war suggests that the apparent closing of the gap between attack and defence in the 1940s was an illusion: the Patriot beat the Scud, and 'smart bombs' were now accurate enough to destroy military targets without harming civilians on the Second World War scale. It has even been suggested that smart bombs may have put the tank finally out of business.)

The first hint that the Germans might be a jump ahead in methods of bomber guidance came in February 1940 when a conversation between two captured airmen, overheard through a hidden microphone in a prisoner-of-war camp, referred to an apparatus in a bomber which appeared to involve radio pulses. This was an early example of one of the two ways (interrogation was the other) in which prisoners-of-war were to provide strategic as well as short-term operational intelligence in the future. A few days later the log of a shot-down Heinkel bomber referred cryptically to *Knickebein* ('crooked leg') in a similar context.

There the matter rested until June, when an obscure Enigma message could best be interpreted to mean that a *Knickebein* transmitter had been erected at Cleves in north-west Germany. Soon interrogation of newly captured pilots, examination of apparatus from their plane, and the discovery of another *Knickebein* station in Schleswig-Holstein convinced Dr R. V. Jones, the Air Ministry scientist, that he had worked out not only the principle – the intersection of two radio beams over the target – of the system but also how to counter it by jamming.

Jones was summoned to attend a meeting of the War Cabinet on
21 June. He convinced Churchill and an initially sceptical
gathering of men twice his age (he was only twenty-eight) that he
had divined the scientific basis of the system; in addition he
secured, against some opposition, an order for an aircraft to test
his conclusions by listening for the beams next day at a position
predicted by him over Derby. The beams were found. Dunkirk
was barely three weeks ago, France was signing an armistice that
very day, and the Battle of Britain had not yet been fought.

In barely ten days the beams had grown from a conjecture to
a certainty. It remained to develop counter-measures. Slow at
first, the process gradually accelerated, taking two other broadly
similar systems, X- and Y-*Gerät* (X and Y apparatus) in its stride
and defeating the last very quickly indeed. By January 1941 all
three had been mastered. Beam bombing had been rendered
ineffective, but the Blitz continued; its accuracy was diminished
but it still caused many casualties and did much damage.[*]

Jones and his scientific colleagues had used their skill and
insight to combine three such different sources of intelligence as
Ultra, prisoners-of-war and captured material to establish
scientific intelligence on a solid foundation and give it access to
the seat of power. The magnitude of the revolution that had
been initiated was plain, as Jones says, when in February 1942
'Bomber' Harris was appointed to conduct the air assault on
Germany 'by the radio aids about which he had been so
scathing' two years before. Science and scientific intelligence
were henceforth to play a leading role both in offence (antisubmarine measures and the atom bomb) and defence (the

---

[*] Although it has often been contradicted, it may still be useful to repeat
that the legend that Churchill allowed Coventry to be bombed on the
night of 14/15 November 1940, although he knew that it was the
Luftwaffe's target, in order not to endanger the security of Ultra, is
entirely without foundation. It was known that a raid was planned for the
Midlands, but that Coventry was the target was not known until far too
late to strengthen the anti-aircraft defences, even if any such action had
been contemplated.

detection of U-boats and of the V-weapons and the development of counter-measures against both). The Second World War was to become increasingly a war of science.

By the end of 1940 several intelligence sources had begun to hint that they might in future be able to assist operations on a large scale, but none had yet managed any great feat: radar and the victory over the bombing beams can be claimed as first-rank successes, but only with the reservation that they were entirely defensive, means of survival not signs of victory. Progress had been fitful and subject to relapses. Even Ultra, soon to overtop every other source, had become almost dormant by the New Year.

The greatest advances had so far been made in air intelligence, to which Ultra had made a notable contribution. Since Britain's need was most urgent in air defence, this was a happy accident. But it gave no hope of finding ways to confront the victorious German army on land, should a new theatre of war be opened up to replace the vanished battlefields of France, still less of suggesting how to take the offensive. It was in a mood of resolute desperation which reflected this that on 16 and 17 July Churchill ordered SIS to take urgent steps to increase the number of its agents in occupied France and went on to found the Special Operations Executive and tell it to 'set Europe ablaze', although he knew that he could not stoke the fires it might set burning because after Dunkirk Britain lacked the resources to do so.[*]

---

[*] 'He sometimes came nearer setting Whitehall ablaze,' was Cadogen's rueful comment (Dilks, *Cadogen Diaries*, p.31).

Whether or not British interests would be best served by encouraging resistance in occupied territory posed a dilemma which plagued SOE throughout its life. It has recently been given new prominence by the release (in August 1998) to the Public Record Office of papers recounting a plan to kill Hitler. It is difficult, though not impossible, to reconcile what these papers say with the story of the same years told in Peter Wilkinson and Joan Bright Astley, *Gubbins and SOE* (Leo Cooper, 1993). The authors' credentials are beyond question (SOE 1940–45, British

Two other entries which were to show profits in the future can be made on the credit side of an intelligence balance sheet which was still deeply in the red at the end of 1940. The refounded Intelligence Corps was now recruiting suitable candidates widely, and had started courses of instruction to give them a broad general training before they were posted to active duty and began to discover that all the finer points of intelligence work can only be learned 'on the job'. Secondly, by the end of 1940 every German agent who had landed in Britain had been rounded up (a feat so unexpectedly complete that none dared believe it until well into 1941) and either executed, imprisoned or 'turned' to become a double agent purveying disinformation to his Abwehr controller. Thus were created the first features of the setting in which the FORTITUDE deception plan – to disguise the Allies' chosen landing place in France and keep the Panzer divisions away from it – could be launched before D-Day in June 1944 in the confident knowledge that the Germans had no certain means of distinguishing truth from falsehood.

Another development in 1940 and early 1941 held still more

Ambassador to Austria later; Head of Secretariat of Chiefs of Staff Committee 1941–45), but they were evidently forbidden to mention the murder plan when they were writing their book. It would have been to the Allies' advantage to have Hitler assassinated in 1941 or 1942, when things were going badly for them, if it had been possible to arrange it along the same lines as the assassination of Heydrich (which was planned in England by SOE); but by late 1944, still more in the spring of 1945, when SOE again had the matter under consideration, Hitler had made so many mistakes (the attack at Avranches, for example) that he was likely to make more, so that his survival would be a positive advantage to the Allies. Many senior members of SOE pointed this out at once, but there were others who believed (quite erroneously) that his removal would trigger resistance to the Nazi regime.

The same tensions within SOE as were apparent in 1940 still remained in 1945. They stemmed from doubts whether support for guerrilla operations (supposing that adequate means could be found to nourish them) would or would not 'set Europe ablaze'. They had been a main reason why the threat of abolition had hung over SOE until at least 1943, they had prevented SOE from forming a true grasp of strategy, and had thereby hindered it from becoming a really useful instrument of war.

promise. The rigid barriers between departments and their reluctance to compare information from different sources and draw common operational deductions from evidence had been among the chief defects of pre-war intelligence. Any sign of change was therefore an augury of better things to come. The first indication of a greater flexibility of attitude and of a greater sensitivity in the handling of evidence came when photographic reconnaissance, the Y Service, prisoner-of-war interrogation and Ultra combined to discover the nature of the bomber beams and to counter them. More striking still was the way an even greater variety of sources, none of which could have done the job alone, contributed to the sinking of the *Bismarck* on her maiden voyage in May 1941. Because she was the newest and the most powerful battleship afloat, she would be difficult to deal with, yet it was absolutely essential to neutralise her because the Atlantic supply route was now more important than ever and she could do far more than the *Graf Spee* eighteen months earlier.

It was plain that *Bismarck* was likely to break out into the Atlantic for a prolonged commerce-raiding voyage as soon as she was ready for sea. The first hint that she had sailed came when a Swedish ship sighted her in the Kattegat on 20 May. The head of the Swedish SIS told his friend the Norwegian Military Attaché, who passed the news on to the British Naval Attaché, who in turn signalled the Admiralty that same evening. This confirmed a tentative inference from a GAF Enigma decrypt of a day or two earlier which showed that long-range aircraft had been reconnoitring the sea route (the Denmark Strait) along the ice-edge between Iceland and Greenland which led into the Atlantic. A little later the Norwegian Resistance sighted *Bismarck* off the west coast of Norway and managed to inform London. Coastal Command photographed her in Bergen on 21 May. Braving dreadful weather another reconnaissance aircraft discovered next day that she had left Bergen, presumably northbound. Despite poor visibility HMS *Suffolk*, one of the first naval vessels to be fitted with radar, managed to keep contact as *Bismarck* passed through the Denmark Strait, only to lose it again early on 25 May after *Bismarck* had sunk the *Hood*. There followed many anxious hours, during some of which the British ships hunting her misinterpreted the only indication of *Bismarck*'s whereabouts (a mediocre D/F 'fix') and steamed in the wrong direction. Was *Bismarck* making for home northabout, or was she shaping course for a Biscay port? No sooner had Admiral Tovey, commanding the hunting squadron, at last decided on the evening of the 25th that the latter was the more probable, than Enigma, entering the lists decisively this time, confirmed the rightness of his conclusion: a senior Luftwaffe officer in Athens had a son serving aboard *Bismarck*, inquired his destination in GAF Enigma and received the answer 'Brest'. This finally solved the puzzle which had been troubling Tovey and the Admiralty alike ever since *Suffolk* had lost contact with *Bismarck*, and it substantially narrowed the sea area to be searched. Next morning a Catalina flying boat located her. Tovey's relief was tempered by the discovery that he was by now too far behind *Bismarck* to catch her before she entered the zone protected by land-based aircraft. Unless *Bismarck* could be slowed down, neither he nor the warships he had summoned to draw the net round her would be able to bring her to battle and destroy her: she would thus be free to make another ocean foray later on. Swordfish from the carrier *Ark Royal* saved the day, putting *Bismarck*'s rudder-control system out of action so that she could sail only in circles. She was sunk next day.

Naval Enigma played no part in the search for the *Bismarck*, though it did in the subsequent destruction of the supply ships scattered over the ocean to nourish her with food and fuel. The planned capture of two weather ships and the fortunate capture of *U-110* had yielded cipher tables, but decryption was not current until 1 June, after the chase was over. When the operational signals of the critical days were read, however, the enormous potential of Ultra stood revealed. A new chapter in the war at sea was about to open. Given the flying start provided by the three captures, by August the cryptographers had secured a firm hold on the cipher then in use by surface vessels and U-boats alike; with one alarming intermission in 1942, they retained their hold for the remainder of the war.

A combination of sources – a friendly neutral, the Resistance, photo-reconnaissance, radio direction-finding and ship-borne radar – found the *Bismarck* and tailed her for four days; when contact was lost and acute danger threatened, the newest source of all, high-grade Sigint, came to the rescue in the nick of time. Looked at in this way, the story of the *Bismarck* illustrates the co-operation between different types of intelligence which was to be the hallmark of the coming months and years, and perfectly epitomises the inchoate but encouraging stage it had reached by the summer of 1941.

1941–1943

A Brighter Prospect
in the Mediterranean

Having delayed in cowardly fashion until German victories in northern France removed all danger of a French counter-attack on his Alpine frontier, Mussolini declared war on Britain on 10 June 1940. His first aggressive action did not follow until mid-September, when Marshal Graziani advanced with a quarter of a million men some sixty miles into Egypt, meeting only light resistance from the tiny British force there; he then promptly forgot that a timid offensive is worse than none at all, and settled down to construct a line of fortified camps in the desert south of Sidi Barrani. It was at sea, however, that Italy was to receive its first rebuff. The powerful Italian fleet could cut Britain's communications with the Middle East and India through the Mediterranean, yet the Admiralty had to find ships for the Atlantic and Pacific as well, so that Admiral Cunningham, Commander-in-Chief Mediterranean, was compelled to make do with fewer than he wanted. The raid on Taranto, described in the last chapter, checked the Italians and forced them to abandon their southernmost naval base, but it did not entirely obliterate the threat from the Italian fleet; because of it, supplies and reinforcements were routed for safety to Suez round the Cape of Good Hope, making the voyage at best six or seven times longer than the single week to Alexandria via Gibraltar.

Hard on the heels of the Taranto raid came COMPASS, the British reply to the Italian advance on land: in December and

January 30,000 men routed a quarter of a million Italians, taking half of them prisoner and driving the rest of the Italian army 500 miles westward and out of Cyrenaica altogether.

Aerial reconnaissance could easily establish the location of the Italian camps, and armoured-car patrols could test their alertness, but neither could discover Graziani's intentions. A Combined Bureau Middle East had been established outside Cairo to intercept army and air cipher traffic and decrypt it on the spot (later also Enigma traffic, which it passed on to GC&CS for decryption), and both had proved rewarding. Italian air force decrypts gave army as well as air intelligence; the army Y Service in the field was quickly developed and during COMPASS tracked enemy movements – the army order of battle had already been satisfactorily established from soldiers' letters captured on their way to Italy. All these sources, useful as they were, could have been turned to more profit had it not been for the general distrust of intelligence which infected field commanders (with the notable exception of Wavell) as much as the War Office at home. This now scarcely credible attitude stultified much military activity in the desert for another eighteen months, until shortly before Alamein.

General Wavell, Commander-in-Chief in the Middle East, had served under Allenby and had been deeply impressed by his use of deception and surprise in Palestine in 1917 and 1918. He now adapted his predecessor's ideas to trick the Italians into thinking that his troops were more numerous and better equipped than they really were and to delude them about his tactical intentions. Thus there was added to the British armoury a new and powerful derivative of intelligence which was to mislead German generals throughout the war, notably by persuading them, and Hitler too, that the OVERLORD landings of 1944 would come mainly round Calais rather than in Normandy. It is important to stress at once that deception was a derivative of intelligence, not something separate from, though parallel to it. Lieutenant-Colonel (later Brigadier) Dudley

Clarke, the specialist whom Wavell summoned from England to develop his ideas, laid it down as a fundamental principle that the enemy could be persuaded into useful error only if he was fed disinformation based on knowledge he already possessed, though subtly diverging from it – that is to say, successful deception depended on the deceiver being first acquainted, through his intelligence service, with at any rate the main lines of the enemy's thinking.

Neither Ultra nor any other source was yet quite fulfilling this requirement when, at Wavell's bidding, Dudley Clarke and a handful of others – collectively known as 'A' force – set out to deceive the enemy about British strengths and intentions. Their first headquarters was in a converted bathroom in GHQ Cairo, but they soon moved into a partially converted brothel in the town. For the first twelve months or more of its existence 'A' force remained small, secret* and entirely personal (to begin with Wavell gave Dudley Clarke all his orders by word of mouth) and was in a sense the first of the 'private armies' which were later such a feature of the desert war. Early success led to a widening of its aim from simply relieving pressure on the desert front to embrace the strategy of the whole Middle East. This was its all-engrossing concern from the launching of its first grand strategic plan, CASCADE, in the spring of 1942, with the object of persuading the Germans that British forces, and therefore their capabilities, were far greater than they really were. A 50 per cent inflation was soon achieved, and 'A' Force managed to preserve the illusion throughout the war. This widening of its horizons necessitated some modification of its hitherto personal character and an enlargement of its staff, as did the induction in 1943 of Americans into something so quintessentially British in its ways. But by this time the manifest benefits which the addition of a 'notional' force to their actual strength conferred on

---

* So secret that even Hut 3 knew almost nothing about it until Christmas 1943, when from its point of view 'value' began to replace mere 'interest'.

operational commanders' freedom of choice and action was so apparent that Dudley Clarke's experience and advice were being called upon to assist those whose task it was to diminish the risks attendant upon an invasion of mainland Europe by methods similar to those he had practised with such tremendous success.

Outstanding in significance as his new departure was – German attempts at deception were feeble and fragmentary by contrast – it was not Wavell's only contribution to intelligence; he also founded the Long Range Desert Group, which sent small but highly skilled patrols hundreds of miles into the open desert flank of the Axis armies in Libya, dominating the northern fringes of the Sahara and producing intelligence of all kinds, most valuably by setting up almost permanent observation posts along the coast road to count the number of tanks and guns delivered to the front from the main supply port of Tripoli. These two initiatives, rather than his generalship, were Wavell's chief contribution to victory.

COMPASS began at dawn on 9 December, and for two months the tiny British force, greatly benefiting from Italian air force decrypts, outwitted and outfought its vastly superior opponent. Sidi Barrani was captured in two days, Sollum and the frontier in three, Bardia in three weeks, Tobruk on 22 January; such rapid progress was made that the defeat of the Italians was completed on 8 February. The surprise thrust along the chord of the Cyrenaican arc to intercept the Italians at Beda Fomm as they retreated by the coast road was made possible by the Y Service, which showed that no significant opposition would bar its path.

Upon news of this, Hitler determined to come to the aid of his humiliated Axis partner. Four days after Beda Fomm, Rommel landed at Tripoli with the advance part of what was to become the Afrika Korps. He quickly pushed patrols out eastwards, and by a strange coincidence their first contacts were with a British armoured car reconnaissance unit commanded by Lieutenant (later Brigadier Sir Edgar) Williams, who was to be Mont-

gomery's Chief Intelligence Officer from November 1942 until
the end of the war.

A little earlier, on the same day as Beda Fomm, the Greek
government asked for preliminary conversations about the
possibility of British assistance against the growing German
threat in the Balkans.

Another development in these same weeks was a new Enigma
break: a second key, used for army–air co-operation in Libya,
succumbed to the cryptographers at the end of February. Thus,
soon after Rommel landed, new information bearing on his
activities became available, and it was clear that it could be
useful to Wavell and his fellow commanders provided it reached
them quickly enough. Much red tape must have been cut in
record time, for a direct service of signals from Hut 3 at
Bletchley Park to Cairo was inaugurated a fortnight later, on 13
March. In retrospect, this was an extraordinary, indeed a
positively astonishing innovation, and it was to have remarkable
consequences. The object was to cut out a stage in the
intelligence-producing process, but there were novel overtones.
The SIS, under whose wing GC&CS at Bletchley Park
functioned, had never had a direct hand in military matters
before. Though they were, of course, under the general
supervision of the War Office and Air Ministry, the men now
empowered to communicate directly with generals and air
marshals were all recently commissioned civilians, some of them
assigned to MI6 and all no more than amateur soldiers and
airmen, unversed in the ways of military intelligence (as I well
remember, having been one of them). As they gathered
exerience in setting the Enigma-derived information into an
intelligible context and in drafting signals to embody it, they
gradually created an entirely new brand of professionalism which
eventually formed one of the foundations upon which the
intelligence community of today is built. The experiment

abundantly justified itself, but its foundation may have been a 'close-run thing'.

It is often said, and with good reason, that Menzies seized on Enigma before others realised its potentialities, in order to bolster SIS's failing fortunes as its share in intelligence waned after the Venlo débâcle. On the other hand, it is difficult to believe that the armed services would have acquiesced in Menzies's swift takeover or have countenanced the hold his 'amateurs' were gaining over the application of intelligence to war if their habit of undervaluing all intelligence had not been so deeply ingrained. If their oversight in 1940 and early 1941 was the price they paid for past blindness, then it was unusually well recompensed: Enigma soon outshone all other sources of military intelligence and, armoured at first by civilian ignorance of military conventions, accustomed to giving reason and logic precedence over hierarchical authority, and unencumbered by inherited prejudices, the 'amateurs' marched forward into the almost unknown with a boldness hidebound Whitehall officers would not have displayed – and yet it was the War Office and Air Ministry which drew the ultimate benefit, access to unexampled riches of information.

Whitehall retained a residuary right of advice and comment on the doings of the 'amateurs', of course, and made increasing use of it as the value of the new source became more and more apparent. But the 'amateurs' of Hut 3 soon outgrew tutelage, and before long became professionals of a new kind, ready to argue doubtful points with equal authority.

Regret that their oversight had cost them too dear first came to the surface in representations by War Office and Air Ministry early in 1941 and lay at the heart of their abortive attempt during the winter of 1941/2 to break SIS's hold over Hut 3 and restore their own pre-war monopoly in a radically different situation. After a disturbed period made still more unhappy because it coincided with the production – it seemed profitlessly – of more intelligence than ever at the time of the CRUSADER battles of November and December 1941 and Rommel's resurgence in January and February 1942 (see pp. 86–7), the fundamentals of the prevailing situation were reaffirmed and badly needed administrative changes were made which satisfied all parties and brought peace[*] to a Hut 3 which had recently been at odds with itself.

Naval Enigma was subject to none of these vicissitudes. None was read until the captures of the early summer of 1941 already mentioned (see p. 66–9) which had marginally affected the *Bismarck* operation, but from August that year the main key was broken regularly. Because the Admiralty was an operational headquarters as well as a Whitehall ministry, all action had to originate there, after co-ordination in its Operational Intelligence Centre, and there was therefore no place for the quasi-independent activity which began in Hut 3 with the inception of the signal service to the Middle East in March 1941. Naval decrypts were translated and telegraphed direct from GC&CS to the Admiralty.

The purpose of the new departure was to exploit army and air Ultra operationally, but it was naval traffic which was to bring the next British victory in the Middle East. The Greek appeal of February 1941 combined with a sense of moral and political obligation to deter the aggressor and led to the despatch of military assistance. The existing plan to continue the desert advance to Tripoli and expel the Italians from their North African empire was shelved. Instead, the Cyrenaican front was weakened (almost fatally, as Rommel was soon to show); so that a strong expeditionary force could be sent to Greece, but its prospects were deemed so frail that the staff of the GOC, General Sir Henry Maitland Wilson, was prudently making contingency plans for evacuation at the same time as the first troops landed on 7 March.

[*] Much of the credit for this was due to the calming influence of Wing Cdr E. M. (later Group Captain Sir Eric) Jones, who was appointed head of Hut 3 in the spring of 1942. After the war he became Director of GCHQ.

Their passage across the Mediterranean lay at the mercy of the Italian fleet, for Admiral Cunningham's protective force at Alexandria was inferior on paper. The danger from the Italians was almost completely removed by a piece of uncovenanted good fortune in the intelligence field.

The Italian naval book cipher became unreadable in the summer of 1940, and although the Italian version of Enigma was broken soon afterwards it carried little traffic until late March 1941,[*] when it most conveniently disclosed that the Italian fleet was preparing to intercept British convoys on passage from Alexandria to the Piraeus. An aircraft sent out to seek confirmation spotted Italian cruisers heading towards Crete from Sicily. Bringing his ships to instant readiness but deferring his departure until after dark so that it should not be known in advance, Cunningham[†] ostentatiously went ashore carrying his golf clubs on the afternoon of 27 March: he knew that the Japanese Consul-General in Alexandria was extremely inquisitive. He surprised the Italians off Cape Matapan on the 28th, sinking three cruisers and two destroyers. It was the first Mediterranean operation to owe its inception entirely to signals intelligence.

When the Germans invaded Jugoslavia and Greece a week later, the Italian fleet made no attempt to come to their assistance. The GAF was more than enough for Wilson in Greece and Freyberg on Crete to deal with; Matapan saved them from a still worse double peril.

The overwhelming power which the Germans deployed on

[*] For its immense later value, see p. 84.
[†] By reacting so swiftly to intelligence and by turning the advantage it gave him to immediate operational effect, Cunningham proved once again that there are exceptions to every rule. He had long been the very epitome of the 'blue-water school' against whom the 'intellectuals' of the 1930s had railed, a 'salthorse' all of whose service had been at sea, because he had spurned staff appointments and all specialisms, whether gunnery, torpedoes or signals (intelligence did not even merit listing) – yet he had remained alert and mentally resilient enough to become the first British commander to forge a victory out of Ultra.

land and in the air over Greece meant that although Wilson was well provided with intelligence he was unable to use it offensively. From almost the first day he was compelled to fight on the retreat and to confine his purpose to withdrawing to his ports of embarkation as expeditiously as possible in order to save his men to fight another day elsewhere. The two Y service sections he employed discharged their duties magnificently, supplying the immediate tactical intelligence which was essential if annihilation by superior force was to be avoided, but Ultra almost at once equalled them at their own game. More than 150 Enigma messages were deciphered and signalled back to Wilson as Ultra, in many cases within five or six hours of their German time of origin, and just in time to affect the next day's operations. For example, an instruction to postpone the opening of the offensive from 0530/6 April until half an hour later was broadcast in Enigma the previous evening and signalled as Ultra before midnight. Thereafter messages reporting positions reached by the German spearheads, or outlining intentions for the next day, were often despatched by midnight, confirming what the Y Service had usually discovered earlier. The most valuable were probably those giving either the withdrawal routes the British were believed to be following or the intended lines of German advance, early warning of air raids on the two main British supply ports, Volos and the Piraeus, and notice that there would be a twenty-four-hour pause before an attack at Thermopylae to open the route to Athens. First-hand testimony to the value of this kind of intelligence in enabling General Wilson to 'duck under the blow' of German might is provided by Sir David Hunt, who was a member of Wilson's own staff.

If Ultra had played an unspectacular part in assisting the withdrawal from Greece, it had at least demonstrated its potential as a source of practical intelligence beyond the possibility of doubt. Within another month it was to go one better by bringing off a far more dramatic coup – the disclosure of the complete German plan for the invasion of Crete a fortnight before the event. This remarkable feat riveted the attention of the few, from Churchill down, who knew about Ultra as nothing else could have done: for a moment's reflection was enough to show that no other source could have given such full and explicit warning.

Surprisingly, in view of the island's strategic position between Greece and Egypt, neither side made up its mind what to do about Crete until late in April. Hitler's directive for the assault was not issued until the 25th, while the British decision to defend Crete was still uncertain before Wavell flew there on the 30th to greet such troops as had reached the island rather than Alexandria and to appoint General Freyberg, GOC of the New Zealand Division (who had arrived from Greece only the previous morning), to take command in the island with a mission to defend it.

At their hurried meeting in the garden of a villa outside Maleme, Wavell told Freyberg that he would receive Ultra (of which he had never heard) and explained exactly what it was and why its existence must be kept completely secret – so secret that he was not to discuss it with his staff. Further, he was to take no action based on Ultra alone, lest the Germans suspect that he got his knowledge from Enigma (there being, it was erroneously believed, no other plausible explanation) and in consequence change their code to a new and perhaps unbreakable system, thus depriving Britain of a promising source of high-grade intelligence.[*]

---

[*] Crete affords an illustration of the difficulty of protecting the secret that Enigma had been broken. Freyberg was strictly forbidden to disclose it to anyone and enjoined to keep it to himself (Lord Freyberg, *Bernard Freyberg, VC* 268–9; *Intelligence Investigations*, 196-201). Yet one page of OL 428 (Germans have reached coast east of Maleme and intend attack on Suda Bay; despatched 2130/23, received Crete 0648/24) was somehow left lying about and captured when Crete fell. The question almost asks itself: how could information like this (it is marked 'Telegram from London') have become known so soon in London save through intercept

Indications that Crete would soon be attacked had been accumulating since 25 April, but on 6 May the complete scope of the German plan was revealed. Parachute landings on the 17th would seize Maleme and Rethymnon airfields and hold them so that reinforcements and a corps HQ could speedily follow by the same route; additional troops, armour and anti-tank guns would come by sea. Later signals added that some 30,000–35,000 men would be employed, roughly two-thirds coming by air and one-third by sea; they also indicated the likely strength of the accompanying air effort and announced a postponement of the assault from 17 to 20 May.

Thus forewarned, Freyberg prepared a hot reception for the parachutists, within the limits of the inadequate resources available to him (Wavell could not spare him the reinforcements for which he pleaded). Large numbers of parachutists were killed, either in the air or as soon as they landed, but after twenty-four hours' bitter fighting Maleme airfield was in German hands. More men, heavy weapons and supplies were flown in, and it soon became clear that the defence would be overwhelmed. British forces evacuated Crete on 31 May.

The high cost of victory disillusioned Hitler with airborne operations (German losses in killed, wounded and missing were approximately 6,000, British and Commonwealth less than 4,000, prisoners excluded). During the spring of 1942, when Rommel was beating at the gates of Egypt and Malta was at its last gasp, he cancelled a projected air-landing operation against Malta at the last moment in favour of more support for Rommel. As élite infantry, parachute divisions fought stubbornly in Italy later on, but they were never again employed in the role for which they had been designed. Had Malta fallen, the British

and decrypt? Yet although signal and German translation were sent to Berlin no suspicions were aroused and no action taken – as in so many comparable cases later (for instance Medenine, see page 126 below).

The document is in the Imperial War Museum (file EDS AL 500/1/3). I am indebted to Miss Bindu Mathur for drawing my attention to it.

position in Egypt and in the whole Mediterranean would have been in great jeopardy. If losing Crete was the price of preserving Malta, the price was worth paying. But for the Ultra warning, the paratroops would have gained a much less costly victory in Crete and consequently earned Hitler's favour; if their Malta operation had then gone ahead, it might well have succeeded.

Freyberg's conduct of the defence has been criticised on three main grounds: that he misunderstood or misread Ultra; that he overestimated the threat from the sea; and that he took insufficient steps to protect Maleme airfield. The first two charges can be satisfactorily rebutted, but there is substance in the third. A discussion of them would range more widely than is appropriate here, but because they have recently been the subject of renewed controversy they are considered in Appendix II.

The land war in Egypt and Libya, now settling into a pattern which lasted two further years, was a war of transport and supply more than of set-piece battles. The British supply route round the Cape was maddeningly slow – strategic decisions taken in Whitehall could not be reflected in desert action for the better part of three months – but at least it was safe. Axis ships could cross the Mediterranean in twenty-four hours, but only at the price of risking attack on the surface and from the air. Moreover, the destination of almost all of them was necessarily Tripoli, the only satisfactory port in Italian territory (Benghazi and Tobruk were too small), although so far behind the front that time and much precious petrol were unavoidably consumed in ferrying tanks, guns, fuel and food to the forward areas, several hundred miles away by road. Information on future sailings and routes was soon regularly provided by the German air and Italian naval ciphers, but cargo manifests were rare and German army Enigma traffic was as yet indecipherable. Information on reinforcements for Rommel could sometimes be pieced together from movement orders in the Reich, and more came from SIS agents working on the Balkan railways, but it was not until the winter of 1941/2 that the Enigma army keys made fuller surveillance possible.

Superior intelligence – mainly but not exclusively Ultra – gradually began to compensate for the delays of the Cape route by enabling the initially weaker RAF and the depleted Mediterranean fleet (its losses in Cretan waters had been serious) to inflict disproportionately heavy damage on the Axis' cross-Mediterranean traffic; by the late summer of 1941, for instance, the GAF in Libya was almost grounded by severe fuel shortage,[*] so many tankers were sunk before Alamein that the mobility of Rommel's Panzer divisions was dangerously restricted, and the German surrender in Tunisia in May 1943 was almost as much the consequence of severed supply lines as of military defeat.

Operationally, on the other hand, intelligence could not prevent successive disasters in the desert during the next twelve or eighteen months. Dazzled by the vista of endless victory which Ultra seemed to promise despite the setbacks in Greece and Crete, Churchill drove Wavell on to two premature offensives in May and June; both quickly collapsed because British radio security was so bad that Rommel always knew where our tanks were and what they intended to do next. The RAF needed guidance about how to interpret Ultra in order to make maximum use of it while maintaining complete security, and 201 Group RAF at Alexandria, charged with sea reconnaissance and spotting Axis convoys, was uncertain how to use Y safely. (Some examples of inadvertent breaches of security and the rebukes which followed have survived.) Inferior equipment lessened the effectiveness of Army Y, although the long series of running commentaries on current events issued by the reconnaissance units of the two Panzer divisions, which often gave

---

[*] Illustrations of the extent to which Ultra revealed this will be found in Appendix VII.

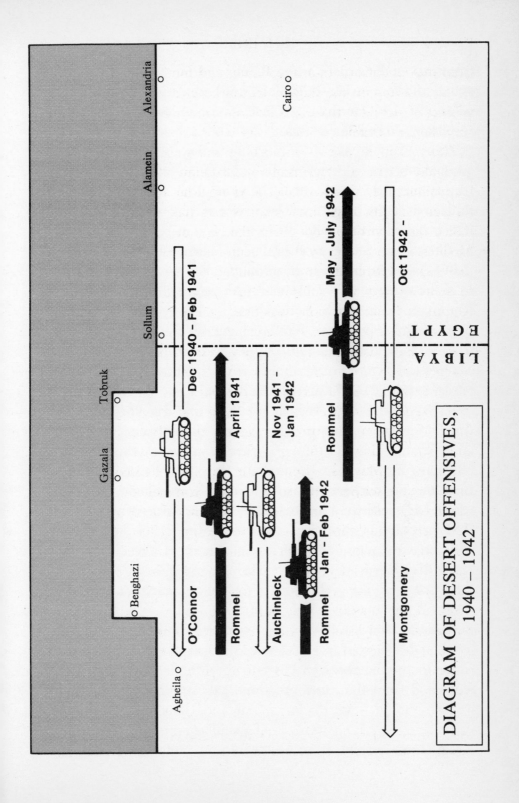

DIAGRAM OF DESERT OFFENSIVES, 1940 – 1942

clues about Rommel's whereabouts and intentions, was beginning, and some tricks of exploitation had already been learned.
(For instance, German advances were ordered according to
arbitrary 'thrust-lines' based on coded map-references. By
shelling likely areas in the morning and waiting for the fall of
shot to be reported in terms of standard map-references the day's
thrust-line code could usually be worked out. (The process was
known as 'gardening'; a similar device was later used to discover
the location of minefields in western waters.)

Once Rommel's onrush had been halted, its impetus blunted
when he threw his tanks headlong against the strongest part of
Tobruk's defences, a tense and nervous calm descended upon
the Cyrenaican front as both sides struggled with the recalcitrant
problem of supply and reinforcement. British intelligence was
the better, and by the autumn they were reaping the benefit –
double the number of tanks and aircraft and the chance of first
strike in the new offensive that both would gladly have launched
sooner – advantages which were to be frittered away by
indifferent generalship in November and December.

As always in quiet times, prisoners were few and the Y Service
able to offer less, but because the very heavy radio traffic in
German air and Italian naval ciphers was being read, Ultra
gained a stranglehold on Rommel's lifeline. Stocks of aircraft fuel
in Libya sank by 90 per cent between May and September, for
instance, and although it secured no figures Ultra showed that
the Afrika Korps' tanks were suffering corresponding restrictions
and that there was a shortage of the flak ammunition needed to
beat off the superior numbers of the RAF.

Unfortunately, not all this valuable knowledge was fully
exploited. The staff in Hut 3 were still learning their job, but so
were those who received Ultra in the Middle East. Both were
recruited from the same predominantly academic background
(which should have made mutual understanding of common
problems easy), both were serving similar apprenticeships, both
were slowly turning from amateurs into professionals. But the

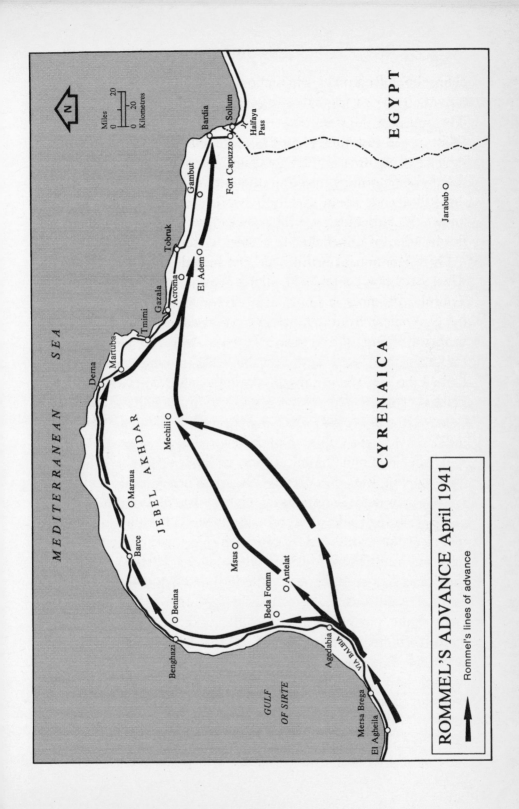

MEDITERRANEAN SEA

EGYPT

CYRENAICA

JEBEL AKHDAR

GULF OF SIRTE

N

Miles
0   20
Kilometres
0   20

Bardia
Sollum
Halfaya Pass
Fort Capuzzo
Gambut
Tobruk
Acroma
El Adem
Gazala
Tmimi
Martuba
Derna
Maraua
Mechili
Barce
Benina
Benghazi
Msus
Beda Fomm
Antelat
Agedabia
Mersa Brega
El Agheila
Jarabub

VIA BALBIA

ROMMEL'S ADVANCE April 1941

→ Rommel's lines of advance

former received too little well-informed backing from War Office
and Air Ministry, and the latter were under the handicap of
having to communicate with generals and air marshals who for
the most part had little regard for, and only limited understanding of, intelligence and its problems, so they set them down
disapprovingly (but no doubt with some justification) as 'more
scholars than soldiers' and needed to have the finer points
interpreted before they could use them.

An illustration of the harm which the current imperfect state
of intelligence could cause occurred in January 1942. Greater
British resources had eventually ground down Rommel's
capacity to improvise resistance to the CRUSADER offensive,
and he had reluctantly withdrawn to a defensive line at Marsa
Brega on the Gulf of Sirte. Then, to the consternation of
Auchinleck, Wavell's successor, he suddenly counter-attacked.
'On 21 January the improbable occurred and without warning
the Axis forces began to advance,' ran Auchinleck's official
Despatch. But there *had* been adequate warning. Auchinleck had
been misled by the failure of his intelligence staff to grasp the full
implications of the various scraps of information which had
come their way and to fit them together properly or to realise
that German radio deception was putting out false positions for a
convoy carrying tanks so that the RAF looked for it in the wrong
places. The jigsaw puzzle was never complete – only air, not
army, keys were being broken; cargo manifests of the Axis supply
ships were rare and in any case listed only GAF deliveries – but
there were sufficient hints[*] to have suggested to alert minds that
it was quite possible that fifty-odd tanks of a new type had
reached Rommel as he retreated and that front-line British units
were not fantasising when they reported meeting them in

[*] Brigadier Shearer was Chief Intelligence Officer, Middle East when
these hints were missed. One of Brooke's first actions as CIGS was to
persuade Auchinleck to dismiss him. Shearer was also responsible for a
flawed deception plan which centred round a 'Gauleiter of Mainz',
having overlooked the fact that there was no such post. (Mainz was in
Gau Baden). See INS 8/1 67–69 and 74.

combat. Because of the consequent miscalculation, Rommel attacked with two or three times more tanks than he was reckoned to have, caught Eighth Army by surprise and off-balance, and advanced halfway back across Cyrenaica before coming to rest at Gazala.

Neither the War Office nor Hut 3 was entirely guiltless in this and other misunderstandings which led to charge and counter-charge of folly during these months. These were partly the by-product of the internal disturbances which led to the reorganisation discussed earlier (see p. 75), partly the result of the lack of personal contact consequent upon the distance between England and Egypt and the near impossibility of travel between them in the prevailing conditions, and partly the consequence of sheer misjudgment on all sides. Wider experience, though thus dearly bought, had smoothed out all these and other problems by the summer; most influential among the changes was the replacement of some members of the intelligence staff in Cairo and the desert by new men under Major-General (as he later became Sir) Francis de Guingand. The new arrangements included the establishment of a section to analyse transport and supply information in order to avoid further damaging miscalculations like that of January. Most of the heads of the new team went on to hold key posts in British intelligence for the remainder of the war. Even before it became a famous fighting force under Montgomery, therefore, the Eighth Army had begun to put its intelligence house in order.

Mistakes were made between autumn 1941 and spring 1942, but essential lessons were learned from them and seldom forgotten thereafter. The whole episode is instructive. It shows that if an effective intelligence staff has to be improvised after war has broken out the cost may be high (as had been pointed out as long ago as 1895, but shamefully forgotten between the wars), because recently civilian 'amateurs', however talented, cannot become professionals in an unfamiliar field except after a prolonged period of experience and self-education, the length of which may be fatal to the cause they serve. Had Hitler turned back against Britain instead of deploying 120 divisions against Russia in June 1941 we should evidently have been as unready in intelligence as in arms and equipment. The success in this particular case does not prove that civilians should be recruited for the purpose when the need arises, as was urged by one of the earliest and still one of the best books about Second World War intelligence; it was simply by the enemy's choice that the 'amateurs', and the whole country with them, were spared a more testing ordeal before they had learned their trade.

The publication in 1990 of the official history of deception has cleared up a small but intriguing mystery. Why did Rommel make a one-day raid into Egypt on 14 September? The facts are simple: 21 Panzer Division advanced some fifty miles across the frontier at dawn, without observable objective unless it was an abandoned British supply depot which Rommel may have believed to be still occupied; the British withdrew, the German tanks ran out of petrol and were bombed – Rommel himself only just escaping death – and returned whence they came the same evening. Why? The answer is now plain: Rommel was lured into it, and this helps to explain the timing of the CRUSADER battle of November.

Auchinleck could not be ready to launch his planned offensive until the late autumn, and it was thought that Rommel might await it quietly instead of beginning his own attack first, if he could be persuaded that Auchinleck would strike soon. (The reasoning was questionable: Rommel would attack as soon as he could, to prevent his besieging forces outside Tobruk from being taken in flank and rear, but the starting-date was dependent on the state of his supplies.) To delude Rommel thus, 'A' Force employed a double agent to suggest three successive dates for the British attack. The latest was 15 September. Rommel's raid was doubtless intended to disrupt British preparations in their final stages. In fact he only betrayed his own petrol shortage and, by construing the British withdrawal and a fake Eighth Army order of battle which he captured as signs that no offensive was being planned, he misled himself as much as 'A' Force could possibly have wished. Early in November he met his wife in Rome for a fortnight's sightseeing holiday and was in Athens on his way back when Auchinleck struck on the 18th.

The occasion marked the arrival of operational and strategic deception on the stage where it was henceforward to play a prominent part, guided, in accordance with Dudley Clarke's principle of feeding the enemy with dishes for which he was known to have a taste, by the fast-growing volume and significance of the information supplied by Sigint. A natural consequence was the hiving off of tactical deception – the dummy tanks and the bogus water-pipeline before Alamein are the best-known illustrations (see p. 107) – to a separate section of the main body, concerned only with the more limited effects which visual deception could produce, while Clarke was freed to concentrate on wielding strategic influence over the whole Mediterranean theatre.

If Rommel's otherwise mysterious September raid marked the first stage in a closer relationship between operations and intelligence, an incident a couple of months later showed that their former segregation could still exercise its evil influence. On the night of 17/18 November, just as Auchinleck's CRUSADER offensive opened, Lieutenant-Colonel Geoffrey Keyes led a raid on what he believed to be Rommel's HQ at Beda Littoria on the 'bulge' of Cyrenaica. Rommel was not there, and Keyes was killed (he received a posthumous VC). No attempt had been made during the planning stage to discover from GHQ whether Rommel was likely to be at Beda Littoria at that time. But Ultra knew that, still believing that Auchinleck was not ready to attack, Rommel had gone to Italy on 1 November and that there had been no sign of him going back. In fact he returned on the 18th, but to his operational HQ at the front, not to what was only an administrative HQ 200 miles further to the rear. The raid could never have served any useful purpose at all.

It was scarcely to be expected that, even though it was now beginning to draw its intelligence from a wider selection of sources, Ultra could be able to throw much light on the confused mêlées swirling across the face of the desert with a rapidity which baffled the commanders on both sides during the British CRUSADER offensive of November and December 1941. More surprising was Y's failure to do much better, in spite of its advantage in quick-moving situations. Neither offers any explanation of Rommel's second and more puzzling aberration, his famous 'dash to the wire'. On the sixth day of the battle, 24 November, with the outcome still uncertain, Rommel suddenly led 15 and 21 Panzer Divisions in a lightning thrust from the neighbourhood of Tobruk to the Egyptian frontier, thus voluntarily removing himself from the hub of events and denying himself all chance of controlling the action. He was away for four days. Soon after midnight on the 24th, a few hours before he started, Ultra reported that he intended to move to the Sollum front, but that was all. Not one of the seventy-six signals which his operations officer Oberstleutnant Westphal, left in charge at headquarters, sent to his absent commander, seems to have been intercepted, and none of the dozen (many of which told him nothing, Westphal wrote later) he received in reply. Any of them might have yielded useful news about the way the kaleidoscopic events looked from the German side, and on the reason why Westphal eventually had the courage to contravene Rommel's instructions and order the two divisions back to the danger-point round Tobruk on his own initiative. Even General Ravenstein, commander of 21 Panzer Division, the first senior officer to be captured, revealed nothing of importance save that there was some discontent with Rommel's impetuous leadership.

More welcome to the British command than any of this would have been, in all probability, was confirmation that the war of supplies was still being won – two tankers sunk on 24 November had been carrying three times as much petrol as there was in the whole of Cyrenaica when they sailed – and advance warning of a

major shift of Axis strategy: Feldmarschall Kesselring, together
with HQ Luftflotte 2 and Fliegerkorps II, were to be moved from
central Russia to the western Mediterranean, Kesselring himself
being appointed Commander-in-Chief South and Rommel's
superior. The significance was clear: a stepping up of pressure on
Malta, the main base for British attacks on the cross-Mediterranean convoys, and thus an intention to defend the Axis supply
lines more strongly. Meanwhile, glaring faults of generalship on
the British side did not prevent CRUSADER, that most
confusing and obscure of offensives, from grinding on towards its
prescribed conclusion, the expulsion of Rommel's army from
Cyrenaica.

While British eyes were fixed on a fluctuating struggle in the
desert between a handful of divisions on each side, momentous
strategic shifts had occurred elsewhere.

Hitler invaded Russia (Operation BARBAROSSA) with 120
divisions and three million men on 22 June 1941, changing the
scale of the war against Nazism in a flash. Britain at once made
common cause with his latest victim, but 'my enemy's enemy is
my friend' counted for little and the new ally was at first more of
a hindrance than a help. No preliminary conversations between
the two had taken place, and no military plans were concerted
now. Stalin told nothing of his resources or intentions, but
demanded assistance (the first convoy of war material sailed for
Murmansk in August); as the Germans pressed forward into
Russia their advance on the southern front conjured up the
nighmare of an envelopment of the Middle East by a thrust
through the Caucasus to join up with Rommel as soon as he took
Cairo, and of a junction with the Japanese somewhere between
Suez and Singapore. (The decrypted despatches of Baron
Oshima, the Japanese Ambassador in Berlin, repeatedly hinted
at this during the spring of 1942.)

On 7 December the Japanese bombed the United States fleet
in Pearl Harbor, Hawaii. Simultaneous attacks on British

territories imposed tremendous new burdens on Britain and the
Commonwealth for the defence of the Far East (reinforcements
on their way to Egypt via the Cape were diverted to Singapore
while at sea), as well as straining American resources. Hitler
declared war on the United States on the 11th, a suicidal move
which brought America openly on to Britain's side at last. 'Now
it is impossible for us to lose the war,' Hitler declared on hearing
the news of Pearl Harbor. 'The accession of the United States
makes amends for all,' said Churchill, 'and with time and
patience will give us victory.' Churchill's was the better
prophecy, and the decision to tackle Germany first, which he
and Roosevelt made on 22 December, ensured that American
men and equipment would reach Europe sooner rather than
later. A combined Anglo-American general staff was set up at
once; complete co-operation in planning and material assistance
followed quickly, in intelligence after rather more hesitation.

Commending Sir Stafford Cripps, Great Britain's new
Ambassador to Moscow, at the end of May 1940 Churchill had
offered to discuss with Stalin 'any of the main problems' created
by Germany's attempt to dominate Europe. This veiled hint that
Germany might one day turn against Russia was based on
nothing more than Churchill's personal reading of strategic
probabilities. As intelligence accumulated during the next twelve
months, the different ways in which the two governments
reacted offered an instructive contrast.

Stalin liked to act as his own intelligence officer, demanded to
see the raw material, disregarded any intelligence and any
comments on it by his professional advisers which did not fit his
own preconceptions and in general so blinded himself with his
own conviction that it was not in Hitler's interests to denounce
the Nazi–Soviet pact agreed by Molotov and Ribbentrop in
1939 that he gained no advantage from the delay (whatever its
precise length) which Jugoslavia and Greece imposed upon
Hitler, so that BARBAROSSA took him by surprise and found
his armies unprepared. Churchill was inclined at first to take the

same line, with regrettable consequences in some cases; fortunately he soon learned how unwise this was and from the New Year of 1942 he allowed himself to be restrained by the CIGS whom he had just appointed, General Sir Alan Brooke. Stalin never learned. Paranoid in 1940 and 1941 about anything that might provoke Hitler (he even ordered Soviet anti-aircraft guns not to fire on the numerous intruders and repeated the order after a German plane crashed while carrying a camera, unexposed film and photographs of Russian defences) and determined to avoid war at all costs, Stalin disregarded the eighty or more warnings he received from Soviet intelligence, and dismissed another from Churchill in April 1941 as proof of an anti-Soviet conspiracy, an error to which Hess's flight to Britain in May seemed to lend colour. Churchill's telegram began, 'I have sure information from a trusted agent . . .', but was in fact mainly based on recent Ultra. Tsarist cryptographers had held a deservedly high reputation, but so far as is known Soviet intelligence never managed to break Enigma at any time during the war. There have been several circumstantially persuasive attempts to suggest the contrary, but none has survived confrontation with such evidence as is at present available; only the opening of the Soviet archives (which is now proceeding) is likely to change this opinion; for hitherto information about Soviet intelligence has been 'either contentious, speculative or hard to obtain'.

Government and people in Britain were alike profoundly ignorant of Russia in 1941. In the absence of regular agent reports since the fall of France and of fully developed intercept coverage, the former found reliable information about German intentions towards Russia hard to come by. From the beginning of the year a scattering of SIS reports, most originating with the Polish underground, spoke of preparations for an attack on Russia; in March, Enigma decrypts mentioned troop movements in eastern Europe, thereby giving some credibility to the

otherwise improbable idea that Germany would soon deliberately destroy the harmony on her eastern frontier which she had
so dramatically secured only a few months before. Diplomatic
sources, however, offered little in the way of confirmation.

What was to be deduced from this ambiguity of evidence?
Russia itself was not yet a major concern of Britain's, but if
Germany was bent on attacking Russia it would have to transfer
troops from west to east on a large scale, thus confirming that
SEALION was not merely postponed but cancelled for the
indefinite future. Air intelligence was inclined to the view that
this was indeed the case, but War Office and Cabinet remained
sceptical and hesitant longer than reasonable caution prescribed.
Was Hitler simply bringing enough pressure to bear on Stalin to
extract further concessions from him? Were the two secretly
negotiating, as some reports insisted? Was the apparently
belligerent German stance a bluff disguising a plan to reverse the
troop movements suddenly and launch a surprise cross-Channel
invasion in the summer or autumn?

Something like certainty that Hitler would open an eastern
front before he had completed his victory in the west seems to
have started at GC&CS, as decrypts showing an eastward move
by army and air units and formations accumulated in April and
May, confused though interpretation was at first by the
temporary diversions occasioned by the assault on Greece and
Jugoslavia. By the last week in May the JIC, just beginning to
settle into its stride as the prime assessor of intelligence for
Cabinet and Chiefs of Staff, was now prepared to concede that
war might come, but hedged its final conclusion by reiterating its
previous opinion that agreement was more likely. Not for the last
time his enemies were crediting Hitler with rational policies
when his actions were in reality dictated rather by mere
conviction and deep-seated emotion – long ago *Mein Kampf* had
proclaimed the need for *Lebensraum* in the east – and it was not
until a bare fortnight before BARBAROSSA that yet more
evidence, mainly from Enigma and Oshima's despatches to

Tokyo, removed all doubt that the unbelievable was about to happen.

The raising of the Mediterranean stakes – already foreshadowed by the transfer of six U-boats from the Atlantic and by the appointment of Kesselring to the new post of Commander-in-Chief South (Oberbefehlshaber Süd) in November – demonstrated that, notwithstanding BARBAROSSA, from the Axis point of view Libya was no longer quite the sideshow it had been in February when Halder (army Chief of Staff) had defined Rommel's task as no more than to ensure that the Italians did not 'go right back to Tripoli without fighting'. Britain's dominance over the Axis supply routes was temporarily reversed, partly because Fliegerkorps X's new aricraft strengthened convoy escort in the eastern Mediterranean, partly because Italian mines sank or damaged a number of ships during an engagement in the Gulf of Sirte and Italian human torpedoes immobilised the battleships *Queen Elizabeth* and *Valiant* in Alexandria harbour in December, keeping them out of action for several months.

On land, Rommel's intelligence suddenly improved in January 1942. The Italian secret service managed to steal a copy of the Black Code in which Colonel Bonner Fellers, the US Military Attaché in Cairo, communicated with the Pentagon, and since GHQ Cairo saw to it that their new ally was kept well informed this meant that Rommel knew nearly as much about British plans as London or Washington, and almost as quickly. His 'good source', as he called it, which could also draw on captured call-sign lists identifying army units, did Rommel excellent service (by revealing British tank strengths and unit locations, for instance) during his great advance in May and June from Gazala by way of Tobruk to Alamein, only sixty miles from Alexandria. But the 'good source' suddenly dried up on 24 July, almost certainly because Ultra had shown that the Germans were reading Fellers' signals; any possibility of a revival was ruled out when Hauptmann Seebohm's listening company, which

intercepted Fellers' signals, was overrun and wiped out at Tell el
Eisa on 10 July during the fighting in front of the Alamein line.

The closing down of the 'good source' brought to an end the
only period of the desert war when the two sides' intelligence was
roughly equal; material captured at Seebohm's camp simplified
and speeded up the work of the British Y Service, Seebohm's
successor was not as effective as he had been, and the Black
Code was of course replaced by another which the Germans
failed to master. Panzer Army's new Enigma keys (like a number
of army keys on the Russian front) could now be read with
regularity, and in August the breaking of the Mediterranean U-
boat key began to tilt the naval balance back to where it had
been in the autumn of 1941. For several months the intelligence
war raged silently, then settled in favour of the British. Rommel
lost the initiative at Tell el Eisa in July, Montgomery seized it at
Alam Halfa in September, and thereafter the intelligence issue
was never in doubt. The salutary (from the British and Allied
point of view) outcome is attributable to several causes: the
Allies' superior cryptographic skills (Enigma was increasingly
penetrated, the equivalent Allied Sigint systems proved invulnerable); the multiplicity and internecine rivalry of the German
intelligence organisations; and the failure of the formally but
only superficially centralised control of the OKW to become
even remotely as effective as the Allied Combined Chiefs of Staff
backed by occasional meetings between Churchill, Roosevelt
and Stalin.

The RAF, unhappily, was hard put to it, in the summer of
1942, to cope with the assaults of the two Fliegerkorps, which
were inaugurating Malta's period of greatest agony. Then in
May, after some of Kesselring's aircraft went back in April to the
Russian front whence they had come, raids on Malta slackened
and Hitler mistakenly cancelled the airborne attack on the island
which he had been contemplating. With this, the strategic
balance finally changed; so long as the British held Malta,
Rommel could not drive towards the Delta with a quiet mind,

because his supply lines were too vulnerable to sustain the troops he needed – difficult or impossible though it was for the British to feel confident of this while Eighth Army was hurriedly and uncomprehendingly falling back past Tobruk to Alamein in June and July. The new and more plentiful intelligence helped Auchinleck to improvise the defence which kept intact the line from Alamein to the impassable Qattara Depression forty miles to the south, and at the same time pinpointed tankers for the RAF and the navy to sink. The quantity and quality of intelligence was at last sufficient for victory, given enough men, tanks and guns to take advantage of it.* One task remained: to persuade the generals to use it properly.

Precisely how this change took place is now impossible to discover, though it can be illustrated. Rather than a sudden rational conversion, a new mood gradually came over command circles in Cairo and the desert during the first half of 1942, notwithstanding the disasters in the field. Better intelligence slowly led to a greater willingness to heed it, and this willingness was also partly based on the growing experience and skill in presentation on the part of the new senior intelligence officers who were displacing less gifted men. Many of these men went on to reach positions from which their good influence radiated ever more widely during the next three years; with a single exception (Major-General Kenneth Strong joined Eisenhower in North Africa in February 1943, and moved with him when he took command of OVERLORD) all the senior British intelligence appointments were later held by men who had won their spurs in the desert.

At all events, there is a striking contrast between the usual attitude towards intelligence in January 1942, when Rommel's

---

* Just how enormous an advantage is strikingly illustrated by Appendix I in PRO.HW3 174, which sets out tank returns in date order and tabular form according to type. The thickness of armour, and the hitting power of the guns, of each type was usually known in advance – there is a summary in UMS Appendix VIII. See also p. 98 below.

counter-offensive was facilitated by GHQ's mistake in crediting the Afrika Korps with too few tanks, and that six months later when, after only a few days in command of Eighth Army, Montgomery used Ultra to consolidate what his military instinct had already dictated and at Alam Halfa in September restored confidence and self-respect to a disheartened Eighth Army in a defensive battle which finally halted Rommel's seemingly irresistible progress towards the Nile Valley.

A significant indication of the benefits a better organisation of intelligence could confer was the mutual support which different sources could lend each other. The opening of Rommel's Gazala offensive at the end of May offers an illustration. Ultra had for some time been hinting that preparations for 'the coming projected operation' would soon be complete, but had not managed to provide more than an approximate date for it: Panzer Army was to receive an increased allocation of petrol from the beginning of June, for instance. Under interrogation, a captured NCO outlined the enemy plan. Then on 25 May Ultra correctly interpreted the news that Kesselring's HQ would transmit 'a most secret communication' that evening and Y realised that the codeword 'Venezia' (doubtless the 'most secret communication') which they intercepted at that time was the signal to attack, thus giving Eighth Army a good twenty-four hours' warning of the opening moves in a campaign which only came to a temporary halt in mutual exhaustion at the end of July.

Two months earlier Ultra started to receive occasional tank strength returns from Panzer Army (similar returns continued sporadically throughout the war); Y had been doing so for some time, and once the fighting began listened in almost nightly to the Panzer divisions' repair workshops reporting the number of runners and write-offs, and the estimated dates for the completion of repairs to damaged machines. A certain Major MacLean (presumably the descendant of a Scottish Jacobite emigré), who commanded 15 Panzer Division's workshops, unaccountably but obligingly sent his evening reports in plain language, thus speeding up the delivery of valuable information to his adopted country's enemies. The ability to count on regular and trustworthy statements of the enemy's armoured strength (even if an occasional report was missed, there was still a firm basis for an estimate) was an enormous advantage to a beleaguered army which had hitherto been compelled to depend on little more than inspired guesswork. Evidence came in from other quarters too and, by cross-checking Sigint, helped to ensure accuracy, now that there was an intelligence section devoted exclusively to the collection and assessment of this sort of information. The Long Range Desert Group, for example, kept an almost uninterrupted watch on eastbound traffic along the Via Balbia, the only metalled road along the coast, at a point near 'Marble Arch' on the Gulf of Sirte, and maintained it with scarcely a break from December 1940 until Rommel evacuated the area in November 1942. Photo-reconnaissance (a relative novelty in the Middle East until late in 1941, when a crippling shortage of photo-interpretation staff was gradually remedied) was already becoming productive. All these sources in combination, with Y outstanding among them, were adding a new and solidly dependable ingredient to operational planning and sometimes to critical tactical decisions as well – knowledge of Rommel's battle strength from day to day played a vital part in Auchinleck's defence of the Alamein line in July.

Meanwhile another element was exercising a serious influence on the land war in Africa: deception. Starting in 1940 with simple tactical measures like dummy radio traffic to suggest a thinning out of British forces in the desert when in reality the COMPASS campaign against the Italians was being prepared, 'A' Force gradually spread its net more widely until large-scale strategic disinformation became its main purpose.

Even before the trick which misled Rommel about the date of CRUSADER, already described (see p. 88), some of the elements of what in March 1942 became Plan CASCADE to delude the enemy into believing British strength in the Middle East to be far greater than it really was had been assembled. At least one bogus division had been successfully planted in German intelligence records, where it stayed until the end of the war. Xan Fielding, who later won fame with the Cretan Resistance, amusingly describes how, during the summer of 1941, when there was barely one brigade of British troops in Cyprus, he established the notional presence of 7 Division by commandeering houses as brigade and battalion headquarters, sending despatch-riders with imaginary messages between them and (since he was the only real live officer of the division) visiting these headquarters in turn to receive the messages he himself had sent.

Intelligence is the nursing mother of deception; without intelligence, deception would be blindfold, ignorant whether or not it was inducing the enemy to believe palatable falsehoods. Deception can therefore legitimately claim a place in a history of intelligence, although it uses its essential nourishment in its own peculiar ways and seeks to defeat the enemy by psychological rather than material means.

Before the middle of 1941, 'A' Force had begun to pursue systematically its new and grander objectives by creating a network of double agents, the most influential of whom was given the extraordinary cover-name 'Cheese'. An Italian Jew, he was recalled to Italy under suspicion and imprisoned soon after making contact with GHQ Cairo, but his radio set was taken over by a notional friend (in fact a member of the Royal Corps of Signals) who managed to establish regular communication with Italian control in Bari. In this guise, 'Cheese' was accepted by the Italians, who before long were passing his reports direct to Rommel. Not suspecting that they were all concocted in Cairo, Rommel formed a high opinion of them. Unfortunately, like much else about 'Cheese' and others of his kind (and in contrast with the similar 'Double Cross' system operated from London), nothing is yet accessible either about the content of 'Cheese''s radio messages or about the extent (if any) to which they influenced events.* It is clear, however, that the design to inflate the British strength in the Middle East by introducing bogus divisions proceeded apace, and the surveillance of the degree to which it achieved its object was facilitated by ISOS and ISK (decrypts of the Abwehr hand cipher and Enigma respectively, which were being used as the basis of signals from 1944 onwards; the files are not yet in the PRO), which enabled Clarke, and later Colonel Bevan and the London Controlling Section for the western theatre, to follow the ideas and activities of the main Abwehr controllers and to monitor the degree to which their deceptions had taken root among them and were bearing fruit in enemy fears, hopes and expectations. Before the end of 1941 when, according to Dudley Clarke, 'the organ was now built and the stops were ready for us to pull at will' the aim was to make the enemy believe that there were eight armoured and twenty-one infantry divisions in the Middle East, just twice the true figure. Documents captured after Alamein showed the Germans overestimating British strength by 50 per cent.

This policy was pursued energetically in the ensuing two years, and the ground on which its seeds were sown grew increasingly fertile. By 1944, when the successes of Tito's Partisans in Jugoslavia were feeding Hitler's conviction that the Allies would exploit victory in Italy by invading the Balkans, 'A' Force seized on the opportunity to infiltrate hints that there were enormous reserves of battle-ready British troops in the Balkans. The resultant threefold threat kept thousands of Germans in Jugoslavia and Greece, away from the far more crucial battle-fields of Russia and France, thus once more illustrating Dudley Clarke's principle that fear can best be inculcated where apprehension already exists.

*

* But now see INS 5/3 176–183 and the articles quoted in note to p. 72 on p. 367.

The new era in intelligence, so long in preparation, dawned on
17 August 1942. Longing to be 'the man on the spot, instead of
sitting at home waiting for news from the front', Churchill, on
his way to the Moscow Conference with Stalin, flew first to
Cairo, where he dismissed Auchinleck and appointed Alexander
and Montgomery Commander-in-Chief Middle East and
commander of the Eighth Army respectively. Montgomery came
out from England at once, took over on 13 August and
immediately began injecting new vigour into the bewildered and
dispirited troops. Two days later Rommel informed Hitler of his
plans for the offensive which was to give him Egypt: provided he
received regular shipments of petrol and ammunition, he would
strike for the Delta by a southabout sweep at the end of the
month. On the 17th, only forty-eight hours later, the text of his
message was in Montgomery's hands. Ultra was repeating its
Cretan performance, but this time there was enough force to
take advantage of the warning.

On the busy 13 August when he took over Eighth Army,
Montgomery's tactical instinct had at once shown him more
clearly than his predecessor that the Alam Halfa ridge would be
the key defensive position if Rommel chose to start his drive for
the Nile in the south, still the least protected sector of the forty-
mile front between the sea and the impassable Qattara Depression; he therefore set about strengthening its garrison. Within
four days Ultra confirmed that he had divined Rommel's
intentions correctly and had taken appropriate steps to counter
them. Admittedly, 44 Division, newly out from England, for
which he asked Alexander, had only just reached Suez and had
yet to become acclimatised and receive desert training, but the
plan was made, there was a fortnight to put it into effect, the
army was regaining confidence and the RAF was primed to
perform its usual task of sinking tankers and supply ships with a
more than usual sense of urgency.

With Seebohm silenced and Fellers inscrutable, Rommel
knew nothing of all this; the balance of advantage in intelligence

had swung to the British side for good. There is still some question how much the Afrika Korps was misled by a deliberately 'lost' haversack containing a falsified map which diverted its tanks from good 'going' into bad, but none that the RAF sank so many tankers that Rommel's whole force was halted by fuel shortage in front of the Alam Halfa ridge and bombed so severely that it was compelled to turn back.

In such circumstances, what need was there for other sources of intelligence? So complete a monopoly could not endure, but Ultra had established its primacy in the special conditions of desert warfare; two army keys which had hitherto resisted the cryptographers' best efforts now yielded up their secrets with some regularity, bringing to an end the imbalance in intelligence which had been so frustrating. For the last few weeks, too, Ultra had even sometimes usurped Y's function of tactical intelligence: an army–air co-operation key, of which the settings required for decryption could be predicted, had come into use during the Afrika Korps' summer advance. The settings were wirelessed to Cairo from Bletchley Park early each day and a Hut 3 officer sent out to service the decrypts; thus much precious time was saved.

Alam Halfa saw operations welcome intelligence into full partnership for the first time. 'Montgomery won his first battle by believing the intelligence with which he was furnished,' wrote Sir Edgar Williams, his Chief Intelligence Officer. Intelligence had played a useful part in Auchinleck's desperate fight to halt Rommel's advance in July, but it had always been a subordinate part, its usefulness often restricted by hasty and unreflecting action. Hitherto intelligence had been 'the Cinderella of the Staff, and information about the enemy was frequently treated as interesting rather than valuable. We had had good intelligence before; henceforward we were going to use it.'

The revolution thus accomplished, and the lessons now learned, redressed the neglect and misjudgments of the past. As yet, however, they were understood and appreciated by only a few in Cairo and the desert. These few were destined later to leaven the whole Anglo-American lump (this was the great accumulated credit-balance of the war in Africa), but the leavening process was inevitably slow. The unblooded British and American armies which attacked Tunisia in November had to discover the advantages of the new system in a hard school, and some among the generals were still discovering them even in France two years later. On the debit side, it is difficult to escape the conclusion that by giving him victory in September 1942 intelligence fostered in Montgomery that conviction of his own inerrancy which some, notably the Americans, eventually found intolerable.

Changes in habits and modes of thought, even of institutions, underpinned the revolution at the top and kept the whole system in working order. Under the influence of Tedder, AOC RAF Middle East, army–air co-operation had greatly improved during the summer of 1942, and it became customary for the headquarters of the two services to be located close together at army and corps level. For their mutual advantage, operations and intelligence needed to know as much about each other's capabilities and requirements as possible. The obvious solution was to live and work in close contiguity. At army headquarters the command vehicles of the senior operations and intelligence officers now usually formed up at night in a quadrangle with those of army–air support and Y, thus promoting easy and rapid exchange of information. To ensure his plans the maximum chance of success, the Eighth Army commander allowed his senior intelligence officer direct access at any hour of day or night, while the latter's staff were on hand to brief him with constantly updated information about the enemy's order of battle and dispositions, gathered from Y, photo-reconnaissance, captured documents and prisoner interrogation. The relative value of the different sources varied with time and circumstance: Y, which from about midsummer grew in volume so much that

Sir Edgar Williams could write later that by the time Ultra delivered the Panzer Army 'evening report' about midnight he expected to have reached the same conclusions from Y, was nevertheless fuller and more informative at times of movement than in quieter periods; photo-recce revealed the development of defence positions and the location of German artillery concentrations, thus facilitating counter-battery work and general bombardment in the weeks before Alamein, whereas it was less useful in mobile warfare. More prisoners than before were taken during the July battles and by patrols between Alam Halfa and Alamein, and these combined to keep the order-of-battle records abreast of tactical movements and to ensure that, when confronted with aerial photographs and asked leading questions, they could be induced to explain the full meaning of what they and their interrogators could see – one of many examples of a new depth of co-operation between different intelligence sources. To supplement the immediately usable intelligence, GHQ Cairo could now provide reliable estimates of the enemy's supply and reinforcement state – material highly relevant to operations at a time when every tanker sunk critically reduced enemy mobility on land or in the air, and when 164 Division was being hastily flown in from Crete to thicken the defensive front which Eighth Army would have to penetrate.

Together with the sensation of uninterrupted success under a general whom they had learned to respect and trust in spite of his peculiar manner, innovations like these had turned Eighth Army into a confident and efficient fighting force by the time it reached Tunisia in January 1943. But a drastic shake-up was needed in operations as well as in intelligence. The mutual distrust of infantry and tanks which had paralysed action in the past, for instance, had to be remedied if a future offensive was to stand a chance of success. There was more than one layer of meaning in Churchill's phrase about Alamein being 'the end of the beginning'.

The instrument of victory into which intelligence was developing played an unprecedented role between Alam Halfa and Alamein. Ultra sank more tankers than ever before. There were only two or three days' supply of petrol behind the front just before the British attack on 23 October, and the news that 4,000 tons had gone to the bottom that afternoon greeted Rommel when he arrived back from Austria on the 25th to resume command of Panzer Army.* 'Now we are really up against it,' he remarked as yet another tanker carrying a much needed cargo of fuel was bombed and sunk. The dire consequences of losses like these were driven home at a critical moment in the battle a week later. The Panzer divisions were so short of fuel that Rommel knew he could not reposition his last remaining armour if he proved not to have placed it where it could best meet the final British assault. When a Y Service intercept showed 21 Panzer Division's Reconnaissance Group moving northwards, and experience suggested that the whole division would probably follow (Ultra shortly confirmed that the deduction was correct), Montgomery shifted his point of attack further south than he had originally intended, bypassed the German armour and pierced the defensive front. This was the decisive moment, but Ultra had prepared the way for it by chronicling the chaos into which the whole German supply system had fallen as a result of the merciless air and sea onslaught on cross-Mediterranean transport, while all through the battle Y had logged over 300 intercepts a day giving details of tactical movements and recording the number of German tanks remaining serviceable after each day's action.

To strengthen the strategic threat represented by the notional divisions it had already inserted into German intelligence

---

* The news of his earlier departure from Africa for medical treatment and a rest, and the illness which caused it, posed a new security problem to the guardians of Ultra. It was solved by the creation of a new category of peculiarly gossipy items the dissemination of which was restricted to a few specially selected recipients only.

appreciations before Alamein, 'A' Force had mounted a comprehensive deception plan designed to play down the scale of any
immediate operation in the desert by putting it about that the
primary British concern was with the threat to their rear
presented by the German advance in the Caucasus: a notional
conference was even arranged, to take place at the end of
October in Teheran, thus diverting attention to both a false
place and a false time. Tactical measures to disguise the intended
point of attack – a difficult task on a forty-mile front bounded by
the sea at one end and the impassable Qattara Depression at the
other – including hiding artillery batteries under dummy lorries,
and the last-minute replacement by dummies of armour which
had been openly displayed at the southern end of the front until
the tanks themselves moved forward by night and were covered
up by what were called 'sunshields', which gave the appearance
of wheeled vehicles to reconnaissance aircraft, whose intrusions
could be shepherded in the desired directions by the RAF's air
superiority and were prevented altogether for the five days
before the battle. Prominent among these measures was the
apparent construction of a water-pipeline which was gradually
being extended southwards (ostensibly to provide for an attack
there) at a speed which suggested completion by the first week in
November. That these ruses were successful was shown by
documents captured at Jalo shortly before Alamein, by Rommel's departure on leave and unhurried return after the opening
of the offensive and the death of his temporary replacement, by
decrypts from the Enigma key used by the Abwehr (this
broadened the hold which had already been obtained over
Abwehr correspondence with its agents), and by the absence of
all contradictory signs in Ultra. Panzer Army clearly expected an
attack in the south rather than the north, and an evening aerial
reconnaissance report, issued only six hours before the artillery
barrage opened just before midnight on 23 October, reassuringly
read 'Situation quiet. Slight increase in British forces in the
south.'

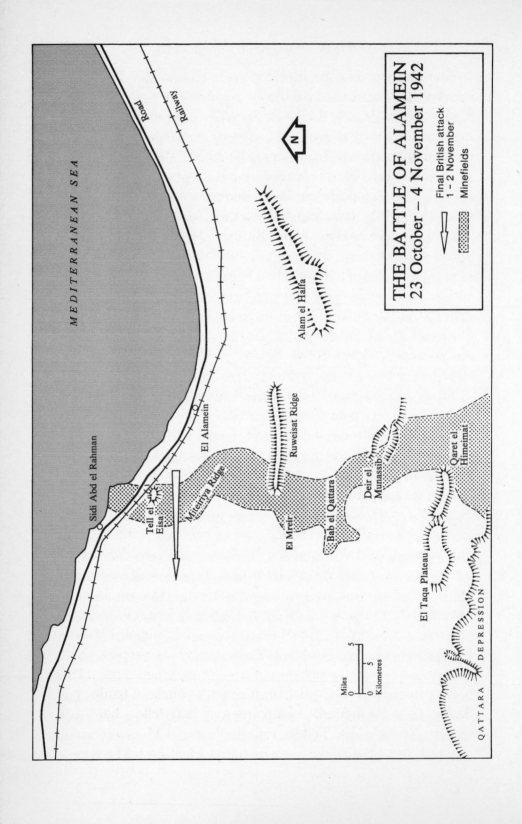

THE BATTLE OF ALAMEIN
23 October – 4 November 1942

Final British attack
1 – 2 November

Minefields

N

MEDITERRANEAN SEA

Road

Railway

Sidi Abd el Rahman

El Alamein

Tell el Eisa

Miteirya Ridge

Alam el Halfa

Ruweisat Ridge

El Mreir

Bab el Qattara

Deir el Munassib

Qaret el Himeimat

El Taqa Plateau

QATTARA DEPRESSION

Miles
0   5
0   5
Kilometres

Knowing that his line had been pierced and that he had no reserves to plug the gap, early in the evening of 2 November Rommel formally asked Hitler's assent to a withdrawal which he had already set in motion, because otherwise 'the possibility of the annihilation of the army must be faced'. With the militarily absurd stubbornness which later led him to order even divisional commanders to report their intentions direct to him personally in time for him to countermand them if he thought fit, Hitler refused. For twenty-four hours Rommel loyally tried to put the rearward movement into reverse, but the situation had deteriorated out of control; Hitler had 'demanded the impossible', and early on 4 November he renewed his request, asking permission to withdraw to Fuka. This time Hitler and Mussolini accepted the inevitable. Ultra put this exchange of signals into Montgomery's hands within twelve hours in every case save the last, when the reply was decrypted before the question.

The precise degree to which all this and other Alamein information was converted into military advantage is obscure and a matter of some controversy. There is nothing to suggest that Montgomery was beginning to distrust intelligence so soon after welcoming it at Alam Halfa, yet it is manifest that he did not act upon it with the alacrity it now seems to merit. His own excuse for what appears dilatoriness, first put forward only after the war, was the rain which made the desert temporarily impassable on the 5th and 6th, but since the rain did not fall until three days after the breakthrough the excuse is unconvincing. Intelligence must not direct Operations – this would be to surrender the initiative – but Intelligence is little more than a parlour game unless Operations follows the main lines it indicates. Similarly, hindsight finds it easy to propose facile answers and actions which would never have entered the minds of men forced to make quick decisions in the heat of battle or in the moment of unguarded elation which may follow hard-won victory. Nevertheless, Tedder repeatedly urged Montgomery on so that he could seize the airfields round Martuba for fighters to protect a badly needed convoy on its way to Malta, Montgomery knew that the commander of 7 Armoured Division was eager for the pursuit and had twice as many tanks in his division alone as there remained in the whole Afrika Korps (fifty-two against twenty-four on 5 November), and visual as well as signal evidence showed that Panzer Army was scuttling back as fast as it could go.

No satisfactory answer has been propounded to the question Why did Montgomery not strike at once, destroy Panzer Army on the spot and thereby fulfil the promise of his Operation Order of 14 September, which proclaimed his object as 'to trap the enemy in his present area and to destroy him there'? His slowness to follow up his crushing victory was plain at the time and has drawn adverse comment since, but the discrepancy between the intelligence about Panzer Army's plight and the use made of it has attracted far less attention. The authors of *British Intelligence* scarcely notice it, for instance, and recent books by Field Marshal Lord Carver (who was Staff Officer to General Harding, commander of 7 Armoured Division at the time) and General Richardson (in succession Montgomery's Chief Planning and Chief Operations Officer) pass it over in silence. The discrepancy is nevertheless a fact which cannot be overlooked, particularly as it followed so closely on the heels of the newly forged alliance of Intelligence with Operations. It was probably due to a combination of factors: Montgomery had set aside an armoured group in readiness for a swift pursuit, but had milked it so dry to strengthen the repeated thrusts which eventually broke through the enemy line that it no longer existed by the time the need for it arose; he had prepared meticulously for the battle of attrition but had given less attention to ways of exploiting the victory he intended to win; and he was already beginning to earn his later reputation for extreme caution and over-insurance against an enemy counter-attack.

The same discrepancy was apparent at critical moments all the way from Alamein to Tripoli. Plentiful Ultra demonstrated

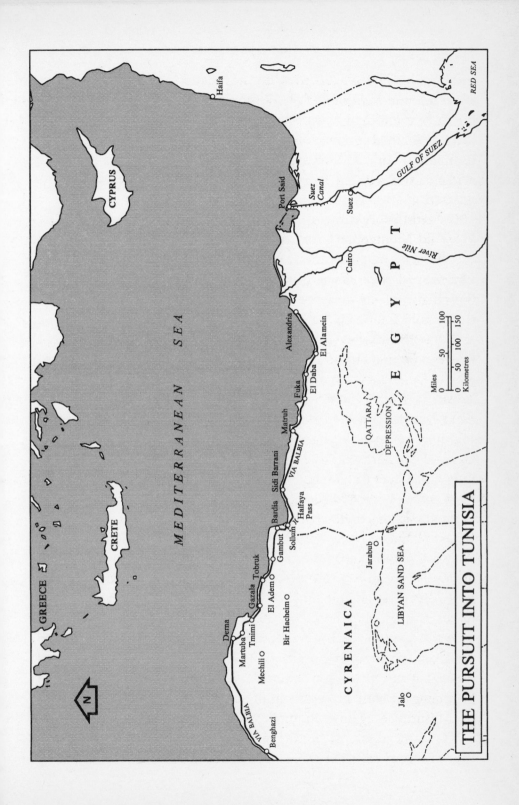

THE PURSUIT INTO TUNISIA

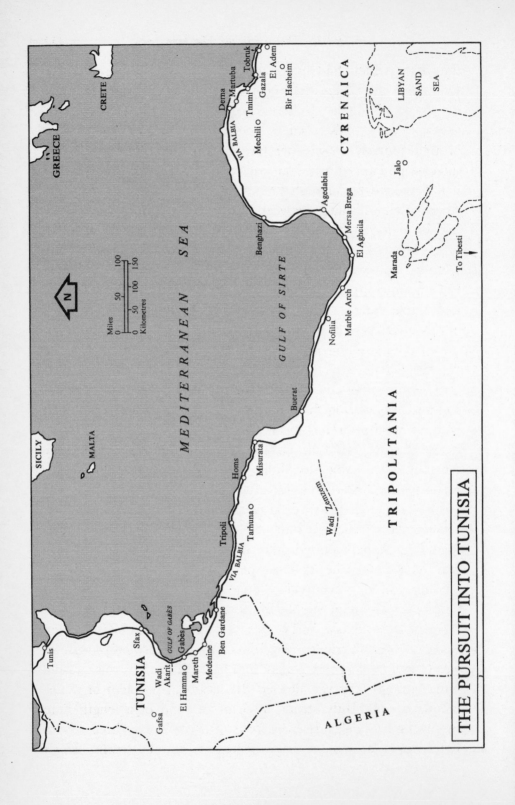

THE PURSUIT INTO TUNISIA

the chaos which had overtaken the Axis supply organisation. Even after the Italians had been left to be taken prisoner, there was hardly enough wheeled transport to lift the Germans the thousand miles back to safety, and too few tanks to protect them on their journey. It was therefore obvious that a few swift blows might wipe Panzer Army out before it could get away and before it had moved far enough to subject Eighth Army to the same stresses as the distance between base and the fighting spearheads had been forcing upon its own transport and supply arrangements throughout the summer. The mirage of speedy victory vanished when Montgomery missed the chance to repeat O'Connor's outflanking move through Mechili in February 1941 and catch Panzer Army as it crawled painfully (because of a petrol shortage so acute that Rommel called the situation 'catastrophic') along the coast road towards the shelter of the Agheila defences.

A certain repetitive quality in the intelligence supplied to Montgomery during the three months after Alamein, combined with his apparent reluctance to seize the opportunities it offered, made this a period of anticlimax after the elation of early November. In cables to Hitler, monitored currently by Ultra, Rommel made no secret of the difficulty he had in keeping out of harm's way in front of Eighth Army, as fuel and tank replacements reached him late, grudgingly and in smaller quantities than promised, and as transport earmarked for him was filched for the defence of Tunisia after the TORCH landings on 8 November. Tunis and Bizerta soon replaced Tripoli as his main supply bases, adding many extra miles of road haulage via Sfax and Gabès through a no-man's land which was developing between two fronts. Amply informed though he was of Rommel's predicament and of the anxiety it was causing him, Montgomery yet allowed the logistical problem of maintaining a sufficiently strong force at the end of a lengthening supply line to delay him in front of Agheila for three weeks. Later, he claimed to have feared a counter-stroke which

intelligence repeatedly showed him that Rommel was incapable
of delivering, and asserted that he bluffed Rommel out of his
defences. In reality he was himself tricked into allowing Rommel
a pause in the long retreat, albeit a far shorter one than that
which Mussolini was constantly demanding. There may be a link
with the allegation that Eighth Army superstitiously believed
itself fated never to get beyond the point it had reached twice
already; however, Montgomery was not the man to be deflected
from his purpose by others' emotions.

After Agheila came Buerat, where Rommel vainly hoped to
make another stand – more to satisfy Mussolini than because he
really expected delivery of the anti-tank guns and artillery
indispensable for the purpose. The threat of another 'left hook',
which persuaded him out in the first week of January, also threw
up a lot more evidence of the acuteness of his supply problem as
well as signs of a quarrel about it between him and Kesselring.
This at last encouraged Montgomery to contemplate bolder
tactics than of late, and a ten-day offensive secured Tripoli by 23
January 1943.

The long chase was over, the victory of Alamein at length
exploited to the full. The English Army had become Britain's
first professionally capable fighting force of the Second World
War, confident of its abilities and flexible enough to carry out its
commander's orders whatever they demanded. But as it
emerged from the desert, its training ground, and approached
the frontier of Tunisia, Eighth Army, like Panzer Army on the
other side of the lines, was compelled to recognise that it was
exchanging a secondary theatre where battles were fought within
strictly definable limits for one where the strategic prizes were far
greater and where co-operation with allies and a possible future
invasion of mainland Europe presented it with far larger strategic
issues than it had faced before. Its horizons were about to be
widened, the bounds of its experience enlarged: the discovery at
Enfidaville in April that it knew how to fight and win on a flat
plain but had no idea how to tackle mountains was something of

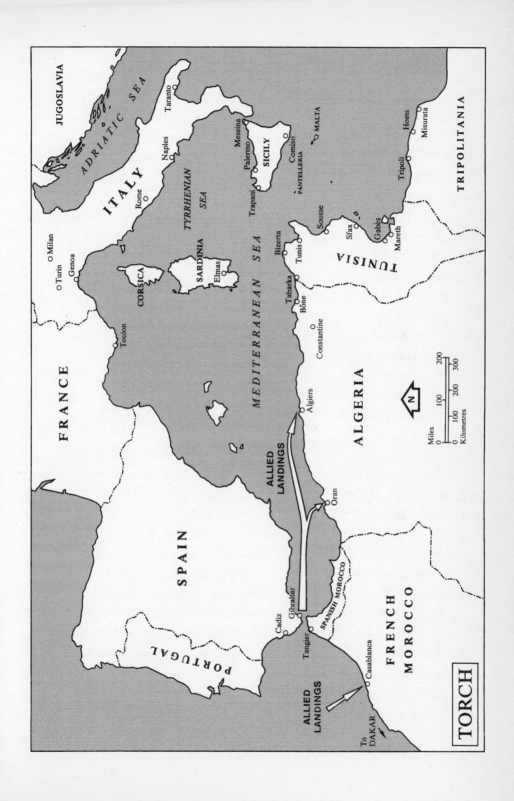

a shock. One great asset, however, would help it to face the future: despite Montgomery's recent dialtoriness, on the level of daily practice Eighth Army and its commander had learned in the desert how to integrate a new and powerful intelligence weapon into the rest of its armoury and how to utilise it in formulating operational plans. As events in Tunisia were already beginning to show, no other land force knew how to do this – or even that it needed doing.

The decision to invade French North Africa (Operation TORCH), taken at the end of July 1942, was a compromise between the aggressive instincts of the Americans, eager to land on the coast of German-occupied Europe at the first possible moment, and the experience-based caution of the British, who regretfully urged that such a landing in 1942 would almost certainly be speedily annihilated. The practical hazards of the compromise were nearly as alarming as the political debates which produced it had been fierce. Such precedents as there were for what was to be the largest combined operation ever undertaken were not encouraging. The attempt to occupy Dakar in 1940 had been leaked before the convoy sailed; the raid on Dieppe, launched in August 1942, three weeks after the decision for TORCH, was a disastrous failure, though it was later found to have taught valuable lessons.

How was the safety of the troop-carrying convoys – some sailing direct from the United States, some from British ports – to be guaranteed, given that the GAF could not be prevented from reconnoitring the British Isles and the surrounding waters and that since the loss of GC&CS's power to read their code (see pp. 192–3) the location of U-boats on hostile patrol in the Atlantic Ocean could not be predicted with much accuracy nor convoys routed to avoid them? How could the transports' passage through the Straits of Gibraltar be hidden and their Mediterranean targets disguised? How was the last part of their journey through the Axis-dominated western Mediterranean to be protected?

The deception planners played their part by putting out rumours via the 'Cheese' network that the objective was Sicily, Crete, the Balkans, the resupply of Malta or support for Eighth Army as it advanced towards Tripoli. Luck took a hand when German intelligence totally failed to realise that these were all red herrings and at first made Malta its most favoured explanation for the appearance of more and more aircraft on the newly extended Gibraltar airstrip and for the crowding of shipping in Gibraltar harbour. When the body of a British officer drowned when the aircraft in which he was travelling crashed off Cadiz on 26 September was held by the Spaniards for thirty-six hours, there was a moment of alarm, for he had been carrying letters which indicated the date (but not the target) of TORCH with tolerable clarity. Mercifully, investigation on the spot showed that it was most unlikely either that the Spanish authorities had found the letters or that they had shown them to the Germans; Abwehr decrypts subsequently made it plain that this was the case and that no suspicion of the real target of the convoys had arisen.

The Cabinet recognised the status of Ultra as a primary source of intelligence when for the first time it gave the Ultra cryptographers advance notice of an intended operation. When individual Fliegerkorps were given their own Enigma keys in January 1942, the key allotted to Fliegerkorps II (based in Sicily and responsible for the western Mediterranean) proved relatively easy to break; but it had not been given high priority in order that as much bombe-time as possible might be devoted to the more immediately rewarding army keys, a policy which had paid handsome dividends between the fall of Tobruk and the Battle of Alamein. Now GC&CS was asked to change its emphasis so that German reaction to the convoys' movements between Gibraltar and the chosen landing-places might be studied. The reward of this forethought came when it was discovered that Fliegerkorps

II was lending fighter and bomber aircraft to eastern Mediterranean commands as late as 5 November (the TORCH landings began on the 8th) and that the purpose of the Allied operation was now presumed to be the delivery of supplies to Eighth Army as it moved farther away from its Egyptian bases. Against all odds, strategic surprise – usually so difficult to achieve – was unexpectedly attained.

This was all the more remarkable in view of what the Germans called 'Operation BODDEN'. Since the beginning of the year it had been apparent from Abwehr decrypts that with Spanish connivance the Germans were supplementing the ship-watchers they had already put in place on both shores of the Straits of Gibraltar by installing a series of infra-red observation posts which, by noting the heat they emitted, could count the ships passing through the Straits by night as well as by day. The serious danger this presented was countered by a curious mixture of science and diplomacy. Aerial reconnaissance showed where the installations were, and scientific investigation revealed what they were capable of achieving. Direct action to destroy them was ruled out, lest it provoke the Spanish government enough to make them abandon their neutrality and join the Axis. Diplomatic representations were the only alternative, in the hope that General Franco would suppress the Germans' activity. This entailed the difficult task of explaining what was wanted to the British Ambassador in Madrid by signal in diplomatic cipher without revealing the source of the information – ISOS decrypts – or taxing his slender scientific understanding too severely. Happily, the task was accomplished; BODDEN installations, operational since March, were dismantled by the end of 1942, and though one or two new installations were detected in the autumn they gave no more information about the purpose of the TORCH convoys than that given by watchers on neutral territory.

The obvious question – how much was known about German

penetration of the French North African possessions and about German preparations (if any) to defend them should the Allies attack – is surprisingly difficult to answer.

The Americans, particularly Robert Murphy, political adviser to General Eisenhower and personal representative of President Roosevelt, had been busy with political negotiations, and General Mark Clark had paid a secret visit to Algeria by submarine. A few of the French cryptographers who had worked on Enigma in 1939 and 1940 had escaped to the unoccupied zone after the fall of France and had continued working there. Their results were passed to London via MI6, but whether they duplicated Bletchley's decrypts or amplified them seems not to be on record. Commander 'Biffy' Dunderdale, MI6's pre-war station head in Paris and one of its few really capable operators, retired to London when France fell and continued to collect information from his remaining contacts (mainly Poles who had fled to France in 1940; see pp. 120–1 below), but MI6's value as a source declined sharply after 1940, while the Resistance provided little information in these early days.

In parenthesis it may be worth remarking that this will also serve as a rough generalisation covering all contacts with occupied Europe before mid-1943, at least until more is made public about the information which was gleaned from all the effort put into their task, and all the risks run, by so many brave men and women. Aircraft were transporting SIS agents from Britain to France and back from June 1940 onwards. SOE soon supplied other passengers, though in rather smaller numbers, together with a growing quantity of sabotage material. Contact with Norway, in similar proportions, became regular a few months later, and as suitable aircraft became available the frontier of air operations was extended gradually further south and east (they were brushing against the Balkans late in 1942, for instance). Seaborne operations followed a similar but better-known pattern. SOE's so-called 'Shetland bus' service of fishing-boats,

whalers and a few faster craft was plying to various points on the
Norwegian coast from an early date. SOE had also been
maintaining clandestine contacts between Cornwall and Brittany
since mid-1940, but transferred its centre of gravity to the
Mediterranean two or three years later. Working from bases in
French North Africa, its main concern was to nourish resistance
in Vichy France.*

The pilots who flew the aircraft to pre-arranged pick-up points
knew nothing about the business of their passengers, though the
captains of the naval vessels were usually better-informed. Both
means of transport carried supplies and sabotage materials,
much the greater tonnage going by air. This was SOE's primary
task, but the naval officers could hardly avoid incidentally
picking up useful information about prevailing conditions. The
securing of intelligence was not SOE's province, however, and
friction occasionally arose with SIS when the delicate frontier
was crossed.

Strangely enough, the only systematic account of the work of a
clandestine intelligence-gathering group which has been published concerns North Africa in 1942. 'Agency Africa' owed its
existence to the courage, initiative and determination of Major-
General Rygor Slowikowski of the Polish army, who had escaped
to North Africa; his more than 2,000 agents contributed
information which made the Agency the largest single source of
intelligence about the state of French military readiness for battle
and French co-operation with the Germans over the transport of
reinforcements and supplies to Rommel's army.

Useful as they no doubt were, nothing contained in the
thousand or more reports Slowikowski sent out in the British and
American diplomatic bags to which he was allowed access seems
likely to have had any bearing on the strategic decision to launch
TORCH or on the course of events in November and December

* See notes to p. 120 on p. 369.

1942. Indeed, since (as Slowikowski later discovered) it was MI6, not the Polish government-in-exile, which assigned him his various lines of inquiry, sadly the whole episode illuminates the irrelevance of MI6 as much as the bravery and determination of the Poles.

The fortuitous presence of Admiral Darlan in Algiers set the political alarm bells ringing but seemed not to have delayed operations unduly when the Allies' eastward advance began on 14 November. It was unavoidable that all the Americans, including the Allied Supreme Commander, General Eisenhower, and most of the British, had no experience of battle, but not that the intelligence staffs should have been as raw as they were in fact. A few lessons had been learned – the topographical department, for instance, provided almost completely accurate information about beach gradients and the like, the lack of which had caused much of the slaughter at Dieppe in August – but military intelligence arrangements were woefully inadequate. Eisenhower received Ultra at Gibraltar until he moved his HQ to Algiers, but the British commander of First Army, General Anderson, did not receive it direct until the last weeks of the campaign and little even through Algiers until after Christmas. Completely inadequate arrangements seem to have been made for Army or Air Y (in the latter case it was not so much the intercept personnel as their controllers, whose job was to utilise intercept intelligence, who were at fault) until the New Year, yet the planners should have foreseen that operations would be piecemeal and scattered during the early weeks and have deduced that Air Y needed the highest priority in order to give early warning of the raids that were bound to come, and Army Y the same so that enemy order of battle and movements might be known in good time and suitable counter-measures prepared.

Instead, almost every conceivable planning error was made. The training of Y detachments began in England only in the late summer, and operational conditions at once showed it to have been insufficient. Equipment was often of poor quality, and careless loading schedules meant that much of it could only be assembled where it was needed many weeks after the landing. Scarcely any provision was made beforehand or during the first two months for the interception of either high- or low-grade traffic, the life-blood of all Sigint.

That there were exceptions to this broad generalisation is clear, but why better advantage was not taken of them is far from plain. One Y Service cryptanalysis party, for instance, was trained at Bletchley Park on one of the more difficult hand-cipher systems, double Playfair, for almost a year, partly under well-simulated battle conditions, and shipped out to Algiers on 8 November. A scare that German traffic had become unreadable following a change of cipher was soon proved groundless, and daily breaks became regular; yet Major Noël Currer-Briggs, a member of the party, reports no important operational intelligence from this source until the last days of January. It would seem that a first-rate intelligence-gathering source was wasted for at least a month, for it was plainly of immense value from mid-February onwards.

It might have been possible to dismiss these grievous errors as just another example of British 'muddling through', had not a still greater lack of foresight imperilled the whole enterprise. From the early stages of planning in July and August, the Chiefs of Staff and JIC, misled by their assumption that Hitler could behave rationally* and would not weaken the endangered Russian front by diverting reserves to a new theatre of lesser importance, had persuaded themselves that German reaction to an Allied occupation of French territory would be slow and

---

* Yet his shelving of the attack on Malta in June, which if successful would have given him control of the Mediterranean, in favour of encouraging Rommel's drive for the Nile at the price of leaving his supply line in grave danger, suggested the contrary, not to mention the whole concept of invading Russia and, more recently, his 'Stand fast' order to Rommel of 3 November. By the following autumn the British, but not the Americans, had learned that Hitler did not conduct his strategy logically (see pp. 218, 237–9, 271).

negligible. They added the proviso that the Allies should make all speed to occupy Tunis, but did not place this in the forefront of their recommendations. American fears of Spanish intervention – fears that proved groundless in the event – prevented landings from being made further east than Algiers (500 miles from Tunis), thus increasing the distance the land forces would have to cover in order to drive the Germans out.* Perhaps overwhelmed with relief after Alamein and the quick ending of French resistance, the responsible authorities seem to have taken the will for the deed and assumed that Tunis would fall into Allied hands quickly and cheaply. It was in many ways a repetition of Montgomery's mistake in September and October: fuller preparations to secure surprise than to exploit it once it was secured. Ultra disillusioned them almost at once.

The move of German aircraft to El Aouina airfield outside Tunis, which had previously been written off as very unlikely, was signalled at midnight 9/10 November, an enemy ground force was being scraped together next day, men and stores were flown in by the 12th, and supplies already earmarked for Rommel were diverted to Tunis and Bizerta by OKW order on the 14th. Further similar evidence showed that, by the time the Allies' eastward advance began, it faced an entirely different situation from that which had been anticipated. It was at this moment that the absence of Y, which could have given notice of the points occupied by the hastily assembled opposition as it pushed west and south-west from Bizerta and Tunis, became a matter for instant regret.

At first sight it is not easy to understand why, at the planning stage of TORCH, more advantage was not taken of Eighth Army's recent experience of the way Intelligence and Operations should be integrated, and thus to ensure that the Allied intelligence staffs were better prepared for their task. The

---

* There was a railway, but it was mainly single-track, and the roads were inadequate to the demands made on them even before the December rains made them virtually impassable.

explanation must lie first in the relative isolation of the Middle East from the home commands by distance and communication difficulties since late 1940, and secondly in the simple fact that when TORCH planning began Eighth Army had scarcely begun to learn the lessons which made Alamein a victory. Yet the difference between those who had and those who had not had desert experience was well understood in Cairo, and it would not have been impossible, even in the early autumn, to bring a few of those who had already practised intelligence back to leaven the lump of inexperience in the training camps at home; even as few as the two or three who were sent out from Hut 3 to service Ultra intelligence at GHQ Cairo would have made a useful contribution. Major James Mark, who had served as an intelligence officer in the desert since August 1941, composed an official paper entitled 'Intelligence at an Army HQ' in October 1942. 'The chief weakness of many intelligence officers arriving from England,' he wrote, 'is that they appear to place more importance on scholarship than soldiering . . . they know how the enemy should be organised but not how he behaves.' His opinion was transferred verbatim to the official War Office manual *Military Intelligence Organisation*, published soon after the war. When a senior intelligence staff officer was sent from Cairo to Algiers in mid-November 1942 to find out what was really going on, news from Eisenhower's HQ having been thoroughly unenlightening, he found that the almost entirely British intelligence staff 'did not know what they ought to be doing and had learnt a whole lot of things which they ought not to be doing'. It was many weeks before an effective remedy was supplied.* But until then the – surely avoidable – difference between those with and those without Middle Eastern experience remained wide. One of the best Y sections sent to Algiers

---

* Again, however, the badly needed lesson was learned in the end. The American intelligence officers who were to mediate Ultra to American generals in OVERLORD were sent on indoctrination visits to Mediterranean commands in late 1943 and early 1944, to the great benefit of their later service in the field.

seems to have been so unaware of its Eighth Army predecessors that it believed 'we had shown that cryptanalysis could be carried on successfully in the field' – as if this had not been demonstrated in the desert long before. Y unavoidably gave less useful results in country where hills restricted interception. Continuous contact along a far longer front line made for many more prisonrs, so that 'first phase' interrogation became the main source of order-of-battle information, yet required more fluent German-speakers than were usually available, while arrangements for 'in-depth' interrogation at base were made only in the last weeks before the surrender on Cape Bon.

These and other shortcomings of the TORCH intelligence organisation go a long way towards explaining the shattering though temporary disaster at Kasserine in February 1943.

By the time Eisenhower was compelled, by the fragility of the only spearhead he could point eastwards, by the speed of the Axis build-up and by some exceptionally bad weather, to call a halt to the advance on Tunis in December, Sigint had revealed a significant shift in the enemy's mood. Towards the end of November Ultra showed General Nehring, temporarily commanding Axis forces in Tunisia, doubting whether he could hold out for long, and Kesselring a prey to gloomy forebodings. Yet only a few weeks later Kesselring had managed to convince himself that he now held the initiative. Even more telling – because it provided the framework or context of Kasserine – was evidence that, barely three weeks after the TORCH landings, the Axis command was already bent on extracting the maximum defensive advantage from its position between the two fronts by treating the whole North African theatre as a single unity for strategic purposes, rather than waiting to be crushed when the two fronts converged. The despatch of a dozen tanks from Tunis on 28 November to protect the tenuous link between Tripoli and Tunis, the coastal road round the Gulf of Gabès, was the first of many signs of this. By mid-January Kesselring, Rommel and von Arnim (now commanding Fifth Panzer Army in Tunis) were disagreeing about the application of this strategy. Rommel, who favoured a quick withdrawal to Tunis as the best defensive measure, was persuaded into sending 21 Panzer Division across to Sfax (its slow progress confirmed the Axis fuel shortage), although the depletion of his strength would force him, against Mussolini's wishes, to hasten his retreat. Arguments like this, monitored by Ultra, showed how the lack of a unified command,* the inevitable consequence of developments since TORCH, was handicapping the Axis in Africa, but it does not seem to have been realised that this was, at least in part, the reason why the evidence for an attack in mid-February was difficult to interpret: there was, in fact, no single plan before Kasserine, as was assumed, but several rival plans, all under discussion at the same time. The emergency was soon to show that the same ills affected the Allies too. The Axis never remedied them; the Allies did – in the nick of time – by establishing a unified command, 18 Army Group, under General Alexander.

Command changes consequent upon the imminent junction of the two Allied fronts were discussed, and the next Mediterranean operation (HUSKY, the invasion of Sicily) decided upon at the Casablanca Conference in mid-January, as Montgomery braced himself for the assault on Tripoli and von Armin prepared to strike back in Tunisia. Y got first wind of an early version of one of the Axis plans on 20 January, and was now delivering a steady stream of intelligence about tank strengths and divisional locations. Considerable as the Y Service had now become as a source of intelligence, however, it could not compensate for the deficiencies (unprecedented in the desert for more than a year) which impaired Ultra during February. It is

---

* The need for a reorganisation of the command structure was second only to a solution of the supply problem in the opinion of General Warlimont (deputy head of the OKW Operations Staff) after the official mission to Tunisia in early February; he likened the Axis position to 'a house of cards' (OKW/KTB iii. 130–3). Ultra got wind of the intended visit but not of its outcome.

sometimes suggested that Y was the better guide during the critical weeks of mid-February, and Eisenhower later implied as much; he blamed his (British) Chief Intelligence Officer for relying too much on a single source, Ultra, when he dismissed him after the battle in the Kasserine Pass. It is fairer to conclude, however, that since several key pieces of the intelligence jigsaw puzzle were missing because they were never transmitted by radio (although Y followed 10 and 21 Panzer Divisions closely for several days, for instance, and gave notice of Rommel's advance towards Le Kef on 19 May, and of his withdrawal three days later), W/T silence denied both Y and Ultra* the chance to warn Eisenhower of the attack on Kasserine, and that this laid a more than usually heavy burden of interpretation upon shoulders too weak to bear it, with the result that wrong deductions were plausibly drawn from questionable premises.

When unblooded and over-confident troops were suddenly faced with an entirely unexpected attack by the battle-hardened veterans of the Afrika Korps at Kasserine on 20 February, defects of command and tactics combined with the absence of warnings to cause a local defeat which, though shattering for the moment, did not develop into a disaster of greater magnitude because Rommel, the attacker, was prevented by his own comparative weakness and by superior authority from exploiting his victory boldly. He was forced instead to abandon his intended line of advance and substitute one which favoured the mustering of Allied resistance (an identical mistake was to muffle the impact of the German Ardennes offensive in December 1944). Only by making unjustifiable use of wisdom after the event can the riddle of conflicting and incoherent intelligence before Kasserine be solved even today; it was entirely reasonable – but utterly wrong – to deduce from the Ultra signals that the main attack would strike westwards from Fondouk rather than north-west from Gafsa and Faid. Less inexperienced and more

* The outward and technical W/T aspects of both were now profitably studied together by the 'fusion room' in Hut 3.

sceptical analysts would have taken alarm at the inconsistencies accumulating daily in the material, have paid more attention to the information collected by the Anglo-American Y Section attached to II US Corps, and have ordered more aerial reconnaissance. Probably at no juncture in the last four years of the war (with the possible exception of the Ultra-less months of 1942* in the battle of the Atlantic) was a body of intelligence so hard to interpret correctly, but the staff called to work under the earlier handicap had been hardened by experience and were not, like the staff in Tunisia, relatively new to the game of intelligence.

Having thus lashed out against the Americans to good effect, Rommel now planned to use the interior lines for a thrust in the opposite direction by all three Panzer divisions against Montgomery as he advanced towards Mareth and the defence line the French had built long before to protect Tunisia against Italian aggression. He changed front with astonishing speed, but Sigint, which had just played the Americans false at Kasserine, now relented and scattered its accustomed favours upon Eighth Army. By 23 February Montgomery knew of Rommel's intentions, and shortly afterwards that he proposed to attack Medenine (which Eighth Army had occupied just before Kasserine) with 31,000 men and 135 tanks on 6 March. It was a copy, though a less dramatic one, of the situation before Alam Halfa. Montgomery dug in 600 anti-tank guns at the precise spot which both Y and Ultra indicated, backed them with 400 tanks in case a counter-attack was required, and beat back the assault in a matter of hours, destroying more than a third of Rommel's armour in the process.

Only a few days later, the LRDG performed its last great service by showing how the Mareth Line, which blocked the narrow coastal strip leading to Gabès and the wider plain of southern Tunisia, could be outflanked. The Mareth defences

* February–December 1942. See pp. 159–60 and 192–4.

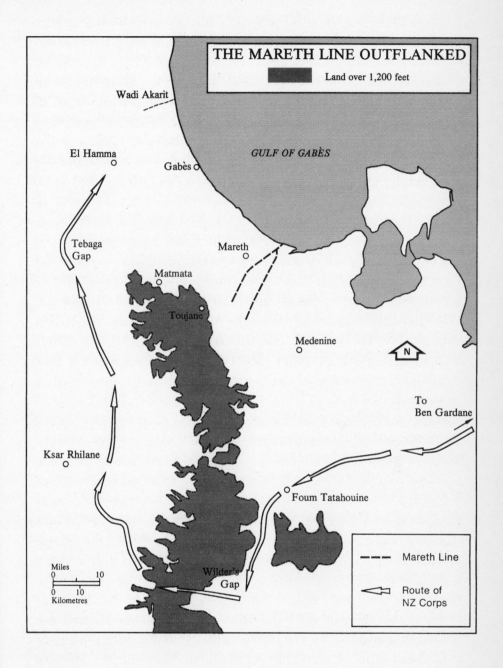

THE MARETH LINE OUTFLANKED

Land over 1,200 feet

Wadi Akarit

El Hamma

Gabès

GULF OF GABÈS

Tebaga
Gap

Mareth

Matmata

Toujane

Medenine

N

To
Ben Gardane

Ksar Rhilane

Foum Tatahouine

Miles
0   10

0   10
Kilometres

Wilder's
Gap

Mareth Line

Route of
NZ Corps

were formidable, and Montgomery was quick to seize on the possibilities of the discovery the LRDG had made three months earier – a gap in the Matmata Hills (upon which the landward end of the Mareth Line was anchored) through which tanks and men could be passed to turn the old French defences by a 'left hook'. When his frontal attack stalled, Montgomery reinforced the 'left hook' and, kept fully abreast of slowly dawning enemy realisation of what was happening by both Y and Ultra, forced Rommel to withdraw on 25 March to the Wadi Akarit, the last defensible position before the heights round Tunis. Two days later the 'left hook' force of Generals Freyberg and Horrocks, assisted by a massive heavy-bomber raid arranged (contrary to Air Ministry doctrine, which deprecated the use of heavy bombers against tactical targets) at short notice by the new commander of the Desert Air Force, drove north-eastwards through to the coast at Gabès. Thoroughly rattled, the Axis put up a show of resistance at the Wadi Akarit, but the fighting was over in a few hours; as the Italian General who had taken over Rommel's old command admitted, 'it was not a good battle'. Rommel himself, ill and dispirited, had already left Africa for good.

An important, though on the face of it unlikely, conversion to and understanding of the value of intelligence in war had taken place during the previous few weeks. Eisenhower had dismissed General Fredendall, the commander of II US Corps at whose door much of the blame for the débâcle at Kasserine was properly laid, and replaced him with General George S. Patton on 6 March, ordering Patton to harry the rear of the forces which were impeding Montgomery's advance. Patton's first impetuous rush into battle came to grief, but in the course of it he learned how useful the Y Service could be, and indeed gained his subsequent success at El Guettar with its help. (Unfortunately over-enthusiasm for it led him to proclaim its merits in a plain-language radio broadcast to his tank commanders, thereby causing an immediate change of key. The incident taught him the lesson that intelligence demands security and security limits exploitation.) He was, of course, not in receipt of Ultra, which was never distributed at corps level, because the risk of the loss through capture of men or material capable of betraying the secret that Enigma was being broken was judged too great so near the front line. Thus a second and greater conversion awaited Patton when he came to command an army in Normandy.

The Allied command, unified under Alexander by the establishment of 18 Army Group on 20 February, was by now so far superior in power that it was clearly certain to prevail. As the fighting became concentrated in built-up areas where civilian telephone systems existed and could quickly be extended for military purposes, Enigma traffic diminished, making every break more difficult to achieve and more subject to delay. Ultra contributed little to the final eclipse of the Axis, save by the light it threw on the steady worsening of the enemy's supply situation and the wild emergency measures taken to improve it: a large number of the transport planes and gliders employed to ferry men and material, most now impossible to feed or to use, were shot down because their routes and destinations were known in advance; the unwanted reinforcements which Hitler insisted on sending served only to swell to almost a quarter of a million the total of prisoners at the surrender on 13 May. In this situation Y came into its own and continued to produce a greater volume of useful intelligence every day, notably showing that there was no reason to suspect that either the shift of two of Eighth Army's best divisions (7 Armoured and 4 Indian) across the front from right to left or First Army's disguise of the point at which it would deliver the decisive blow had been recognised.

Triumphant, Alexander telegraphed to Churchill, 'We are masters of the North African shores.' Had he been minded to give reasons for the victory, he could have explained that prominent among them were not only the penetration of the enemy's most secret cipher, which gave access to the thoughts and intentions of theatre commanders, of OKW and even on occasion of Hitler himself, but almost equally importantly the conversion of British (and lately some American) generals away from ignorance of and contempt for intelligence to a lively appreciation of its usefulness in shaping operations and strategy and to a daily familiarity with the processes by which this was accomplished. It was these novelties which marked the North African campaigns out from all previous conflicts.

Intelligence in the ordinary sense of the word – information about the enemy sought and used in order to discomfit him – may be called 'active' because it influences events. So too may intelligence used for the purpose of deceiving the enemy, though it does so at one remove. But there is another type, best described as 'passive' or 'negative', which protects the rear of the others by preventing the enemy from discovering that advantage is about to be taken of him. The former is the more glamorous – it is the inspiration of all spy stories – but the latter is essential to the other's life. If all the German agents in Britain had not been rounded up, they would have seriously imperilled the defence of the country in the emergency of 1940; four years later, the fiction that the main thrust of OVERLORD would come round Calais would never have been accepted as truth had Berlin been able to discover by air reconnaissance that there were insufficient signs of military encampments or road movements in Kent and Essex to support the double agents' stories and the apparent evidence of (spurious) radio traffic.

In the Middle East, where long and open land frontiers offered easy access to clandestine infiltrators, the protection of Eighth Army's rear by an agent-proof security system was potentially as difficult as it was vital. The rudiments of such a system were nevertheless in place before war broke out ('field security' and 'military intelligence' were almost interchangeable terms in the Middle East, as at home and in France, until 'active' intelligence came to the forefront in and after 1942). Postal censorship was fully operational by the summer of 1939, for instance, and by the end of 1941 all diplomatic facilities for non-Allied powers had been withdrawn. Long before this, 20,000 or more persons had been interned as a precautionary measure (the 60,000-odd Italians resident in Egypt when Graziani invaded in 1940 had to be treated as a possible threat to stability, though in the event they caused no trouble).

The primarily political purposes of the handful of Defence Security Officers (DSOs) already operating under MI5 in Gibraltar, Malta, Cairo and a few other places in the Middle East were necessarily subordinated to military needs as war approached. Already in January 1939 the JIC had recommended the establishment of a Middle East Intelligence Centre (MEIC) to correlate local intelligence; before long SIME (Security Intelligence Middle East) took over its counter-intelligence functions and for this purpose settled more DSOs in Palestine, Iraq (after the collapse of Rashid Ali's revolt in May 1941), Beirut (to protect Syria, through which enemy agents had found it easy to pass, after the destruction of the Vichy regime in July) and Istanbul (whence German spying activities were controlled, but where Cairo developed a close and friendly relationship with the Turkish secret police as a counterweight).

The task of seeking out would-be infiltrators and other suspicious characters was carried out by a number of Field Security Sections, whose work varied from supervising the repatriation of French families from Syria after the brief conflict with the Vichyite administration to pursuing suspects wherever they were thought to be lurking. The magnitude of the task in the northern areas is indicated by the contemporary estimate that some 200 German agents were at work in Syria alone in 1941, apart from various local trouble-making groups like the self-styled Society to Commend Virtue and Condemn Vice. When arrested – as eight were at Aleppo between the loss of Tobruk in June 1942 and Alamein – suspects were interrogated, a few executed, some 'turned' to act as double agents and many

more interned. It was not only new incomers who needed to be
carefully watched: agents returning to Turkey after completing a
mission might be in possession of sensitive information useful to
the enemy.* By constant alertness, by meticulous care in the
pursuit and cross-examination of suspects, and by other means,
security was maintained in the rear of the British and Allied
forces in the field. So successfully were German agents eliminated that in 1944 every single name on a captured Abwehr list of
its agents in the Middle East belonged to a man or woman who
had in fact become a double agent working under British
control.

That the ill-success of the Abwehr was due to its own
incompetence as well as to British counter-measures can be
illustrated by the suppression of the attempt (known to the
Germans as Operation Condor) to plant two agents in Cairo.
During the summer of 1942 Count Almasy, a Hungarian desert
explorer of repute now working for Germany, guided them
across the northern fringes of the Sahara and into the Sudan,
whence they travelled to Egypt. They were supposed to make
contact with Rommel's headquarters, but were apprehended
when they flung British banknotes round lavishly in the bars and
nightclubs of Cairo – their controllers evidently being unaware
that these had ceased to be legal currency in Egypt many months
earlier. The official history dismisses them in a short and sober
paragraph, but several more colourful accounts are in circulation; they speak of a popular belly-dancer, a Nile houseboat used
as a brothel, and other scandalous details.

Arrested and interrogated at the Combined Service Detailed
Interrogation Centre (CSDIC), these two men at first refused to

* The wagons-lits conductors on the Taurus 'express' which ran between
Ankara and Tripoli in Syria all worked for the Turkish intelligence
service. In 1943 one of them was also working for the Abwehr and the
Sicherheitsdienst (each unknown to the other), the Italians, the Japanese
and the British. On one occasion he asked Nicholas Elliott of the SIS to
carry through customs a bomb he had been given by the Japanase
Military Attaché to throw on to the line between Aleppo and Tripoli
(Elliott, *Never Judge a Man by His Umbrella* (Michael Russell, 1991), 117).

co-operate, but their resistance was broken by a simple ruse. Placed together in a room they correctly supposed to be 'bugged', they guarded their conversation and kept to innocuous subjects. Later, housed in a bell-tent they supposed to be 'clean' but where a microphone had been cleverly inserted into the top of the tent-pole, they became careless, talked freely and soon gave themselves away. Thereafter they supplied valuable information about the Abwehr, and helped to identify newly arrived German infiltrators.

Over the whole territory of the Middle East, the detection and neutralisation of the agents was immeasurably simplified by breaks into the Abwehr hand and Enigma ciphers in the course of 1941. In consequence it was possible to discover the names and purposes of many of the men and women (Paula Koch, who at one time worked as a nurse in a Muslim hospital in Beirut, was among the most skilful of them) sent to collect information for the enemy, and to imprison them or otherwise nullify their efforts while still allowing the Abwehr to believe that it was operating a spy network behind the British lines. Details of how this was done are obscure because, as has been remarked already, the relevant files are still closed to public inspection, but it is abundantly clear nevertheless that Field Security swept the rear areas remarkably clean and that, by guaranteeing that the Allies were doing something which the other side could not do, greatly enhanced the value of 'active' intelligence.

The two years between spring 1941 and spring 1943, the years of the desert war, saw momentous developments in every aspect of military intelligence. By Alamein in October 1942 it was being generated on a large scale and with a degree of sophistication which deserved the respect with which it was at last being treated by senior commanders. Britain's American allies were beginning to follow suit. The ascent of intelligence to a position of high regard had been slow and sometimes painful, but it was now a sharp instrument ready to inflict deep wounds on Germany's power to make war.

1939–1945

Ten-Tenths Cloud Cover:
Intelligence and Bomber Command

With the fall of France in June 1940 the land front in Europe disappeared, and with it Britain's chance to attack Germany anywhere but in the air. The struggle was necessarily defensive at first: the Battle of Britain and preparations to resist invasion took precedence over all else. But even before the danger was past Churchill's mind was already turning to the offensive. In an often quoted minute of 8 July 1940 to Beaverbrook, the Minister of Aircraft Production, he wrote, 'There is one thing that will bring Hitler down, and that is an absolutely devastating, exterminating attack by very heavy bombers from this country upon the Nazi homeland. We must be able to overwhelm them by this means, without which I do not see a way through.'[*][†]On 3 September, in a memorandum for the Cabinet, he added,

[*] Six weeks earlier, however, the Chiefs of Staff had proposed to the Cabinet what was to become the triple Bomber Command objective – economic damage leading to shaken morale and revolt. See Sir Brooks Richards, *Secret Flotillas* (HMSO, 1996), 20. See also Foot, *SOE*, 18 and PRO. CAB 66/7 W P (40) 168.
[†] In 1917, as Minister of Munitions, he had expressed a contrary opinion: 'It is improbable that any terrorisation of the civil population which could be achieved by air attack would compel the government of a great nation to surrender ... We have seen the combative spirit of the [British] nation roused, and not quelled, by the German raids ...'
Quoted in P. Calvocoressi, *Causes and Course of the Second World War*, 2nd ed., 1989, p. 514; from Churchill, *The World Crisis 1916–18*, 1927 edn, pp. 573–4, without attribution. I am grateful to Mr Allen Packwood of the Churchill Archives Centre for locating the original source for me.

'The Navy can lose the war, but only the Air Force can win it.'
This belligerent enunciation of the prevailing Trenchard doctrine, to which the Air Ministry remained firmly attached for the
next six years, did credit to his defiantly bulldog spirit: but as a
realist he knew that he was whistling in the dark to keep his
country's courage up. There were as yet no heavy bombers at all
(if we allow the word its normal later sense – four-engined
Halifaxes and Lancasters – for the heaviest then were twin-
engined Wellingtons), Bomber Command could not normally
muster more than fifty or sixty aircraft for a single raid and could
drop only a puny tonnage of bombs – less than 600 tons in May
1940, for instance. (The figure for March 1945 was almost
150,000.)

Thus was displayed the unhappy divergence which governed
British air policy right down to 1944: a laudable – indeed a
necessary – desire to carry the war into enemy territory, but a
distressing lack of the means to do so. Published accounts of the
air war dwell mainly upon this divergence, tracing also the
chronology of the technological improvements in navigation and
bomb-aiming by which the gap was narrowed and the scale and
quality of Bomber Command's performance raised. In addition,
these accounts sometimes reflect on the moral issue – the
slaughter of thousands of German civilians – which came more
and more into prominence as a result of the improvements and
of the policy of area bombing until, in the last twelve months of
the war, the decline of the Luftwaffe into near impotence
allowed the British and American bombers to range almost at
will across the skies of the Reich and to deal death and
destruction with something like impunity.

Critical as most of these accounts are, none has much to say
about intelligence and the use Bomber Command made of it, or
about the lack of reliable information concerning the effects of
bombing on German industrial output.[*] They rightly deal at

[*] Because it was published sixteen years before Ultra could be
mentioned openly, Webster and Frankland's monumental study could not

great length with technical intelligence (navigation and bomb-sights) and with photographic evidence of raid damage, but not with the kind of intelligence which the army and the navy were procuring in growing measure and learning to assess and utilise better in the same midde years of the war.

Part of the reason for this is not far to seek: there was scant means of getting such intelligence, and practically none of securing it deliberately and for a particular purpose.[*] There were no British agents in Germany, and few as yet in the occupied countries. Above all, however, until later on from

refer to it in any way. Volume ii, p. 294, for instance, merely lists 'secret reports' last in a catalogue of sources, and does not elucidate.

[*] Little seems in fact to be known about how and how quickly military information came out of occupied countries: some SOE records have survived, but most SIS papers are still embargoed.

Deliberately planted agents could report by wireless, but they had to be careful to avoid the fate of those trapped by Operation North Pole (see p. 263) or that of the unlucky man who was inadvertently assigned the wavelength of a Panzer regiment stationed near the point where he was landed: he was arrested as soon as he used his radio. The return flights of the Lysander aircraft which planted agents could (weather permitting, and if arrangements could be made quickly) bring back even fairly bulky articles. This was how the plans of the Atlantic Wall, which René Duchez's quick thinking enabled him to purlion from an Organisation Todt office (see p. 253), reached England, for instance. Much, however, depended on unplanned local initiative, like the Oslo report (see pp. 32–3), or the debris of a V2 which landed in Poland, a sackful of which was transported 200 miles by bicycle to a secret airstrip from which it was flown to England via Brindisi. It was of great assistance to Dr R. V. Jones's investigations (see Jones: *Most Secret War*, pp. 443–4).

Of direct relevance to Bomber Command's activities is the fact that it does not seem to be known how quickly the 'Stockbroker' circuit's ingenious plan to blackmail the staff of a factory which made tank turrets into sabotaging their own plant was reported. Damage done surreptitiously in this way could put the factory out of business for weeks at a time and render bombing wasteful and unnecessary; two pounds of plastic explosive, applied by 'Stationer', brought the Dunlop tyre factory at Montluçon to a complete standstill in September 1943. (Most of the information in this footnote depends heavily on M. R. D. Foot, *SOE in France*, pp. 437–41 and on correspondence and conversations with Professor Foot, to whose generous guidance in everything concerned with SOE and the Resistance I have been indebted over the years.)

inside Germany there was practically no Ultra, the novel type of intelligence which by 1942 was inexorably advancing to the foremost influence on the plans of Cabinet, Chiefs of Staff, Admiralty and War Office. The fact that there was so little that was relevant to its operations may be the reason why, so far as can be ascertained, Ultra was not sent direct from Hut 3 to Bomber Command at this time.* The staff at High Wycombe, Bomber Command's headquarters, though arranging operations nightly, were therefore in some sense isolated and deprived of the intellectual discipline of having to juxtapose completely reliable, factual, current intelligence with prevailing theoretical concepts and merely plausible hypotheses and of observing the solvent effect of the one upon the other – as their equivalents in the desert were doing from early 1942 onwards. The consequences for the lack of rigour in their mental approach to evidence must remain a matter for speculation. Bomber Command cannot be blamed for not making use of what it did not receive, but it can be censured for not recognising the limitations of what it did acquire.

The reason for the lack of air Ultra in Europe in the middle years of the war is plain: ample land-line communications existed in Germany and France, so there was no need for the Luftwaffe to use radio except in the occasional emergency. Nor, because there was no land front, were prisoners of senior rank, who might possess operational information worth discovering, likely to be taken. (There were notable exceptions, but they were soldiers, not airmen. After their capture in Libya, for instance, but before they realised that their prison room was 'bugged', Generals Cruewell and von Thoma not only gossiped about criticisms of Rommel within Panzer Army but in the course of conversation let out precious details about Peenemünde and the V2 rockets at what was an early stage in the rumours about

* For further discussion of what Ultra Bomber Command received, see pp. 167–8.

them. Most Luftwaffe prisoners were only of junior commissioned rank, and they were in any case not numerous.)

The result was that no worthwhile assessment of the effects of
bombing could be secured. Yet this was what Bomber Command, if it rightly appreciated what it was about, needed above
all. When PR had shown how inaccurate the early raids were
and how far later technical improvements had managed to better
them, information essential to a proper estimate of the damage
done was still missing. Air photographs did not, and could not,
deliver all that was needed, however intensively they were
studied. Suppose them to show a factory or an oil plant to be
badly hit, its workshop unroofed and so on. How many of the
machines in the workshop had been put out of commission?
How long would it take to bring them back into operation? For
how long would production be interrupted? How soon could the
flow of oil or the manufacture of fighter aircraft be restored, and
to what percentage of the former rate? What was the mood of
the workforce after the raid, and would this give rise to
absenteeism or disaffection? Answers to these questions were
needed, but air photographs could not provide them. Analytical,
not merely pictorial, evidence could alone provide satisfactory
answers and consequently a sound basis for bombing policy; yet
this was almost impossible to obtain. Factory managers' damage
reports and estimates of repair-time and the return of something
like normality went by telephone or teleprinter, so that there was
an almost complete dearth of information comparable with that
which Ultra was beginning to provide for the Mediterranean
theatre and which became almost routine there in 1943.* Here

* Two points require emphasis in this context. First, such intercept
evidence as there was is not open to inspection; the accounts of Bomber
Command in *British Intelligence* do not suggest that it was of much value.
Second, although there does not appear to be any published statement to
this effect, it must be presumed that Air Ministry passed on to Bomber
Command such Ultra as it thought helpful. But (as will become apparent)
Air Ministry was usually disinclined to question Bomber Command's
decisions or attempt to alter them.

was Bomber Command's irremediable handicap. Portal, Peirse and Harris (successively AOCs Bomber Command, 1940–5) do not seem to have realised that in consequence of it they were forced to base their actions on their own *a priori* conviction and on evidence too weak to justify the conclusions they drew from it.

The inability of even the best air photographs to see beneath the surface, and therefore the possibility of error if deeper inferences were drawn, can be illustrated in another way. In order to gain tactical surprise before Alamein, Eighth Army used deception on a large scale to disguise the place and time of its attack. Ammunition dumps, tank and artillery concentrations were made, by means of specially designed covers, to look like innocuous lorry parks; above all, a simulated extension to the genuine water-pipeline which ran south from the coast road was laid at a rate which suggested that it would be finished a week or two later than Montgomery intended to strike. German air reconnaissance quite failed to penetrate any of these disguises, and Panzer Army expected an attack much too far south. Did no one point out to Bomber Command during the winter of 1942/3 how successful deliberate deception could be, and that there was always the possibility of accidental deception, because of the limitations of photographs taken at a great height, and that it would be wise to take both into account?

*

Chamberlain having forbidden any offensive action which might provoke the Germans to retaliate, Bomber Command dropped leaflets not bombs over Germany throughout the winter of 1939/40; this gave valuable practice in navigation but in no way atoned for the astonishingly complete absence of any pre-war training in an art which was absolutely fundamental to the doctrine that aerial bombardment could destroy industry and thereby an enemy's capacity to wage war. Slow and obsolete aircraft carrying only a handful of small bombs gave their pilots opportunities for suicidal bravery in May 1940 but did nothing to halt the German *Blitzkrieg* in France. Repeated attacks on the invasion barges assembling in the Channel ports helped to persuade Hitler to call SEALION off in September, but were far from the strongest deterrent.

When all physical links with the continent of Europe were cut in June 1940 it was the RAF which suffered most from the isolation which followed. The navy was not comparably affected; maritime contact with an enemy could never be more than occasional, and by that time the *Graf Spee* and the Atlantic U-boats had kept it alert to new developments. Although there was no home-waters Ultra until August 1941, lower-grade keys and radio direction-finding told something of shipping movements in the Channel and the Atlantic. Six months after Dunkirk the war in Libya renewed the army's battle contact, and within a short time this began to generate first a trickle and then a steady flow of intelligence about the war in the Mediterranean. The specifically army information, though small in volume at first, nevertheless threw light on the structure of the whole German army, its fighting methods and equipment; most of the far larger bulk of intelligence concerning the Luftwaffe was relevant only to the theatre in which it originated.

This was not all, however. It was non-contact evidence, information generically distinct and derived from a higher level than most contact evidence, which the RAF most lacked. It was a symptom of the informational imbalance in the west that when technical details were required of a new German radar device, of which little more than the name – Würzburg – was known from intelligence sources, a commando raid had to be mounted to capture essential parts of it from a site which PR had pinpointed on the coast of Normandy.

From the RAF's point of view, the most important type of non-contact evidence was that concerning German industry. The prevalent belief in London was that Hitler, having planned to fight, had as a natural preliminary placed German industry on a war footing. In fact he had done nothing of the kind, and did not do so until the dawning prospect of losing the war led him to appoint Albert Speer Minister of Armaments and War Production in July 1943. Under Speer's direction, output was very considerably increased even after four years of war and fifteen months after the first thousand-bomber raid on Cologne. Yet all this time the Cabinet and Air Ministry had been believing that in Bomber Command they possessed a weapon which had already done appreciable damage to the German economy and was well on the way to destroying it altogether. This was, of course, very far from the truth. So gigantic an error is a measure of the handicap under which Bomber Command laboured. It badly needed intelligence qualitatively different from that which satisfied the other services if it was to play a commensurate part in the war and fulfil its self-chosen function. Unhappily, this type of information was well-nigh impossible to obtain, because it could come only from sources within occupied Europe which were few, unreliable and irregular in supplying it. Much remained unknown until the United States Strategic Bombing Survey discovered it after the war was over. In comparison, the army and navy could satisfy far more of their needs through information acquired from operational intercepts. The non-fulfilment of Bomber Command's real needs not only deprived it of vital intelligence but preconditioned it to misinterpret such intelligence as it did manage to secure.

It is largely this discrepancy which made the bombing offensive far and away the most controversial aspect of the 1939–45 war; beside it, other disputes within the RAF or between the RAF and other services were of less significance – army co-operation, which was negligible in 1939, first developed on the periphery in the Mediterranean and was of little account in the west until 1944, for instance, or the Admiralty/Air Ministry disagreement about the supply of modern aircraft to Coastal Command. Most accounts of the bombing offensive begin by dwelling on the early discorrelation between ends and the means to achieve them and then proceed to chronicle improvements in navigation and target acquisition before moving gradually into a debate about both the strategic wisdom and the morality of the large-scale killing of civilians. Crucial as this debate must always be for a final verdict on the offensive, it has one great drawback as a tool of historical analysis. It imports an element of value-judgment into the discussion and cannot escape measuring actions against a climate of opinion which has perceptibly changed since the 1940s.

The Dresden raid of February 1945 caused a revulsion of feeling greater even than that which followed the dropping of the atom bombs in Hiroshima and Nagasaki in August of the same year, because there appeared to be less military justification for it. But in neither case was there anything comparable to the public reaction of horror when napalm was used in Vietnam in the 1960s. In 1945 civilians and airmen alike felt 'They started it, let them have a taste of their own medicine'; in 1991 it was reported that some pilots refused to continue the carnage on the road along which the Iraqi troops were retreating northwards from Kuwait – an attitude unthinkable fifty years earlier. Yet the history of the one has to be written in the atmosphere of the other.

An unavoidable element of hindsight here intrudes into historical investigation; emotion strains judgment in ways which can be neither measured nor eliminated. To use the intelligence available when actions were taken as the sole criterion of judgment, noting the impressionistic, subjective character of the evidence upon which Bomber Command was so frequently forced to act, while army and navy could increasingly rely on objective sources, may escape at any rate part of the danger of hindsight, as well as being a relative novelty.*

---

* Most of the books about Bomber Command pass over the intelligence issue in silence, and none gives it much prominence. The air-war chapters in *British Intelligence* carefully record what was known but lay no emphasis on the small proportion this represented of what was needed to

For almost fifty years Sir Arthur Harris has borne the brunt of the criticism directed at Bomber Command. Grievous as were his mistakes, this is not entirely fair. Under his three immediate predecessors (Ludlow-Hewitt, 1937–40; Portal, April–October 1940; Peirse, 1940–2), Bomber Command had failed to make its mark as the offensive weapon it was designed to be, and it is generally agreed that its fortunes were at their lowest ebb when Harris became AOC in February 1942. Whatever else Harris did or did not do, he certainly made Bomber Command a more effective striking force than it had yet been, and one of which the general public was far more aware.

The death sentence on the Trenchard doctrine was in reality pronounced as early as December 1939, when raids on naval targets landed bombs on Denmark and failed to hit two cruisers in harbour. Given the small pre-war attention to navigation and bomb-sights, this is not surprising. What is more difficult to understand and forgive is the five-year stay of execution imposed by some senior officers' refusal to credit unwelcome evidence. Its malign effects lasted throughout the war, from Ludlow-Hewitt's belief in 1939 that he could carry out 'the major part of our plans by precision bombing at night', although Bomber Command lacked the training and the equipment to make this possible, to Harris's refusal even in 1945 to admit intelligence or argument which ran counter to his preconceived opinions. It is particularly striking in view of the quicker and more intelligent reaction of the Lufwaffe to the same problem at the same time. Daylight bombing of London having proved too expensive in men and machines (as it was for the RAF over Germany), like the RAF the Luftwaffe turned to night bombing instead – but with greater effect.

Although it had not been intended as a long-range strike force, as Bomber Command had been, but for army co-operation, the Luftwaffe soon brought in science to make up for human incapacity; the *Knickebein* beams chose the exact position at which

justify the bombing programme.

the pilots should drop their bombs, and by this means set the centre of Coventry on fire in November 1940. In contrast, the RAF's revenge attack on Mannheim next month scattered its bombs too widely, and by Christmas PR had shown that two successive raids by a total of 300 aircraft had dropped 260 tons of explosives, plus incendiaries, on Gelnhausen without causing major damage to the oil plants which were their target. Photography could never fulfil all intelligence requirements, but it could hardly make a mistake in locating bomb craters. Yet it was some time before its evidence was generally accepted, and meanwhile no attempt seems to have been made to bridge the gulf between PR's sobering objectivity and the impressionistic optimism of aircrew. By the time Harris took over, inaccuracy was taken for granted. In 1940 Peirse had reported that only one in five of his bombers found their target; summing up the situation he inherited two years later, Harris admitted that his aircraft were 'hardly ever able to find their targets'. Modern writers claim that in early 1942 it was generally accepted that less than 10 per cent of bombs fell within five miles of the point aimed at. The official history of British intelligence remarks that 'Despite the fact that a big effort went into the study of bombing targets, intelligence could do little before the end of 1942 to increase the effectiveness of British bombing raids,' but without offering explanation or comment.

Much of this 'big effort', it is worth recalling, was undertaken by the Ministry of Economic Warfare. But, however carefully the Ministry might analyse the weak points in the German economy, it was not equipped to judge either the difficulty of hitting them (hence in part the ill-success of the brief strategic oil offensive of early 1941) or the effectiveness of the raids it suggested, for it had no better means than Bomber Command of collecting intelligence from inside the Reich. This was to restrict the value of its advice throughout the war.

Significantly, Churchill's original commitment to bombing Germany had been made only a week before he founded the

Special Operations Executive and told its first head to 'set Europe ablaze' by stirring up resistance movements. Both occurred in the middle of July 1940, during the tense weeks between the Battle of France and the Battle of Britain, when the country was at its loneliest under the threat of invasion. Both represented his and the country's determination to fight on whatever the odds, not a carefully thought-out strategic plan. The two were clearly linked in his own mind: the sentence about bombing Germany, quoted earlier, followed another which lamented Britain's lack of military power on land. SOE was another way of making up for the loss of a 'continental army' at Dunkirk.

Disillusion soon set in under both heads. Two few bombs were dropped, and most missed their target. Occupied Europe gave no hint of rising against the oppressor until faint and contradictory signals began to come out of Jugoslavia in the late summer of 1941, and by then it was already plain that Europe could not resist unless it was first supplied with arms – for which Britain itself had more urgent need. Resistance remained on the periphery of Anglo-American strategy until 1944.

This left Bomber Command to wield the only offensive weapon, but both edges of its sword were blunt. As soon as the immediate fear of invasion had passed, Churchill voiced his anger at Bomber Command's disappointing performance. On 17 September 1940 he complained bitterly that its aircraft were too few, demanding a rapid increase in numbers together with an improvement in aim: Bomber Command should on no account be diverted from the 'accurate bombing of military objectives', he wrote, and severely rated Portal (now Chief of the Air Staff) on 1 November because 'the discharge of bombs on Germany is pitifully small'. A year later his scepticism had bitten deeper, and he even showed signs of abandoning his earlier conviction that bombing could bring Germany down on its own. 'It is very disputable,' he minuted to Portal on 21 September 1941, 'whether bombing by itself will be a decisive factor in the present war.' Its effects had been exaggerated, though the raids had stimulated the British people, but ground defences and night fighters might soon neutralise the attackers' skills, and only a quarter of their bombs hit their targets. Hence 'I deprecate placing unbounded confidence in this method of attack.' In this he was more prescient than most of those around him, as the future was to show. Yet in the autumn of 1941, when the USA was still neutral, the Russians in full retreat and there was no prospect of a British land front for years (the little conflict in Libya was insignificant in this context), there was still no other way of hitting Germany. So Churchill ended, 'The only plan is to persevere.'

Between these two almost directly opposed views Churchill was to fluctuate for more than three years, coming down against bombing at the end only because of the huge civilian casualties it caused.

When he took over from Peirse as AOC Bomber Command at the beginning of February 1942, therefore, Harris knew that a tremendous task confronted him, and that not least among his problems was that of a Prime Minister who harboured doubts about the policy which he (Harris) was to make increasingly his own – that of the ruthless bombing of Germany. He tried hard to convince Churchill that he was right. On 17 June he sent the Prime Minister a memorandum setting out his ideas. Adapting a phrase of Churchill's own, he wrote, 'Victory, speedy and complete, awaits the side which first employs air power as it should be employed.' Churchill was unmoved, his doubts unresolved. 'You must be careful not to spoil a good case by overstating it. . . . I do not think air bombing is going to bring the war to an end by itself. . . .'

How far did Harris allow himself to be guided by intelligence in the pursuit of his aim? He inherited only about 400 aircraft, barely a quarter of which were heavy four-engined machines (ordered in 1937, they were at last beginning to come into service), but the weakness of his hand had been very clearly shown up six months before he took office. The Butt Report, drawn up by a member of the War Cabinet Secretariat, studied 650 photographs of raid damage in conjunction with the related operation orders for two summer months of 1941; it demonstrated that only one-third of the crews claiming to have attacked had in fact dropped their bombs within five miles of the target and that most of the aircraft despatched on a given raid had not even reached the target area at all. This was 'hard' evidence so far as it went; no certain inferences about industrial damage could be drawn from it, but it was clear that much effort had been wasted and many casualties suffered for little gain – the bombs which Butt showed to have been dropped in open country had plainly not harmed the German economy at all. Yet Peirse, still AOC Bomber Command at the time, commented that these figures 'could not have produced the damage *known* [my italics] to have been achieved', forgetting that only the placing of the bomb craters was *known*, while the consequent industrial damage was mere surmise. Harris, then in command of 5 Group, was guilty of an even greater distortion when he boasted of his crews' accuracy without considering the evidence to the contrary; he never surrendered this totally irrational position.

The distinction between 'hard', objective evidence on the one hand and subjective supposition or estimate on the other is fundamental. One depends on provable facts, the other too often on faith, hope or guesswork. It is a distinction which lies at the heart of historical, as of all scientific, research, but it has consistently been denied its due prominence in the historiography of the bomber offensive.

Ironically enough, an example of the undervaluing of objective intelligence occurred in the same February 1942 as Harris became AOC Bomber Command. For the first time since the Battle of Britain, Ultra – that is objective – evidence about the GAF in western Europe was accumulating in sufficient volume to suggest action. It showed that attrition on the Russian front was weakening the GAF, particularly the fighter arm, more than at any time since the outbreak of war.* In consequence, the Air Ministry suggested that Bomber Command should carry this process a stage further by concentrating its attacks on the aircraft industry. Only a very moderate response was secured, and Harris accelerated his area bombing plans, notably in the dramatic thousand-bomber raid on Cologne on 31 May, for which he mustered every possible aircraft and crew, including a number of crews which had not yet completed their training, on a 'one-off' basis for publicity purposes. Although a large part of the city centre was set on fire, even the Ministry of Economic Warfare estimated that life had returned to normal in Cologne after a fortnight and that only a month's production was lost. Other raids in spring and early summer were less successful in hitting their targets and caused little serious damage. Twelve months later a special police cipher, used in the Ruhr for a week after the Dam Busters' raid, yielded the disappointing news that, after all the ingenuity of invention and meticulous training which had gone into the raid and the extraordinary bravery with which it had been carried out, the damage done was quickly brought under control. Sad to say, intelligence steadily accumulated to show that a mountain of effort might often bring forth only a ridiculous mouse by way of result or – if this be thought too severe – at any rate an extremely disproportionate return.

MEW was itself largely responsible for misjudging the effects of Bomber Command's raids, but for another and more fundamental reason. As is now well known, everyone in Britain, with the Ministry in the forefront, took it for granted that the German economy had been placed on a war footing in 1939 or 1940, and that therefore raid damage in 1941 or 1942 was

* However, figures in the OKW War Diary (OKW/KTB i.110E) show that overall numbers remained static in 1941 but that the serviceability rate (i.e. the average number of aircraft available for operations) fell from about 64 per cent to about 44 per cent in the four months since June 1941, mainly no doubt because of adverse weather conditions on the eastern front. The serviceability rate was not very much better in Libya in better climatic conditions.

bound to have taken something away from an already achieved maximum production capacity. A wrong assumption led to a false conclusion. German industry had not yet been fully geared up for war – it only reached that pitch under Speer in 1943–4 – and raids merely served as a stimulus to restore it to its former level. Agents being non-existent and Ultra uncommunicative on internal German affairs, there were negligible ascertained facts to argue from: the resultant inaccuracy can be pardoned, but not the confidence with which opinions which rested upon a questionable basis were defended. The assumption that the logical Germans had of course done in advance what the British had only begun to do when need arose – gird their loins as fast as possible – was, given the differences between the two peoples (much more marked then than now), so blatant a *non sequitur* that it should not have survived a moment's reflection. Ignorance of the Nazi Party and its chaotic methods, so different from the logical image, was probably at the root of the faulty assumption. This in turn is surely in part attributable to the reluctance of the pre-war (and alas also often the post-war) Foreign Office to pay proper attention to economic matters, and to the distaste of its educated and gentlemanly staff for the coarse and tawdry squabbles of vulgarians; here in fact is another aspect of British unpreparedness, and one with unfortunate repercussions.

A similar combination of illogical argument with insecure assumptions rather than reliable evidence, spiced this time with a little sharp practice, can be descried in the contemporary debates about the effects of bombing on German morale. Area bombing, to which the RAF had been committed since 1940 because it could not hit precise targets, soon received approval in its own right. A directive from the Air Staff in early July 1941 ordered Bomber Command's main effort to be devoted to 'the weakest parts of the enemy's armoury', namely civilian morale and the transportation system. At the end of the same month the Chiefs of Staff elaborated this in a remarkable statement which spoke of making 'a planned attack on civilian morale' as soon as the RAF was strong enough; 'there is increasing evidence', it went on, 'of the effect which even our present limited scale of attack is causing to German life' – the 'evidence' was of course nothing but the fruit of self-delusion – and that if the scale were raised in future 'the economic system, the machinery for production and destruction, the morale of the nation' would be so weakened as to cause Germany to sue for peace and thus reduce the role of the British army to that of an army of occupation. This, at a time when the British army at home had not yet recovered from Dunkirk and when the fragment of it fighting in the desert was licking the wounds Rommel had inflicted, struck the note which Harris was to strike with 'damnable iteration' – that Bomber Command could deal with Germany on its own, and that there was no need for an invasion.

The Chiefs of Staff view* was repeated in instructions to Bomber Command – 'the primary object of your operations should now be focussed on the morale of the population and in particular of the industrial workers' – a week before Harris took command in February 1942. Harris shut his eyes to the ill-expressed intention of finding a way of hitting targets more accurately as soon as possible, and thereby changed the emphasis. But a few months later Churchill was telling Stalin in Moscow that 'morale is a military target. We seek no mercy and shall show none.' Stalin agreed that that was 'the only way'. In the course of correspondence in November, Churchill and Roosevelt took a common decision that US long-range bombers should attack Italian industrial targets 'to terrorise and paralyse the population'. A year later the JIC chimed in to the same effect, optimistically but groundlessly asserting that before the end of the year the German people might decide that to continue the war would be more harmful than to accept defeat. By this time Harris had the bit between his teeth, launching heavier and more indiscriminate raids: the twelve months from

* It became joint Anglo-American policy at Casablanca a year later (see p. 165, below).

March 1943 to March 1944 have been called his period of independence. Arriving to share in his task, 8 USAAF found to its dismay that in spite of their defensive armament Flying Fortresses could not safely penetrate far into Germany by day without escort any better than Bomber Command three years before, because German anti-aircraft and fighter defences had been strengthened; it had consequently almost to suspend operations until the long-range Mustang fighter came into service at the beginning of 1944.

On what basis of evidence or rational deduction did the theory that widespread bombing could fatally undermine German morale now rest? 'On nothing but wish-fulfilment. There never was any objective evidence for it' must be the answer. In the first place, it does not seem to have occurred to anyone in authority to question the theory by confronting it with Britain's own experience. There had been one, though only one, attempt to examine the effects of bombing on British morale scientifically, the so-called Hull–Birmingham Report compiled by Professors Zuckerman and Bernal early in 1942, which had come to the conclusion that there had been no sign of panic, lowered morale or defeatism in either city. No attention appears to have been paid to the report. Admittedly, the difference in scale between the raids of 1941–2 and those which could be mounted in 1943–4 laid the prognostic value of the report open to question, but the failure to take any account of such evidence as there was before planning future action (an unwelcome obligation which fell unavoidably upon the shoulders of army and navy commanders and their staffs every day) throws into sharp relief the disastrous priority of blind belief over cool reason which marked the entire bombing campaign. 'London can take it' was always too rose-coloured a picture of the Blitz, but the real sufferings of Londoners had never led to a moment's weakening of the will to win, let alone to murmurs of revolt.*

---

* Goebbels ensured that the same was true of Germans under the heavy RAF/USAAF bombing of 1944–5 (Calvocoressi, pp. 330–1).

Post-war investigation found the same reaction in Hamburg, the Ruhr and Berlin after the tremendous pounding (far worse than the London Blitz) they received in 1943 and 1944. Harris and those who thought like him forgot that the natural reaction to great discomfort imposed by an enemy from outside would indeed be complaint mixed with anger, followed by lowered morale and furious if fruitless defiance – but nothing more; disaffection leading to revolt would need other, internal stimuli such as distrust of the government's ability to exact retribution from the offender. So hag-ridden were they by the conviction, inherited from pre-war days, that bombs must inevitably fall that they developed an abstract quasi-philosophical theory about it to which ascertainable facts were almost irrelevant.

A variety of sources, ranging from Ultra to German newspapers, were reporting by the end of 1943 that Bomber Command's raids were causing a decline in German morale. It would be easier to regard them as in some sense a justification of Harris's policy were it not that careful analysis, undertaken at the time, could find no sign of political disaffection in them. SIS reports from Berlin in April and May 1944 to the same effect – weakened morale but no hint of resistance – had convinced the JIC by June that there was after all 'no evidence to suggest that Allied bombing may shortly foment any effective opposition to the regime', and of course after the failure of the 20 July Plot against Hitler the SS and Gestapo clamped down on the slightest manifestion of it more firmly than ever. Nevertheless Harris continued with the greatest confidence to proclaim that if left alone he could finish Germany off in a few months through popular revolt as well as economic ruin: in December 1943 he was sure he could do it by April and even as late as at Eisenhower's final run-over of D-Day plans, 'Harris told us how well he might have won the war had it not been for the handicap imposed by the existence of the other two services,' noted Brooke. Having failed in his announced intention of achieving this in time to make OVERLORD unnecessary, he was subordinated, much against his will, to SHAEF between April and September 1944 and forced to use Bomber Command in a tactical role. On his release and return to Air Staff control he deliberately disobeyed orders to concentrate on oil targets and instead redoubled the weight of area bombing. Portal has been blamed for letting him get away with his disobedience and not dismissing him, but the Chiefs of Staff and the War Cabinet are equally implicated because they did not use their superior authority to insist that Harris cease his mutinous conduct.

Since it must be presumed, in the absence of any indication to the contrary, that agent intelligence from inside Germany was still on a negligible scale, it is natural to ask whether intercepts of any kind were by now giving enlightenment on the industrial effects of bombing. The intelligence black-out caused by the use of land lines still prevailed until the last months of the war, and applied as much to the Enigma key used by senior police commanders (which was broken from February 1944 onwards) as to any of the operational keys. Though the solution of all intercepts was at this stage greatly hampered by German precautions, which several times threatened to make them unbreakable, police hand ciphers, used by fire services and the ARP organisation as well, were a little more informative, giving positive information about damage to factories and the state of public opinion in the last months of the war as land lines were more frequently cut by bombing. Unfortunately, however, few details are recorded by the secondary sources and the original material – apparently of considerable bulk – is not open to inspection.

So far, the indictment (if that be not too strong a word) of Harris rests on his disregard of such objective evidence as there was that his raids were neither smashing German industry fast enough nor awakening resistance to Hitler. Defence counsel acting for him would certainly begin by pointing out that the evidence was too scanty to be conclusive and then, passing lightly over its cogency, would urge that his client could therefore be forgiven for overlooking its importance. Far more voluminous evidence can be proffered in support of another set of charges which, however, would be challenged by the defence on the ground that they were too oblique to the main issue to be allowed to carry much weight.

They merit careful consideration, on the other hand, because they are entirely contemporary, owe nothing to hindsight and, by introducing comparisons with other branches of the RAF and with the army and navy, serve as a reminder that Bomber Command should not be viewed in isolation from what was going on around it. However much Harris underestimated or even despised the other arms, he was aware of events in the desert, Italy and the Atlantic and may legitimately be held to have had a duty to profit from others' experience wherever it was relevant. The heads of all the services were joined in a common purpose to win the war, not simply to seek the greater glory of their own battleships, tanks or Lancaster bombers. Another advantage of a broader approach is that by drawing others into consideration as associates or accessories it spreads the responsibility and shows how little was done to restrain Harris's headstrong tendencies.

Harris had an innate scepticism of intelligence. In November 1941 he scouted the importance of beam-bombing, which had so recently proved its worth in the Blitz: 'We use no beams, but we bomb just as successfully as the Germans. . . . [The beams] are not really useful' – an opinion wholly at variance with the experience of the previous eighteen months and indicative of a mind wilfully unreceptive to even the most promising new ideas. Denigrating the validity of PR and implying knowledge which he did not possess, he confidently told an unimpressed Churchill in 1943, 'What actually occurs is much more than can be seen in any photograph.' Discussing his evasion of orders to bomb oil targets in 1944, *British Intelligence* remarks on Harris's disregard of unpalatable news about the enemy which conflicted with his own ideas. He was less intransigent about scientific intelligence originating at home, and willingly accepted a succession of scientific improvements to navigation systems in 1942 and 1943 – Gee, Oboe and H2S, followed by Pathfinders and Mosquitoes to guide the main body to its 'Target for Tonight' – but he showed no marked enthusiasm for them and admitted to surprise when, after the raid on the Trappes marshalling yard in northern France on 6 March 1944, which had been arranged as a test of Bomber Command's suitability for precision targets (already affirmed by the Friedrichshafen raid of June 1943, and then being demonstrated by the destruction of even quite small bridges in narrow valleys during Operation STRANGLE in Italy), PR showed that the target had been hit with great accuracy* and a satisfactory scale of damage inflicted, while not one of the 263 aircraft engaged had been lost.

Although he does not say so in his account of the circumstances, Harris's surprise was rueful at best. The Trappes raid opened the way for Bomber Command to contribute to the Transportation Plan, which aimed to restrict rail traffic round Normandy, reduce it to chaos and so prevent the swift arrival of German reinforcements, a plan which in his opinion would divert Bomber Command from its true function and which he had already denounced in round terms – 'the irremediable error of diverting our best weapon from the military function for which it has been equipped. . . . Though this might give a specious appearance of supporting the army, in reality it would be the greatest disservice we could do them. It would lead directly to disaster.' (In fact, of course, the Transportation Plan greatly relieved the pressure on the bridgehead during the first perilous days after the landing.)

Science alone created Oboe and the other novelties, but most

* Portal and Leigh-Mallory later 'had a good laugh over Bert Harris and his operations, particularly on the point of how strange it was that the very things he said his Command could never do, they were now doing to such good effect and he was so pleased about it' (Leigh-Mallory's diary, 11 and 12 July 1944, quoted in B. Newton-Dunn, *Big Wing* (Airlife, 1992), 160.

of the information from which a picture of the anti-aircraft and night-fighter defences (named the Kammhuber Line after its architect) could be pieced together and counter-measures devised was provided either by listening to the jargon conversations between night fighters and the ground stations which controlled them or by Ultra. So great an obstacle to the prosecution of British raids did the Kammhuber Line's guns and aircraft present, with their constant exploitation of new electronic devices (beginning with the Würzburg ground-control radar which had been captured at Bruneval in 1942), updated regularly to take account of each new British device and neutralising each new British airborne radar instrument within weeks of its introduction, that it might have been expected to awaken curiosity about the source of so much invaluable information. If Colonel Charles Carrington, the 'Soldier at Bomber Command', had been privy to the Ultra secret, he might have been able to dent the hard surface of Harris's refusal to pay attention to external intelligence. As things were, neither Harris's own writings nor those of his subordinates and subsequent defenders show any sign of recognising the value (or even the existence) of Ultra or any other form of intelligence except scientific, or that their own lack of interest in it was at all regrettable.

Responsibility for ensuring that lessons drawn from other areas, in which intelligence was more plentiful, were passed on to Harris if they seemed likely to help him rested with the Chief of Staff and the Air Ministry. The accusing finger points directly at Portal, whose task it was to oversee RAF activity in all theatres and who was the only channel along which digested Ultra, increasingly the dominant source of reliable information, and inferences from it reached Harris, but the Chiefs of Staff Committee and the JIC cannot escape blame for failing to bring more pressure to bear on him.

The Mediterranean was the obvious source of lessons. There, by the middle of 1942, Tedder had built up a comprehensive body of information about the Luftwaffe and its habits from intelligence of the same type as that which was at last beginning to come Harris's way – in the latter case, for instance, about the activities of the new night-fighter squadrons in Holland and the Rhineland. Furthermore, Tedder had found that co-operation with army and navy, rather than scorn for them, could be beneficial to all three, and had looked benevolently upon Broadhurst's (commander, Desert Air Force) experiment in using heavy bombers in tactical support of armour, thereby ensuring that Montgomery's 'left hook' round the Mareth Line was able to punch right through to the coast at Gabès in a single night. The exploitation of intelligence was by no means the whole story, but it had induced a salutary scepticism of pilots' claims on the one hand and on the other had helped towards the conclusion that the best results were achieved through the co-ordination of all arms – the policy which Tedder was to make so peculiarly his own during the four months (April–September 1944) when Bomber Command was nominally under the authority of Eisenhower as Supreme Commander, and effectively under that of Tedder, his deputy. Harris and Spaatz, the USSTAF commander, might have been less recalcitrant subordinates had their attention been more decisively drawn in advance to the Mediterranean, and Harris might have been persuaded that he was not the sole repository of all RAF wisdom. Portal has often been criticised for not using his formal authority over Harris more firmly during the winter of 1944/5: here is an instance of his failure to do so at an earlier stage.

Portal stood shoulder to shoulder with Harris in what has been called 'the most important single British strategic debate of the war' – that about how to win the Battle of the Atlantic – and the particular concern of both was the Admiralty's efforts to secure the allocation of more long-range aircraft to Coastal Command for use against the Atlantic U-boats. In March 1942 Pound, the First Sea Lord, followed Churchill when he declared, 'If we lose the war at sea, we lose the war,' and demanded the

transfer of some eighty Liberators and Flying Fortresses to cover
the mid-Atlantic gap, the wide strip of sea over which
surveillance could not be exercised from either shore because no
aircraft hitherto in service had the necessary range. This was the
U-boats' second 'happy time', as they played havoc with
unescorted coastwise shipping silhouetted against the brightly lit
and unprotected east coast of newly belligerent America as well
as continuing their depredations in the Atlantic. Sinkings rose to
an alarmingly high level, and when the Germans added a fourth
rotor to the naval version of the Enigma machine, thus making
messages enciphered with it unreadable between February and
December 1942, the ten-month blindness of Bletchley saw it rise
still further to potentially lethal heights. There was a real chance
that Britain's Atlantic life-line might be cut, the supply of food
and petrol so reduced that civilians would starve and Harris's
bombers be unable to take off.

No close study of intelligence was required to appreciate the
severity of the danger. Yet Portal, who was privy to all
intelligence and to MEW's estimates of what might lie ahead,
took the same negative line as Harris, denying that the danger
was as great as the Admiralty maintained; he even asserted that
there was insufficient evidence to justify a gloomy view at all, and
labelled every transfer of aircraft to Coastal Command as a
transfer from an active to 'an uneconomic defensive role'.

Harris, it has been said, saw the Admiralty, Coastal Command and Tedder in the Middle East (who also demanded more
aircraft) as 'vultures tearing at the entrails of his command'. In
one sense, he was no doubt right. But a just appraisal of the
intelligence and of the strategic risks to Britain if the Battle of the
Atlantic were lost should have convinced both him and Portal,
whose responsibilities and angle of vision were wider, that the
plain and concrete needs of the Atlantic for more long-range
aircraft ought to be preferred to the uncertain rewards of
bombing Germany.

In no field was Bomber Command's obstinately blind spot

about intelligence more clearly illustrated than in its commander's attitude towards flying bombs and rockets (V1s and V2s), for it was by intelligence that his every action against what at one time threatened acute danger was directed. Because the evidence was at first fragmentary and inconclusive, it could be dismissed as unworthy of credence – Churchill's scientific adviser Lord Cherwell was still calling it 'a mare's nest' in October 1943 – but as time went on the accumulation of detail became overwhelming. Directly this stage was reached, something approaching panic broke out among the few politicians in the know, and Herbert Morrison (Home Secretary) even had a plan prepared to evacuate London in the event of a rocket bombardment. Admittedly, the near panic was magnified because quasi-scientific theorising by a few unqualified 'experts' on the basis of imperfectly understood material greatly exaggerated the explosive charge which either type of weapon could carry. Nevertheless, against a background like this, it is hard to understand why, once Harris had been persuaded to interrupt area bombing to raid the Peenemünde research station on 17 August 1943, he did not show more interest either in the process which had led first to a request for photographic cover of Peenemünde and then to the raid, or in sharing the whole business of gathering and interpreting the evidence upon which his actions depended. It would seem, however, that Harris's interest, great though it could be in the fine details of a single raid like that on the underground storage site at St Leu on 4 July 1944, did not extend beyond the immediate and factual into abstract and general issues.

Yet the intelligence story of how both types of V-weapons were discovered was not only fascinating in itself but provided a good example of the way in which careful analysis of evidence from a variety of external sources could lead to urgent operational decisions and to an escape from an unexpected and possibly very serious reverse just when the war seemed on the point of being won. Two years after the Oslo Report, rumours of

a secret experimental and research establishment at Peenemünde in East Prussia began to reach SIS, but the first evidence
that could be taken seriously was the 'bugged' conversation
between Generals Cruewell and von Thoma in March 1943
which has already been mentioned, for it showed that at some
time before his capture the previous October von Thoma had
been given information about rocket development and that he
expected progress to have been made since then. Within a short
time Ultra showed that two companies of a GAF Signals
Regiment known to have been connected with beam-bombing
were on the move to Peenemünde (this was quickly elaborated
by the French Resistance) and a sketch of a rocket was received
from Luxembourg. When PR showed rockets at Peenemünde,
the devastating raid of 17 August followed, forcing the opening
of a new V2 station at Blizna in Poland. Within a week or two a
pilotless aircraft landed on the island of Bornholm in the Baltic
(reports of a 'bomb with wings' had been coming in since April)
and a disaffected German indicated that both V1s and V2s were
being developed. More information about the V2 came from the
'Alliance' network of the French Resistance, and before long
Ultra proved the existence of the V1, thus ending a period of
painful uncertainty whether one or two new weapons were
planned. By Christmas, 159 SIS and 35 prisoner-of-war reports
about V-weapons had accumulated (many of the former from
Poles or members of the forced-labour gangs at Pennemünde,
and a particularly valuable series from Michel Hollard and
André Comps of the French Resistance making clear the nature
and construction of the launching sites and their alignment on
London) and V1 launching sites had been discovered in
northern France and heavily bombed. The first V1 landed in
London on 13 June 1944. A little earlier a rogue rocket came
down in Sweden; when another fell in Poland, a Resistance
leader carried a sackful of debris miles across country to a secret
airstrip, whence it was flown to Britain for examination. By the

time the first V2 landed in London on 8 September, documents captured in Norway had given further information.

Practically every known source of intelligence contributed something towards answering the questions What novel weapons are being prepared in secret? How dangerous are they? When will they be ready for action? Only analysis of a high order, partly deductive but mainly scientific – for instance, proof that it was technically impossible to deliver more than a one-ton warhead from a rocket perhaps ten times as large (sizes of forty tons and even more had been rumoured), given the equipment known from sketches and air photographs and fuel of the type reported – could have worked out the true meaning of the confusing and contradictory mass of material. Had the warning been less timely and the analysis less rapid, then German preparations could not have been so seriously disrupted by bombing, and V1s and V2s might have rained down on southern England well before D-Day, disrupting the invasion preparations perhaps fatally and greatly protracting the war, if not altering its outcome altogether. To divert part of Bomber Command's effort (and much of 8 USAAF's as well) away from a policy of area bombing, which by the spring of 1944 was already showing itself unable to produce the results claimed for it, was to turn from marginal to decisive action. Yet not a word in the book of either Harris or his second-in-command Saundby suggests the slightest awareness of this.

Harris was completely impervious to intelligence; as Hastings says, this was Bomber Command's cardinal weakness. The carapace of his resistance to it was impenetrable. Neither he nor the Air Ministry nor the Ministry of Economic Warfare grasped the simple fact that unroofed factories[*] had not necessarily

---

[*] M. R. D. Foot made a tangential but relevant point when he wrote (*SOE in France*, 436–8) that the amount of critical damage inflicted on French industry and French transport by SOE was comparable to that inflicted by Bomber Command, and at far less cost. SOE's share used

ceased production, and their failure to do so upset all calculations on the subject dearest to Harris's heart, the state of the
German economy and the morale of its workforce. This empties
his plaintive 'We never had sufficient information about German
industry' of most of its meaning. There was indeed a serious
shortage of reliable evidence until the last months of the war, but
a critical appraisal of what there was, conducted along lines
already becoming familiar to the army and the navy, might have
been expected to raise doubts in his mind about his own
methods of target-selection.

The youngest service, or at any rate a large part of it, had the
hardest arteries – a strange paradox. What else but a hopelessly
blinkered outlook prevented Harris from seeing that Berlin was
simply too big to be flattened as Hamburg had been, and
therefore that many of his raids were attempting the impossible
and losing men and machines to no good purpose? Why, even at
a late date, did Harris pay no attention to the paper written by
the air commander in Italy, Sir John Slessor, after the fall of
Rome in June 1944? Among many other points (some of them
highly critical of the OVERLORD air policy) Slessor emphasised that air power 'cannot by itself defeat a highly organised and
disciplined army' or 'enforce a withdrawal by drying up the flow
of essential supplies'. Should not Bomber Command's mounting
casualties have been reason enough to question whether area
bombing was really justified?

Against all this it was argued by Harris, who has been followed
by many since, that Bomber Command diverted so much
German effort away from Russia (60 per cent of German fighters
were defending the Reich against attack from the west in

only 3,000 lb of explosive, less than the load of a single Mosquito
bomber. A small charge set in the right place by SOE could bring
several workshops to a complete halt while a big bomb, less precisely
aimed, might only take off a factory roof. SOE, rather than Bomber
Command's cutting of railways, was responsible in June 1944 for delaying
2 SS Panzer Division on its journey from Toulouse to Normandy and II
SS Panzer Corps from the Franco-German frontier to Caen, in each case
for between two and three weeks.

September 1943) and into the defence industry that it must be deemed a success. But granted Great Britain's duty to help its Russian ally – the same duty which condemned so many sailors and merchant seamen to die on Atlantic convoys – was the construction of so many thousands of Lancaster bombers, which occupied as many men as were engaged in production for the entire British army, the best use of the country's limited industrial power? More and better tanks would have speeded victory in the desert and in France. More Liberators for Coastal Command (Harris released them very grudgingly, but aircraft killed more U-boats than surface vessels did between autumn 1942 and spring 1943, for example – 86 out of 161) and more Sunderlands on anti-U-boat patrol would have speeded victory in the Atlantic, so would more frigates and escort vessels. More sparing discharge of bombs would have saved steel for other purposes (twice as many tons of bombs were dropped in the last eight months of war as in the previous five years). Military and industrial effort was diverted away from its natural wartime objectives in both England and Germany; in Germany the diversion was involuntary, but on the Allied side it was deliberate, avoidable and mistaken.

The Directive for the Bomber Offensive issued by the Casablanca Conference in January 1943 called for 'the progressive destruction and dislocation of the German military, industrial and economic system, and the undermining of the morale of the German people, to a point where their capacity for armed resistance is fatally weakened', and was in effect licence for the construction of unlimited numbers of Lancasters and Flying Fortresses. Yet when the strategic situation changed (Casablanca was four months before the fall of Tunis) and no sign of the collapse of the German economy or morale appeared in any intelligence source, priorities were not reappraised nor the rival merits of different kinds of expenditure weighed against each other. Nothing therefore prevented Harris from continuing on his chosen course.

Ill-founded in intelligence and sound reasoning though so many of Harris's actions were, others must share some of the blame for the militarily needless deaths – British and German – which will always be associated with his name. Neither Brooke nor Tedder saw eye to eye with him, yet neither did much to thwart him. Portal, after a disagreement over the priority to be assigned to oil targets, virtually surrendered to Harris in January 1945.* But there is an unsolved mystery about how much relevant intelligence Harris actually received, and this naturally affects the allocation of responsibility.

Until shortly before OVERLORD, intelligence from continental Europe which could guide target selection was scanty, and this applied particularly to Ultra, for reasons already given. This may explain why Bomber Command was not put on the Ultra distribution list in earlier years. But, even when Ultra began to produce information useful to Harris early in 1944, it was still not sent to him, although from 1 January it was sent to the former Fighter Command (now renamed Air Defence of Great Britain), the Allied Expeditionary Air Force (the air component under Eisenhower) and the US Strategic Air Force; the reason for this discrimination is obscure. From May 1944, when Bomber Command was still not on the Ultra list, the US Strategic Air Force had a specialist Ultra officer (Bomber Command never had one), Colonel Lewis F. Powell Jr, the future Associate Justice of the US Supreme Court, who was Chief of Operational Intelligence under General 'Tooey' Spaatz, the commander of USSTAF. The two bomber forces collaborated in designing their policies (unfortunately Powell has little to say about this). How could they do so satisfactorily if one had vital information the other lacked? (It was normally a fixed rule

---

* In the light of this (of which the authors take no account), it is difficult to understand the view of Portal expressed by General Sir William Jackson and Field Marshal Lord Bramall – *The Chiefs* (Brassey's, 1992), 199 – that Portal was marked out by his 'intellectual capabilities, integrity and moral courage' and an ability 'to concentrate upon critical issues'.

of Ultra distribution to send identical information to authorities with related or overlapping responsibilities, for this very reason. The breach of the rule on this occasion is unexplained.) It has to be presumed that Portal and the intelligence staff at the Air Ministry kept Harris abreast of information from what amounted, from his point of view, almost to a new source, but in fact it can at present only be a matter of speculation whether Bomber Command was informed by this means of Ultra reports of the location and strength of fighter units in France and Germany, for instance, matters capable of influencing Bomber Command's actions closely.

Bomber Command received a direct service of Ultra material from D-Day, it is said, but this does not appear to have been taken very seriously at first. A report of the weather over Germany and France issued at 1230 on 6 June, transmitted to other recipients just after midnight, was not addressed to Bomber Command, yet it could surely have been as useful to them as to the fighters and the Americans. A more surprising omission than this or several other signals which could be cited is a warning from OKL (Supreme Command of the Air Force) to Parachute Army on 5 June, decrypted next day, which showed how wrong Harris was to underestimate the extent to which bombing was restricting German oil supplies and in consequence battle operations.* 'As a result of interference by Allied action,' it began, only fuel quotas for bombers, fighters and ground-attack aircraft could be honoured in June, and units would have to manage as best they could for training and so on. The July delivery date was uncertain, and it had already been necessary to break into the strategic fuel reserve. Where possible, rail was to be used for supplies and duty journeys.

One inference is possible from these and other omissions to route appropriate Ultra signals to Bomber Command in early June, and one question arises. Evidently Hut 3 were not at once

---

* Just as it had done before Alamein (p. 106 above). The lesson does not seem to have been learned.

instructed to route them thither: such instructions were always obeyed, and either the Air Ministry or Hut 3's Air Section (which was in almost hourly contact with Air Ministry) would have pointed out any disregard of them immediately. The question goes deeper: did Bomber Command have an intelligence staff capable of analysing and putting to effective use the information, had it been sent to them? Hut 3's Air Section had long been familiar with this sort of material and was used to analysing it; Colonel Powell was soon doing the same at Spaatz's HQ. 'Ultra shaped operations,' he recalled later. Bomber Command had no similar background, nor did it show any inclination to acquire the requisite skills. A service of Ultra to Bomber Command opened on 16 August, and was still in operation in mid-November.

It is beyond belief that the Chief of Air Staff, Harris's direct superior, would not supply Harris with such Ultra information as seemed useful to him; there is positive evidence that he did so on one occasion, for in a comment to the Prime Minister on 8 June about the signal from OKL to Parachute Army about oil allocations quoted above, he wrote that there were several oil targets in the Ruhr 'which Bomber Command think they can destroy with Oboe'. But there seems to be nothing to show how regularly and in what volume Harris received Ultra from Portal. The matter is critical for an assessment of the grave differences of opinion between them about the advisability or otherwise of a concerted attack on Germany's oil industry during the second half of 1944. As a glance at the reference notes to Chapter 54 of *British Intelligence* will show, much of the best evidence for Germany's growing shortage of oil and for the way it was restricting the Wehrmacht's operational freedom of action came from Ultra – that is to say, it was an absolutely solid basis for concluding that the bombing of oil targets would restrict this freedom still further and thus shorten the war. Portal called this 'the irrefutable evidence of Sigint'. Harris took refuge in bluster, refused (as he had done before) to accept the evidence, disobeyed

Portal's instructions to concentrate on oil targets, repeated that area bombing was effective and continued to devote most of his raids to it. German oil stocks rose considerably (see Appendix III).

Government awareness of the effects of the strategic bomber offensive as seen from the German side came soon after the end of the war, but not, it seems, an equal awareness of the conclusions to which the new information pointed. On 13 March 1946 John Strachey, Under-Secretary of State for Air, made a statement to the House of Commons on the subject, and began by asking whether, in the light of a preliminary study of evidence newly available, Bomber Command had employed its resources well in the closing months of the war. He concentrated on what he said were its two principal objectives, the transportation system and the oil industry. For the latter, he relied entirely on the testimony of Albert Speer as manifested in captured documents (Speer's reports to Hitler) and as given under interrogation. If hydrogenation plants and refineries were not protected against air attack by September, Speer told Hitler on 30 June 1944, 'an impossible situation' would arise; again, on 30 August, 'the last stocks will be consumed'. The shortage of fuel for the Luftwaffe became 'insupportable' from September onwards and 'catastrophic' at the time of the Ardennes offensive. In answer to the direct question 'Do you believe that strategic bombing alone could have brought about the surrender of Germany?' he replied, 'The answer is Yes. The attacks on the synthetic oil industry would have sufficed, without the impact of purely military events, to render Germany defenceless.' Strachey then turned, without comment, to a consideration of the next year's air estimates.[*]

---

[*] How hard it is to decide whether there was one single tender spot in the German economy upon which attacks should have been concentrated is illustrated by what Speer was telling the Chief of Air Staff only three months later, in June 1946. Concentrated attacks on the ball-bearing

Here, at one and the same time, was a possible, if hypotheti-
cal, justification of Harris's claim that he could have won the war
by air attack alone, and also evidence that by neglecting
intelligence he had ruined his chance of doing so. Once the
precision-bombing skills which he had once despised had been
demonstrated in the summer of 1944, single refineries were
targets as attackable as rail junctions, the Peenemünde works or
the shipyards where Bomber Command's raids were fatally
retarding Germany's development of a new and potentially
lethal generation of U-boats. There were ample signs in Ultra –
Portal's 'irrefutable evidence of Sigint' – that accurate strikes at
them would pay handsome dividends. Harris rejected them.

Who, then, deserves the greater blame – Harris for what
amounted to mutiny, or Portal for not disciplining his subordinate?

Whatever may now seem the right conclusion, it must be
remembered that at the time Harris's raids had the approval of
the whole country, until right at the end some began to feel that
with victory approaching it was superfluous to continue the
killing. When, after dinner on 27 July 1943, Churchill suddenly
started up from his chair during a showing of films taken in the
course of raids on German towns, exclaiming, 'Are we beasts?
Are we taking this too far?' he was the first to call into question
the policy he had so long supported. But, though the seed of
doubt was sown in his mind, it obtained only a feeble lodgment:
six months later he could tell the House of Commons that the air
offensive 'constitutes the foundation upon which our plans for
overseas invasion stand'. He long withstood soldiers and airmen
over the Transportation Plan for bombing French railways in
preparation for OVERLORD on the ground that too many

industry along the lines of the USAAF raid on Schweinfurt on 17 August
1943, he said, would have 'crucially weakened' armaments production in
two months and would have brought it to a complete standstill in four
months (Albert Speer, *Inside the Third Reich* (Weidenfeld & Nicolson, 1970),
284–5).

innocent French civilians would be killed ('You will smear the good name of the Royal Air Force across the world') but eventually yielded to their insistence that military necessity must take precedence over moral and humanitarian scruples. Only in the aftermath of the Dresden raid of February 1945 did he carry his point that the time had come for a drastic review of bombing policy, and only by then was public opinion beginning to be of the same mind.

Until then, however, by what would, had its author not been transparently (if misguidedly) sincere, have amounted to a massive 'con' trick, Harris had persuaded all and sundry that he was right on military grounds, and had got away with it for three whole years. It is as impossible today as it ever was to determine whether the gradual occupation of territory by the Allies, the disruption of communications or the oil shortage was most responsible for the collapse of Germany. But it is at least clear that it was not area bombing.

Controversy has long raged over Harris's actions; it has centred mainly round the appalling casualty rate among bomber crews (a total of 55, 573[*]) and the ethics of area bombing. It is therefore worth noting that Ronald Lewin, author of the first book about Ultra[†] after the secret was revealed, seized upon the crucial point at once, writing of Harris's '*delusion*' (my italics) that only 'massive raids by heavy bombers could bring Hitler to his knees'. Lewin had been an artillery officer in North Africa and Europe, had known nothing of Ultra until long after the war, and therefore came to it without preconceptions.

[*] Terraine 682.
[†] Ronald Lewin, *Ultra goes to War* (Hutchinson 1978). The quotation is from p. 292.

Three books about Bomber Command were published during the winter of 1997–8.

Richard Overy's *Bomber Command 1939–1945* (HarperCollins 1997) has a Foreword by Marshal of the RAF Sir Michael Beetham, was linked to a TV programme and much hyped. Outwardly, therefore, it has an air of authority which the contents do little to deserve (it consists mainly of quotations from the diaries of former members of the RAF).

The apparent authority which surrounds the book makes it all the more of a shock to find that the text contains much (disguised) loose reasoning as well as many errors of omission and commission. A few concessions to unfavourable views of Bomber Command (e.g. p. 182) and an only tolerably fair assessment of Harris himself (scattered over pp. 63–80) scarcely mask a uniform complacency. On the other hand, much is repeatedly made of Bomber Command's contribution to the war at sea, although it has long been known that Harris many times refused to allocate even a few long-range aircraft to Coastal Command, which urgently needed them to increase the protection it was struggling to give to the Atlantic convoys which brought food, petrol and American soldiers to Britain. Only towards the end did he reluctantly yield to pressure and grudgingly part with a handful.

Next to the appalling cost in lives and material destruction, the most novel feature of the Second World War was the vastly greater volume of intelligence (most of it from radio intercepts and code-breaking) available to commanders in the field than in any previous conflict. It is therefore alarming to discover that the words 'intelligence' and 'Ultra' do not appear even once in this book, particularly since, as the foregoing chapter has shown, it was his contempt for intelligence which prevented Harris from realising that there were flaws in his policy of area bombing.

More recently (March 1998) two wartime documents, long known to scholars, have been edited with introductions by Sebastian Cox, senior Air historian at the Ministry of Defence.

Thus they have greater authority than Overy's book. But they arrive at much the same conclusions.

The first is Harris's official *Despatch on War Operations, 23 February 1942–8 May 1945*. Cox makes some pertinent criticisms of Harris's conduct, notably of the way in which he managed by obstinacy and selective quotation from the Air Ministry Directive issued a week before Harris took over Bomber Command, to escape from its (admittedly too loose) provisions and to persist in the area bombing which it was intended to replace as soon as it became practicable to do so. However, he only makes a single passing mention of Ultra, and never discusses intelligence at all. How can a serious account of Harris be composed unless he is set against a background of the information he received and that which by the nature of the case he could not secure, particularly in view of the criticisms which have been levelled at him by, for instance, Max Hastings, John Terraine and myself?

The second, *The Strategic Air War against Germany, 1939–1945*, a document dated 1947, like the first, has a Foreword by Marshal of the RAF Sir Michael Beetham,[*] but also another by Major General John Huston, USAF (because the report itself incorporates the findings of the US bombing survey, which was much more thorough than the British equivalent. Cox's Introduction follows the same lines as in the previous volume, and contains no direct discussion of intelligence.

Cricitisms of Harris are, on the contrary, to be found scattered through the Report itself but – as Cox rightly points out – they must in part be discounted because the final draft was written by Sir Solly Zuckerman, who had long opposed Harris's single-minded devotion to area bombing and was co-author of the so-called Hull–Birmingham investigation into the effects (it found them very slight) of German bombing on British morale in 1941. The last few pages (pp. 169–70) rightly blame unsound intelligence and the misinterpretation of it on 'preconceived

[*] Wartime bomber pilot, Gp. Capt. (Ops) Bomber Command 1962–4, Chief of Air Staff 1977–82, President Bomber Command Association.

ideas and wishful thinking' (vices from which naval and military intelligence had escaped by 1942–3), but complaints of the lack of factual information about the effects of area bombing serve only to underline Harris's refusal to let this deter him from pressing on with a policy for which there was no real evidence.

* * * *

Both Huston and Cox make much (pp. xi, xviii, xxix) of the obstacles (including the most brazenly bureaucratic) which Churchill put in the way of the British bombing survey, and regard it as a puzzle without a solution. Admittedly, at first sight this is in sharp contrast with 'Action This Day' which so colours his popular image. But surely there is no great mystery here?

There had always been a humane and emotional element in Churchill's make-up. Completely lacking experience, like everyone else in 1939, he expected bombing raids to be far more lethal than they ever were, even in 1945 (p. 5, above). Harsh reality compelled him to suppress his fears after Dunkirk (p. 133) 'only the Air Force can do it' (But can one detect an air of wistfulness and regret in 'the only plan is to persevere' (p. 148), of late 1941?). About the same time he warned Harris not to think that he could win the war by bombing alone (p. 148). Twelve months or more of contemplating Harris's treatment of Germany caused the 'Are we beasts?' outbreak of July 1943 (p. 170), and he was slow to reconcile himself to the Transportation Plan because he feared it would kill so many French civilians (p. 171). The Dresden raid finally turned him against bombing, but the policy dilemma was settled by then.

Only the *absence* of secret service intelligence about the effect of bombing on Germany, it is to be presumed, prevented David

Stafford from considering the subject in his brilliant *Churchill and Secret Service* (John Murray, 1997). This was regrettable, though understandable. Churchill endeavoured to reconcile, in swiftly changing circumstances, the conflict between the morally acceptable and the practically attainable, and thereby revealed the high intellectual level at which he conducted his wartime policy. This aspect of his character merits more attention than it has received.

5

1941–1945

Shadow and Sunlight Over the Atlantic

The war at sea presents the sharpest possible contrast to the war in the air from the intelligence point of view. In the Operational Intelligence Centre (OIC), the Admiralty had an organisation in place by 1939 ready to filter naval intelligence to operational commands if war should come: its staff was already fifty-strong. Bomber Command's adamant refusal to consider seriously any target or damage evidence except PR (belatedly), and the unscientific and inevitably rose-tinted impressions of returning bomber crews, show up badly beside a carefully planned organisation already two years old – one which had proved its usefulness at the time of Munich by tracking the movements of the battleship *Deutschland* in Spanish waters and showing that they did not suggest war, and which quickly managed to distil valuable intelligence from scrappy and unpromising material when war broke out.

The OIC's chief regret, indeed, was that during the first few months of war it could not find enough solid food to satisfy its appetite. This was frustratingly evident while the Yellow key used for the invasion of Norway was current in April and May 1940. In somewhat over-sanguine anticipation that GC&CS's attacks on Enigma might soon yield operationally useful results, the Admiralty had warned the Commander-in-Chief Home Fleet that he might soon receive specially secret high-grade

Sigint. War Office and Air Ministry had done nothing comparable and could not now explain the new source over insecure radio communications. But Yellow was an army and GAF key, and only carried naval information coincidentally. Thus those who might have used the traffic could not be sent it, while those who were ready to use it were left unsatisfied. Only when the variety of Enigma used by the German navy was broken in August 1941 did more grist come to a mill which had until then been grinding less nourishing grain. Soon after the *Bismarck* was sunk in May, sea-going admirals began paying fuller attention to the higher-quality information purveyed by the OIC and to the Admiralty's tactical directions based upon it; their lamentations when U-boat Enigma dried up between February and December 1942 showed how much they had already come to rely upon it.

Paymaster Lieutenant-Commander 'Ned' Denning had proved the ideal head of the OIC from the moment of his appointment in 1937. In January 1941, just in time to profit from the Enigma break of that spring, the other now legendary figure of wartime naval intelligence came to prominence: Rodger Winn, a barrister who had been a member of OIC's Submarine Tracking Room since 1939, was appointed its head although he was a civilian (his position was at once regularised by the grant of a commission). Both men possessed a lucid reasoning power and achieved remarkable insight into the enemy's mind which fitted them admirably for their tasks. They owed much to the intelligence work, as well as to the cryptographic skill, of the Naval Section at GC&CS, but the successes of OIC depended in large measure on the personalities and skill of these two men. Upon them, and upon their staffs, rested the responsibility of issuing the operational signals which made it possible for commanders at sea to convert intelligence into action.

It has long been clear that U-boats were the great enemy of the Anglo-American alliance in the middle years of the war, when

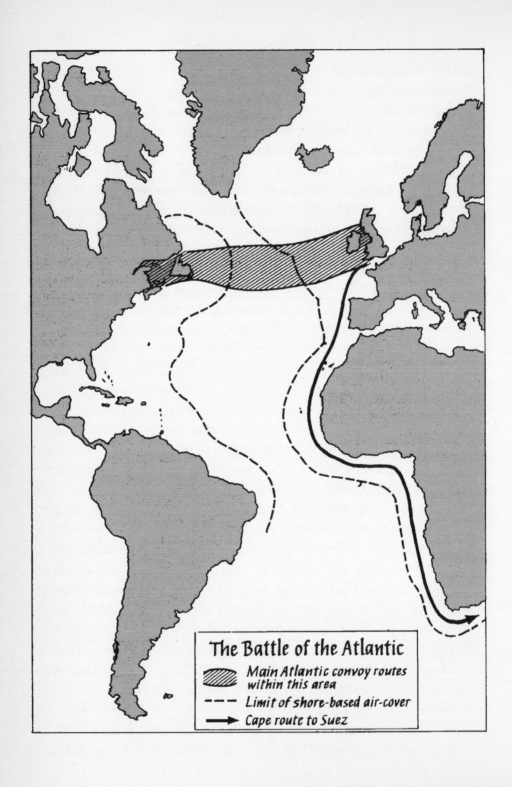

The Battle of the Atlantic

▨ Main Atlantic convoy routes within this area

- - - Limit of shore-based air-cover

→ Cape route to Suez

under the command of Admiral Dönitz they almost cut the Atlantic sea route along which food, industrial supplies and American soldiers came to England. But this was not at first apparent, for two reasons. Although it permitted the construction of U-boats, the Anglo-German Naval Agreement of 1935, which sanctioned breaches of the Treaty of Versailles, focused more attention on surface ships, and the Admiralty believed that they, rather than U-boats, were the chief danger to British trade. The Atlantic sorties of the *Graf Spee* in 1939 and *Bismarck* in May 1941, the Taranto raid in November 1940 and the sinking of the *Prince of Wales* and the *Repulse* off the coast of Malaya in December, followed by the Battle of Midway in June 1942, confirmed that the long reign of big-ship fleets was over, brought to an end by aircraft and carriers. One of Churchill's first actions when he became Prime Minister in May 1940, on the other hand, was to ask Roosevelt for some First World War destroyers (much rusted and in need of repair, it was found) to supplement Britain's inadequate convoy-protection forces. From this grew the deal which exchanged fifty old destroyers for bases in the Caribbean and signified the beginning of Lend-Lease.

A quite different reason also helps to explain why, though it seemed almost lethal in 1942–3, the U-boat threat was slow to develop. By what Correlli Barnett has called 'a crass error of judgement' on Hitler's part, which perhaps cost him victory, Germany was in this respect (as in so many others) insufficiently prepared for the war towards which the Führer's political manoeuvrings tended. Wegener's book (see p. 17) should have served as a lively reminder of what U-boats had done in 1914–18, but it was in no sense a foretaste of what Hitler was planning to do twenty years later. Dönitz, Commander-in-Chief U-Boats, constantly pressed the need for new construction upon him, but Hitler paid far more attention to Raeder, Commander-in-Chief Navy, who urged the merits of a powerful surface fleet. The consequence was that in 1939 Dönitz had too few U-boats to dominate the Atlantic; not until the summer of 1941 could he marshal over thirty there at once, for instance, but by the time he succeeded Raeder in January 1943 over 200 were regularly operating. Peak numbers were not reached until well into 1943, but up to a hundred were infesting the Atlantic convoy routes before the end of 1942. In ironical contrast to the hectic activity of Dönitz and his crews, the greatest triumph of the German surface ships was won in these years. The *Tirpitz* never took to sea for a war cruise but remained holed up in Norwegian fjords, where she engaged the constant attention of Admiralty and Air Ministry until she was sunk by the RAF on 12 November 1944.* Though usually immobile, her mere presence halted Arctic convoys and compelled the Home Fleet to remain in permanent readiness at Scapa Flow lest she attempt to break out and follow *Bismarck*'s plan to interrupt the Atlantic sea route.

In no respect was the inner significance of the Admiralty's signal to the navy 'Winston is back' on the evening of 3 September 1939 better shown than in Churchill's first request for information when he took over as First Lord. With the Atlantic peril of twenty years earlier in mind, he asked how many U-boats were known to exist and how many were in prospect. The torpedoing of the liner *Athenia* that same day emphasised his fears, and *U-47*'s penetration of the Scapa Flow defences six weeks later was even more menacing. The Admiralty wisely reconstituted the convoy system during the first week of war, but (with Churchill's backing, though with less wisdom) also returned to another 1914–18 practice, that of dividing a substantial part of its (now exiguous) anti-U-boat force into hunter-killer groups. While U-boats combed the seas for convoys, these groups searched for U-boats, but with less success. Both sides were eager enough for battle, but the currently available means of finding the object of their search were unequal to the task in the wide spaces of the Atlantic.

For a variety of reasons, the absence of radar good enough to

* In consequence, there was not a single German capital ship available on D-Day.

locate U-boats (which spent most of their time on the surface) at a distance and the shortage of suitable aircraft and escort vessels prominent among them, it was found that offence was by no means the best defence. If the hunter missed his prey, the U-boat commander was free to attack the unprotected convoy, provided that he could find it. Paradoxically it was found that the best way to protect convoys was for them to avoid the enemy, not to fight him; this remained the case even when new construction at last enabled such a powerful escort to be given that part of it could peel off, briefly turn itself into a hunter group and kill U-boats as soon as they revealed themselves by attacking.

The evasive routeing of convoys thus became the first line of defence for Britain's ocean supply-line, particularly when Dönitz inaugurated his favourite 'wolf-pack' method of attack as soon as he had enough U-boats for the purpose. Given sufficient information, a reasonably safe route could be planned before a convoy sailed. This was where the OIC's Submarine Tracking Room came into its own and first demonstrated the indispensable service it was to render to the British, and later the Allied, cause. It was giving admirable assistance to convoy-planning, using HF/DF (high-frequency direction-finding) bearings and aircraft and other sightings, even before the first naval Enigma break added so much to its resources in May 1941.

During most of the eight months for which this first break into naval Enigma lasted, evasive routeing became much quicker and more effective. Every signal to or from U-boats at sea could be read, with the consequence that the OIC could maintain an almost complete check on their positions and update it from day to day, diverting convoys in good time if (as was the case more often than not) decryption was current. For three of the first four weeks of June 1941, for instance, the U-boats made no sightings at all, and when they did find homeward-bound convoy HX 133 from Halifax, Nova Scotia, and converged on it OIC could safely take away escorts from two other convoys to hunt them down (two U-boats were sunk, and only five merchant ships were lost). Reading naval Enigma did not make the Atlantic entirely safe, of course, though it is estimated to have saved more than a million tons of precious shipping, but it significantly reduced losses and enabled OIC to feel that it had some control over the Atlantic situation – an astonishing change in comparison with the bad days of 1939 and 1940. This period marked 'a decisive setback' for Dönitz, who, as he was later to admit, ended the year 1941 'in an atmosphere of worry and anxiety', wondering whether he would be able to win the Battle of the Atlantic after all. This, though of course unknown at the time, is the measure of what Ultra had done in eight months to raise British hopes.

Sadly, however, there was a shadow side to all this: if a movement of U-boats towards a convoy, like that towards HX 133, was detected, then a suitable diversion could be signalled to it and all would be well – provided that the code or cipher used for the signal was secure. Until the summer of 1943, unfortunately, this was not the case for lengthy periods.

Dönitz's great advantage was that for much of the time down to the middle of 1943 he quite often knew British convoys' intended routes even before they sailed.* The German B-Dienst (*Beobachtungsdienst* – (radio) observation or monitoring service) managed with the help of traffic analysis to reconstruct the British convoy code and later to read with comparative ease three-quarters of the signals transmitted in Naval Cipher No. 3 (introduced in June 1941 for convoy routeing). Its output was handled in much the same way as the British Admiralty had handled the German High Seas Fleet decodes thirty years earlier – by being passed direct to the appropriate operational commander, without the interposition of an intelligence agency like the Naval Section of GC&CS or the OIC. Most seem to have gone through the hands of Dönitz himself or of one or two of his most trusted staff officers. Many British and Allied ships were sunk, but whether the tally would have been higher had

* Though it is to be noticed that honours were often even: Dönitz lost his advantage while Enigma was being broken in 1941, but regained it when Enigma dried up in 1942.

Dönitz possessed something like an OIC of his own can only remain a matter of speculation. Yet it is worth noting that here, as in the whole field of intelligence, Germany failed to develop the analytical and investigative institutions which, on the Allied side, were eventually able to squeeze the maximum possible operational advantage from sometimes unpromising material. Even without such institutions, however, the B-Dienst made a good start on both the merchant navy code and the current naval cipher before the war, and this, despite some ups and downs as new codes were introduced and new captures solved old problems, enabled them for the next two or three years to learn almost all they needed to know about British and Allied Atlantic convoys.

The war on and under the surface of the Atlantic can therefore with great justification be presented as a conflict between British and German cryptographers, a terrible poker game with the makers and breakers of codes and ciphers as the players, and the survival of Britain and the overthrow of Nazism as the stakes. This was probably its essential feature, but it is not the whole story. The building of new ships to replace those destroyed or sunk – of U-boats on one side and merchant ships, frigates and corvettes on the other – the provision of torpedoes, guns and depth-charges and technical improvements in the means of close- and long-range detection ... all these were critical elements in the fluctuating balance between the two sides, because they governed the use to which intelligence could be put. Above all, the Battle of the Atlantic was a matter of nerve, endurance and speed of decision by U-boat captains and escort commanders and their respective crews, exhausted after days or even weeks spent vainly gazing at empty seas in storm and cold but suddenly faced with emergency action upon which their duty and probably their own lives too depended. The human and dramatic side of the conflict is the more striking because the men engaged in it had to be on the alert against surprise for far longer periods at a time than was usual on land or in the air: a U-boat's war cruise might last a month, and a slow convoy might take almost as long to cross from a US or a Canadian to a British port.

Two other, contradictory features of the bitter ocean conflict deserve mention. It was greatly to Dönitz's advantage that he could base his U-boats on Atlantic ports in France and Norway. When Germany occupied the Biscay ports after the French capitulation in 1940 (he moved his own headquarters to Lorient until Hitler ordered him back to Paris after the St Nazaire raid in 1942), U-boats no longer had to start their war cruises from the Baltic and proceed to their hunting grounds through the waters north of Scotland; this shortened their operating period by several days. On the other hand, the British gained from the fact that every time a U-boat reported by radio during a cruise its transmission could be heard, and by a simple application of direction-finding technique (two ground stations take a bearing on the same signal; where the bearings cross, there is the source of the transmission) the U-boat could be located at least approximately, and the convoy it was thought to be shadowing diverted. There was no way in which Dönitz could nullify this risk, and he realised that he was enlarging it when he imposed his centralised command system, which required U-boats to report their movements regularly (though with the aid of a manual of 'short signals' to hamper D/Fing by minimising transmission-time) and to obey his tactical orders. A firm system of control from the centre – something which the Wehrmacht as a whole lacked – was admirable in itself, but it proved in this case to be a fatal weakness when U-boat Enigma (Shark) was broken at the end of 1942 and every detail of Dönitz's orders was laid open to the Admiralty's scrutiny.

In the first years of the war, however, central control enabled Dönitz to extract maximum advantage from Britain's woeful shortage of escort vessels. The self-sacrifice of the captain and crew of the *Jervis Bay* in November 1940 (an armed merchant cruiser, converted from peacetime use, with six-inch guns but no armour) in taking on the pocket-battleship *Admiral Scheer* (eleven-inch guns) in defence of convoy HX 84 is well known. What is less often remembered is that *Jervis Bay* was the *only* escort and defence of the thirty-seven ships in her charge. There were so few escorts available that often none could stay with a convoy for more than the early stages of its journey or meet it more than a short distance from the Irish coast as it returned fully laden (one of the first convoys to be escorted throughout sailed in May 1941). The U-boats had free rein between these two points. A little further out there lay the fearsome 'Atlantic gap' where aircraft too had to turn back because until 1942 none had the range to stay longer and still get home before its fuel ran out. A convoy was on its own in the gap, and the underwater peril might come upon it suddenly if, as was the rule to begin with, and during the 1942 black-out period, too little was known about U-boat movements to divert it to safety. Only in 1942, when more escorts had been constructed and long-range Liberators were at last assigned to Coastal Command did the gap begin to diminish, eventually disappearing altogether.

Partly because of the time required to compose, print and distribute new codebooks, and partly because the Admiralty was reluctant to believe that its signals were insecure until Ultra provided incontrovertible proof, the B-Dienst retained the advantage which its ability to read British signals conferred upon it longer than it should have done. Only when the Admiralty at last grappled with the scale of the risks involved and adopted securer communications in June 1943 was the B-Dienst shut out completely. The Germans took the same line, utterly refusing to credit that Enigma could be decrypted, even after a series of investigations following apparently inexplicable cases of British advance knowledge of their intentions. The stiff-necked 'Our systems cannot possibly be insecure' attitude was common to both sides; it is a matter for thankfulness that we were flexible enough to see how dangerous this attitude was, though only after prolonged hesitation, whereas the enemy was not.

Deprived though it was for long by the Enigma machine and its naval operators' good discipline of any means of discovering what Dönitz and his U-boat captains were saying to each other, and for long denied all hope that the situation would ever change for the better, the Submarine Tracking Room could nevertheless piece together scraps of information about U-boats and their ways with some profit even before May 1941. Direction-finding could trace them from their working-up exercises beyond the Kattegat until the moment when they set out westwards from the Bay of Biscay (the SIS could also report this sometimes), but it could not tell what direction the U-boat would then take. PR, together with lower-grade codes, could ascertain a U-boat's type, and therefore its designed range and speed; from its known speed could be calculated how far it could travel each day (and therefore whether it was capable of reaching a given convoy or not), from its range could be predicted approximately when it would be returning to one of the three swept channels which were always kept open for homecoming craft. Prisoners occasionally provided information about U-boat tactics and details of torpedoes and other equipment. The so-called 'Dockyard cipher' and others gave occasionally useful information about inshore waters, and from time to time weather broadcasts were also of value; but when it was later found that certain messages were transmitted in these easier codes and also in Enigma they were broken mainly because they offered 'cribs' into Enigma, not for their operational value. By establishing signal patterns, Traffic Analysis (the study of the external characteristics of radio communications) could discover much about the command set-up and even on occasion suggest possible German intentions by noting sudden increases or decreases in traffic volume at a particular place or time – indeed, suggestions of this kind were among the earliest triumphs of the Naval Section in Hut 4 at Bletchley Park.

Finally, even before Coastal Command and the navy's Western Approaches Command (responsible for Atlantic defence) opened a joint headquarters at Liverpool in February 1941, the two had begun to integrate their operations as far as possible. But the former would have been of more use to the latter if it had not been so consistently starved of aircraft by the Air Ministry, in spite of continual protests by both. Successive requests for long-range aircraft without which Coastal Command could not extend the air protection it gave convoys nor reduce the Atlantic gap (it was not finally closed and convoys given air cover throughout their voyage until spring 1943) were turned down in favour of an allegedly more profitable investment in bombing operations. So strong was the Air Ministry's faith in bombing, and so vigorously did the Americans protest that they were not supplying four-engined Liberators (the first entered service with the RAF early in 1942, after Hitler had declared war on the USA and Britain and America had agreed on the policy of 'Germany first') for them to be diverted to what they called 'marginal purposes' like ocean patrols,* but solely to increase the weight of bombs dropped on Germany, that there were still only five of them under Coastal Command in August 1942. In reality, of course, it would have been infinitely wiser to employ them to protect the Atlantic life-line (they could spend three hours over a convoy in mid-Atlantic a thousand miles from base) than in scattering bombs at random over German cities (or, as Barnett unkindly says, in 'ploughing up German fields').

For the first eighteen months of the U-boat war Germany unquestionably had the upper hand. Intelligence (through the B-Dienst) and force (because of the British shortage of escorts) were both on her side. Sinkings of British ships by all means, aircraft and mines as well as U-boats, rose inexorably from a monthly average of a quarter of a million tons in the second half of 1940 to twice as much in the three months March–May 1941, when U-boats contributed half of the total. It was in the middle of this period that Dönitz made 'wolf-packs', tactically directed from his

---

* Since Atlantic convoys carried US troops, this seems a strange opinion.

headquarters, the regular method of attack, since by now he had sufficient U-boats at his disposal to make this the most economically remunerative method of applying his strength. The situation was not yet as dangerous as it was to become in the spring of 1943, but it was alarming enough for Churchill to warn Roosevelt in December 1940 that unless Britain could feed itself, import the munitions it required and move armies at will 'we may fall by the way, and the time needed by the United States to complete its defensive preparations may not be forthcoming'. When the spring of 1941 saw the loss-rate still rising and anxiety growing about how to make good the losses, alarm rose to almost fever heat: we might well lose 4.5 million tons in the next twelve months, Churchill told Roosevelt in May, the USA might manage to build 3.5 million and Britain one million, but this would be 'just marking time and swimming level with the bank against the stream'. The danger signs were plain to see. Before long Britain might be starved out and rendered powerless in self-defence, let alone in finding ways to take the offensive.

From these fears the breaking of naval Enigma in May 1941 provided welcome relief. Large-scale evasive routeing at once became possible and average monthly sinkings quickly fell to 120,000 tons between July and September, but the sailing, also in May, of the first west–east convoy to be given surface escort throughout its journey is a warning not to attribute every improvement to signals intelligence. The warning was not heeded in Whitehall, it appears. Carried away by excitement and relief at the breaking of naval Enigma and the immediate fall in the loss-rate, less than three months later the War Cabinet debated whether to take away even the few Liberators Coastal Command had managed to acquire and add them to the bomber force. So extraordinary a misjudgment so soon after Churchill's words to Roosevelt and the despatch of a mission to Washington to plead for maximum possible assistance in shipbuilding is hard to understand. Fortuntely the fierce objections of Admiralty and Coastal Command ensured that the aircraft stayed where they were, but this was not to be the last of the argument.

Looked at in another light, however, the incident makes plain the tensions of the time. The anxiously awaited but delayed break into naval Enigma came at a time of mounting anxiety. Was Britain doomed to lose the war because she could not feed herself? Was she now suddenly freed from this fear at a single stroke?

When, at the end of May 1941 Hut 4 at GC&CS began teleprinting translations of great numbers of U-boat and other naval decrypts to the Admiralty, the unprecedented novelty could hardly fail to bring tremendous relief, even if by no means every decrypt was at first current enough to have immediate operational value. It was perhaps natural that those who knew little or nothing of cryptographic problems or of the accumulating warnings that they might soon escalate alarmingly (that is to say, practically all recipients) should harbour exaggerated expectations, notably of the bearing the decrypts might have on the Atlantic battle. Ultra of any kind was effectively only a few months old, and no one had yet discovered how best to use it operationally: all through the summer and autumn of 1941 Churchill himself, misinterpreting the underlying significance of GAF Ultra, repeatedly harried Wavell and Auchinleck into offensives against their better judgment. It is a curious reflection that the OIC, latecomers in the Ultra field, were now to become the first to find out how Ultra could best be applied to action; a sailor, Admiral Cunningham, had already been the first to apply it in a single case (see p. 77).

In one respect at least the ability to read the German Home Waters key (called Dolphin at GC&CS) did bring about a radical change. It led directly to the destruction of all the supply ships which had been scattered round the Atlantic for *Bismarck* and her partners; this ruined the prospects of other raiders, including U-boats, and by extension forced Dönitz to rely in future on specially constructed submarine tankers and supply carriers, less suitable for the task because of unavoidably smaller capacity.

Forced in consequence to take refuge at Brest and La Pallice, and severely damaged there by the RAF, *Prinz Eugen, Scharnhorst* and *Gneisenau* were out of action for months at a time while repairs were carried out. They were later removed for greater safety to Baltic and Norwegian waters. What was left afloat of the German surface navy presented a latent threat for the next three years, but it was mostly a passive not an active one.

The effects of reading Dolphin on the U-boat danger are more difficult to assess with precision. There is an undeniable time-correlation with the rate of shipping loss, which immediately fell to a much lower level than in the previous six months. It fluctuated around this level for some time, and in one instance (November) dropped well below it, then suddenly rose much higher again in December. But the arrival of high-grade Sigint on the scene was not the only novelty in the second half of 1941. The number of U-boats also rose sharply – to double the June figure – at the end of the year; on the Allied side corvettes (miniature and in some ways primitive destroyers), now entering service in considerable numbers, were soon to be the workhorses of the Atlantic as convoy escorts; the newly invented high-frequency direction-finding apparatus (HF/DF), which made it easier and quicker to find U-boats and hold on to them as targets, was being fitted to a growing number of escort vessels; so was another innovation, Anti-Surface-Vessel (ASV) radar.

Historical events can seldom be traced to a single cause, and where several causes operate it is unwise to offer comparative estimates of the responsibility of each. However, the balance of informed opinion in this case favours Ultra as the decisive element which created a new situation. The best sign of this is the increased confidence with which OIC's Submarine Tracking Room could recommend changes in a convoy's route to avoid the wolf-packs whose location and plans were revealed by the daily Dolphin decrypts: among much else, they showed more than one U-boat group searching the ocean for two or three weeks on end without sighting a single ship. This is convincing indeed, but to accept it is not to overlook other things. Intelligence is of no value unless there is force to take advantage of it.

One consequence of the vastly increased flow of information into the Tracking Room during the second half of 1941 transcended all others and was of permanent importance. Eight months' exposure to German communications enabled Rodger Winn and his staff (now enlarged but hardly enough to cope properly with increased work and new responsibilities,* except at the cost of the overwork and strain which caused Winn to collapse in December 1942 and at doctor's orders take a month's sick leave) to familiarise themselves with U-Boat Command's standard procedures and study Dönitz's reactions to information received. The patterns thus revealed were of the greatest value when, eight months after Dolphin was first broken, a separate U-boat cipher came into operation and cut off the flow of oceanic intelligence; the Tracking Room could now make intelligent estimates during the blank period which followed, rather than repeat the guesswork on which it had so often had to rely before. A single illustration of this: the knowledge accumulated from Enigma and other sources about minefields and swept channels along the coasts of France, the Low Countries and western Germany made it possible to persuade Harris to bomb them, sink a number of ships and distract a significant proportion of German manpower to a purely defensive role, as well as to store up knowledge that proved of immense value before and during OVERLORD in 1944.

However the balance of advantage at the end of 1941 be

---

* Similar pressures already affected Hut 3. The cryptographers in Hut 6 and Hut 8 were so shorthanded that they took the unusual step of writing direct to the Prime Minister on 21 October 1941, asking for his support. Next day Churchill minuted, 'Make sure they have all they want on extreme priority' (BI ii.656–7).

assessed between a German naval command discouraged by the elusiveness of so many convoys and an Admiralty unable to control the fluctuations of a sinking-rate which still sometimes rose disconcertingly, it was destroyed by the blow which fell on 1 February 1942. The U-boat key suddenly became unreadable. The relief felt in May 1941 was proved only temporary; as the next ten months ground relentlessly on and losses rose more alarmingly than ever, it seemed that it might never return.

The deprivation of U-boat intelligence which the key-change signified could scarcely have come at a worse time for Britain. The United States had become an ally after Pearl Harbor at the beginning of the previous December, but this meant that more shipping would need to cross the Atlantic from west to east with much less protection than of late. Moreover, sharp competition for scarce resources soon developed to defend or recapture British and United States possessions round the Pacific rim. Hong Kong fell in December 1941, Singapore in February 1942, Burma and the Philippines between January and May. News from the Mediterranean was equally bad: Rommel attacked unexpectedly in January, captured Tobruk in June and was only halted in his progress towards Cairo and Alexandria in front of Alamein in July; reinforcements to stop him had to traverse the Atlantic from north to south on their way to the Cape of Good Hope and Suez. The need for defensive intelligence had never been so great nor the lack of it so painful.

The need and the lack were about to be intensified. After a period of transition since mid-December, during which U-boats and surface ships at sea had used the same or related Enigma keys, the two were finally separated on 1 February 1942.[*] Surface ships and U-boats in the Baltic and Mediterranean continued to use Dolphin; Atlantic U-boats were given their own key, called Shark by GC&CS. For the previous twelve months there had been indications that a new key would soon be

---

[*] See Erskine in INS 3 162–183, especially footnote 69 on p. 180.

introduced: although the investigations already mentioned had exonerated Dolphin from blame for some curious British anticipations of U-boat movements, OKM (Supreme Command of the Navy) felt that a new key with a four-rotor system of encipherment (Dolphin and all other known keys used only three rotors) would bring welcome additional security. The fourth rotor vastly increased the difficulty of decryption by enormously increasing the number of possible solutions to a given encrypted text, and decryption would require four-rotor bombes unless it were to be extremely slow. Yet no four-rotor bombes existed, and to design and build them would be a slow process which would disrupt the three-rotor construction programme urgently needed to deal with Dolphin and the many other keys (covering the Mediterranean and Russian fronts) which were now vulnerable.

In the event a happy accident shortened the delay which would otherwise have occurred, possibly with disastrous consequences. Cryptographic material recovered from *U-559,** sunk in the eastern Mediterranean on 30 October 1942, helped to break Shark on 13 December (see p. 203), six months before the first four-rotor bombes were delivered to GC&CS the following June. In August the first American-built bombes came into regular service and eventually took over the whole task of decrypting Shark, which from that time onward was broken daily, and often currently, until the end of the war.

The intelligence famine which began in February threatened disaster. The Tracking Room plot of convoy and U-boat positions soon lost the accuracy of detail to which everyone had become accustomed. Although, as already indicated, lessons learned during the time of plenty permitted rational hypotheses

---

* These five bald words hide the extreme bravery (posthumously rewarded by George Crosses) of Lieut Antony Fasson and AB Colin Grazier who, in their eagerness to retrieve from *U-559* everything that might be of value, stayed a moment too long in the sinking U-boat and were drowned. The full story is told in David Kahn, *Seizing the Enigma* (Souvenir Press, 1991) 218–27.

to be advanced, these were not always precise enough for evasive routeing to reach the high standards which had brought so many convoys safely through the perils of the Atlantic in 1941.

Two months before the onset of the famine, Pearl Harbor had brought the USA into the war. But instead of being the deliverance which Churchill had expected, it was at first the opposite. Dönitz diverted his main effort to the eastern seaboard of America where, in the absence of a convoy system which the US authorities astonishingly failed to introduce until the middle of May 1942, his U-boat captains enjoyed what they called their second 'happy time'.* When, with four times the number of boats at his disposal in August as at the beginning of the year, he switched them back to the Atlantic, they found ample prey. By September the AOC Coastal Command, seeking the allocation of more long-range aircraft, was pointing out that the Allies were losing more tankers than they were building, and merchant ships at an only slightly lower rate. Sinkings continued to rise frighteningly, reaching their peak in November at almost three-quarters of a million tons. The bells rang out for Alamein in the same month, but TORCH had already taken escorts away from the Atlantic to protect transports and supply ships entering the Mediterranean.

Very little could be done to fill the wide intelligence gap that now developed. U-boats still had to signal sighting and success reports to Dönitz, thus giving away their positions, and better fixes could now be achieved; improved HF/DF techniques enabled surface ships to locate U-boats and to inform any patrolling aircraft which happened to be in the vicinity so that it could run down the bearing indicated quickly enough to sink a U-boat by shellfire or depth-charge before it could submerge (by the beginning of 1943 a great many escorts had HF/DF and could often do their own 'killing'); but the content of the U-

* An additional reason for this was, of course, that the US entry into the war happened to coincide with the ten-months' 'black out' which afflicted Ultra for most of 1942.

boats' signals could no longer be understood, and a prime source of information had disappeared. Better PR could add something, prisoner-of-war interrogation laid the foundation for a more complete technical grasp of torpedo types and U-boat speeds and armament; the French Resistance added to what Dolphin revealed about the beginnings and ends of war cruises, about the number of boats at sea and about the construction programme. But nothing could compensate for the loss of the ability to direct convoys away from danger areas with confidence and thus save their precious cargoes.

The danger was greater than could be appreciated at the time. The same February which deprived GC&CS of U-boat traffic saw the B-Dienst complete its mastery of Naval Cipher No. 3. Although according to one calculation only 10 per cent of British signals were decrypted in time to affect immediate operations, the remaining 90 per cent enabled the B-Dienst to build up a convoy picture as good as that which the OIC had had of U-boat movements until February. Thus the material captured from *U-559* brought an immediate and welcome relief.

Four events occurred during the black-out months of 1942 which to a greater or lesser extent affected the Battle of the Atlantic and showed up the current state of intelligence.

The battleships *Scharnhorst* and *Gneisenau* had been holed up in Brest since early 1941, their projected commerce-raiding hindered by the Ultra-inspired destruction of their supply ships; the cruiser *Prinz Eugen* joined them after the sinking of the *Bismarck*. All three were heavily bombed and put out of action for lengthy periods; but by the turn of the year evidence piled up from Sigint, PR and SIS indicating that repairs were complete enough for them to be preparing to move. No source gave any hint of date or direction, but opinion gradually became convinced that 'early February' and 'up-Channel' were the likely answers. By 8 February Coastal Command predicted 'any time after the 10th'. No motive for the move was proposed, but in fact it originated from Hitler's intuition that the Allies were planning to land in Norway and his desire to strengthen the defence.

When Ultra showed on 3 February that destroyers and other vessels were being drafted in to act as a protective screen, existing preparations to intercept any attempt at a breakout were stepped up. It was easy to calculate that the journey up-Channel would take about fourteen hours. But when would it start? The subsequent inquiry discovered that some influential officers in the Admiralty were so convinced that the ships would sail by day in order to pass the dangers of the Narrows by night that they omitted to consider the alternative carefully enough. At all events, when the ships left Brest just before midnight on 11 February, no source gave news of their departure (Ultra for the 11th and 12th was not decrypted until the 15th) and everything now proceeded to go wrong.

Two aircraft patrolling for the purpose of watching the ships failed to give any warning because their radar broke down. Against all odds the squadron sailed on undetected all night and was not spotted and identified until 1100 on the 12th, when it was almost off Boulogne, with the result that attacks now had to be mounted in haste instead of with the intended deliberation. Slow, obsolete Swordfish biplanes, carrier-borne, had braved *Bismarck*'s AA guns and launched the torpedoes that had jammed her rudder, but against land-based Messerschmitts as well as AA fire, and deprived of their own promised fighter escort (it failed to turn up on time), they were completely outclassed. Lieutenant-Commander Esmonde RN pushed his hurriedly arranged attack through with the greatest courage, but not a single torpedo found its mark. Partly because of a few days' (8–22 February) hiatus at the apex of Bomber Command, it was mid-afternoon before another raid was launched against the ships, now off the Belgian coast; over 200 aircraft scored no hits. These are only the highlights of a shameful affair.

The lessons were too plain to need labouring: unexpected gaps in intelligence and extraordinary misinterpretations can occur at the most inconvenient moments and without warning, so precautions against them must be taken; preconceived ideas must not be allowed to obscure objective judgment; abnormal alertness and foresight are needed whenever an emergency is thought likely to occur; most immediate of all, better co-operation between the services than on this occasion was urgently needed. Public indignation at a missed opportunity and a German triumph drove these lessons home.

Something was saved at the last minute. During the evening *Scharnhorst* and *Gneisenau* both struck mines laid a few hours earlier by Bomber Command on the strength of route information worked out at the eleventh hour by OIC. Both reached Kiel, where bombing soon destroyed *Gneisenau* and put *Scharnhorst* out of commission for a year. So the net result of the 'Channel Dash' was that the German navy lost a large unit, the defence of Norway was unaltered, and the possibility that the Battle of the Atlantic might be complicated by surface ships was greatly reduced.

It was still further reduced by the raid on St Nazaire at the end of March, a completely successful stroke aimed at preventing *Tirpitz* from using the docks there as a base from which to terrorise Atlantic shipping. *Tirpitz* had been still in the last stages of construction and so unable to accompany her sister ship *Bismarck* to sea six months earlier, but was now ready for action and had recently been in Trondheim. By showing inter-service co-operation in a far better light than during the flight of *Scharnhorst* and *Gneisenau*, the St Nazaire raid also fulfilled the most urgent recommendation of the Board of Inquiry set up after that incident.

The raid was planned by army and navy intelligence and operations departments working together under the aegis of Combined Operations (newly revitalised under Mountbatten), which compiled a dossier on shore defences. The Inter-Services Topographical Department (ISTD) contributed other valuable shore information, as did members of the French Resistance. Special air photographs were commissioned and rigorously interpreted at Medmenham, while OIC settled route and timing in the light of Ultra. An old destroyer, filled with explosives behind specially strengthened bows, crashed through the lock gates, and a landing party damaged the locks; so great was the combined destruction that the locks could not be used again for the remainder of the war. If *Tirpitz* dare not use Brest, *Gneisenau* was destroyed and *Scharnhorst* damaged though operational in Norway, the most immediate surface threat to the Atlantic convoys was gone, though not the latent threat which the remains* of the German navy inevitably presented so long as any of it was still afloat.

Tirpitz was again the villain of the piece, off-stage but controlling the action, during the fatal voyage of PQ 17 two months later. Convoy PQ 17, of thirty-seven merchant ships laden with military equipment for Russia, left Iceland on 27 June, destination Archangel, by a route which kept it as far away from the German aircraft stationed round the northern tip of Norway as the southern limit of the ice-edge would permit. The close escort was six destroyers, two AA ships, four corvettes and two submarines, supported by three fleet minesweepers and four ocean escort trawlers; but, because *Tirpitz* was known to be in Trondheim and other heavy ships in the vicinity, the convoy was also given the First Cruiser Squadron (four cruisers, three destroyers) as close cover, while the Home Fleet (two battleships, two cruisers, a fleet carrier and fourteen destroyers) gave distant cover well to the westward. Eight days out, on 4 July, the First Sea Lord in London overrode OIC and Admiral Tovey, Commander-in-Chief Home Fleet, and took a controversial decision, based on his own reading of the intelligence available at the critical moment, to order the convoy to scatter. As a result, U-boats and aircraft (but not the surface ships) sank two-thirds of

* Two pocket-battleships and several cruisers and destroyers.

the convoy which was carrying 210 crated aircraft, 430 tanks and 3,350 M/T. Within a few hours intelligence and unfolding events showed up the devastating consequences of Pound's decision – but not, of course, what would have happened had he acted differently. Opinions about its wisdom are still divided today: would worse (the destruction of the whole convoy) have befallen had he allowed the convoy to proceed or ordered it to reverse course until the position became clearer? This was the crux of the decision he had to take.

The essence of an extremely complicated story illustrates the problem of applying intelligence to the conduct of military operations perhaps better than any other comparable incident in the Second World War. Apart from agents in Norway (but in the summer of 1942 there were none with adequate access to relevant information as well as the means of passing it on quickly), information obviously could only come from Ultra. Dolphin was still being used in home waters, and it could be broken with fair regularity (although Eighth Army was in retreat before Rommel at the same time, by special arrangement the majority of the still insufficient number of bombes was allotted to Dolphin). But for technical reasons it could be broken only by fits and starts, two days at a time; there was an awkward gap, devoid of decrypts, between midday on 3 July and late evening on the 4th, when up-to-date intelligence was urgently needed. It had always to be borne in mind that, even when it seemed most complete, Ultra might not record material of particular relevance because for some reason it had never been put on the air; in this case it did not reveal that Hitler, over-sensitive to dangers *Tirpitz* had only narrowly escaped when she set out to destroy PQ 12, had ordered that *Tirpitz* should on no pretext leave port if there were any risk of the Home Fleet catching her; had this been known, it would have sharpened attention to Ultra's discovery that German reconnaissance planes had erroneously reported a battleship with First Cruiser Squadron and believed that a British carrier might be off Trondheim.

Late on 3 July Pound visited OIC for almost the first time in
his life – as an 'old salt' (he had commanded a battleship at
Jutland) he had never had much use for intelligence. Where was
Tirpitz, and what was she likely to do? he asked. As PQ 17
rounded the North Cape, these were the vital questions, for, as
Churchill had said earlier, *Tirpitz* 'exercises a vague, general fear
and menaces all points at once'. Ultra soon answered the first
question by locating her in Altafjord, a protected anchorage
close to North Cape. Ultra then fell temporarily silent, though
the next break was expected soon. Late on 4 July Denning gave
Pound – many years his senior and vastly his superior in rank –
several cogent reasons, grounded in his deep experience of the
source, to suggest that *Tirpitz* was not at sea at that moment and
probably would not sail for some time; but he could not be
definite, because the necessary information was lacking, and he
did not feel able to insist too strongly on his opinion against that
of the operational head of the navy. In the absence of that
absolute certainty which intelligence can so seldom provide, and
contrary to the opinion of several of his advisers and to the
strongly expressed views of Admiral Tovey (who received the
same Ultra information as Pound, but mediated through OIC),
shortly before midnight Pound decided that the risk that *Tirpitz*
and other heavy ships might get among the convoy and
annihilate it was too great to run. He therefore ordered the
cruiser force to withdraw and the convoy to scatter, although he
knew that his action might well leave the ships at the mercy of
U-boats and aircraft as well as of *Tirpitz*.

Tirpitz and a strong escorting force did eventually emerge
from Altafjord next afternoon (5 July), when air recce had
established that both the cruisers and the Home Fleet were
leaving the area, but returned shortly after, on realising that U-
boats and aircraft could do the job of destruction by themselves.
This they did, sending more than twenty ships to the bottom.
Pound's reasoning, and what would have happened had he

trusted Denning and not interfered, can be endlessly debated; in the context of a study of intelligence in war, the main interest centres on two things: the relationship of an intelligence officer (almost certain to be a specialist and junior in rank) with the operational commander who is bound to outrank him and to be older, but lacks specialist knowledge of the peculiarities of intelligence; and the delicate business of turning a mixture of ascertained fact and experience-based 'hunch' into irrevocable action on the battlefield.

Since it had nothing to do with the Atlantic and little with the navy, the ill-starred Dieppe raid in August would not rate a mention here did it not further illustrate the condition of the intelligence/operations interface in the late summer of 1942. OIC and the Submarine Tracking Room, starting out with the advantage of a ready-prepared organisation and hampered only by the irregularity of their main source, had developed it to a high state of efficiency in purely naval affairs. Eighth Army, handicapped by the tactical and strategic unsophistication of most of its officers, and hindered recently by Seebohm's skill and Fellers's indiscretions (see pp. 95–6), had just taken the first steps towards better things in ground fighting and was about to link intelligence firmly to operations at Alam Halfa. Experience had been the main teacher of both, but neither army nor navy had any experience of combined operations, which were henceforth to open the way to every new advance. Dieppe was thus the first foray into unknown territory. It demonstrated that without experience the link between intelligence and operations in the British Isles was weak or non-existent – even Montgomery's rigorous training of South-Eastern Command did not make up for the combat experience which the troops engaged at Dieppe (and later in Tunisia), in common with almost the whole of the army in England, had had no chance of acquiring since Dunkirk. This experience, gained at great cost in six hours at Dieppe on 19 August, taught elementary lessons, some of which were put to good use in TORCH three months alter and led to successive improvements in Sicily, at Salerno and Anzio and in Normandy.

The laudable purpose of the raid was to test the Germans' defences and their reactions in order to gain guidance for the future, and then to withdraw on the same day. The intention was fulfilled, but at the cost of 1,000 dead and 2,000 taken prisoner out of the 6,000 men in the raiding force. This can only be called failure. Combined Operations was put in charge of the planning and the conduct of the raid. There were marked shortcomings in its arrangements for intelligence-gathering, partly because of its own casual methods and partly because of the difficulties under which those who supplied it worked. SIS provided a little advance information but was restricted by German security precautions. Special air photographs were taken, but it was still not properly understood that photographs cannot show every detail of importance for a particular purpose – in this case, for instance, guns mounted in caves. ISTD had much to say about local topography, but unaccountably omitted to investigate the angle of slope of the beach, which proved too steep for men or tanks to negotiate easily in the face of hostile fire. An elaborate plan for making immediate use of R/T and Sigint broke down because the channels provided became choked.

All these defects were remedied in due course, none more strikingly than by ISTD, whose accurate measurement of beach gradients was of major assistance to the OVERLORD landings. From all these points of view, a small failure paved the way for a greater success. The same is true of non-intelligence lessons learned – that it was a mistake to delete the heavy preliminary air bombardment from the initial plan (Trenchard's deadly legacy exacted its price here) and another mistake not to provide supporting naval gunfire during the operation itself. Finally, the raid showed that a port could be captured only at the cost of damaging it so much that it was rendered unusable – thus stimulating the development of the artificial harbours which were a principal key to victory in 1944.

To return to the Atlantic situation in late 1942: with the loss-rate still threatening to outstrip the construction-rate and with the need to increase the available tonnage growing daily, anxiety mounted throughout the autumn. In November the Admiralty prodded GC&CS firmly but with surprising gentleness, urging 'a little more attention' to Shark. Less than a month later came the welcome news that Shark had succumbed. The explanation was not simply greater cryptographic effort, however, but also one of those lucky windfalls without which Enigma might have remained for ever intractable.

It had been found in the past that the code in which German weather reports were transmitted offered cribs into Dolphin when the same message was sent in both. The weather code in use since 1941 had been captured long before and was used for this purpose. But it was changed early in 1942, and there were no more cribs. Then in October the new weather code was captured from *U-559* in the Mediterranean, and it was discovered that when Shark was used for weather signals the fourth rotor was set at neutral, that therefore the three-rotor bombe could decrypt them, and that the remaining part of the day's key could then be reconstructed with comparative ease.

While, because of Dönitz's centralised control system, the air was filled with decryptable transmissions and the breaking of Shark which followed undoubtedly saved many ships and many lives, this did not solve the whole of the Atlantic problem. Many days' keys could only be broken with so much delay that the decrypts were too old to assist operations, and the B-Dienst quickly overcame the obstacles imposed by changes which had been made in the British Naval Cipher No. 3, strangely enough only two days after Shark was first broken. (The parallelism between the two opponents is striking.) The Allied loss-rate fell, but still remained too high for comfort: in December 1942, forty-six ships of 262,000 tons were lost, but even January's lower figure of twenty-seven of 175,000 tons represented not far from two million for the whole year by extrapolation.

Thus the breaking of Shark did not at once determine the mastery of the Atlantic. As the New Year 1943 dawned, the bitterest convoy battles were still to come. More U-boats than ever (sixty-six in the North Atlantic alone in March) were ready to take advantage of everything the B-Dienst could tell them – so many were there, in fact, and so well distributed, that there was no space between them into which a convoy could be diverted without fear of discovery. The prospect of losing the war loomed ahead again even before disaster overwhelmed HX 229 and SC 122, a slow and a fast convoy which became mingled in mid-Atlantic when one overtook the other: a destroyer and thirty-two ships totalling 187,500 tons went to the bottom in a running four-day battle in mid-March, and only one U-boat was sunk in return. As if this were not enough, there had just been a final alarm about Shark. On 10 March Dönitz brought into force a new codebook for the weather reports which, as explained above, had been so useful in providing cribs. It was at first feared that Shark would become unreadable again, but by prodigious cryptographic efforts and by commandeering every available bombe, GC&CS overcame the new obstacle in nine days, and by 20 March (the same day that the HX 229 battle ended) Shark was in full spate again.

After a period of despondency in March, the balance now shifted in the British favour in April and May. Although there were sometimes distressing gaps, Shark was now more often than not providing almost current intelligence. New and improved means to make the best use of its wealth of information were coming into service: independent and highly trained support groups, sometimes including small aircraft-carriers (converted merchant ships), directed to points where the escorts sensed danger and needed strengthening (the attacking policy which had to be discarded in 1940 now matched the case); HF/DF and centimetric radar as standard fittings for aircraft and escorts; more Liberators to complete the closing of the air-gap; multiple

forward-operating depth-charge throwers ('Hedgehogs') . . . separately or together all these prevented any repetition of the
March disasters.

The effectiveness of these measures in resolute hands was
demonstrated during the outward voyage of convoy ONS5
(forty-two merchant ships, destined to fetch supplies from
American ports) at the end of April. Dönitz lined up some thirty
U-boats across the convoy's route and drafted in another dozen
once contact had been made. In a week-long running battle one
of the most highly trained escort groups under Commander
Peter Gretton RN restricted the attackers' bag to twelve
merchantmen and sank seven U-boats in return, with five more
seriously damaged – almost one for one, a score never before
remotely approached.

By the end of May, OIC had statistical proof of the change
which had been so suddenly brought about: in the preceding
three months fifty-six U-boats had been sunk, but only fifty-one
had begun war cruises in that same period. Not surprisingly in
the circumstances, the morale of captains and crews was shaken:
Shark revealed their growing fears of air attack, and in May the
decrypt of a rather half-hearted exhortation by Dönitz to his U-
boat commanders to do their duty and show determination
confirmed that he feared the opposite. Unable to scent victory
any longer, he withdrew all his U-boats from the North Atlantic
on 24 May, ostensibly for a period of rest and regrouping only;
but when on 10 June the Admiralty at last replaced Naval
Cipher No. 3 with No. 5, which proved quite secure, it was plain
that the U-boats could never regain their former authority.

Dönitz' retreat in May 1943 and the shutting down of his main
source of intelligence in June, it could be seen later, marked the
effective end of the Battle of the Atlantic. But this was far from
clear at the time, for it could not then seem more than a
temporary and very welcome intermission in a struggle which
had already been going on for nearly four years. The number of

U-boats in service continued to rise: there were always more than 400 from the summer of 1943 until the end of the war, in a proportion of roughly one-third operational and two-thirds undergoing training or sea trials.

Dönitz represented his withdrawal of U-boats from the Anglo-American supply and reinforcement routes in the North Atlantic as a momentary interruption of the assault, but his first show of a return was only to the Bay of Biscay, where furious battles were fought during the late summer against U-boats setting out on passage to distant waters. By September, Ultra was giving warning that there would shortly be a new offensive against Atlantic convoys, but the Allied counter-measures proved so effective that it was broken off after only two months. A succession of relatively minor new problems caused by further modifications in Enigma procedures was overcome by the autumn, after which decryption was regular and usually current or only slightly in arrears. Signs of coming victory were plain. Shipping losses fell from just under eight million tons in 1942 to a little over three million in 1943 and U-boat 'kills' rose; by December 1943 almost half of the German U-boat captains had held their commands for less than six months.

Allied fears were kept alive right up to the surrender of May 1945 principally by two things: reports of novel developments (they would have brought wartime U-boats even nearer Polaris than Bletchley's decoding machines approached modern computers) which would enable U-boats to remain submerged for longer and to travel faster under water, and nervousness about what even existing types could do if concentrated against the large numbers of fighting vessels and transport craft which would be required on D-Day for the invasion and thereafter to maintain the invaders ashore. If U-boats could travel great distances unseen, how could their presence be predicted accurately enough for action against them to be prepared? What were the chances that an invading force could survive if large groups of U-boats were massed in the narrow waters of the

Channel? If all the new developments could have been perfected in time, by D-Day Dönitz would have controlled a force of speedy underwater craft which could not be located by D/F and whose signals could defy cryptanalysis, but which could find their enemies with new and improved equipment and destroy them with more accurate torpedoes. The nightmare of starvation at home returned, this time with a new horror in addition – that of the Anglo-American armies in Europe immobilised and weaponless for lack of petrol and ammunition.

These fears were dispersed by the teething troubles which all remarkable scientific advances experience on the one hand and by Bomber Command's attacks on shipyards and the inland communications along which prefabricated parts were transported on the other. As it turned out, there was far less need for apprehension than was anticipated, but this became clear only very gradually.

Evidence that OKM was urgently experimenting with new types of U-boat began to accumulate towards the end of 1943, heralded by reports from Ultra, PR and the German press that the construction of existing types was being phased out: if the Allies had by now mastered the traditional model, the underwater offensive could be resumed with much prospect of success only by the application of new techniques. The most familiar of these today is the *Schnorkel*, a retractable air tube which allowed a U-boat to run its diesel engines for propulsion or to recharge its electric batteries while submerged, instead of having to surface for air and risk detection. The *Schnorkel* was first reported in January 1944, but tests had been going on for six months previously. For several weeks it was mistakenly believed that the *Schornkel* had something to do with the most alarming aspect of current intelligence from prisoners-of-war – that a new type of engine was being developed by a Professor Walter to give higher underwater speeds to a new streamlined hull, and it was not until February 1944 that the confusion was cleared up.

This was not enough, however, to remove all the Admiralty's

fears. Prisoners (the source of a great deal of information at this time) did not, and PR could not, distinguish between U-boats with or without the new engines. If, therefore, the many small boats of the new type which had been seen or otherwise reported were both fast and able to remain submerged for long periods, they would be capable of inflicting immense damage on the OVERLORD shipping. The Admiralty therefore remained in a high state of alarm until at the end of April Ultra – in the form of decrypts of messages from the head of the Japanese naval mission to Germany – revealed that the Walter engine was still not ready to go into production and that as an interim measure the new streamlined hulls were being fitted with 'old-fashioned' but much more powerful diesel engines and *Schnorkels*. Later, the same source gave full technical details of both the new types, large and small (of 1,600 and 250 tons displacement)* which were being developed for ocean-going and inshore work respectively.

A feeling of relief at the diminution of the U-boat threat therefore prevailed well before D-Day. In fact the relief could have been even greater than it was. Allied precautions kept tight control of the seaways, and more than half the U-boats trying to operate in the Channel were sunk. By August 1944 Dönitz abandoned the vain effort to interfere with reinforcement and supply, and bombing so disorganised production that only six of the smaller new-pattern U-boats operated in March and April 1945, while the first of the larger type did not even sail until 3 May.

Is it possible to determine the principal cause of victory in the Atlantic? On the one hand, there is a distinct, though not a perfect, correlation between the tonnages lost at sea and the decryption in turn of Dolphin and Shark. From this arises the common oversimplification that 'Ultra won the Battle of the

---

* The standard-type U-boat displaced 740 tons.

Atlantic.' On the other hand, intelligence is useless without men and weapons to use it. Had the shipyards of Britain and America not outstripped the huge shipping losses by new construction, had better radar not been invented and long-range aircraft designed and produced in great numbers, had seamen not been ready to serve as commanders and crew of merchant ships (particularly of the tankers which carried petrol and oil for the aircraft which bombed Germany and for the tanks and jeeps of the OVERLORD armies, but which a single torpedo could turn into a flaming furnace in a few seconds) – without these, Ultra alone could not have prevented defeat.

A stark choice between such alternatives has only to be stated to be seen as absurd, and no serious historian has ever made it.

Patrick Beesly and Jürgen Rohwer were the first to write with knowledge of Ultra; their books were published in 1977. Having said (strangely ignoring the role of Coastal Command) that the Royal Navy and merchant navy crews 'bore the brunt of the battle and deserve most of the credit for its outcome', the former turns to the important part played by OIC and GC&CS, without which, he says, victory would have come later and been more costly. In his book on the convoy battles of 1943, the latter (who had served in German destroyers in the Atlantic) points to 'the efficient use of HF/DF' as the decisive factor, but in saying so plainly has tactical matters in the forefront of his mind. Ten years later, at a conference held at Exeter University, both came down decisively on the side of Ultra, Rohwer clearly taking a wider view on this occasion. The official British intelligence history carries indecision to great lengths: the fact that the convoy battles of 1943 were so protracted 'suggests' that Ultra 'must have been of crucial importance' but victory hinged on so many factors that 'it is not easy to establish the extent to which it was influenced by the Allied decryption of the signals of U-Boat Command'. Its chief author, Harry Hinsley (formerly the Chief Intelligence Officer of the Naval Section at GC&CS), went only a little further when he said at the Exeter conference that Ultra was 'directly instrumental' in shortening the war by two years. Most recently Correlli Barnett, with action rather than intelligence his chief concern, has written that it was 'the sailors ranged against each other . . . and their willingness to endure and dare', and particularly the advent of support groups, which had most influence on the issue of the Atlantic conflict.

There can be no question that Ultra had even more to do with the winning of the war at sea than it had with victory on land or in the air. A break in the Atlantic supply route, had it occurred, would have been more disastrous, and in quicker time, than any other form of defeat except possibly the V2 offensive on the scale which Hitler intended but was prevented from delivering. The inescapable circumstances of command and control over oceanic distances compelled Dönitz to put his orders and wider operational plans at the mercy of the cryptanalysts; and when they overcame the many difficulties placed in their way, naval Ultra had access to more operational and quasi-strategic information than was normally derivable from decrypted army of Luftwaffe messages: only Hitler's order for the Mortain attack in August 1944 (see p. 271) bears comparison with Dönitz's signal of 24 May 1943, with its implied acknowledgment of at least temporary defeat.

This said, however, no broad conclusion is possible save that here as elsewhere intelligence and action depended inseparably upon each other: it was co-operation between the two, rather than the destructive contribution of either, which brought the final victory.

1943–1945

Clear Skies in Italy,
Storm Over the Balkans

The two years between the preparations for the Sicily landing (Operation HUSKY) in the spring of 1943 and the surrender of Army Group South at Caserta on 29 April 1945 saw the longest continuous campaign in which Ultra and its foster-child, deception (often with important backing from other forms of intelligence) provided daily operational guidance to field commanders and occasional strategic information of the greatest value to the Supreme Command and the Chiefs of Staff. The famous 'Man Who Never Was' marked its beginning and a long despairing assessment of his plight by the German Commander-in-Chief its end; at intervals between the two came up-to-the-minute news of Hitler's reaction to Italy's change of sides and of his long-range intentions about the defence of Italy and the Balkans consequent upon it. The Italian campaign is often depicted as a long and tedious grind up the peninsula which caused needless destruction and loss of life. The geography of Italy favours defence against an invader from the south, and Kesselring took skilful advantage of this to inflict periods of frustrating stalemate upon the Allies, but a fair appraisal shows not only how intelligence helped to overcome these handicaps but also how it made possible the integration of the Italian campaign with convergent attacks on Nazi Europe from east and west so that it substantially weakened resistance to them all.

Intelligence played no part in the decision to invade Sicily, however. The decision was taken, after considerable American objection, at the Casablanca Conference in January 1943, because it was the only way in which the armies already deployed along the southern shores of the Mediterranean could coalesce to open something like the 'second front' which both Stalin and Anglo-American public opinion loudly demanded. Yet there were two undeniable objections to it. A combined operation on the scale required had never been attempted before, and the ill-fated Dieppe raid had just shown how much there was to learn about ways and means. Secondly, Sicily rather than any other point on the Axis-held northern Mediterranean coastline was so obviously the Allies' target ('Anybody but a bloody fool would know it was Sicily,' said Churchill) that resistance strong enough to repel any attack would surely be prepared: Eisenhower even sought to impose conditions on the Chiefs of Staff – no landing if there were reason to believe that there were more than two German divisions on the island. The first objection was only partly overcome: joint planning by the land, sea and air commanders was hindered by the fact that their HQs were many hundred miles apart; the second was triumphantly neutralised by a deep-laid and many-faceted deception plan which completely fooled the Germans; soon after its inception General Jodl, head of the OKW operations staff, was heard shouting down the telephone to Rintelen, Military Attaché in Rome, 'Forget Sicily, we know it's Greece.'

Contrary to commonly held opinion, Operation MINCE-MEAT was not the prime mover in the deception, but only a carefully designed and amazingly successful feature of it. 'Major Martin's' body was floated ashore at Huelva in Spain on 30 April; the 'despatches' he carried confirmed OKW in beliefs it had already been conditioned to accept. Their great merit was that they occasioned Enigma messages[*] which by 14 May

---

[*] CX/MSS 2751/T4, the version sent to Churchill (at sea on the way to Washington) shows that the Spaniards had passed the MINCEMEAT documents to Berlin by 12 May, and that OKW accepted them as

showed that the Germans believed them to be genuine, that the Peloponnese and Sardinia were considered the Allies' chief objectives, and that appropriate military measures – they soon culminated in the hasty transfer of a newly reconditioned Panzer division from France to Greece, where it arrived on 14 June – were being taken. Jodl's remark, made soon after all this (but of course unknown at the time) is interesting because it shows OKW roughly dismissing the quite correct view, from which they never deviated, of Rintelen's Italian associates, that the Allies would land in Sicily.

MINCEMEAT was not in itself decisive because, following upon CASCADE, its outline plan for 1942, 'A' Force had devised a successor, BARCLAY, with the object of continuing to infiltrate into the German mind (through agents, bogus radio transmissions and the like) the idea that a notional British army of nine divisions or more (by the time of the Sicily landing Keitel, head of OKW, believed that there were forty in the Mediterranean as a whole) poised to stage a major operation in the Aegean to bring Turkey into the war and attack the Balkans via Greece. Since Hitler had long been confident that to occupy the Balkans would better serve Allied interests than to secure Italy, this was a perfect illustration of Clarke's principle that deception could be most effectively practised by playing on an intended victim's existing anxieties. So effective was BARCLAY that a fortnight after the Sicily landing OKW still believed that the Balkans were the ultimate objective (the otherwise ill-starred expeditions against the Aegean islands of Cos and Leros in September prolonged the illusion) and that Italy had been invaded only as a stepping-stone into the Balkans. German fears of this kind (illustrated in August by a reorganisation of command in the Balkans and the establishment of a new Army Group) did not

genuine and immediately informed OB South and OB Southeast in an Enigma message which was being studied in Hut 3 just after midnight 13/14 May. (This version (in PRO HW1) fills out and slightly corrects UMS 223 and note, and BI 111/1 78.)

abate until the end of the year – by which time Tito's Partisans were emerging as the leading anti-German party in the Balkans and Whitehall was considering lending them greater support.

Ultra rendered the incomparable service of demonstrating well in advance that BARCLAY was having its intended effect, but the deception plan must not be given all the credit for the German reaction to the post-TORCH situation. It follows from what has just been said that, even had there been no deception, OKW would have taken precautions in the Balkans and would probably have refused to commit more troops to Sicily in support of the Italian Sixth Army lest they be lost in the aftermath of an Italian defection which it had already begun to fear. Hitler set in train Operation ALARICH,* to occupy north Italy if the Italians deserted the Axis, at about the same time as MINCEMEAT. On 4 May Ultra located Rommel with a mysterious 'Planning Staff' outside Vienna. When Mussolini fell on 25 July, Rommel moved to Munich with Army Group B (as the 'Planning Staff' was renamed), which crossed the Italian frontier and began moving south a few days later. Ten divisions strong, Army Group B spread over Lombardy and eastwards into Slovenia, more than doubling German strength in Italy and protecting the Balkans (into which further additional troops were moved) as well as Italy. By the late summer BARCLAY, HUSKY and the threatened change of regime in Rome had transformed the military situation in the central Mediterranean.

To go back a little: Ultra apart, intelligence gave small assistance to HUSKY planning. The SIS had no agents in place, and Army Y provided few items of consequence. Information about beach gradients and the holding quality of the sand was better than at Dieppe, but was insufficient as well as too late in reaching those who could use it. No significant improvement occurred during the five weeks (10 July–17 August) that the fighting lasted; Ultra kept good track of army movements and

* Alaric the Visigoth had entered Italy from the north-east and sacked Rome in 410 AD.

was particularly useful on Luftwaffe strengths and the transfer of units from place to place.

As the battle drew to a close the command authorities on the spot and the JIC at home seem suddenly to have become blind to intelligence from the source they had been relying on for twelve months or more. Plainly, the Germans would lose many men and much equipment unless arrangements for ferrying them across the Strait of Messina were made in good time; both sides had vivid memories of what had happened at Cape Bon in May. As early as 14 July, only four days after the landing, a series of Ultra signals showed that Kesselring had appointed a certain Oberst Baade to command 'Fortress Messina', organise the defence of the northern tip of Sicily and prepare for evacuation. If confirmation were needed, it was provided by a map, captured by Eighth Army on 31 July, which outlined evacuation measures, and by a practice evacuation held the same night. Yet Alexander and Eisenhower, like the JIC in London and its satellite in Algiers, saw no signs of withdrawal for several more days, even after the first ferries began to operate at full blast on the 11th (120,000 men and a multitude of tanks, guns and M/T got away). It is hard to understand how officers who had been accustomed to Ultra for a year or more can have made such a mistake; the defensive tone of some of their later pronouncements suggests a consciousness of guilt.

Not until the end of May, little more than two months before HUSKY, and only after much inter-Allied wrangling, did the Trident Conference in Washington decide that an invasion of Italy should follow the conquest of Sicily. That conquest was still incomplete when Mussolini fell on 25 July and the new Italian government made overtures of surrender. After tortuous secret negotiations, the two events coincided in point of time. Terms of surrender were signed on 3 September, a few hours after the British Eighth Army landed unopposed at Reggio on the toe of

Italy; they were officially announced on 9 September, as the US Fifth Army fought its way ashore at Salerno on the west coast.

How, and with what speed, would the Germans react to the new though not wholly unexpected situation? This was the prime intelligence problem in the early autumn of 1943. Just a year after its tactical/operational triumph before Alamein, Ultra was now to pass its first strategic test with equal success. Although he had long foreseen that Italy might desert the Axis, and had taken some preliminary steps to deal with the consequences which would arise, Hitler had not yet decided what he would do after seizing power in Rome. He took a month to make up his mind. Ultra was able to follow his hesitations and to report his decision within a fortnight of his taking it – an intelligence feat of immense value which enabled the Allies to frame their own response in the light of Hitler's intentions. No other source could have gained access to his inner circle nor have reported its discoveries so quickly. Only by intercepting German communications could this be done, and OKW's awareness of the faint possibility of it was shown when it sent a special representative to explain a crucial decision to Kesselring in person and delivered four of the eight copies of the relevant order by courier rather than by radio.

ALARICH had a Balkan twin, KONSTANTIN, under which Rommel was to take command in Greece. No sooner had he reached his destined HQ in Salonika on 25 July than he was summoned back to meet Hitler on news of Mussolini's fall that same day, and was at once given command of Army Group B. ALARICH and KONSTANTIN, which had only been precautionary measures, were now merged as ACHSE ('Axis'), an operation to occupy Italy and Italian-held territory in Croatia and along the Dalmatian coast. Ultra gave the first hint of this on 5 August, less than a week after Army Group B had begun moving south into Lombardy, and had identified every German division in the Army Group, with an indication of their tank-strength, before the end of the month.

Thus, only a few weeks after the Allied armies set foot in Italy, the Combined Chiefs of Staff knew that Hitler's reaction to recent events had been to weaken his eastern front (despite the Russian advance after the collapse of his Kursk offensive in July) and the Channel coast of France – for almost all Rommel's troops had come from one or the other – in order to meet the emergency in the south. This showed that one of the main aims of the Trident Conference was already being achieved. What it did not show, however, and could not show because Hitler had not yet made up his mind about it, was whether Rommel's Army Group B would be milked to reinforce Kesselring as he retreated from Salerno and Apulia, or whether Hitler would take the more rational course of withdrawing to the line of the Alps, where fewer men could put up an indefinite resistance at a far lower cost in lives and equipment. Not only was the latter the more rational strategy (but after BARBAROSSA and his 'Stand fast' order at Alamein, were Hitler's military decisions likely to be rational?), there was positive evidence that it would be German policy. So the German Foreign Office told the Japanese Ambassador, who informed Tokyo (and the Allies, via Ultra), so ran the plainest deductions from German divisional moves in northern Italy. The JIC was convinced that a withdrawal to the line of the Alps was in the offing.

Behind the scenes, however, a struggle was raging, often in Hitler's presence, between Rommel and Kesselring over precisely this point. For a month he could not, or would not, decide between them. Eventually he sided with Kesselring, and in doing so made one of his many mistakes. So long as Hitler hesitated, Rommel's Army Group was not called upon to provide reinforcements for Kesselring, in whose favour Hitler decided at the end of the month. Ultra knew nothing of the dispute which preceded the decision, but quickly discovered the essence of Hitler's conclusions. Signs that Kesselring would make a stand south of Rome accumulated on the first days of October; they included a plan for three lines of defence to protect the city.

During the same week Rommel was reconnoitring another defence line 150 miles farther back, in the mountains north of Florence (this was the later Gothic Line) and his divisions were being redistributed, some going south to Kesselring, some back to the Russian front, where the alarming speed of the Russian advance was causing a major reappraisal of defence plans only six weeks after the front had been weakened to furnish Army Group B for the take-over in Italy.

Despite these kaleidoscopic shifts of policy, German strategy in Italy for the foreseeable future lay open to view by the middle of October. Only a month had passed since the Salerno landing, but all Allied hopes of a quick thrust northwards were at an end. Alexander had been expecting to reach Florence by December, but now he knew that his armies (soon to be depleted by transfers to England to prepare for OVERLORD) would have to fight their way laboriously northwards through country which favoured the defence at every step. But it was now certain that in spite of the intensified pressure on his eastern front Hitler was prepared to co-operate, in what he supposed his own best interest, with the Allies in their policy of containing as many German divisions as possible in Italy in order to keep them away from fronts where they could do more harm.

From the strategic point of view, Rommel's had been unquestionably the wiser advice: a shortage of manpower, caused by attrition on the Russian front, was already becoming a crisis, clearly evident in the decline of Kesselring's air power as squadrons were moved to protect the Reich against ever heavier Allied raids and the troops in Russia against further losses. Hitler's rejection of Rommel's advice marked another stage in the irrational refusal to face unpleasant military facts which he first showed at Alamein and Stalingrad and continued until the end. But it did make the Allies' progress up the Italian peninsula very slow. This has sometimes led to criticism of the whole Italian campaign ('a long and painful slog up Italy') as a strategic mistake. To do this today, however, is to forget what was thoroughly appreciated at the time and has since been re-emphasised – that the obstinate German resistance helped the Allies to fulfil their prior purpose of drawing troops away from other theatres and grinding them down in Italy (1 Parachute and Hermann Göring Divisions were notable sufferers). Kesselring was repeatedly outwitted by his opponents, only to restore a temporary balance by skilfully improvising counter-measures, and this has strengthened the impression, created also by the defensively inclined topography at Cassino and elsewhere, that he imposed delay on the Allied advance.

On the other hand, it would be scarcely an exaggeration to say that the delay was a calculated risk, part of a policy of continual pressure that gave Kesselring no respite. Even after losing eight of his best divisions to OVERLORD in late 1943, seven more for the invasion of southern France in August 1944 and three more – making eighteen in all – to the west in the spring of 1945, Alexander and his replacement force continued the work of attrition. Although they enjoyed the advantage of easily defensible terrain, Kesselring's armies suffered considerably more casualties than the Allies: four or more for every three on the Allied side. No German division left Italy for the western front in 1944, and only one for the eastern. With only very short-lived exceptions, the Allies always disposed of fewer divisions in Italy than the Germans, so that the task of 'containing' the enemy was fully accomplished.

Too much cannot be claimed for a single piece of intelligence, but it is clear that the discovery in October 1943 that, contrary to expectation, Hitler would not give up Italy without a fight was pivotal to subsequent Allied strategy. Any judgment which overlooks this is doomed to superficiality.

Even before the German surrender in Tunisia in May 1943, Jugoslavia had begun to exercise a discernible influence on Mediterranean strategy. The way it happened is enlightening for the manner in which Balkan intelligence was gathered – by SOE

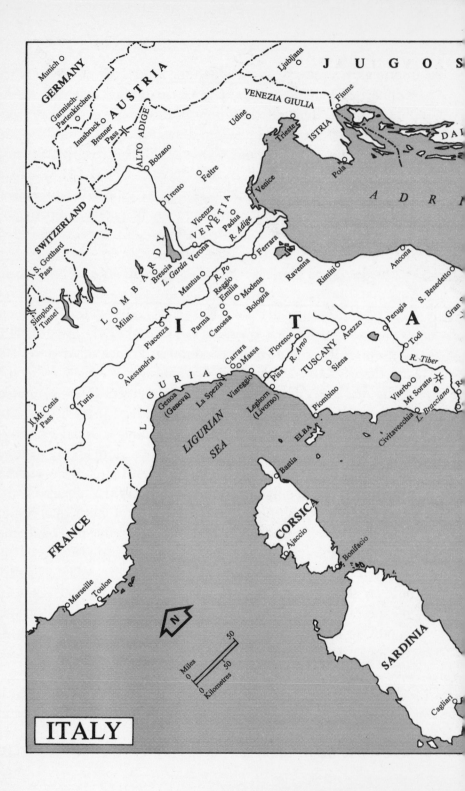

ITALY

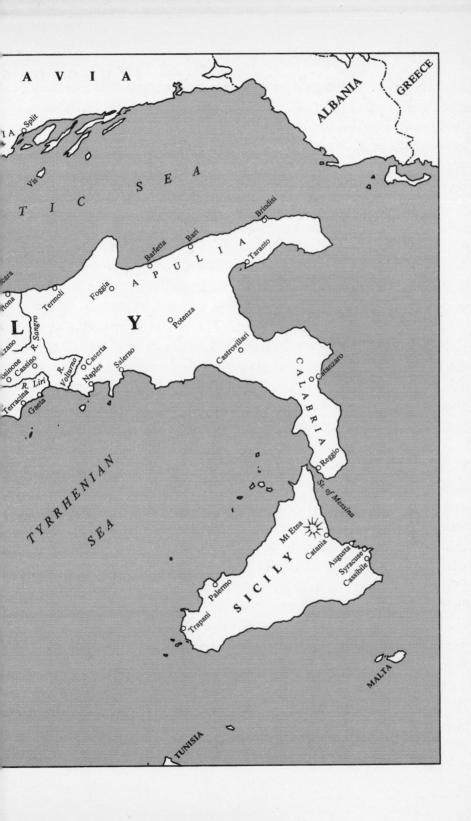

as well as by SIS, in an unusual variation of their normal roles –
and for the manner in which it was handled at a time when SOE
London and SOE Cairo acted almost independently of each
other. In retrospect it is also notable for the passion and
prejudice which has distorted some writing on the subject in
recent years and for the secretiveness which has withheld much
of the surviving evidence.[*]

Two Resistance leaders emerged in Jugoslavia soon after the
German invasion of April 1941: Colonel Draža Milhailović, a
regular army officer, a typical representative of the ruling
Serbian elite, soon appointed Minister of War by the royal
government-in-exile in London, and Josip Broz, known as Tito,
a Moscow-trained communist Croat. The fact of their resistance
qualified both for the attention of SOE, with its mission to 'set
Europe ablaze'; in so far as they were keeping German and
Italian occupation forces engaged they were fulfilling the aims of
the British deception plans CASCADE and BARCLAY by
holding Axis divisions away from other fronts.

Until shortly before Alamein, however, Britain was far too
concerned with survival in the Middle East (not to speak of
finding resources to combat Japan in the Pacific) to pay much
attention to the Balkans, and for lack of reliable information
found the greatest difficulty in arriving at a true assessment of the
military situation in Jugoslavia. SOE's prime purpose was to stir
up trouble in occupied territory, not to collect intelligence. Yet,
because information was at first so scanty, SOE was often
obliged to perform both tasks in Jugoslavia, and in any case
could not support local Resistance groups without first knowing
something of their purposes, nor carry out acts of sabotage
without reconnoitring the ground and discovering whether, and
by whom, its planned targets were being defended. Moreover, it
would be scarcely an exaggeration to say that, at any time before
the end of 1943, there were almost two separate SOEs and that

[*] See pp. 296–8, below. The release of some of the SOE information
was promised in 1993.

they seldom worked in harmony together. SOE London was largely staffed by bankers and businessmen, like-minded with the founders of the organisation who had recruited them; SOE Cairo was broader-based, included men of a more liberal outlook and was more military and less exclusively political in viewpoint. These differences in sympathy could hardly avoid having a bearing on the different actions taken or proposed by either, but differences in the intelligence available to each and in their interpretation of it were at least as influential.

The first attempt to find out what was going on was made in the autumn of 1941, when Captain (later Colonel) Hudson, a mining engineer long familiar with the country and fluent in Serbo-Croat, was sent on a fact-finding mission. He met both Mihailović and Tito and soon reported that Tito was being much the more active in resistance to the Germans, that the two leaders had met but could not work together, and that their followers frequently came to blows. After this, unfortunately, Hudson's radio was out of contact until August 1942. During the interval SOE London certainly, and SOE Cairo probably, collected such information as it could, but was forced to rely for most of it on nothing better than a careful scrutiny of the European press.

SIS in London, however, was far better off for intelligence about Jugoslavia. The hand cipher (ISOS) of the Abwehr had been broken in December 1940 and its Enigma cipher (ISK) twelve months later. Both sets of signals were intercepted in the Middle East, re-enciphered and transmitted back to England for breaking. They remained unread in Cairo until a senior SIS officer was installed there in 1942. On his arrival he received ISOS and ISK intelligence from London and divulged items from it to whomsoever he thought appropriate, but never to SOE. However, for reasons not now clear, some material, almost certainly ISOS, was made available to Brigadier Keble, Chief of Staff of SOE Cairo, and two of his officers in January 1943, and was used to plan the parachute drop of Captain (now Sir

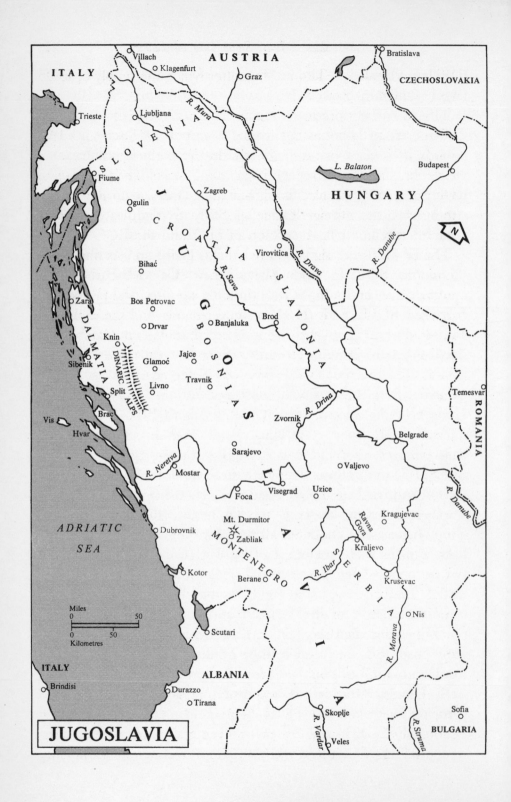

JUGOSLAVIA

William) Deakin to Tito in May, after which the supply of ISOS was withdrawn from SOE.

ISOS had not produced much strategically usable intelligence of interest to London, but from December 1941 onwards ISK released 'a flood of new information' from the traffic between Abwehr outstations in Jugoslavia and Abwehr headquarters in Germany. SIS received it all, but none was sent to the service ministries, the Foreign Office or SOE. Summaries of it were passed to Churchill, the Chiefs of Staff and the JIC.

Since Hudson's signals were sent to Cairo and forwarded to London, SOE in both places knew his views; the most informative items in SOE London's file for this period are marked BULLSEYE (Hudson's cover-name) and the same will no doubt have been the case in Cairo. But whereas Cairo as yet had no strong leaning towards either Tito or Milhailović, but was ready to favour whichever was doing more to thwart the enemy, SOE London was constrained by the Foreign Office's preference (shared by the Chiefs of Staff, whose eyes were focused elsewhere) for King Peter and his London-based government-in-exile. When Lord Glenconner, a senior member of SOE London, was appointed head of SOE Cairo in August 1942 and tried to impose London's views, divergences began to appear and tension between them to mount. The divergence and the tension soon mounted all the more for another reason too. As soon as some members of SOE Cairo – less political and more military than London – saw the ISOS decrypts in January 1943, they became aware for the first time what a powerful case could be made for the Partisans and against Mihailović.

Mihailović had long been inactive (he had warned Britain at the outset that he could do little on his own and would remain quiescent until we could invade in force – this corresponded with the Foreign Office's own expressed preference) and declined during the interim to fulfil General Alexander's request to sabotage the Belgrade–Athens railway and thus cut one of the routes along which Rommel's supplies travelled. On 17 January

1943 one of the first Ultra signals[*] on Balkan military affairs revealed that the Germans and Italians were planning a large-scale operation called WEISS against the Partisans. By May MINCEMEAT showed the Chiefs of Staff recognising that there was a close connexion between events in the eastern and western basins of the Mediterranean.

The slow progress by which British support was switched from Mihailović to Tito began in Cairo that same January; its origin has always been attributed to the new knowledge which SOE Cairo had possessed for the last few months. Early in January, Glenconner's Chief of Staff, Brigadier Keble, handed certain intercepts to two members of his Jugoslav section, Major Davidson and Captain Deakin; they were presumably among the ISOS intercepts now being decrypted in Cairo, which showed the Partisans to be more actively fighting the occupation forces than had hitherto been realised.[†] Keble based a report on them which he showed to Churchill when he passed through Cairo at the end of January 1943. Churchill's interest was

---

[*] ISOS and ISK decrypts are still classified secret and are not in the Public Record Office. The Ultra signals in the PRO are all from army, navy and air decrypts.

[†] The old story that Keble had access to Ultra at this time because he had been entitled to Ultra in his previous appointment and had somehow managed to keep himself on the secret list can be discredited on several grounds. (1) Security regulations limiting the circulation of Ultra were so strictly enforced (new regulations had been promulgated five months previously to ensure extra secrecy for the news that Rommel was ill, for instance) that breach of them in Keble's case is highly improbable, in spite of the lukewarm support which BI iii/1.141n gives to it. (2) Sir Peter Wilkinson, who was set by General Gubbins, executive head of SOE, to keep an eye on Keble during the latter part of 1943, authorises me to say that he has no reason to dissent from my reconstruction of events. See now Wilkinson's account in his *Foreign Fields*, 132–7. (3) Mrs Annette Street, who was Keble's secretary between February and November 1943, assures me that she had access to Keble's safe and recalls no secret file containing information not available to her in the normal course of duty. (4) Only three army/air Ultra signals, none of which carried information about the Partisans' activities, had been sent to Cairo by mid-January 1943. See now also Peter Wilkinson and Joan Bright Astley, *Gubbins and SOE*, 132–6.

aroused, and when he returned to London he handed the report to Selborne, the head of SOE.

It is plain from the revelation that Churchill had been made aware more than twelve months earlier of the Abwehr Enigma decrypts convicting Mihailović of collaboration with the German occupying forces that Keble's report can have told him nothing new. He and the Chiefs of Staff had obviously paid little attention to these decrypts, however, for several reasons, including the impossibility of acting on them at that stage and sympathy with the exiled King Peter and with Mihailović himself. Keble's action, it has usually been said, was motivated as much by the hope of advancing his own career as by a genuine desire to spread new intelligence. This may have been the case, but in the event it merely served as a stimulus to action on a far larger scale than Keble could have anticipated. In the post-Alamein climate, still more after the whole southern shore of the Mediterranean had been cleared of the enemy in May 1943 and HUSKY was being prepared, Churchill and the Chiefs were much less ready to be governed by old loyalties and much more inclined to support a side whose aims coincided with their own. A decision between Tito and Mihailović was becoming urgent, quite independently of anything in Keble's report.

Tension between London and Cairo over which side to support mounted throughout the summer of 1943, with the latter advocating the immediate transfer of support to the Partisans and the former still wedded to Mihailović for mainly political reasons. The decisive stage, with direct personal contact replacing dependence on Sigint evidence, began when Deakin and Captain Stuart of SIS (who was killed almost at once) were parachuted to Tito on a fact-finding mission in May and at once began reporting back that Tito was fighting hard but that Mihailović was collaborating with the Germans. In the post-Alamein and post-HUSKY climate, the Chiefs of Staff soon came to accept the natural inference – to support one but not the other; and when Brigadier Fitzroy Maclean, despatched to Tito by Churchill with a political as well as a military brief, composed a report in November which firmly advocated directing all aid to Tito and withdrawing it from Mihailović, the die was finally cast. By the end of 1943 the necessary action had begun.

Contemporary German sources confirm that, if the object of British policy was to cause maximim embarrassment to the Germans, then by the autumn of 1943 the time was ripe for a transfer of support to the Partisans. Hermann Neubacher, Hitler's Plenipotentiary in Serbia and Montenegro from August 1943, soon became convinced that the Partisans were gaining ground everywhere and that, having disarmed most of the Italian occupying forces in September and October and taken over their weapons, they were becoming a formidable fighting force, while the German policy of repression was increasingly counter-productive. Mihailović's support, on the other hand, was disintegrating, several groups regularly collaborating with the Germans. In October 1943 von Weichs, the new Supreme Commander South-east, told Hitler, 'Tito is our most dangerous enemy.'

Sigint never again wielded the influence over the course of events in Jugoslavia which it had exercised in late 1943. One of its last major contributions was to pass on an estimate by Army Group B (during its brief reign in the northern Balkans) that Partisan strength along the Dalmatian coast was between 160,000 and 200,000; a month later Fitzroy Maclean assessed Tito's supporters at 200,000 or more, that is to say, at a figure of the same order of magnitude. While neither figure can be regarded as more than a guesstimate, the approximate mutual confirmation is interesting. The strength of the Axis occupation forces is still a matter of dispute. Before the Italian withdrawal, their combined strength was some thirty or thirty-five divisions; thereafter, when the Germans were on their own, they could spare only a fluctuating handful of six or seven weak German divisions (which, however, included one first-rate Panzer division, the SS Prinz Eugen) backed up by several non-divisional units, some of considerable firepower, and by a slightly smaller number of Bulgarian and other satellite divisions of poor quality.

While it was possible to keep track of the movements of these troops into and out of particular areas and their participation in successive drives against the Partisans, nothing emerged from the considerable bulk of Ultra traffic which bore at all closely on the vexed question of the numbers at the disposal of either Tito or Mihailović; and, although it is clear that the Y Service could read Partisan and related ciphers, nothing has yet been revealed about the significance of the intelligence thus obtained, nor of that provided by the British liaison officers and the SIS.

A Balkan Air Force HQ was established at Bari in southern Italy in June 1944, and SOE soon joined it.[*] Together they did good work in increasing the flow of supplies to Tito. But it must be remembered that at no time was an operational Allied force permanently established on Jugoslav soil, so that the degree to which intelligence could be used there was severely limited.

Despite plentiful intelligence from a variety of sources (among which SIS must increasingly be counted, along with others already mentioned), the strategic consequences of the recognition of Tito and the Partisans are hard to assess. Any thought there may ever have been of co-ordinating military action on the two sides of the Adriatic soon foundered on American suspicion of British designs in the Balkans, Tito's reluctance to dilute his authority and his brief flirtation with Moscow (whither he suddenly flew without explanation in August 1944) and Anglo-American preoccupation with Italy and the west. Wider considerations apart, Alexander and Mark Clark were much too busy tackling stubborn German resistance and keeping up the pressure on Kesselring with constantly depleted resources to take much thought for Tito, and were content to leave SOE to

[*] SOE's Operation CLOWDER penetrated into German-held territory in Austria during the winter of 1944–5. It was led by Sir Peter Wilkinson, who describes it in *Foreign Fields* (I.B. Tauris, 1977), 167–211. See also pp. 223–33 on Trieste.

organise supply-dropping with the Balkan Air Force in Bari. Not until British and Partisan troops raced each other for Trieste in the first days of May 1945, and General Harding's (commander of XIII Corps) adroit mixture of firmness and tact averted what might easily have become an awkward clash between them, did Allied and Partisan interests seriously impinge upon each other again.[*]

Even though they became much stronger in 1944 and 1945, the Partisans were still not the only reason for the presence of German troops in Jugoslavia, however. 'A' Force continued to encourage Hitler's conviction that in Allied eyes Italy was only the springboard for a leap into the Balkans, so that he must therefore keep troops there to counter a landing. But whether these would have been sufficient to affect the fate of SHINGLE, ANVIL or OVERLORD if they had been moved to Italy or the west must remain extremely doubtful.

It is sometimes said that intelligence in Italy was very different from what the British and Americans had experienced in Africa, because the mountains made it more difficult to intercept long-range radio traffic and because the greater proximity of the front lines to each other led to the more frequent capture and interrogation of prisoners than before. Provided the continuing, even increased, value of strategic information like that which revealed Hitler's hesitant decision about the conduct of the Italian campaign in the autumn of 1943 and its bearing on matters like the ANVIL discussions later (see p. 237–8) is not overlooked, there is much truth in this generalisation. For a number of converging reasons tactical intelligence was greater in volume and more useful in content than hitherto.

[*] A few years ago a violent controversy raged in newspapers, learned journals and on television about the relative merits of support for Mihailović and Tito. Five of us, with widely different sources of knowledge, nevertheless found that our views converged very closely. We published a statement to this effect in INS 10. 527–9 in July 1995. It is reprinted as Appendix IV.

More prisoner interrogation meant that the relief of one division by another was more quickly recognised and its possible operational implications spotted. In 1945, 12 Army Group, which had controlled United States formations in the west, went as far as to say that it had found prisoner interrogation the most satisfactory of all sources of tactical intelligence. Growing maturity on the part of the partially trained Y Service contingents which had come straight from Britain or America for TORCH led HQ staffs to rely on them more; this became of great significance when experienced Eighth Army divisions left Italy to prepare for OVERLORD at home before Christmas 1943. During the fighting on the Winter Line which guarded Rome, for instance, British and American Y Service units monitored the traffic of the best and most mobile German divisions like the Hermann Göring, 26 Panzer and 3 Panzer Grenadier, and gained much useful information as a result. Similarly, in periods of movement like that which shifted the front from Cassino to Rome in June and July 1944, Flivos (Air Liaison Officers) yielded much useful information about the movements of Panzer divisions through decrypts of their reports sent in Enigma. The only blot on all this was that it also revealed careless insecurity on the part of Allied (mainly American) operators which brought similar joy to the German Y Service right down to the end of the war.

New, and not always satisfactory, arrangements were made by SIS and its American counterpart, the Office of Strategic Services (OSS), for agents to supply intelligence – something which had been out of the question in Africa – but little of what they supplied has been published. Significant advances were made in photo-interpretation. Each corps and division was soon provided with its own interpretation unit, thus increasing the speed with which aerial reconnaissance could be turned to account; this became particularly significant as the eventually tremendous preponderance of Allied air power grew evident. Germany was obliged to move aircraft from the Mediterranean theatre to Russia in an effort to stem losses on the eastern front; the consequent reduction of PR on the Italian front was plain to see, while the Allies could increase theirs at will. Once again, one side became blind and the other's vision more penetrating at much the same moment, and a comparison of Allied with German recce reports, made possible by Ultra, revealed this with startling clarity. The advantage this represented was soon strikingly illustrated. DIADEM, the offensive which at last cracked open the Cassino front, was predicated on transferring the bulk of Eighth Army across the Apennines in order to create the 3:1 superiority in numbers which was thought necessary to ensure success. The move was of course carried out mainly at night and in great secrecy. But it was reassuring to know from Ultra that not a single German recce plane had noticed what had happened.

By the time the Allied advance reached the Winter Line which Kesselring had hastily prepared, both sides were exhausted. To break the ensuing deadlock plans were made, though on too small a scale to promise much success, for a diversionary landing south of Rome, but these were abandoned towards the end of November. At Churchill's insistence they were revived and enlarged about Christmas, and a landing at Anzio set to take place before the end of January. Until early March, when it relapsed into an uneasy calm, there was violent action in the new bridgehead, but the main front remained almost static, though hardly quiescent, until late May. Relative immobility did not mean the absence of action, but the topography of Italy now came strongly to Kesselring's aid as the Allies strove in vain to force the defile at Cassino.

Usable intelligence was consequently on the small scale described above, and there is little worthy of record save the assistance provided by the Polish intercept section in the final capture of the monastery. No intelligence justified the bombing of the monastery on 15 February, which went ahead although there was no proof that German troops were occupying it (they were not), and although an *en clair* intercept showed that the abbot was still in residence. (The intercept was taken as proof of military occupation until a senior intelligence officer pointed out that 'Abt' is the German word for 'abbot' as well as the standard abbreviation of *Abteilung*, 'detachment'.)

SHINGLE, the landing at Anzio on 22 January 1944, gained strategic surprise, and almost tactical surprise as well. Kesselring felt no more apprehensive about that part of the coast than any other, and no sizeable German force was either in Rome or between Rome and the coast at Anzio – indeed, as the OKW War Diary later admitted, Rome itself was 'to all intents and purposes unguarded' at that moment. But was a quick advance to the Alban Hills, which dominate the route along which a force retreating from Cassino would have to pass, or even the capture of Rome itself, the object of SHINGLE? The bridgehead at Anzio lengthened the German front by 50 per cent, and so stretched enemy resources that he was compelled to bring down reinforcements to prevent an Allied breakthrough, but Alexander's orders for the exploitation of a successful landing were ambiguous. General Lucas, the American commander, has often been criticised for sluggishness,* but it was the reserves he had accumulated which repelled Kesselring's determined efforts to wipe the bridgehead out in February.

From the intelligence point of view, one of the most interesting features of the defence of the Anzio bridgehead is the way it illustrates both the variety of intelligence and the conflict of evidence. A small undercover OSS intelligence group was established in Rome just before the landing. Its head, Peter Tompkins, was provided with a radio for the purpose of communicating with the US VI Corps in the bridgehead; how he managed to make contact five times a day, sometimes transmitting long messages, for five weeks on end without being

---

* However, he had not been told about Ultra until a few hours before he landed.

detected by D/F is only one of the mysteries of his story. Tompkins's bravery and devotion to duty are not in question, but much of the information gathered by his network of agents was inaccurate and potentially misleading. He repeatedly reported that a heavy counter-attack would come from the direction of Pratica di Mare, some fifteen miles north-west of Anzio on the left flank of the bridgehead. Ultra consistently pointed to an attack straight down the road from Albano through Aprilia, and this proved correct. Fortunately Lucas and his successor, Truscott, completely ignored the erroneous forecast and prepared themselves to withstand Kesselring's thrust down the road; VI Corps did not, of course, receive Ultra direct, but in disguised form via Alexander's HQ.

The Anzio landing produced some notable intelligence triumphs. In order to reduce opposition to it, Fifth Army attacked across the River Garigliano, where the front line then lay, a few days before the landing. Almost at once General von Senger und Etterlin, commanding the German XIV Corps, was crying out for reinforcements for his sector of the defences, and Ultra began tracing how in response Kesselring was commiting his last resources to support him (the divisions in question had to move back north again in the next day or two, thus fruitlessly using up scarce stocks of petrol and diesel fuel). Next came the revelation that plans were being made to 'drive the invaders back into the sea' in accordance with Hitler's demands, followed by Kesselring's operational orders to this end, and a statement of the number of tanks available for the purpose. Thus forewarned, the defenders could prepare themselves to resist at the point where they knew that the attack would come, and were soon able to bring it to a halt. After much bitter fighting, by 1 March Kesselring concluded that he could do nothing but accept that the bridgehead had come to stay. To him, as also to the Allies, it was becoming plain that Italy was a secondary theatre, and that he would have to surrender troops to the greater needs of the

Russian front as they to OVERLORD; but in explaining how he would nevertheless try to prevent the Allies from gaining any more ground he revealed his future strategy: to hasten on the construction of a defence line in the mountains north of Florence. This was known in London and at Allied HQ, Caserta, by 9 February. It was warmly welcomed in both, particularly by the British CIGS, Brooke, for it enabled him to urge on the sceptical Americans the desirability of pressing forward the attack on the new fortifications. Intelligence had unquestionably again penetrated the highest levels of strategic planning.

Two months now elapsed before the DIADEM offensive opened on 11 May; Rome fell on 4 June. During this period the integration of operations and intelligence at the tactical level was as complete as at the strategic. Both forms of Sigint were exceptionally productive, and so was prisoner interrogation, so that the identity of the divisions occupying the front line could often be confirmed from three separate sources. If order of battle could be checked daily in this way, so could divisional strengths from twice-weekly tank returns and intermittent statements of divisional commanders' assessment of the battle-readiness of their divisions according to a new four-point *pro forma* ranging from 'ready to take the offensive' to 'fit only for static defence' (it was noticeable that very few qualified for the first category). From all this intelligence it was possible to deduce with absolute confidence that Kesselring was so misled by his own preconceptions, by rumours of new coastal landings circulated by the Allies, and by his determiantion not to be caught out again as he had been at Anzio, that he was doing nothing to protect his lines at the points where the blows would soon fall and was in fact diverting some of his best troops to fruitless coast-defence duties.

Almost unchallenged air power could inflict heavy damage on supply bases and communications, while new precision-bombing techniques made attacks on pinpoint targets like bridges across narrow valleys practicable. Though great inconvenience was thereby caused to the enemy, who had to divert manpower to repair gangs which were constantly busy, the complete isolation of the front from its bases in the rear was never achieved; the appreciation (already quoted; see p. 164) of the results of the DIADEM bombing campaign by Sir John Slessor, Deputy Commander of the Mediterranean Air Force, explained why this was impossible. The conclusion is inescapable: by showing how ill-prepared Kesselring was for effective defence, Sigint and PR paved the way for the great Allied advance and make it easier to understand why it was several days after heavy fighting began before he realised that he was facing a major offensive.

Alexander ordered VI Corps to break out of the Anzio bridgehead and link up with the forces advancing from the main front on 27 May. Within a few days Mark Clark had shifted its axis northwards towards Rome instead of straight ahead eastwards to cut the Via Casilina (Route 6), block Kesselring's line of retreat and effect a junction with the main body. Except for the discovery and quick exploitation of an unguarded sector in the hills which facilitated the switch, intelligence played no part in Clark's much disputed decision.

Contrary to what might have been expected, the capture of Rome did not release any accumulated diplomatic or military intelligence from the heart of German-occupied territory, the tiny neutral Vatican City centred round St Peter's, nor had any been received from it during the preceding four years. Soon after Italy had entered the war in 1940, the Italian police snuffed out any chance that foreign diplomats accredited to the Holy See might send useful information back to their home governments. Instead, the diplomats became, it has been said, 'virtual prisoners' for four years. D'Arcy Osborne, the British Ambassador, was allowed out only once – to see a religious film – after several times being refused permission to go into Rome; they were forbidden to send coded cables, and their diplomatic bags were opened and searched instead of being allowed to pass with unbroken seals as in time of peace. They were allowed to communicate with home through the papal bags, but they suspected that their letters were censored and in any case the roundabout route the bags took made transit-time inordinately long: using deliberately circumspect language Osborne told Eden in February 1941, 'I have not entire faith in my communications either by bag or by cipher telegram.' Many escaping Allied prisoners-of-war made for the Vatican and were secretly given refuge, but the information they possessed was already stale before they reached even this degree of safety.

The hope that the tide of victory would carry the Allied armies past Rome and enable them to keep the disorganised enemy on the run as far as the Po and beyond (even perhaps deep into Austria) taxed the Allied armies to the limit. The loss of more divisions, this time to the ANVIL landing in the south of France on 15 August, finally signified the reduction of Italy to a secondary theatre. But Alexander did not accept his fate without a fight.

The German intention to construct another defence line in the Apennines north of Florence had been known from Ultra since October 1943, when Rommel (then in command of Army Group B) was ordered to reconnoitre an 'Apennine position'. Subsequent intercepts showed that what was now called the Gothic Line was still unfinished in June 1944 (two assessments by Kesselring's Chief Engineer were confirmed by PR), when Hitler angrily declared that it was 'the final blocking position barring entry to the Lombard plain' and ordered Kesselring to retreat as slowly as possible in order to give time for the fortifications to be completed.

Once more Ultra influenced strategic discussion at the highest level, but it was too late. British and Americans were already locked in argument about ANVIL, the latter urging it on the ground that it would relieve pressure on Eisenhower and the Normandy battle (which had lately seemed bogged down) and that Hitler would soon tell Kesselring to retire to the protection of the Alps, the former arguing that ANVIL forces could be found only by weakening the Italian front, that Hitler would defend every inch of ground as he had done before, and that better and quicker results would be achieved by keeping up the maximum pressure in Italy. Brooke and Churchill now sought to end the argument in their favour by quoting Hitler, but in vain. The Americans remained adamant, and ANVIL was given the go-ahead on 2 July. Just fifteen days later, and only forty-eight hours after the ANVIL landing, Hitler ordered the immediate evacuation of southern France; the Ultra signal revealing this was solid proof that from the military point of view ANVIL (now rechristened DRAGOON) had been a wholly mistaken diversion of effort from a major to a minor objective. So far from leaching away some of the opposition to Eisenhower, it had sent such troops as there were in the south of France scuttling back north to help stanch the wounds which the battle of the Falaise gap was already causing. Had the ANVIL divisions remained in Italy they might well have made the breaching of the Gothic Line and the defeat of Kesselring possible in 1944, thus opening the way for Alexander to fulfil his dream of turning the flank of the Reich defences by marching on Vienna. Churchill had aleady told Roosevelt that ANVIL would be 'the first major strategic and political error for which we two have to be responsible'.

To fulfil his determination to push forward quickly in spite of his reduced strength, Alexander proposed a new offensive (OLIVE) only a short time after the fall of Rome. The first step would be an assault on the Gothic Line north of Florence. General Leese (commanding Eighth Army after Montgomery's recall to direct OVERLORD) objected, and at a hasty meeting with Alexander and his Chief of Staff, Harding, on Orvieto airfield on 25 July persuaded them that it would be better to transfer Eighth Army back to the Adriatic coast (this was achieved unobserved in mid-August) where the defences were known to be least ready, and drive hard for the Romagna plain instead of dashing their heads against the mountains. Some progress was made, but by late September Leese's advance was slowing down against stubborn German resistance on the line of each of the rivers which flow across the Romagna plain to the Adriatic.

Why was this not foreseen? No relevant intelligence seems to have survived. But it is legitimate to wonder why no one had studied a map carefully enough to recognise the risk, whether the extensive PR which showed the unfinished state of the Adriatic end of the Gothic Line did not also show that the high flood-banks of half a dozen rivers a few miles apart offered admirable defensive opportunities despite the 'good tank country' between them, and why no one who knew the area was asked for his opinion.

If apparently unforeseen topographical problems hindered the Allies, a shortage of supplies and fully trained soldiers shackled the Germans. Although Kesselring now had more than a million men under arms, some of his best divisions were known to be suffering more casualties than new drafts could make good, while low fuel stocks and irregular deliveries were so restricting air operations that Luftflotte 2 could not manage more than a dozen or two sorties a day. And yet the defence held. Perhaps it was this which made the Allied command in Italy less susceptible in late August and early September to the over-optimism which briefly infected Whitehall and the West. OLIVE lost momentum in September at much the same time as 12 and 21 Army Groups were crossing the Seine and (as they thought) pursuing a beaten enemy up to and beyond the frontiers of his Fatherland. Arnhem ended the westerners' daydream, but in Italy the Allied commanders remained ruefully wide awake as Fifth Army ground to a halt in the mountains a tantalising five miles short of Bologna and Eighth Army stopped a little north of Ravenna. Exhaustion and bad weather finally closed operations down in December.

Although the purpose of the Italian campaign had never been

the conquest of territory but rather to attract the greatest possible volume of German resources in men and material away from other theatres, the occupied area had doubled between June and October and with it a more than proportional fraction of the population – a more settled and urbanised population, and one of European descent moreover, which therefore presented the occupying force with problems quite different from those which had been met in Africa or even Sicily. This distinction from the past was sharpened in another way too. Because the Luftwaffe was now so weak that it could not undertake enough aerial reconnaissance to discover any hint of Allied intentions, and because the Germans could read none but the lowest-grade Allied ciphers, the enemy was forced back upon agents – whether line-crossers, stay-behinds or parachuted in – as his main source of intelligence. His position was thus not unlike that of Britain in 1939 and most of 1940, but more difficult to deal with because there was now continuous contact along a land front instead of separation by the English Channel.

To satisfy their needs the Germans set up agent-training schools in Lombardy and Piedmont, but quantity rather than quality was the hallmark of most graduates. Many were equipped with identical revolvers and briefcases, and this blew their cover as soon as it was noticed. All fifteen students on one Abwehr training course were later rounded up and put in prison: a group photograph was taken to mark the occasion. The gullibility of some agents and still more of their superiors, and the depths of incompetence to which German intelligence sank after the dismissal of Canaris in February 1944 and the transfer of the Abwehr to Himmler, is suggested by a report which was thought worthy of Himmler's personal attention: it alleged that in January 1945 (that is, just as strenuous Anglo-American efforts had recovered the ground lost in the Battle of the Bulge) there were still 400,000 troops waiting in English coast harbours for a descent on Denmark!

To detect, apprehend and interrogate the agents who now

pullulated in every sector of the Italian front, a threefold system was soon devised. Field Security sections operated between the rear of the battle front and the Rear Army Control Line some miles back (it moved forward by stages as the battle front advanced, leaving everything behind it to AMGOT, the Allied Military Government of Occupied Territories). They ranged their allotted sectors seeking out suspicious characters and set up road blocks to check traffic and detain travellers who lacked the proper permits, sending the more involved cases back to Counter-Intelligence (CI) units for unmasking and possible 'turning' into double agents who could be played back to mislead the enemy. The success of Counter-Intelligence in doing this was illustrated by an incident shortly after the German surrender in May 1945. The British Colonel in charge of CI interviewed SS General Wolff, who had commanded police and security troops in Italy. With a confident air Wolff proclaimed, 'I had seven agent teams in the south, reporting to me by radio.' The instant riposte was crushing: 'I'm sorry, General, every one of them was working for us.' Finally, the Combined Service Detailed Interrogation Centre dealt with the most intransigent captives of all, squeezing out the last scraps of useful information.

Agents adopted various ruses to protect themselves from discovery. Several managed to get hold of a flock of sheep and in the guise of shepherds tried to bluff their way through the front lines in pursuit of legitimate business, like the practitioners of transhumance moving from summer to winter pasture in earlier centuries; others represented themselves as seeking to get back to their homes on the other side of the lines, and these might be returning from a mission laden with news. Not for the first time, brothels were found to be useful sources of information: 417 Field Security Section (which moved with Eighth Army across the Apennines from east to west and back again) interrupted business at the brothel in Aquila, high in the mountains east of Rome, one day shortly after the Germans evacuated the town. They were searching for Nadia Bufarina, a prostitute suspected (rightly) of having betrayed British prisoners who had escaped after the Italian surrender, and the peasants who had protected them. Nadia was off duty that day, but she was soon traced with the help of her workmate Gina. Gina had been forced into prostitution by the Germans for a minor offence some time before, and was willing to display her credentials as one who had unwillingly lost her amateur status by showing off her fiancé's name tattooed over her left breast. Unfortunately, Nadia did not suffer for her sins; higher authority released her on a legal technicality.

The vigour with which anti-agent measures were prosecuted and the severity of the punishments inflicted (death or prolonged internment) had the desired effect. No agent returned north with information of sufficient military value for it to be used in operations, nor was there any significant act of sabotage in Allied territory. On the other hand, every interrogation was likely to turn up something which could assist counter-intelligence to make another arrest.

In sum, the Germans' expenditure of time, trouble and manpower was rendered almost wholly worthless. Field Security and Counter-Intelligence together kept the rear army area clear, thus enhancing the value of 'straight' intelligence by frustrating hostile designs and averting any need to divert men from the front line to mop up behind the lines as the enemy was forced to do in even greater measure after the Italian partisans became a far more formidable fighting force during the last few months of the war.

The Italians' change of sides in September 1943 led to the appearance of scattered anti-German resistance groups which Kesselring was already finding a thorn in his side by April 1944, but their greatest expansion came after the fall of Rome in June. From that time onwards the groups gradually coalesced into divisions and brigades, and Kesselring began a series of ever more stringent measures (at least one of which was detected by Ultra) against them. These culminated with the despatch of the notoriously brutal 162 ('Mongol') Division, which burned, raped and murdered its way through Piedmont and Liguria in the winter and spring of 1944–5 but without destroying the Resistance there. Recognising, as it had done since mid-1944, the potential usefulness of Italian support, the Allied command authorised SOE and OSS to send liaison officers to Partisan brigades to bring them under Allied control as far as possible, and encourage them to harass German troop movements and disrupt communications. This work was scarcely interrupted by Alexander's instructions, broadcast when the advance was checked in the autumn, that the Partisans should wind down their operations; rather the pause enforced by winter weather was but a prelude to renewed activity in March and April when the Partisans materially assisted the Allies by liberating Genoa, for instance, and engaging German troops on the approaches to Venice.

A great deal of order-of-battle intelligence was accumulated by the Partisans and their British and American liaison officers, and transmitted by clandestine radio to Allied HQs, just as it had been in August by means of the famous telephone line laid under fire across the Ponte Vecchio in Florence by Charles Macintosh of SOE. Unfortunately there seems to be no record of the use to which all this intelligence was put, and it is distressing to reflect that, in spite of the bravery displayed by so many men in collecting it, much must have been simply duplication of what was already known from other and more quickly available sources.

By the time the final Allied advance began in April 1945, Kesselring had been summoned away to conduct a last despairing effort to save the west, and von Vietinghoff had taken his place. An Allied victory was by now so inevitable that there was little need for intelligence to assist it; nevertheless right up to the end much evidence of the fragility of the opposition came in. During the preceding three months tank and gun returns of the now familiar type showed that battle wastage was not being made good by new deliveries and that German commanders' opinion of their divisions' state of training was lower than ever. Ammunition was in such short supply that howitzer batteries were not allowed to fire off more than six rounds a day, and even that, they were told, might soon be in jeopardy; in some areas fuel was so scarce that, as with ammunition, it was possible to calculate how long the enemy could continue to fight and manoeuvre.

Hitler had already tied Kesselring's hands by refusing him permission to retire behind the River Po, and it was now discovered that he was restricting von Vietinghoff similarly by ordering that all commanders down to divisional level should report their intended actions to him personally in time for him to countermand them if he thought desirable. Von Vietinghoff proved himself no more skilful than Kesselring in distinguishing between truth and deception in the information he received about Allied plans. That 'A' Force had lost none of its cunning in dispersing German troops unnecessarily was discernible from Ultra decrypts; a particularly striking example was the diversion of a large part of 29 Panzer Grenadier Division to coast-watching north of the Po, where Alexander had no intention of attempting a landing because he (but evidently not von Vietinghoff) had learned that the water was too shallow for the purpose. A fortnight before the end von Vietinghoff signalled its approach in unmistakable terms: continual air attacks had so destroyed signal lines that control was impossible during the greater part of the day, four of his divisions were either exhausted or broken, the only hope of salvation lay in a large enough withdrawal to protect the so-called 'Reich fortress' in Austria.

When Alexander accepted the surrender of the German armies in Italy on 29 April, he was entitled to feel as much satisfaction as when, almost two years before, he had signalled in triumph to Churchill, 'We are masters of the North African shores.' For in spite of repeated reductions in his forces he had won his victory with only three casualties to the five he had inflicted on his enemies, and had gained it a week earlier than Eisenhower, the man who had been responsible for depriving him of divisions at a critical moment.

Continuously over the eighteen months since it had revealed Hitler's intentions for the defence of Italy in October 1943, intelligence – particularly Ultra – had kept Alexander fully informed about what the enemy was up to, what he planned to do next and how well equipped he was to do it. So good had been this guidance that the Italian campaign may rank above North Africa or even the Battle of the Atlantic as the supreme intelligence triumph of the whole war.

1944–1945

Set Fair in the West,
Then Autumn Showers

Just, but only just, in time before D-Day Ultra production at GC&CS became a completely Anglo-American enterprise. Since all Ultra would continue to emanate from Bletchley Park in England, since the land commander was to be a Briton whose supreme self-confidence (not to say arrogance) many Americans had learned to dislike in Tunisia, Sicily and Italy, and since before the end of the year more American than British servicemen would be involved, this was no doubt a timely blessing. Its prophylactic and emollient qualities appear all the greater now it is clear that for the first three months at least after the landings Ultra was an even larger ingredient of intelligence than hitherto.

Co-operation in secret intelligence matters had been delayed throughout the eighteen months which had elapsed since the United States' entry into the war in December 1941 by a combination of circumstances: the very natural fear on the British side that to widen the circle of those privy to the secret that Enigma had been broken would be to multiply the risk of damaging leaks – the Fellers affair of summer 1942 (see p. 95) alone justified this fear – the bitter rivalry between the War and Navy Departments in Washington, which prevented an Ultra-sharing agreement of limited scope arranged to facilitate anti-U-boat operations in the Atlantic from promoting further developments, and a natural American desire to set up its own Ultra centre until a daunting telegram from the head of the first US delegation to Bletchley Park in April 1943 – 'If Corderman of Arlington Hall[*] wants his people to learn what makes this operation tick, he had better send them over to learn it, because they never on God's green earth will learn it from anything Arlington will be able to do in any foreseeable future' – deflated American aspirations. Even an agreement to share information about U-boat movements – a matter of obvious and immediate practical application – which had been proposed earlier, had been held up by American suspicions that the Ultra black-out of February–December 1942 (see pp. 160 and 192–4) was really a British cover-up, not simply the consequence of difficulties arising from the fourth rotor. Confidence was lacking on both sides, and this explains why the British and American authorities concerned spent so long 'walking around each other like two mongrels which have just met', in the words of the official historian[†] of 3US (the collective name of the American party which settled in Hut 3).

Mutual suspicion protracted the delay still further after the American mission already quoted, and it was not until December 1943 that a dozen or so young American army officers arrived at GC&CS to learn about Ultra. There were just six months to go before D-Day, barely enough time for them to familiarise themselves with what had by now become a highly complex business. Some stayed in Hut 3 and by June were sharing the load on equal terms with the British; others were sent, after short visits to Allied commands in the Mediterranean to see how Ultra was used in operations, to the new American headquarters being set up in England and to work out how best to mediate Ultra to generals who were as reluctant to believe in its usefulness as their British counterparts had been three years

[*] Arlington Hall was the American cryptographic establishment.
[†] Lieutenant-Colonel F. W. ('Ted') Hilles, Professor of English at Yale, who acted as a day-to-day head of the American party, under Colonel Telford Taylor, later chief US prosecutor at the Nuremberg Trials.

earlier.* Sufficient was accomplished under both heads to justify the claim that by June 1944 3US had 'come of age'.

Hindsight, that inescapable plague of historians, has been the cause of many misjudgments. Its mellow light blurs the sharp edges of real events, and lends an air of easy inevitability to what were in fact agonising choices between equally appealing alternatives. Thus Eisenhower is remembered rather for post- poning D-Day in 1944 by twenty-four hours on meteorological advice than for his courage in facing the even greater consequent risk of failure: overnight he prepared two communiqués, one announcing a successful landing on the enemy coast, the other a withdrawal in face of insurmountable opposition. Montgomery has often been blamed for slowness round Caen in June and July, although this was probably the one occasion when he was flexible enough to modify his original plan and to avoid both the excessive caution of the post-Alamein weeks and the recklessness of Arnhem. Many accounts insidiously – and perhaps uncon- sciously – make it seem that victory in Europe was always certain. The bitterness of the bombing controversy (see Chapter 4) is enough to show how false this impression is. Everyone knew that the Anglo-US command wielded absolutely overwhelming air power, yet the heated disputes over the best way to employ it reflected fears that all might be lost if the wrong method was chosen. Victory is now often seen as inevitable, but the eleven months between D-Day and the German surrender can best be appreciated if in imagination they are seen as a succession of inscrutably unfolding events and not simply with retrospective wisdom.

* The American system was for a single trained Ultra officer to receive Hut 3's signals and to brief only the general and his senior intelligence officer with their contents; senior British army and air IOs and their immediate staff received the signals and briefed their commanders. At the end of the war the US Ultra officers were required to report on their experiences. SRH–023 at the National Archives, Washington, collects their reports, SRH–006 is an official synthesis of the use of Ultra in the field. Regrettably, there is nothing similar on the British side.

The passage of time has almost erased the memory of one aspect of the anxiety which pervaded the months before D-Day: that Ultra might be lost just when it was most needed. For Ultra was by now far and away the chief source of intelligence, and the possibility that the invasion might be marred by the loss of it, as the fight against the U-boats had been temporarily marred two years earlier, was frightening to contemplate. Yet there were several reasons why it might well disappear. It had never given much information about Germany, because telephone conversations *en clair* were a quicker and better means of communication there than telegrams in cipher. There were plenty of land-lines in France, as there were in Germany, and it was taken for granted that many more would have been laid, so that a similar, or even worse, situation might arise. Only after the war was over did it become apparent that this had never been so; according to General Westphal, Chief of Staff to Field Marshal von Rundstedt, Commander-in-Chief West, insufficient preparations had been made, and in June 1944 a priority message within France might take anything up to twenty-four hours to arrive at its destination.

Hut 3 had begun sending signals to SHAEF, Eisenhower's HQ, in January, but – because of the scarcity of material – at a rate of less than one a day, most of them of no great importance; the daily rate had reached only three or four by the end of May, which was hardly likely to be of much use when hostilities began in earnest. Worst still, cipher change was always on the cards. Army Y might perhaps fill a little of the consequent gap (in fact it did so only very intermittently) but not until after the landing had actually taken place and the interception equipment been landed, that is after the most critical phase. Pre-invasion bombing had more urgent targets than telephone lines, the cutting of which would compel the use of radio, although it seemed that some of the best Ultra was the consequence of raids. Cases in point were the interception of the whole programme of a tour to be made in April and May by General Guderian,

Western and Central Europe

〰〰〰 Approximate front line 30 September 1944

Figures indicate approximate areas
covered by small maps on following pages

Miles
0   100   200

NORTH SEA

Frisian Is.

Emden

Ijmuiden
Amsterdam
THE HAGUE   HOLLAND   Osnabrück

Cardiff   LONDON   Rotterdam   ④   Munster
Bristol   Hamm
                                                               Duisburg
Plymouth   Portsmouth   Dover   Ostend   ⑤   Cologne
                              Dunkirk   Bruges   Antwerp   Siegen
                    Calais   Ghent   Bonn
               Boulogne   Pas de   BRUSSELS   Maastricht   Remag
                                 Calais   Lille   BELGIUM   Aachen
English Channel   Maubeuge   Charleroi   Liège   Koblenz
                                                      Namur   ⑥   Prüm
          Cherbourg   Dieppe   Ardennes
          le Havre   Somme   LUXEMBOURG

               ①   Caen   ②   Seine   Oise   Aisne   Saarbrücken
Avranches   Normandy   Reims   Verdun   Metz
St Malo   ③   Marne   Châlons   Nancy
Brest   sur Marne   Strasbourg
Brittany   Chartres   PARIS   Vosges   Colm
          Rennes   Mulhouse
                    Le Mans   Yonne   Belfort
St Nazaire   Nantes   Tours   Orléans   Vierzon   Dijon   Jura Mts   BERN

                    Loire   SWITZE

          Poitiers   FRANCE
Bay   la Pallice   Vichy
of   Limoges   Geneva
Biscay   Lyons
                    Massif   Grenoble   Turin
          Bordeaux   Central   Vercors
                    Garonne   Anvil Dragoon
                                                                   15 August 1944
     Bayonne   Toulouse   Canne
SPAIN   Pyrenees   Rhône   Marseilles
                                               Toulon

Inspector-General of Panzer Troops, to the bases of all the Panzer divisions in France and to the tank training ground at Mailly-le-Camp (eighty miles west of Paris), from which much information about the strength, equipment and readiness for battle of the German armour was derived. In spite of forebodings and the relative paucity of information, however, by the first week of June Ultra had located all the German divisions in France, and supplementary details about many of them had been added by the French Resistance. The only serious gaps were news of the most recent movements of 352 Division, which later held up the US First Army on Omaha Beach, and of 21 Panzer, which represented the most immediate mobile threat to the British left flank on 6 June.

News like this was as tantalising as it was welcome. Would more of the same follow? I have vivid memories of the tension that built up. Having been on duty during the evening of 5 June, knowing what was about to happen, I had to wait a frustrating twenty-four hours until my next shift to discover that our fears had mercifully been groundless. The first Enigma messages had been decrypted soon after midnight and signalled before dawn. 6 Airborne Division's capture of the Bénouville bridge over the River Orne, thus blocking German access to the British left flank, was reported by early afternoon, and the first orders for air reinforcement an hour or two later. Some twenty operational messages in all were received on 6 June, and the number rose steadily thereafter.

The exclusive merit of Ultra was its capacity to keep a finger on the pulse of German strategy. Its tactical contribution (as the above examples suggest) turned out to be greater in France than it had been in Africa or Italy, and it sometimes usurped Y's position in this respect. No other source could rival it, though others could at times give valuable information provided that obstacles to delivering it before time destroyed its value could be overcome.

The operational value of Ultra is attested by Directive 590

issued by Group Captain Jones, Head of Hut 3, on 25 January 1944 (PRO. HW3. 124). It reads in part: 'Many of our old customers, "Monty" in particular, demanded an immediate service of information "on which we plan our battles" . . . so we have begun signalling to SHAEF and 21 Army Group at once.'

The form of words, and the use of quotation marks, both imply that Jones was repeating words he had himself heard, no doubt from Brigadier Williams, Montgomery's Chief Intelligence Officer, who had given a lecture in Hut 3 that morning (Directive 598).

In February 1942, as one of his last actions before handing over to von Rundstedt in March, the then Commander-in-Chief West toured the Channel coast from Cherbourg to Le Havre to determine what defensive works were needed. SEALION had not long been shelved for good, but already an Anglo-American assault on German-occupied Europe was at least a theoretical possibility. Plans for the fortifications were quickly drawn up, and the Organisation Todt set to work. The offices the builders commandeered in Caen needed minor repair and redecoration, and in May a young Frenchman, René Duchez, a painter by trade and already the leader of the local Resistance, was seeking a contract for part of the work. The Todt officer interviewing him was called from the room for a few moments, and Duchez found himself alone with a map of the proposed defences of Normandy. He managed to remove it undetected, and thus began a train of events which got it to London before a single blockhouse had been completed and even before the Anglo-American command had finally settled on the landing-place: an intelligence coup of the first magnitude which showed the mettle of the nascent Resistance and proved of the greatest value in preparing for OVERLORD.

Improvements and additions were always likely, particularly after Hitler commissioned Rommel to investigate progress in

November 1943 and later gave him charge of coastal defences. Rommel's proposals too reached London via the Resistance, but regular air reconnaissance kept a constant watch on what was being done, above all when beach obstructions began to appear in the spring. There was one limitation to air recce, however; the ten million or more prints which were made by D-Day could not tell what was inside the buildings photographed – as the US Rangers discovered when they found no guns in the Pointe du Hoc battery, their target on 6 June 1944. Expert geologists from the universities had already been consulted about the comparative firmness of various beaches and about relative gradients consequent upon differences in composition (poor information on these points had impeded the tanks at Dieppe), so that the most suitable beaches (quick and easy exit was another important desideratum) within the Baie du Seine might be chosen for the initial assault. Their generalised conclusions had to be checked yard by yard and detail by detail to prevent as far as possible the inadvertent imposition of intolerable handicaps on the first wave of troops. This difficult task was carried out by courageous men in midget submarines and small boats, who brought back samples of sand from night-time expeditions without once by their interest betraying to the Germans any hint of the chosen landing-places. Behind all this lay the Inter-Services Topographical Department, an active clearing-house for the collection of, and research into, every kind of information about the terrain over which the invading forces would pass.

Examples like these illustrate the depth and complexity of the intelligence required and the integration of a variety of sources to make the conclusions drawn from it as complete and as reliable as possible.

Although its main, self-imposed task was to prepare the way for anti-German action at the right moment (thus demonstrating the fallacy of 'setting Europe ablaze' – only in Jugoslavia, where Tito did not care what reprisals followed his actions, because he was, or thought he was, furthering the cause of a higher international cause, Muscovite communism, would an oppressed population rise spontaneously before Anglo-American landings showed that help was on the way).* The French Resistance was often able to supply valuable military intelligence. 'I'm the head of an intelligence service,' proclaimed Marie-Madeleine Fourcade, who took over what became known as the Noah's Ark Resistance organisation after its founder was arrested, and considered her chief function to be that of supplying intelligence to the British General Staff to make up for the eclipse of the SIS after the Venlo débâcle. All the intelligence that Noah's Ark and similar groups (Rémy, which was responsible for the map of the Atlantic Wall, is said by some to have been the most fruitful) supplied reached England through SIS channels, but in almost every case the initiative was French, not English. French telephone engineers, for instance, tapped into the Paris–Metz cable in April 1942 and sent transcripts of messages between German HQs in Paris and Berlin until they were caught and shot in December. French and Belgian railway workers reported

---

* The case of the Vercors in July 1944 shows another aspect of the fallacy. The steep sides of the Vercors plateau, thirty miles long and twelve wide, 3,000 feet above sea-level south-west of Grenoble, offered an ideal defensive position. Yet it fell in a week to the first serious German assault upon the Resistance group which held it, mounted by two (low-grade) divisions and a striking force of 200 SS men in gliders and supported by the Luftwaffe group, Geschwader Bongart, which had been specially set up for anti-Resistance operations. The defenders were equipped only with small arms; a successful defence required artillery, yet the weight of guns and shells (and a regular supply of both) precluded more than occasional air drops several hundred miles into enemy-occupied territory (automatic weapons and ammunition were, however, provided on as large a scale as could be managed). A general rising did in fact take place, though quite when and on whose (certainly local) authority is obscure. The timing was unfortunate: three weeks later the rising would have coincided with the Falaise battle rather than with the stalemate outside Caen; a month later it might have seemed a diversionary measure to distract attention from ANVIL/DRAGOON only a hundred miles to the south; in either case the chances of success would have been much greater. But the chief lesson is that the deepest appeal of a guerrilla movement is to hearts and minds, not to the holding of territory.

train movements – even the movement of a single empty truck might yield clues to the transfer of a Panzer division from, say, Brittany to the Pas de Calais – on a sufficient scale for a special section to be created at COSSAC (the predecessor of SHAEF) to catalogue and analyse it. If the original value of this type of information was mainly for order of battle, it later showed which were the most favoured transport routes, and hence which rail junctions it would best pay to put out of action by bombing or sabotage in order to cripple troop movements.

Here, and on similar occasions, intelligence and operations are inextricably linked. The three little girls who put a mixture of grease and grit into the axle-boxes of the railway flat cars waiting to transport the tanks of 2 SS Panzer Division from Toulouse to the battle area were committing an act of sabotage (the axles seized up when the trains moved), but tracking the delays with which the Maquis afflicted the division on its enforced journey by road was an intelligence matter. Similarly, the greater part of II SS Panzer Corps had to detrain at Nancy, and took four times as long to reach Caen from the Franco-German border as it had spent on the journey from Russia to the border. In each case prior knowledge of some of the stages in the division's adversities enabled Montgomery to get in attacks before reinforcements could strengthen the opposition. The consequence could be read from the Ultra signals the fighting generated. The artillery barrage which greeted the arrival of 9 SS Panzer Division was so severe that one of its officers has become famous for quoting Dante's *Inferno* to express his feelings: 'Abandon hope all ye who enter here.'

In addition to its very considerable value in the long term, the intelligence provided by clandestine sources in occupied France helped those planning the invasion in two ways. In the first place it distinguished tactical targets which could profitably be attacked from those of less moment. Almost a thousand nodal points on the French railways damage to which would disrupt transport had been identified by D-1; almost all were bombed or sabotaged next day. This was one of several advantages the Transportation Plan had over its longer-range strategic rival. The very efficient German repair gangs could replace damaged track before serious harm to Germany's war economy could occur, but a stretch near the front could not be mended quickly enough to permit the movement of reinforcements to the point where they were urgently needed, with immediate effect on operations. The other advantage, often conferred by information from the Resistance, prisoner interrogation and the like, was that of providing satisfactory cover for high-grade Sigint. Intelligence known to be absolutely reliable because it came from Ultra could safely be passed right down the chain of command once it had also been noted in a prisoner's statement or a Resistance report, without in any way endangering the secret that Enigma had been broken.

The best known of all the ways in which the Germans were put off the scent during the spring of 1944 is deception, the 'bodyguard of lies' which protected OVERLORD through a network of double agents. Rather unfairly, less emphasis is frequently given to the Mulberry artificial harbours which, however unintentionally, were the first of the deception measures because they unbalanced the enemy's judgment long before FUSAG (Patton's notional First United States Army Group) seemed to threaten the Pas de Calais. German appreciations were still restating the obvious – that the invaders would probably land 'somewhere between Boulogne and Normandy' – only a month before D-Day. On 8 May von Rundstedt repeated what had always been one of the fundamentals of German thinking: that it would be essential for the Anglo-American command to seize Le Havre, Cherbourg or a similar port to ensure the inflow of the supplies they would need. Twelve months earlier, however, the idea of constructing artificial harbours to escape the risk inherent in assaults on what were certain to be heavily defended ports had been mooted, and the construction of 'Mulberries' was by now far advanced. They were large and difficult to disguise, yet they were never spotted. No air reconnaissance had penetrated as far as London since January 1941, and, although there had been tip-and-run sorties over coastal areas, the reconnaissance planes had been chased away before their cameras could record much.

But even had the Luftwaffe remained strong enough to guarantee them fighter protection, it was discovered after the war, no better results might have been achieved. Interrogation of prisoners and examination of the captured German print library made it clear that the German photo-interpreters did not even use stereoscopes, and that their other methods were equally antiquated. The Zeiss factory at Jena made the best lenses in the world, but the Luftwaffe did not use them to the best advantage. British and American practice had surged so far ahead in just four years that Medmenham held material from which a thousand exact and detailed models were constructed and distributed so that the assault units could familiarise themselves with their objectives before they embarked.

*

The theory and practice of deception, learned and effectively applied in the Middle East, was brought to Britain when the Chiefs of Staff took advantage of a visit by Dudley Clarke in October 1941 to inquire about what he had been doing. His account was persuasive, and the London Controlling Section was set up to replicate 'A' Force in Britain. When preparations for OVERLORD began in earnest, Dudley Clarke's second-in-command, Colonel Noël Wild, was brought home to take charge at SHAEF in the same way as Dudley Clarke at GHQ Cairo. In this capacity Wild became a member of the XX Committee, which selected material for double agents to pass to the enemy in order to delude him. Since enough easily verifiable truth had to be mingled with the fictions to make the whole convincing, permission had first to be sought from the service authorities before it could be transmitted.

Once it was realised, in 1941, that every German agent who had managed to reach the UK had been caught and imprisoned or executed, it was possible (because there was now no chance that an undetected survivor might blow the gaff) to invite some of those who had been rounded up to turn their coats and work for their captors. A few accepted the offer of alternative employment, and by 1942 the 'Double Cross' system had taken shape.

The double agent most successful in planting error in the mind of the Abwehr was, however, not 'turned' but a volunteer. He was a Spaniard, Juan Pujol Garcia, of fiercely anti-fascist views. He had been in touch with both the Abwehr (providing them with bogus information) and SIS in Lisbon and Madrid, and the latter brought him to London in April 1942. He was given the cover-name Garbo, and over the next three years he sent to the Abwehr in Madrid hundreds of messages concocted by his 'case-officer' to deceive the Germans. These messages were accepted as genuine and reliable by the Abwehr and – more importantly – by Foreign Armies West, the intelligence branch of OKW; so high did Garbo's credit eventually stand that he was awarded the Iron Cross by Hitler.

Garbo is deservedly famous for the part he played in persuading the Germans that the main weight of OVERLORD would be directed not at Normandy but at the Pas de Calais. This was a variation on the same theme as HUSKY. Then, the obvious target was also the real one, and a plausible alternative had to be sought. Now, the problem was to pull the wool so far over the enemy's eyes as to make him believe that the obvious was again the real in spite of the possibility of double bluff, although he knew perfectly well that almost any point on the coast between Holland and Brittany would serve the Allies equally well, and although he was already fortifying the whole Channel coast. The false tale was told so well that it still retained some of its persuasive force two months after the 6 June landings.

Seen from the other side, this is less surprising than it appears.

Albert Speer, the Reich Armaments Minister, was at the Berghof above Berchtesgaden by 10.00 a.m. on 6 June. Hitler was still asleep, and the daily situation conference did not take place until 'several hours later'. Speer reports that Hitler had recently been far surer than ever that the Allies were trying to deceive him into committing divisions too soon and in the wrong place and therefore construed what had occurred the previous night as only a diversionary assault. Since he personally decided which intelligence reports were reliable and which not (a dangerous practice which Churchill had often followed in 1941–2 but had since wisely abandoned to the intelligence professionals and the Chiefs of Staff), this was to risk adopting a wrong strategy. '*During the following days and weeks* [my italics],' wrote Speer, 'Hitler continued to hold that the real invasion would take place at another spot – he meant the vicinity of Calais – which would meanwhile have been stripped of troops.' This conference probably occurred before Garbo's first message reached the Führer, and certainly before the second. Garbo was chafing at an already sore spot, and once more deception took a stronger hold because it confirmed self-induced errors.

Long before this, and after the LCS had considered various options and had agreed a broad deception outline, BODY-GUARD, with the Americans and Russians, on 25 January 1944 Montgomery's Chief of Staff at 21 Army Group (which was once more to integrate deception with operations) finally decided that the fictitious main thrust should aim at the Pas de Calais for a date some time after the real main landing in Normandy. FORTITUDE was thus formally launched. Three months later, substance was lent to the threat by the creation of a notional First United States Army Group (FUSAG) with HQ in Kent, preparing for a landing on the opposite coast.

The first of several strange obscurities arises here. Long before, on 9 January, the German Y Service had identified FUSAG in southern England. In fact, FUSAG barely existed at that time, having just arrived from the USA and being a vehicle not of deception but of combat (it was eventually renamed 12 Army Group when it went to France and FUSAG became notional). It seems, then, that German intelligence was already deluding itself and playing into FORTITUDE's hands by offering it a perfect *point d'appui* for its schemes. An additional peculiarity is that this is not mentioned in the history of FORTITUDE[*] written soon after the war by Roger Hesketh, through whose hands all the threads had passed. There is a further puzzle too. Hesketh's book was written for internal circulation, so there was no need for its language to be guarded, yet it makes no reference to information derived from the Abwehr controllers' answers (in ISOS or ISK) to Garbo's and other agents' communications,[†] and offers only passages from German situation reports inaccessible until after the war as proof of the agents' effectiveness.

Garbo's fame rests principally on two messages which he sent on the first three days of OVERLORD. During the night of 5/6 June he went on the air with a warning that the invasion was imminent; by an ingenious device he so timed it that the landing had taken place before his warning was received: operational surprise was not sacrificed, but his own credit with the Abwehr was not thereby diminished. Three days later he confidently predicted that the Normandy landing was only a feint to distract attention from the heavier assault on the Pas de Calais which would follow. Hesketh produced a copy of this message, initialled by Hitler himself, as proof that it was this which kept the tanks

---

[*] It has never been published, but photocopies are in circulation.
[†] Ten years ago I drew attention to the strange air of mystery which hangs over the part played by deception in the invasion of Normandy (INS 4. 482–502. See p. 375, below, at note to p. 259). No solution to it has been propounded since then. The *Times* obituary (8 August 1998) of Colonel David Strangeways who, as head of G(R) at 21 Army Group, was privy to all related secrets, has deepened the mystery: it goes at length into his work in the desert (about which a great deal is now known), but passes over D-Day and beyond without explaining anything about what he did.

away from the beachhead in the first critical days, though the arguments with which he supports his claim are unconvincing.

There are varying accounts of exactly how much armour stayed far from the action as the Allied armies painfully fought their way ashore, and for how long, but there can be no doubt that had it intervened at once the beachhead would have been in great peril and might even have been extinguished. But there were at least two good reasons, apart from Garbo, for Hitler and von Rundstedt to hold the armour back. Just before Garbo's message reached OKW another to the same effect had been delivered. It came from an Abwehr officer (codenamed Josephine) in Stockholm who had in reality no special knowledge of Allied intentions and based his reports on nothing more authoritative than newspaper articles and occasional conversations with the Swedish intelligence staff. Where one warning might have been dismissed, two seemed conclusive, it has been said, and there is independent witness to the high regard in which Josephine was held at the Führerhauptquartier.

There remains another reason, one which has often been given too little weight, for doubting whether Garbo should be given all the credit for keeping armour away from the Normandy beaches. The Channel is narrowest in the Straits of Dover, therefore invasion convoys could receive greater protection there than anywhere else. Simple prudence therefore called for measures to protect the endangered coast from a surprise onslaught. Moreover, it was from here that the Germans had intended to launch their own invasion in 1940, and the temptation to suppose that the Allies would do the same was strong. It is a well-known experience of intelligence practitioners that 'They will do what we would do in like circumstances' has a great (but misleading) appeal to commanders forced to predict the enemy's next move. Precisely because deception must attach itself like a parasite to a body already sick, it cannot later claim to be the sole cause of the patient's death.

None of the foregoing detracts from the hard work of Garbo

and his case officer, or from the whole LCS effort, all of which were abundantly worth while. It serves as a reminder, however, that there are still, and may always remain, some aspects of the deceptions carried out in 1944 which are far from clear.

Why did neither the Abwehr nor the OKW, for whom it worked, ever suspect that Garbo had been 'turned' and was peddling disinformation? Since the Abwehr had itself 'played back' agents whom they had lured into captivity in Holland in 1942–3 (Operation North Pole) and in Lorraine more recently, did it not occur to them that the boot might now be on the other foot? Was it not extraordinary that a German agent in England had apparently escaped detection for two years while constantly chattering on the radio? Garbo did not keep his transmissions short (rather the opposite), and neither Masterman nor Howard suggests that his transmissions were especially short or that he changed wavelength frequently – that is, he did not follow the standard means of escaping detection.

There seems no way of explaining the Abwehr's unsuspecting attitude except by supposing German blindness and stupidity. The Abwehr was only one of half-a-dozen intelligence agencies at odds with each other, and some of its leading officials were anti-Nazi in sympathy. (What Canaris, its head, told his Polish mistress in Switzerland, and what she told the Allies can only be surmised.) The Abwehr lost its influence when it was taken over by Himmler's and Kaltenbrunner's less efficient SS organisation in February 1944.

There are similar and even greater puzzles. Why was every suggestion that Enigma might have been broken rejected? Dönitz was baffled by the way Allied aircraft and surface vessels kept appearing at awkward times and places, yet although he had himself profited from reading the Allied convoy code he did not pursue his inquiries vigorously enough to approach the truth, and his radio security agency, the B-Dienst, did not urge him in that direction. Similarly, 'A traitor in the Naples docks' was surely too easy an explanation of the frequency with which cross-

Mediterranean supply ships were intercepted in 1941–2. Although it was circular reasoning, from the fact that Enigma was believed (wrongly, as it proved) unbreakable, it seems to have been deduced that it had not been broken, however superficially alarming the evidence in a particular instance might be.

Rigidly fixed ideas which nothing can shake are not the bane of dictatorships alone, but they flourish among them. In the west, they were about to cause the Germans to lose France in the course of only a few weeks. Hitler and the OKW were so convinced that the Allies would strike straight from Caen, as soon as they occupied it, towards Paris that by concentrating their armour round the city in response to Montgomery's adaptation of his original intentions they were dangerously weakening their left flank and so facilitating an American breakthrough there. Hitler then committed the fatal blunder of attacking westwards in the direction of Avranches and inviting the encirclement of his armies. 'Whom the gods would destroy, they first make mad' is too facile a conclusion if applied to the whole situation, but there is unquestionably some truth in it.

For by the winter of 1943/4 there was so much to warn Germany of its increasingly gloomy prospects that the need for the acutest attention to the signs of the coming danger could hardly have been greater. Russia had retaken Kiev and relieved Leningrad; the Battle of the Atlantic was lost; Italy was no longer an ally, though Kesselring was still keeping the invaders cooped up south of Rome; the tempo of air attack on Germany was moving towards a climax; the United States' economic power was being deployed on a huge scale to concentrate men and material in Britain for an invasion. The Allies were moving in for the kill.

On top of all this came a clear indication of the wide scope of the Allies' preparations: the now famous 'Cicero' case. The Turkish valet of the British Ambassador in Ankara managed to make impressions of the keys to the safe containing his secret papers, then photographed some of them and sold them to the Germans at intervals between December 1943 and March 1944. The lack of proper security in the Embassy was blameworthy in the extreme (an agreeable and civilised ambassador of the old school was living in a time-warp and had not advanced beyond the habits of the 1930s), but did no serious harm whatever: all that the stolen papers betrayed was that an operation with the cover-name OVERLORD was planned, and that it would absorb the whole of the Allies' military effort in Europe in 1944. Yet German opinion about the genuineness or not of the Cicero documents was divided, and they do not appear to have raised the general level of alertness in any way. Good fortune preserved the Allies from great perils (the theft of more compromising material) and even this stimulus did not make the German command more sensitive to the dangers that might lie ahead. Von Rundstedt pooh-poohed the imminence of an invasion during the evening of 5 June, Rommel was on leave at home, several generals were away from their posts taking part in a war-game, and it was only after some dithering in the early hours of the following morning that a first-degree state of alarm was proclaimed.

Hindsight suggests, then, that by D-Day the Allies held a large credit balance in their intelligence account and the Germans an even larger overdraft. This was not quite how it appeared as tension built up and the time for action approached, however. Forewarned does not always mean sufficiently forearmed, as the Battle of Crete had shown in 1941. Huge risks inevitably attended an assault on a heavily fortified shore defended by a well-prepared enemy standing fiercely at bay, as Eisenhower knew when he wrote out the two alternative press releases during the night of 5/6 June. Hope, confidence and determination abounded as the troops waded ashore, but there was no expectation of instant victory.

The first danger to the landings was from the sea. *Schnorkel* U-boats and destroyers from the French Atlantic ports, torpedo boats and other such craft based in Le Havre, Cherbourg and Dutch harbours, could theaten the passage of ships and landing craft from both west and east. In the event a speedy service of naval Ultra (OIC was often able to despatch its signals within thirty minutes of German time of origin) and quick action neutralised them all to a remarkable degree. U-boats registered no sinkings until 15 June, destroyers were bombed as they sailed from the Gironde estuary and three were sunk when a group of five was brought to battle during the night of 8/9 June. Intended attacks by E-boats (fast torpedo boats) were equally well monitored and their efforts rendered largely ineffective by standing patrols protecting the 'Spout', the wide channel through which Allied shipping passed on its way from the English coast to the beaches.

On land, Army Y located 21 Panzer Division's tanks as they moved up to protect Caen from the immediate capture Montgomery intended, but apart from battle contacts and scraps of news from the local population, the best intelligence for the first day or two was advance notice of raids on shipping anchored off the beaches and of the move of seven *Gruppen* (nominally of thirty aircraft each) of fighters to advance landing grounds. It was a good omen for the future that the first big intelligence stroke came through a combination of sources. Panzergruppe West had been established to control the armour for a counter-attack. It was shot up by fighter-bombers seeking targets of opportunity as it shifted its headquarters northwards from Paris, D/F'd on arrival at its chosen site in Normandy (because of the volume of its outgoing wireless traffic), and finally pinpointed by Ultra (which, surprisingly, was already a main provider of tactical intelligence) early on 10 June. The subsequent bombing raid destroyed its command network, killed a number of senior staff officers and put it out of action for almost three weeks: the nerve-centre of the counter-attack force designed to drive an invader back into the sea was paralysed at the outset.* A replacement was specially created to mastermind Hitler's ill-starred thrust towards Avranches in August, but it was hastily put together as well as burdened with an impossible task.

Signs of German nervousness were encouragingly numerous. On 10 June von Rundstedt issued orders for the immediate destruction of Cherbourg harbour (the American drive to capture the port had not yet begun, and it did not fall until the 26th), and Vichy was known to be in effect continuing Garbo's good work by warning OKW of probable fresh landings. On the 11th Hitler ordered II SS Panzer Corps (9 and 10 SS Panzer Divisions) from the Russian front to Normandy; well over a hundred trainloads got as far as the Franco-German border within a week, but the Resistance prevented them from reaching the firing line until the end of the month, too late to halt Montgomery's EPSOM offensive across the river Odon west of Caen. An appreciation by von Rundstedt covering the week 19–26 June showed how uncertainty about the extent of the threat FUSAG posed to the Calais area was not only holding armour away from Normandy (no tanks moved west for almost a fortnight after D-Day) but causing him to misunderstand Allied strategy, to prepare to counter an imagined British intention of striking direct from Caen towards Paris (perhaps joining up with FUSAG on the way) and – worst of all from his point of view – to overlook the risk he ran by concentrating armour on his right, thereby weakening his left where it faced US First Army at the base of the Cotentin peninsula.

---

* As part of a publication he planned to celebrate the 50th anniversary of D-Day, Mr W. G. Ramsey, editor of *After the Battle*, sought my permission to reprint some passages from chapters 2 and 3 of *Ultra in the West*. These appear on pages 58–75 in the first of the two handsome volumes entitled *D-Day and After* which were published in 1995. Two points are of particular interest: (i) these pages are lavishly illustrated with photographs and reproductions of relevant signals; (ii) the effects of the bombing raid on Panzergruppe's HQ are examined in great detail with maps, the findings of the immediately post-war Bombing Analysis Survey, and modern photographs.

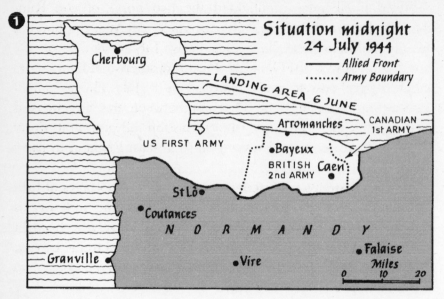

1

Situation midnight
24 July 1944

—— Allied Front
········ Army Boundary

LANDING AREA 6 JUNE

Cherbourg

Arromanches

CANADIAN
1st ARMY

US FIRST ARMY

Bayeux

BRITISH
2nd ARMY

Caen

St Lô

Coutances

N O R M A N D Y

Granville

Vire

Falaise

Miles

0   10   20

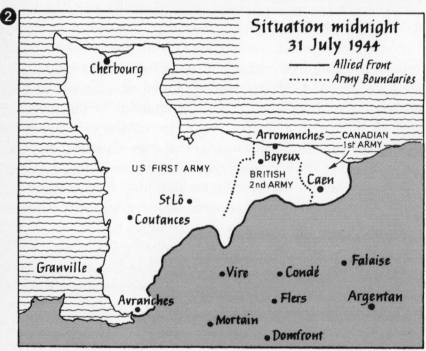

2

Situation midnight
31 July 1944

—— Allied Front
········ Army Boundaries

Cherbourg

Arromanches

CANADIAN
1st ARMY

US FIRST ARMY

Bayeux

BRITISH
2nd ARMY

Caen

St Lô

Coutances

Granville

Vire

Condé

Falaise

Avranches

Flers

Argentan

Mortain

Domfront

Allied intelligence highlighted the two horns of von Rundstedt's dilemma, and by doing so cruelly exposed the flaws in his analysis. In late June and early July evidence of the continuing power of FORTITUDE to mesmerise judgment and create apprehension accumulated. On 8 July Hitler himself forecast new landings on the coast between the Somme and Seine, while the Japanese naval mission alleged that thirty divisions were ready and waiting in south-east England to carry them out.

Von Rundstedt's resources were dwindling. Shortages of fuel, ammunition and transport showed up after the first week's fighting. Petrol, reported II Para Corps, could only be brought up at night, so incessantly did the RAF strafe road traffic by day. Expenditure of ammunition was outrunning supply, according to I SS Panzer Corps on 23 June. On the very next day OKW turned down out of hand an urgent request by von Rundstedt for more lorry-space (Kesselring in Italy was under orders to surrender vehicles to other fronts) and suggested that his 'temporary' fuel problems might be solved by borrowing from the navy or the GAF; the navy objected at once and it had already been reported that GAF operations might soon be jeopardised by petrol shortage! (Only ten days later Luftflotte 3, the western air command, ordered that only absolutely essential air travel should be permitted.) Most conveniently, casualty returns and manpower information was freely available on the American front. Panzer Lehr Division, transferred westward from the Caen front by von Kluge as soon as he took over from von Rundstedt on 3 July, was soon suffering 'heavy casualties' during the US attack on St Lô, where II Para Corps had warned a few days earlier that the German line would soon crack in the face of superior American artillery firepower – as indeed it did in places almost at once. Most enlightening of all was a correspondence between General Meindl, commanding II Para Corps, and General Student, head of Parachute Army, on 20 July. Meindl felt that the fighting power of his men was steadily declining,

complained that he had not received the drafts he had asked for
(the few who had arrived, he said, were raw recruits lacking all
but the most basic training), and feared that he would not be
able to halt an American thrust south-westwards from St Lô if
one developed. This, the COBRA offensive at the end of July,
was in fact little more than a week away.

Thanks to Ultra, General Bradley, commanding US First
Army, knew that he would face only weak opposition whenever
he chose to strike. No sooner had he done so than he was to have
to thank the same source for an even greater opportunity. For
their part, Eisenhower and Montgomery could reflect that the
damage to the Mulberry harbours and the delay in the flow of
reinforcements (to the tune of three whole divisions in the British
sector) caused by the storm which raged between 19 and 22 July
had not given their enemy as great an advantage as they feared.

Happily – for the next four or five weeks were to see frenzied
activity – August was to be one of Ultra's most productive
months, while Army Y yielded more instant intelligence than in
the recent past. During the fast-moving battle which saw the
Germans evicted from France, information poured out from
these well-tried sources at an unprecedented rate, their evidence
confirmed by highly organised aerial reconnaissance, visual and
photographic, more completely than ever before. Command
decisions at all levels revealed enemy plans (or the absence of
them) and the changing positions of every formation could be
traced from day to day, often from hour to hour.

The first act in the drama was, by contrast, slow, its central
action an almost complete surprise. During the afternoon or
early evening of 2 August Hitler – still reeling from the 20 July
plot,* and perhaps with his judgment still impaired by it –
telephoned von Kluge with a sudden order to assemble four
Panzer divisions and cut the narrow corridor which the

_____

* Of which intelligence knew nothing at the time. Aware that even
Enigma could not hide their secrets because their Nazi enemies had the
keys, the conspirators used other means of communication.

Americans had just driven through Avranches and along the west coast, giving them access to Brittany (where the Resistance was strong) and potentially also to the naval base at Brest. There was therefore something to be said for the plan, militarily imprudent though it was, to withdraw troops from Seventh Army's northern front, hard-pressed by the parallel attacks of Americans and British along half its length, and to transfer its centre of gravity westwards. Obediently, though against his better judgment, von Kluge set about disengaging armour from its current battle and collecting it together for the new enterprise. During the whole of this period no hint of what was afoot appeared in any Allied intelligence source. Then, in the early evening of 6 August, Ultra gave warning of a heavy armoured attack with fighter protection to be launched within a few hours from the area of Mortain, some twenty miles east of Avranches. Speedy reaction by the Allied air forces and stubborn resistance by 30 US Division repelled the attack.

By this time the US Third Army, passing through the Avranches corridor, had been ordered to turn left up the Loire valley rather than right into Brittany, and had reached Tours and Le Mans, converting what only a few days before had been the Germans' undefended rear into an unprotected and gravely endangered southern flank. The inflow of intelligence was already almost overwhelming when, in the early hours of 10 August, Ultra broke the astonishing news that nevertheless Hitler had ordered the renewal of the 6 August attack in greater strength next day.

This was to convert the unwisdom of a week ago into sheer madness, and to know it in advance was intelligence beyond price. It was not hard to imagine the consequences which could be made to follow: the destruction of three German armies in what came to be called he 'Falaise pocket'. As they shepherded them down the road to ruin, much of the information which continued to deluge Bradley and Montgomery will have told them little more than they knew already, however, because events were now moving so fast that intelligence was almost bound to lag behind; but indications of intended retreat routes, of future defence 'lines' and of the speed with which the ANVIL/DRAGOON landing in the south on 15 August was driving Army Group G up the Rhône valley gave valuable operational pointers. The 'pocket' was never quite closed, but those who survived it fled helter-skelter, under a hail of bullets and bombs from the RAF and USAAF, for shelter behind the West Wall (neglected since 1940 and in some disrepair, it could give less protection than they hoped) and the water-lines of Belgium and Holland, filling the air with reports of their whereabouts in Enigma at the rate of a hundred a day as they went. The Allies crossed the Seine on 19 August, liberated Paris on the 25th, and reached Antwerp and Brussels on 3 and 4 September.

So vast and so sudden a victory understandably brought with it an immense feeling of relief, but with hindsight it is astonishing how widespread the feeling became and how long its effects lasted. It was natural that the American soldiers who followed the French into Paris, and the British tank crews who raced across northern France at forty or fifty miles a day, should be swept off their feet by the rejoicing with which they were welcomed, and that newspapers should write of a German 'rout', but it is harder to understand why the same unreflecting excitement took such a hold on the higher levels of command.

As early as the middle of July the JIC had rashly predicted that a German collapse might come soon, probably before December, and this may have set the ball rolling. In late August a SHAEF intelligence summary, issued over the signature of General Strong (Eisenhower's Chief Intelligence Officer since February 1943; he was never noted for caution in the appraisal of evidence), confidently declared, 'the enemy in the west has had it'. The normally hard-headed CIGS, Brooke, was already of the same opinion; he had written to Maitland Wilson (Commander-in-Chief Mediterranean) on 2 August, 'the Boche

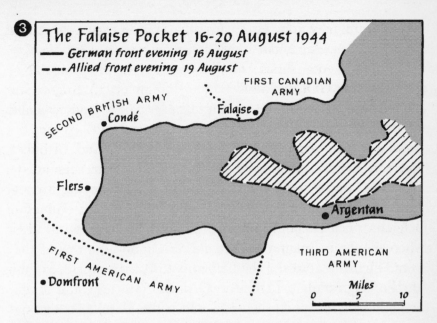

3 The Falaise Pocket 16-20 August 1944
— German front evening 16 August
----- Allied front evening 19 August

FIRST CANADIAN ARMY

SECOND BRITISH ARMY

Falaise

Condé

Flers

Argentan

THIRD AMERICAN ARMY

FIRST AMERICAN ARMY

Domfront

Miles
0   5   10

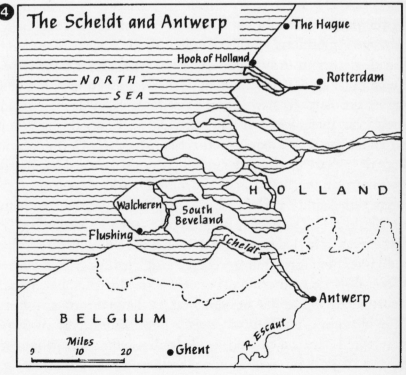

4 The Scheldt and Antwerp

The Hague

Hook of Holland

Rotterdam

NORTH SEA

HOLLAND

Walcheren

South Beveland

Flushing

Scheldt

Antwerp

BELGIUM

R. Escaut

Miles
0   10   20

Ghent

is beat on all fronts. It is only a matter now of how many more months he can last,' and was still in the same state of exhilaration a month later when he assented (influenced, he admitted, along with the other Chiefs of Staff, by the JIC's optimism) to the view taken by the JIC and the Cabinet that German resistance would soon disintegrate and would cease by the end of the year.

Anyone who expressed an opinion of this kind before 4 September could be charged with counting his chickens before they were hatched and with forgetting the talent for improvisation shown by Kesselring in a not dissimilar situation after DIADEM, but perhaps no more. From 5 September onwards, however, there was no excuse for facile optimism, like that voiced by the War Office that day and repeated on the eve of the Arnhem operation (MARKET GARDEN) nearly a fortnight later, that there was 'no way' in which the German command could hold the West Wall with the small forces it could muster for the purpose. On the 3rd, Hitler announced that he attached 'decisive importance' to the retention of 'Walcheren island with Flushing harbour, a bridgehead round Antwerp and the Albert Canal as far as Maastricht', that is, he was determined to nullify the loss of Antwerp (there was soon daily detailed information about the rate at which Fifteenth Army was ferrying troops across to the north bank of the Scheldt). Hitler's instructions were decrypted and signalled to all parties concerned by the late afternoon of the 5th. Churchill was the first to seize on the implications, and the first realist among the advisers accompanying him on the *Queen Mary* (then in mid-Atlantic) to the Quebec Conference. He had been in a despondent mood lately, and had run a temperature, but recovered sufficiently to minute the Chiefs of Staff in the following terms on 8 September: 'Apart from Cherbourg and Arromanches, we have not obtained any large harbours. *The Germans intend to defend the mouth of the Scheldt* [my italics]. . . . It is at least as likely that Hitler will be fighting on the 1st January as that he will collapse before then.'

Failure to make proper use of Antwerp was the first bitter fruit of the recent misguided optimism. Hitler's new order was issued twenty-four hours before 11 Armoured Division captured the Antwerp docks and, amazed by its own feat, halted there. The moment he heard of the capture, Admiral Ramsay, Allied naval Commander-in-Chief, reminded Eisenhower that it would not be safe to use the port until both banks of the estuary (Antwerp is some fifty miles from the sea) were free of enemy. Although both Eisenhower and Montgomery wanted Antwerp as a base for their operations (according to statements made by both of them in the last days of August in preparation for Eisenhower's assumption of office as Land Commander on 1 September), neither of them heeded Ramsay's warning or changed his mind on learning of Hitler's order. On the 9th Eisenhower could tell the Combined Chiefs of Staff that 'Antwerp *having been seized* [my italics]' his main effort would be directed towards the Ruhr and specifically authorised Montgomery to defer clearing the approaches to Antwerp until after the Arnhem operation a week later. Montgomery himself took the same line, writing that 'the Ruhr is our real objective, but *on the way* we want the ports of Antwerp and Rotterdam'. Both later admitted their mistake, but meanwhile a high price was exacted for it. The first supply ship unloaded in Antwerp on 28 November, eighty-five days after the port was occupied.

There is a second count on the charge-sheet. It was a misunderstanding of the significance of a piece of military intelligence – Hitler's stated intention to prevent the use of Antwerp even though he had lost the port itself – which was the chief cause of the logistical difficulties that beset the Allied command until the eve of the Ardennes crisis in December, but now straightforward operational intelligence was to be misread in its turn. However strategically desirable, Montgomery's plan to seize the Meuse and Rhine crossings by a single bold stroke was doubtful as a practical proposition, notably because XXX Corps' advance to rescue the lightly armed airborne troops would have to be up a single road. But apart from this it was

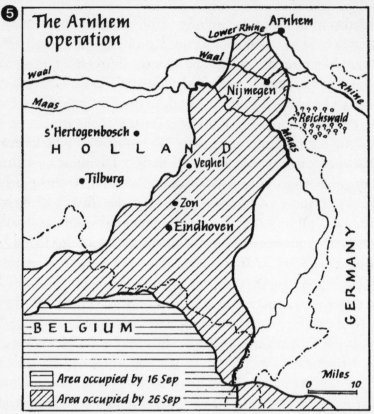

5 The Arnhem operation

Arnhem

Lower Rhine

Waal

Waal

Maas

Nijmegen

Rhine

Reichswald

s'Hertogenbosch

H O L L A N D

Maas

Veghel

Tilburg

Zon

Eindhoven

G E R M A N Y

B E L G I U M

Area occupied by 16 Sep

Area occupied by 26 Sep

Miles

0   10

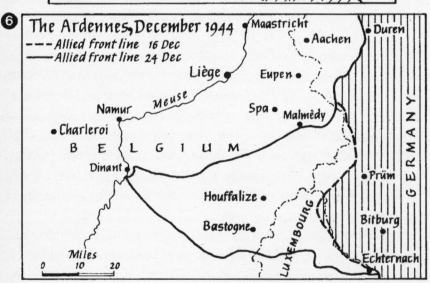

6 The Ardennes, December 1944

--- Allied front line 16 Dec
—— Allied front line 24 Dec

Maastricht

Aachen

Duren

Liège

Eupen

Namur

Meuse

Spa

Malmèdy

Charleroi

B E L G I U M

G E R M A N Y

Dinant

Prüm

Houffalize

Bastogne

L U X E M B O U R G

Bitburg

Miles

0   10   20

Echternach

founded on an almost wilfully misleading interpretation of intelligence at a moment when its quality was (as already explained) irremediably falling away from its recent high standards, and therefore on a botched analysis which repeatedly skated over awkward problems and 'pressed on regardless' in the hope that 'it would all come right on the night'.

Among many illustrations of this the most striking concerns II SS Panzer Corps, whose 9 and 10 Panzer Divisions overcame 1 Airborne Division after bitter fighting around Arnhem bridge. Ultra lost touch with the Corps for the first few days of September, but reported that its component divisions and several others were under orders to rest and refit in south Holland. Its headquarters were at Eindhoven (forty miles south of Arnhem, right in the path of XXX Corps' planned advance) on the 5th, before moving to Doetinchem, ten miles east of Arnhem, by the 17th. Meanwhile Army Group B, its direct superior, had settled at Oosterbeek, a suburb of Arnhem, where 1 Airborne Division landed, to the surprise of both. While this was going on, the GAF had been trying to discover by direct observation and photography whether Aachen or Arnhem was the Allies' next objective. With all this thoroughly reliable high-grade Sigint to guide them (Y, prisoners, the local Resistance and other ground-contact evidence added very little), it is incomprehensible how what appeared to be camouflaged tanks under trees by the roadside near Arnhem could be lightly dismissed as 'battered remnants' or how General Urquhart, commanding 1 Airborne Division, came to be told that he would have to meet only a weak tank brigade. The commander of II SS Panzer was known to have indented for over a hundred new tanks at the end of August, and there had been plenty of time since then for them to have been delivered.

Surely it was at least as likely as any more triumphalist conclusion that these might be signs of a German intention to defend the river crossings which barred the route into the heartland of industrial Germany – that is, that OKW had drawn the same conclusions as Montgomery? For the last two years intelligence staffs had, like the Ultra signals they received, been careful to distinguish between 'strong', 'fair' and 'slight' indications of the confidence with which they presented their deductions, and the commanders to whom they presented them had taken appropriate heed. This seems no longer to have been the case in September 1944: intelligence was losing its hold on operations. Eisenhower's Chief of Staff, Bedell Smith, visited 21 Army Group the day before the airborne drops took place, and warned of possible danger from armour in the MARKET GARDEN area, but his warning was not taken seriously.

Hitler began planning his revenge even before he had time to grasp the scale of the defeat he had suffered in Normandy. During the last ten days of August the Japanese Ambassador in Berlin and the Naval Attaché picked up rumours that the 'coming offensive' would take place in November or December, and their reports back to Tokyo were intercepted and decrypted with only a few days' delay. A month later Ultra revealed that an entirely new formation, Sixth Panzer Army, was being set up under SS Oberstgruppenführer Sepp Dietrich[*] and would consist of several SS Panzer divisions to be based for training in north-west Germany. Other decrypts showed a massive shift of GAF fighters to airfields on the same latitude but east of the Rhine.

   The connexion of all this with a forthcoming offensive seems self-evident now, but it was never made explicit in any intelligence received at the time. It is in the nature of all intelligence-gathering systems that the link between reported fact and enemy purpose is often missing, and one of the prime tasks of an intelligence staff is to determine whether or not there is a link between the two. By the early autumn of 1944 Allied

[*] One of the first bully-boy Nazis, commander of Hitler's guard and leader of the execution squad on the Night of the Long Knives in 1934. The SS rank of Oberstgruppenführer corresponds to army general.

intelligence had been routinely discharging this task with a great deal of success for two years or more. Yet it failed to discover a link on this occasion, although one existed and was absolute and direct. Why?

One possible explanation – German security precautions – may be dismissed at once as merely secondary. Hitler revealed his purpose to only a small circle – even Sepp Dietrich did not know it for several weeks – chose a defensive-sounding cover-name WACHT AM RHEIN (which, however, the Allies never discovered) and imposed radio silence on the lower army formations. This last disarmed the Allied Y Service, but Enigma was still used freely at higher levels and was intercepted and decrypted as usual.

A far greater handicap to Allied intelligence was almost certainly the length of the notice it received, paradoxical though that may seem. Hitherto its problems had almost always been short-term, now there was a four-month interval between the first reports recorded above and the Ardennes offensive in December. The daily pressure of a more familiar kind – items affecting the Canadian army's progress through the mud and water of Holland as it cleared the Scheldt and opened Antwerp, the British advance further south towards the River Roer and the Rhineland, the Americans' capture of Aachen in October and of Metz in November – all pre-empted time and attention. First reactions to the news about Sixth Panzer Army were evidently influenced by post-Falaise euphoria although composed just after the disappointment of Arnhem. The War Office, for instance, could say on 27 October, 'We can dictate to him where his reinforcements must go,' and SHAEF could call Sixth Panzer Army no more than a 'fire brigade' to douse the flames of the next Allied push forward. This was a view which persisted in spite of further information which was not easy to reconcile with it, and tended to dull or even obliterate the earliest news of all – that of the Japanese that an offensive was pending.

Further awkward news continued to accumulate: the SS

divisions would be brought up to strength and given a fresh allocation of tanks and heavy equipment (details were provided); steady movements of men and equipment under fighter protection to a wide area west of Cologne started early in November and continued into December (thirty Ultra signals in forty-five days disclosed the large number of trains involved, their starting points and destinations, and sometimes their loads) as part of a highly articulated transport programme which demanded exact time-keeping and permitted no delays.

The heightened sense of urgency conveyed by these movements was steadily intensified during the next three weeks, but still no exact reason for them appeared. The latest and fastest jet fighters were instructed in late November to carry out daily reconnaissance of the central front, paying special attention to the Meuse crossings round Dinant; this, and the fact that the route thither would retrace that of the victorious 1940 campaign, suggested intended German aggression rather than defence against an Allied attack, for this would entangle them in the narrow and mountainous road network of the Ardennes to no apparent end; Aachen and Metz offered better prospects. On 5 December an evidently urgent conference of fighter-group commanders was called to discuss an unspecified agenda: recent intelligence had shown that fighter numbers were rising sharply on both banks of the Rhine and that planes were being withdrawn from home defence in spite of heavy Allied raids on Reich territory.

In the continuing absence of any indication of the purpose of all these arrangements it was, of course, possible to read them in different ways. It was just conceivable that something like half the German armour was being refitted before despatch into the furnace of battle in Russia (its final destination in January 1945, in point of fact). But now, however, that all the tanks and some of the fighter planes were west of the Rhine, it was more likely that they would be used either as a fire brigade to snuff out the next Allied attack, as SHAEF had predicted, or to launch an offensive on Germany's own part. But which?

The virtual unanimity with which SHAEF and both the Army Groups plumped for the fire-brigade theory without seriously examining the alternative is the single most astonishing thing about the whole Ardennes affair. What mental gymnastics (seemingly performed by the Air Ministry on 6 December) made it possible to suppose that the urgent and elaborate arrangements noted above could be reconciled with the abandonment of the 'lightning blow' of which some of the earlier evidence had spoken? Or with the theory that the Ardennes front was being used to 'blood' the new Volksgrenadier divisions which were being created out of the recent call-up of older men, as SHAEF imagined as late as 13 December? (Ultra had by then reported nine or ten Panzer divisions in the Ardennes, but made scarcely a mention of Volksgrenadiers.) Was it really likely that so much air reconnaissance would be devoted to a sector from which no danger was to be apprehended (Bradley had deliberately thinned out his front line in the Ardennes because of the needs of the 'broad front' policy)? Was a German attack not a more likely explanation?

Major-General Strong, who was responsible for intelligence at SHAEF and was reported to have considerable influence on Eisenhower, later complained that the location of the German armour was not clear: yet Ultra had supplied illuminating if approximate information on the subject, and had shown that some of the divisions crossing the Rhine were detraining only ten or fifteen miles from the American lines. Strong's account in *Intelligence at the Top* (published in 1968) is evasive and equivocal, and tends to self-exculpation in its presentation of the intelligence picture before 16 December, when the Battle of the Bulge began. Like so many others, he stressed that German fuel shortage would preclude a mobile offensive of any duration, and leaned towards the defensive fire-brigade theory, but did not consider whether (as was in fact the case) special reserves to support an offensive had been accumulated during the autumn, or remember that Bomber Command had not pursued its attack on fuel-storage depots and distillation plants as vigorously as Portal had demanded.

Early in the New Year GC&CS (whose normal duties did not include either the preparation of intelligence digests or historical investigation) and the Vice-Chief of the Imperial General Staff conducted inquiries which sought to establish why intelligence had not managed to foresee the German offensive. Both conceded that there had been plenty of pointers in Ultra to an offensive, but nevertheless managed to conclude that too much reliance had been placed on Ultra alone. Neither reflected that for practical purposes there was no other source which could have redressed the imbalance they assumed. Neither SIS nor SOE nor the American OSS produced any useful information (there were no Allied agents in the neighbourhood of the Ardennes), Y was powerless because of the radio silence* Hitler had ordered, bad weather prevented more than minimal PR (which in any case could observe only the massing of troops, not the reason why they were massing). Such prisoners as were taken knew nothing of the higher command's intentions. The intelligence staffs' mistake was not to leave other sources out of the reckoning, but to forget the lesson of experience – that Ultra could never be guaranteed to provide all the answers, and that, although where strategy was concerned it sometimes supplied unmistakably accurate pointers, where it did not deductions from ambiguous evidence had always to be drawn critically and with caution.

Although they were evidently blinded by over-confidence that victory would come almost at once without much effort, the intelligence staffs at SHAEF and the two Army Groups can be partially excused on the ground that they were primarily concerned with current business. The JIC has no such excuse. It

---

* Which, however, did not apply to Enigma transmissions.

was far removed from the heat and stress of battle, and its job was to advise the Chiefs of Staff about long-term intelligence trends. If anyone was equipped to undertake lengthy research and to see that nothing was overlooked, it was surely the JIC. But by mid-November it had apparently forgotten that the Japanese representatives in Berlin, hitherto a very reliable source of information, had used the word 'offensive' even before the men and tanks to conduct it had been allocated; an appreciation it issued on 11 November surveyed all the evidence to date about Sixth Panzer Army but did not mention the August and September decrypts or their possible relevance to later information. Nor, if one may judge from the absence of any record of it in *British Intelligence* (the relevant JIC papers are still withheld from public scrutiny) did the JIC undertake any later review of the whole field or make any new prediction.

Distracted as they were by the unfortunate controversy over the 'broad front' strategy and the personal animosity it induced, and by anxiety about supply,* the Supreme Commander and his immediate subordinates were not well served by their intelligence staffs during the autumn of 1944, when they stood in particular need of guidance.

The very first engagements in the Ardennes on 16 December showed Ultra reverting to its former straightforward ways, yielding a mixture of tactical information and material from which operational inferences could be drawn with more confidence than of late. For the next six months the volume of traffic diminished as the territory under German control grew smaller, but its quality remained as high as ever. One difference from the

---

* As early as 9 October Eisenhower had gloomily forecast, 'All operations will come to a standstill unless Antwerp is producing by the middle of November' (VW ii.85, 94–6). Before then a great deal of American supply was coming in via Toulon and Marseilles to destinations in the north. Bombing by the Allies and sabotage by the Resistance had played havoc with railways and bridges, and some of the damage took a long time to repair.

past was the lengthening of the average interval between interception of a German message and transmission of a derivative Allied signal to commanders in the field; this reflected new complications introduced into Enigma procedure in the search for greater security. Decryption was slower, but nothing deterred the cryptographers nor loosened their stranglehold on German military communications. A more surprising change was a diminution in the proportion of intelligence from other sources: for the next few weeks the Y Service found little traffic to intercept (there was some improvement in March, however); a hostile Nazi population was less willing to co-operate with the advancing Allies than the French, Belgian or Dutch population; no agents had been planted because the Gestapo and the concentration camps were held to be too great a danger; only air photography remained constant in quality and quantity, but within its usual limitations.

Once the Allied command had recovered from the shock of the unexpected, the speed of its reactions in the Ardennes (the southward move of the Army Group boundary to bring Montgomery's forces to bear on what would otherwise have remained a solely American problem, Bradley's order for Patton's Third Army to turn north and the rapidity with which Patton executed it, the stubborn resistance of the US 101 Airborne Division at Bastogne) and its superior economic base combined with the underlying German weakness (of which too much had been made beforehand) to make it plain that the Battle of the Bulge could end in only one way, prolonged and bitter though the fighting might be. Victory was greatly assisted by a steady flow of tactical information, but particularly by evidence confirming the slenderness of the logistical shaft to which the offensive spearhead was attached.

First news that attack was turning into defence and withdrawal beginning came on 8 and 9 January as soon as Hitler sanctioned it (at two hours and twenty minutes, the latter signal was exceptional for its period and near the record for speed of retransmission). This was followed by a protracted search for confirmation of hints, none of them strong enough to bear the weight of more than a tentative conclusion, that Sixth Panzer Army was destined for the eastern front; proof emerged at last on 28 January, but even this was only a week after Hitler's decision to make the transfer.

Although the Y Service is said to have delivered better results in the last two months of the war, these have left few traces on the operational record. Nor have the hundred or more agents which William Casey (later head of the CIA) claims to have placed in Germany when he was put in charge of OSS secret intelligence in December 1944: amid much circumambulatory detail, Casey mentions only two cases where information led to USAAF raids on (unspecified) targets. Ultra itself continued to the end and beyond (the last signal was dated 9 May), but it is doubtful whether it was of much operational value. The vast resources of the USA in manpower and weaponry were by now overwhelming anything the enemy could bring against them, and the Allied advance could continue almost as it pleased. Quite unwittingly, however, Ultra contributed for a time in the spring of 1945 to the mistaken belief that a few irreconcilable Nazis might try to make a last ditch stand in the mountains of Bavaria and Austria.

Rumours to this effect started in the late autumn because the Americans had shown some interest in discovering whether there was such a project, and were taken up for propaganda purposes by the SD. There never was much factual evidence for the idea – PR found no sign of the building of fortifications except in the south, where Kesselring was already known to be constructing another defence line along the fringes of the Alps – but in the way that scare-stories have it took root in some minds; Eisenhower became a true believer and Churchill an adherent. It would probably have died a natural death for lack of evidential nourishment had not Sigint given it a semblance of life in March and April 1945 with a series of decrypts showing the preparation of communication centres for OKW (or a part of it if it were divided; the other half would go northwards) in Bavaria and Austria in case the advances of the western Allies and the Russians bisected the Reich and rendered Berlin untenable. These signs of high-level concern were taken to imply the creation of a 'National Redoubt'. This was a plausible, but, as it turned out, a wildly incorrect deduction. The subdivision and migration of OKW, OKH and OKL became accomplished fact in late April, but the word 'fortress' was never used in connexion with it until Hitler did so on 24 April (less than a week before his suicide), nor was there any attempt to provide a garrison or to stock up with food and weapons. By then, of course, it was far too late in any case.

Had there been any serious will to resist, Norway would have been a better site than Bavaria/Austria. The problem of regular supply would have been the same in each case, but the eleven divisions and five independent brigades (over 300,000 men) remaining in Norway even after several transfers to the western front during the post-Falaise crisis would have put up a far better fight than the disorganised remnants retreating across Germany, and they had ample rations at least for the present. In contrast, Lieutenant-General Andrew Thorne's largely 'notional' Fourth Army in Scotland, which had long sustained the FORTITUDE NORTH invasion threat, had lost a large part of the small substance it ever had for the same reason and was now hopelessly inadequate to capture Norway by force of arms. Here too there were only faint rumours of a 'fortress' until near the end, when the main source of information, Jens Chr. Hauge, head of Norwegian Resistance, radioed that 'the Nazi leaders have decided to go to Bavaria not Norway'. In the event the German General in Norway accepted the inevitable even though he knew that for the immediate future the Allies had no power to subdue him, and the combination of firmness and tact displayed

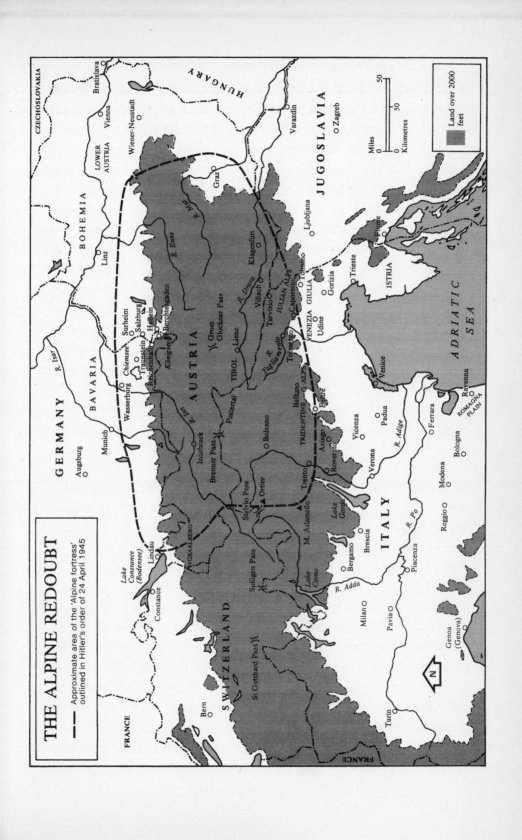

THE ALPINE REDOUBT

- - - Approximate area of the 'Alpine fortress'
outlined in Hitler's order of 24 April 1945

by General Thorne ensured that the process of transferring German forces back to the Reich passed off peacefully after the end of the war.

APPENDIX I

Enigma and Ultra

(for more detail, see Appendix VI)

Early History

Encoding messages by machine was an innovation of the 1920s. The Enigma machine, originally patented to protect commercial secrets, had been adopted by the German Wehrmacht even before Hitler, but its use was greatly extended after the Nazi take-over and many improvements were made in it to preserve secrecy; additional improvements were made right down to the last few months of the war. Because many million cipher versions of a single plain-text original were possible, Enigma was supposed unbreakable; despite occasional alarms, the Germans continued to believe it invulnerable until 1945 and beyond.

Polish mathematicians and cryptographers broke the early pre-war version of Enigma; they handed over copies of their machine and revealed their methods to France and Britain in July 1939, when they realised that they were likely to be overwhelmed themselves. Thereafter, all further progress was made at Bletchley Park in England.

The intelligence derived from breaking the Enigma code was called Ultra.

Content and Treatment

There was in effect not one Enigma but many. Numerous variants of the basic code, used by different organisations, were identified as they came into use in the course of the war, and most were broken. Each changed at least once a day, so the cryptographers' work was never finished and it was always possible to lose touch with a once familiar key: thus, for instance, a technical innovation by the Germans (the addition of an extra rotor to the Enigma machines used for communications between Atlantic U-boats and German naval headquarters) denied Britain and the US knowledge of U-boat movements between February and December 1942.

Because the Admiralty was not only a government office but also an operational headquarters issuing orders to ships at sea, whereas the War Office and Air Ministry were not, translations of decrypted Enigma messages were treated differently according to whether they were of naval or army/air origin. Translated naval Enigma was teleprinted from Bletchley Park to the Admiralty, where the OIC ordered any consequential action. These teleprints can be consulted in the Public Record Office and in Washington.

Raw army and air decrypts were handed over to a translation party which, when it was satisfied that a correct rendering of the German into English had been arrived at, passed it to an intelligence section specially established for the purpose. When this section had provided the translations with such explanatory notes as might be needed to elucidate their full meaning, they were divided into two classes, the more and the less urgent or important. The former were teleprinted immediately to SIS (who kept Churchill informed) and the three service ministries; the latter were made up daily into typed reports and despatched to the same recipients by road. Neither of these two classes of material has been opened to public inspection, but GCHQ is, or will be, reviewing them with release in mind. They were used by the official historians for *British Intelligence in the Second World War*. At a conservative estimate, they amount together to several million items of intelligence.

Early in 1941 this Ultra intelligence department was authorised to send, on its own initiative, signals based on the translations to GHQ Middle East in Cairo and subsequently to other Allied commanders in the field. These signals have been released to the Public Record Office, Kew, and to the National Archives in Washington; they number nearly 100,000[*] and they constitute almost all that is known about the intelligence content of Ultra – save, of course, what is summarised in the six volumes of the *British Intelligence History*.

Because of the distinction between what has and what has not been made available to the public, there are some remarkable anomalies. It is possible, for instance, to follow events in Jugoslavia and Greece in 1944

[*] See Appendix V.

and 1945 in considerable detail, because Balkan information was included in signals to Allied commanders in the Middle East and Italy who might be able to use it, but impossible to do the same about the German campaign in Russia, although a great deal of information about it was intercepted and translated.

Range and Limitations

Ultra information ranged from the momentous to the trivial, and which would come next off the decoding machines was unpredictable. At one extreme there were rare intercepts emanating from Hitler himself (like the order for the counter-attack which led to the German disaster in the Falaise pocket in August 1944), at the other instructions for the transfer of small parties of soldiers or airmen from one unit or one district to another. In between fell such things as orders to theatre commanders which revealed enemy plans and thus gave valuable strategic guidance to the Allies, supply and transport information which, when accumulated and tabulated, could show the fuel or ammunition state of an army or an air fleet (most valuably perhaps in the case of the routeing and cargoes of the ships which supplied Rommel's troops in Libya) or the number of tanks in repair workshops after a battle. Less often, though on rare occasions useful, was tactical information about intended battlefield moves or warnings of air raids.

All three branches of the Wehrmacht used Enigma widely, but they did not use it under all conditions or for all purposes. Where telephone or telegraph lines existed, these were preferred to radio, which carried with it the time-consuming obligation to use the Enigma machine twice. Where land-lines did not exist, or where they were interrupted by sabotage or bombing, radio was used and interception became possible. Thus there was very little Ultra in France between June 1940 and June 1944, but a great deal of it in the desert in 1941 and 1942.

Though voluminous and immensely valuable, Ultra could consequently never give a complete picture of German military power and potential. It was only a random selection of the enemy's private correspondence; it told a lot, but it did not, and could not, tell everything. On the other hand, it was an entirely novel kind of intelligence source, one which no general had ever had before – or perhaps will ever have again in such volume and with such regularity. By the end of 1942 it was accepted as the chief among all sources, providing the framework for the others and guiding strategic decisions at the highest level.

Geheimschreiber

In addition to Enigma, the German armed forces also used, from 1942 onwards, a machine called Geheimschreiber ('secret writer') for communications between Berlin and senior headquarters in the field. Geheimschreiber sent non-Morse signals at very high speed. It was mainly used on the Russian front. Its transmissions were intercepted and a new machine (a direct ancestor of modern computers, which the bombes used to decrypt Enigma were not) devised to decrypt them. The decrypts were classed as Ultra and treated in every respect like Enigma decrypts. The great bulk of them consisted of long lists of supplies needed or sent, and the like, but important high-level operational items were also found among them.

'Fish' (as Geheimschreiber material was called in Hut 3) was at first put down as 'strictly non-operational' and 'of the highest importance but not of the highest urgency', but by May 1943 was being dealt with round the clock in the same way as Enigma.

Note: For further details, see F. H. Hinsley and Alan Stripp, *Codebreakers* (Oxford University Press, 1993), 81–8, 141–8, and *The Oxford Companion to the Second World War*, ed. I.C.B. Dear. (OUP, 1995), s. v. Ultra.

APPENDIX II

The Controversy Over Crete

(see p. 81)

In *Crete: The Battle and the Resistance*, which was published in May 1991 to coincide with the fiftieth anniversary of the Battle of Crete, Mr Antony Beevor revived criticisms of General Freyberg along lines made familiar by others thirty years earlier, but with the benefit of knowledge of Ultra which was denied to them. At the same time the late Lord Freyberg published a biography of his father (*Bernard Freyberg, V.C.: Soldier of Two Nations*) which set out to defend his memory and dealt with Crete at length.

Several points made in the resultant controversy require clarification if a fair assessment of General Freyberg's actions is to be reached.

1.   Lord Freyberg disclosed that his father had told him that he was expressly forbidden to make use of Ultra. So long as this was not known, it had been legitimate to blame Freyberg for not using Ultra to the best advantage. This line of argument is now ruled out; it can be sustained only by doubting the word of two honourable men.

2.   Why was Freyberg given Ultra but forbidden to use it? To today's eyes, this seems illogical and absurd, a needless additional burden upon him. No contemporary explanation has been discovered. A strong possibility is that the pressure of multiplying emergencies (enforced retreats in Egypt and Greece, the growing threat to Syria, Iran and the whole Middle East) was causing confusion and muddle. In the absence of positive evidence it is permissible to guess that Churchill's enthusiasm to utilise the new source of intelligence outran his discretion when he ordered Freyberg to be given Ultra, but that in the overriding interest of security Menzies forbade its use but forebore to tell Churchill that he had done so.

Admiral Cunningham later wrote that Churchill did not understand the Mediterranean. On 10 May, for instance, he thought that 'tanks [there were hardly any in Crete] and special assault parties [none existed]' could 'destroy the intruders' when the parachutists landed, and on the 14th he wrote that he 'would welcome the chance for our high-class troops [exhausted and without heavy weapons after Greece]' to get to grips with them, adding 'we can surely reinforce [with what, and how?] more easily than he can'. Even as late as 26 May, when the die was already cast, he signalled Wavell, 'Victory in Crete is essential at this turning point in the war. Keep hurling in all aid you can.' The loss of Crete did not cool his ardour to make use of Ultra: less than a month later he was spurring Wavell to attack Rommel on insufficient Ultra evidence, although Wavell lacked the wherewithal to do so effectively, and he badgered Auckinleck to the same effect later.

3.   That Menzies silently countermanded Churchill's instructions is pure speculation,* but one of the certainties is that the security rules governing the dissemination of Ultra were in a primitive, imperfectly formulated and (by later standards) inconsistent state in the spring of 1941, and that anomalies abounded. For instance:

(a) No evidence exists to show that Wilson was forbidden to make use of Ultra in Greece. He did use it. Why should he have been treated differently from Freyberg? Using Ultra to facilitate retreat would be no less, but also no more, likely to give away the secret than using it to arrange the defence of Crete to the best advantage.

(b) Before long, security regulations restricted Ultra to the level of army commanders in order to minimise the risk of men or papers being captured. Neither Wilson nor Freyberg commanded an army, but lesser *ad hoc* formations, W Force and Creforce respectively. Again, the 'value not interest' rule also denied access to information which the recipient could not use to prosecute the war. Yet between 7 and 15 April, forty-four Ultra signals were sent to the British Military Attaché in Belgrade, who commanded no troops at all, could not use the knowledge constructively (that is, for him 'value' was nil, 'interest' all) and was in imminent danger of capture and interrogation.

---

* Barely two months later, however, 'C' did take just that sort of action. On 16 July he prevented Churchill from sending Stalin the news that 4 Panzer Army intended to surround the Russian forces at Smolensk, on the ground that to do so would imperil Ultra, the source of the information (Bradley F. Smith, *Sharing Secrets with Stalin* (Univ. of Kansas Press 1996) 52). The speculation in the text is thereby made the more persuasive.

(c) There is no evidence that either Wilson or Freyberg was instructed to disguise Ultra beyond recognition – as was insisted upon later – if he embodied it in orders to subordinates. Freyberg seems to have made fairly transparent use of it in this way.

4.   Critics have accused Freyberg of paying too much attention to the threat from the sea. They forget two things:

(a) No island had ever before been captured *except* from the sea. It was therefore natural for Freyberg to take the seaborne threat seriously. Like every other historical event, his decision can be judged fairly only in the light of the probable assumptions and thought-patterns of the time.

(b) Although the event showed that the sea landing was designed simply to deliver supplies and heavy weapons, and although the convoy of caiques was sunk at sea before it reached the coast (which of course tends to hide its importance from the eyes of later writers), there was very little in the Ultra signals available to Freyberg to suggest that he would not have to face an armed assault from the sea. The word 'attack' was used to describe the landing on OL 389, for instance. Nothing in the two chief operational signals, OLs 2167 and 302, distinguished the airborne from the sea landing save the intended method of delivery and the proportional weight of attack, stated to be two-thirds air and one-third sea, the latter amounting to about 10,000 men. OL 278 of 11 May announced that twelve ships totalling 27,000 tons were available for the 'attack' on Crete, and that 'some' of them would carry rations and ammunition; the implication was that the remainder would carry a formidable contingent of armed men.

Freyberg's assessment of the danger from the sea proved to be wrong, but on the evidence it is difficult to fault him.

5.   Freyberg can, however, be blamed for not taking steps to protect the western side of Maleme airfield better. He apparently believed that the dried-up bed of the River Tavronitis was unsuitable for an air landing. On second thoughts he changed his mind and wanted to move the Greek brigade thither, but felt bound by the 'no action on Ultra' rule. He should have devised a better plan for the defence of the airfield during the first five days of his command, before the first Ultra signal designating Maleme as a primary target (OL 2167) reached him. Gliders landed in the river-bed; he had probably not envisaged this unprecedented action because he did not think that the German commander would accept the risk of so many casualties from rough landings.

6.   With hindsight, it is easy to see that obvious precautions like the all-round defence of an airfield could not possibly have betrayed the Ultra secret: but again it was only later experience which showed this. An air

landing was bound to be a part, even if only a secondary part, of any attempt to capture Crete: an earlier defence commander's appreciation had made this point six months before. It was not more logical to refrain from all-round defence than from using Ultra intelligence to 'duck under the blow' in Greece, but logic is seldom the guide in conditions of haste and emergency, and the prohibition rule fulfilled the primary requirement of secrecy – 'better safe than sorry', even if Crete were to be lost in the process.

See also a paper I read at the National Army Museum in 1991, reprinted in *Intelligence Investigations* 195–203.

APPENDIX III

Harris and Intelligence

(see p. 169)

A striking example of the casuistry with which Harris could misrepresent what he either would not or could not understand occurred in the spring of 1944. Examining possible reasons for a known decline of U-boat construction, an Admiralty report of 1 March attributed the decline to policy rather than air-raid damage, giving reasons (the report was in fact correct, as was discovered later. Fewer 'old-fashioned' U-boats were being built because the revolutionary new Walter boats were about to come into production; see pp. 206–8.) Harris read the report and commented on 7 March, 'It seems to me, however, absurd to suggest that this decision to curtail U-boat building has been voluntarily taken and is not, in large measure at least, the result of our bombing and mining policy. Such a suggestion might perhaps be plausible if no account whatever is taken of the known effect of our bombing of supplies of basic products . . . a general reduction . . . in U-boat construction is precisely the result which might be expected to follow on the destruction of industrial centres. . . . I note also that no credit has been given to Bomber Command for the considerable switch over of resources to ship-building which has beyond doubt been forced upon the enemy almost entirely through the destruction caused by the mine-laying of this Command.'

There are many flaws in this argument, including (1) 'absurd to suggest' – but how else seek an explanation of unexplained phenomena except by suggesting solutions? (2) 'known effects' – what had become *known*, since the Japanese Ambassador's conversation with Feldmarschall Milch on 17 August 1943, to invalidate the Ambassador's estimate that 'the damage done [by bombing] to production establishments was very small in comparison with the damage done to ordinary potential'? (3) Harris can hardly claim credit for minelaying, since he had only recently been converted to it under pressure and had for so long done his best to deny Coastal Command the aircraft required for it.

APPENDIX IV

Mihailović and Tito

(see p. 222, above. Reprinted from Ralph Bennett, Sir William Deakin, Sir David Hunt and Sir Peter Wilkinson, 'Intelligence and National Security', vol. 10, no. 3 (July 1995), pp. 527–8.)

Fifty years ago the undersigned were intelligence officers concerned *inter alia* with Balkan affairs. We wish to place on record some of our views about the switch of British support from Mihailović to Tito in 1943 because (i) the motives for the switch are at present under attack on what we consider ill-conceived grounds and (ii) because we find that our very different wartime experiences lead us to almost identical conclusions.

Briefly:

Bennett was a Duty Officer in Hut 3 at Bletchley Park for the relevant period. He read all the Balkan Ultra signals and was personally responsible for issuing some of them.

Deakin was posted from London to SOE Cairo in November 1942. He was parachuted to Montenegro in May 1943 on an exploratory military mission to contact Tito's forces and seek direct firsthand evidence whether they were effectively fighting the Axis. From December 1943 to mid-1944 he served with SOE in Cairo and Italy.

Hunt was a senior army intelligence officer in the desert, Tunisia, Sicily and Italy, and later wrote Alexander of Tunis' official *Despatches*. In the course of his duties he received all Balkan Ultra signals. They were so numerous and specific from September 1943 until the end of the war that he entrusted one of his staff with the special task of entering German dispositions in Yugoslavia on a map which was kept up-to-date daily.

Wilkinson, on the staff of SOE London, held a senior appointment in

SOE Cairo between September and December 1943. From December 1943 until the end of March 1944 he was head of an SOE mission with the Partisans in Bosnia, Croatia and Slovenia.

Our various publications document our opinions.

We make the following points:

1.   About a thousand Ultra signals concerning Balkan affairs were sent to Allied Forces Headquarters (AFHQ) Algiers and GHQ Cairo, and later to Field-Marshal Alexander's successive Army Group HQs in Tunisia, Sicily and Italy, between the beginning of May 1943 and the end of December 1944. Many of them were based on several intercepts. It is therefore not true (as has been alleged) that Ultra produced little Balkan intelligence.

2.   These signals were summaries of decrypts of Wehrmacht Enigma messages. The originals emanated from all three services at all levels of authority – from OKW and Army Groups as well as from lowly German Air Force (GAF) units. Copies of these can be read in the Public Record Office.

3.   Most of the signals conveyed intelligence about the location, movements and intentions of German troops and recorded their attempts to combat Tito's partisans, notably listing the forces deployed in the three leading German offensives of 1943 and in their almost successful operation to capture Tito at Drvar in May 1944. Far fewer dealt with the activities of Mihilović's forces or with contacts between Chetnik groups (whether loosely subordinate to Mihailović or independent) and the German command. It was evident from Ultra that – as von Weichs (German C-in-C South-East and Army Group F from August 1943) told Hitler and OKW (who promptly agreed) on 1 November 1943 – 'Tito is our most dangerous enemy.' (In this context it should be remembered that the British government had told Mihailović to await an Allied landing before attempting active resistance, and that this accorded with Mihailović's own stated policy.)

4.   Other relevant secret intelligence available in London (and occasionally in Cairo) included decrypts of Abwehr Enigma, Abwehr hand-ciphers and a variety of German, Italian and Partisan hand-ciphers. None of these are at present open to public inspection.

It is pertinent to remark here

(a) that in the present state of knowledge it seems unlikely that these decrypts significantly contradicted Ultra evidence or told much in Mihailović's favour, particularly since it is said that Abwehr Enigma convicted Mihailović of collaborating with the Germans.

(b) the shift of support was carried through on the orders of the Prime Minister and the Chiefs of Staff in the light of all the intelligence available to them.

(c) the shift ran directly counter to the long-standing and strongly-held convictions of the Foreign Office and to the views of King Peter and his Yugoslav government-in-exile.

5. It has been alleged that certain junior members of the staff of SOE Cairo who were either communists or left-wing sympathisers were biased in favour of the Partisans and exercised an undue influence on policy in their favour. No evidence for this supposition has been produced.

6. In our opinion the reason for the change of sides can be amply demonstrated from German evidence available at the time (it has, of course been reinforced since) – that is to say, by a simple calculation of military advantage.

7. Wild accusations and the violently pro-Mihailović views expressed in current controversy may reflect praiseworthy loyalty to the leader and the cause to which certain British liaison officers were attached, and may understandably originate in resentment and disappointment at the switch to Tito. We are nevertheless confident that they bear little relation to historical truth.

RALPH BENNETT   DAVID HUNT
WILLIAM DEAKIN   PETER WILKINSON

I associate myself fully with the views expressed above.

ALEXANDER R. GLEN

(Royal Navy Intelligence Division 1938–54. Assistant Naval Attaché Belgrade, January 1940 until German attack April 1941. Closely associated with SOE and SIS. Returned Yugoslavia September 1943, Peljesac offensive May–October 1944, Eastern Serbia and Danube, with Partisans and Red Army.)

APPENDIX V

Signals to Commands Abroad

Very approximately, the number of signals despatched daily from Hut 3 to commands abroad at different periods was as follows:

March–November 1941	10 or less	First clashes in the desert
December 1941–May 1942	30–40	CRUSADER
June–October 1942	70–80	Tobruk to Alamein
November 1942–April 1943	90–100	Alamein to the surrender in Tunisia
May–June 1943	70–80	Between campaigns
July–September 1943	100–120	Sicily and Salerno
October 1943–March 1944	70–80[*]	Anzio
April–May 1944	80–100	DIADEM
June–August 1944	120–140	Advance to Florence; D-Day and Falaise
September 1944–April 1945	90–100	The Gothic Line, OLIVE; Arnhem, crossing the Rhine

It is of some interest to note that fewer than 2,000 signals were despatched during the first six months, only about 8,000 by the fall of

[*] Signals were sent to SHAEF and other western commands from January 1944.

Tobruk in June 1942, and 15,000 by Alamein. By the end of the war, almost 100,000 had been sent.

In the early days, only two or three headquarters in Egypt were served, but the service was progressively extended, and by 1945 sixty or more navy, army and air headquarters had at one time or another been recipients.

Signals were prefixed OK, MK, etc. (usually 9999 of each series), as quoted in the reference notes. The complete series, in historical order, was OL, MK, MKA, QT, VM, ML, JP, VL, KV, XL, HP, BT, KO. All are now in the Public Record Office, in class DEFE 3, together with the small C series.

APPENDIX VI

How It Was Done

(Reprinted from *Ultra and Mediterranean Strategy*)

Decrypting Enigma

Machine encipherment was still a novelty in 1939. The Enigma machine had been patented in 1919 and marketed without much success during the 1920s by a German firm as a means of safeguarding commercial secrets. It used a system of wheels or drums to complicate the path followed by an electric current when a key on its keyboard was depressed, thus making the relationship between the letters of the plaintext and the enciphered version so erratic as to be undiscoverable by any process of decryption then known. Soon after they seized power, the Nazis bought up the patent and improved the machine, and by the late 1930s it was in use by all branches of the Wehrmacht. It looked like a rather large and clumsy portable typewriter, but it was compact and sturdy enough to stand up to rough treatment. The electrical circuits it contained were immensely complicated, but anyone could learn to use it. Thus it was ideal for its purpose – simple in operation, yet it could make radio signals secure against the eavesdropper. Its only drawback was that it did not print out the encrypted text; instead, each letter was lit up in turn on a display screen, so that two or more operators were needed, one to type out the plaintext, another to copy down the encrypt as each letter appeared. The three wheels or drums could be chosen from a set of five and were interchangeable; each had an outer metal rim which could be locked to it in twenty-six different positions, one for each letter of the alphabet. Each time a key was depressed, the right-hand wheel moved on one place (i.e., made one twenty-sixth of a revolution); once in every twenty-six times the wheel also moved; and all three moved together when the middle wheel had made a complete revolution – just in the way a car's milometer does. The current passed through all three wheels and a fixed drum (the *Umkehrwalze*), which sent it back again by a different route. Later on, another complication was introduced: after leaving the wheels, the current was made to pass along loose wires ending in *Stecker* (plugs), which could be plugged in pairs into the machine in any order. The positions of the wheels and the order of the plugs were frequently changed in accordance with standard instructions; there was usually one major rearrangement every twenty-four hours, with minor adjustments at shorter intervals. In addition, the sender chose different settings of the wheels for every message, telling the receiver what he had done by means of an 'indicator' – two groups of three letters with which every message began. (The receiver would set his wheels to the position shown by the first group, and by decrypting the letters of the second group discover the setting at which the body of the text could be decrypted.) In order to decipher a given group of traffic, it was necessary (and sufficient) to know the choice and order of the three wheels, the positions of their outer rims, and the *Stecker* pairings. Wheels and rims together could provide something over a million possible arrangements, and the introduction of the *Stecker* pairings multiplied this to a total of approximately 150 million million million possible but unpredictably different versions of a single original text. It might take months – perhaps years – of unremitting application by a roomful of expert mathematicians to find the right solution to even a single day's key, and the Germans therefore believed that an Enigma message could safely be transmitted by wireless in ordinary Morse code, for although it was sure to be intercepted, it would certainly be unintelligible. They never seriously questioned this belief.

The Polish government, fearful that it was to be Hitler's next victim and anxious for warning of his army's moves, trained a party of mathematicians and set them to work to break the Enigma cipher; they devised a machine to test possible solutions and read many signals until the Germans introduced new complications into their procedure in 1939. France and England were also tackling the problem, and the three countries began to concert measures, most notably when the Poles handed over a reconstructed Enigma machine to the British shortly before the outbreak of the war. Anglo-French co-operation continued until the fall of France in 1940, after which all the work was concentrated at Bletchley Park.

Possession of an Enigma machine gave indispensable familiarity with its circuits, but otherwise did not help toward reading its messages; for this, it was essential to discover the settings used, and the mathematical problem thereby posed was formidable indeed. Only a machine could consistently defeat the machine; certainly nothing else would do if the messages were to be read in time to be useful. A young Cambridge mathematician, Alan Turing, who had worked on the theory of a universal calculating machine, was brought together with cryptanalysts skilled in all the tricks of their trade, and they had the benefit of the Poles' experience with the machine they had constructed. By the early summer of 1940 an electromechanical engine (always referred to as the bombe) had been built at Bletchley and had proved its designers' genius by decrypting several days' traffic.

Human ingenuity had to give the machine a start, however. In theory, the bombe could try out all the millions of possible solutions to a day's key, but it would take an immensely long time to do this. And how was it to tell its attendants that it had come upon the right solution because it had found one that was in German, not gibberish? Before starting the bombe, it was necessary to make a correct guess at the original version of a bit of the text. In the early days it was sometimes possible, because of the slack cipher discipline of some of the Luftwaffe signalling staff, to guess the initial settings of some of the messages, and this provided decrypts of the last three letters of their indicator groups. The first breaks were achieved during the spring of 1940 in this way – that is, by hand and without the help of the bombe. Before long the Germans tightened up their cipher discipline, but by that time the damage had been done. For as soon as a few days' traffic had been read, a second careless habit was discovered.* The tightening up of cipher discipline had made future breaks by hand impossible or hopelessly laborious, but the second bad habit was enough to start the bombe off and to give it a good chance of finding the right solution to the day's key.

Success came just in time for the Battle of France and the Battle of Britain, though as yet it was by no means always possible to break a given day's key while it was still current. If the bombe occasionally faltered, however, it never failed: the flow of decrypted messages was soon regular and remunerative enough for shift-working round the clock to be

---

* Military operations call for regular reports from the front line back to headquarters; they are likely to be rendered at much the same time each day and may be of much the same length. Thus there is a reasonable chance of identifying them on external evidence alone. If the same opening formula is used every time, decryption becomes immeasurably easier.

necessary for the intelligence staff which translated and appraised them. From then on, the output showed a constant tendency to rise, except for rare and fortunately brief intervals. Temporary declines in the volume of traffic accounted for one or two of these intervals and progressive improvements in the Enigma machine for others. But although these improvements eventually raised the number of possible versions of a given plaintext to over 10^{33}, none of them proved insuperable.

All three branches of the Wehrmacht used Enigma, but differently, and within each service different forms of it were used for different purposes. Thus by 1945 there were more than a dozen species, so to speak, of naval Enigma – one for surface ships in the North Sea and the Atlantic and another for U-boats in the same area, a third for Mediterranean surface vessels, a fourth for Mediterranean U-boats, and so on. Naval Enigma proved difficult to break, and the first successes were not gained until early in 1941. GAF Enigma was easier game – partly because there was much more of it, so that the cryptanalysts' foundations were laid sooner, partly because of the slack signals discipline resulting from hasty expansion and low-grade operators – and it was the first to be broken, in spring 1940. Again, there were several 'species' – one for general GAF use in northwestern Europe, another for the Mediterranean, several for aerial reconnaissance and army co-operation in particular theatres of war. A great deal of ground information was thus transmitted over GAF links (the Flivos – *Fliegerverbindungsoffiziere*, air liaison officers – were later one of our most prolific sources of information about the panzer divisions or corps to which they were attached), but in the desert it was a severe handicap that army signals discipline was good enough to delay regular decryption of army Enigma until 1942. All told, there were almost fifty different army and air Enigma keys, several of which might, in the last two years of the war at any rate, be 'running' at the same time, at least one of them currently.

Signalling Ultra

As soon as decrypted messages were plentifully available, a new requirement promptly became evident. Cryptanalytic skill and mathematical insight were no longer enough; an exact and fluent knowledge of German and an aptitude for intelligence work were now also needed if the miracle was to be exploited to the full. The two sets of qualities complemented each other; the latter was only called for because of the success gained by the former, of course, but henceforth it was just as essential.

Inescapable differences between the best methods of handling intelligence by the three British services now imposed organisational distinctions. Evidence about the movements of German surface vessels and U-boats could be properly appraised and acted on only by those who knew where British ships and convoys were – that is to say, by the Admiralty, which was an operational command headquarters as well as a government ministry. Naval decrypts were therefore translated at Bletchley Park and teleprinted, almost without annotation, to the Admiralty, which rerouted convoys or took other necessary action. Similar considerations scarcely applied to army and air intelligence. Except for advance news of German bombing raids on English targets (for which the Air Ministry acted in the same way as the Admiralty did for all naval intelligence), very little of it could be immediate and operational in the circumstances prevailing during the winter of 1940–41. The War Office and Air Ministry had much in common with each other, and many things distinguished the attitude of both toward Ultra from that of the Admiralty. A common intelligence organisation for these two services was therefore set up at Bletchley Park. It was always known as Hut 3,* even after it moved into more convenient brick premises; it was this organisation which I joined in February 1941, and it is Hut 3 and its output with which this book is mainly concerned.

As soon as the Germans invaded Jugoslavia and Greece and began to intervene in Africa in the spring of 1941, a further common characteristic of army and air Ultra became evident, and this too shaped our organisation in a fundamental way. Like the Naval Section, Hut 3 teleprinted its hottest information to ministries in London (less urgent material was typed and sent up by bag), but in addition it had already begun to annotate and elucidate each item from background information derived from previous decrypts and accumulated in its card indexes. The swift movement of events in Greece and Cyrenaica, and the direct bearing of Ultra evidence on the fate of British troops there, soon made it plain that much would be gained if the decrypts were fully processed in Hut 3 and if signals based on them were immediately sent to commands in the field. Many perhaps vital hours would thus be saved. The first signals were sent to Cairo in March 1941. Other receiving stations were

---

* Decrypts were supplied to Hut 3 by Hut 6. In a similar pairing, Hut 8 supplied Hut 4 (the Naval Section).

established as need arose – the air and naval headquarters in Malta and Alexandria were the next – until by the time the Allied armies broke out of the Normandy bridgehead in July 1944, Hut 3 was currently serving forty or fifty subscribers in northwest Europe, Italy and the Mediterranean. Each of these subscribers was serviced by a Special Liaison Unit, a signals and intelligence link established for this sole purpose and operating under stringent security rules.

The veil of official secrecy which had hidden Ultra was lifted in October 1977 when some 25,000 of these signals, covering the period November 1943 to August 1944, were placed in the Public Record Office.* Subsequent releases completed the series from March 1941 to May 1945. These signals are the evidence upon which this book is based. Each signal drew its authority from one or more decrypts, which were themselves translated and teleprinted *in extenso* to the service ministries along with copies of the Hut 3 signals derived from them. The teleprints have not been released. Because the Hut 3 signals were not only checked meticulously at the time of drafting for accurate statement of fact and appropriately qualified comment but also rechecked later on both in the Hut and in London, it is safe to assume that their wording fairly represents the information received, though usually in summary form. Moreover, nothing which was regarded, either at the moment of receipt or during subsequent rescrutiny, as being important for the conduct of Allied operations was left unsignalled. Even unsupported by the teleprinted translations, therefore, the signals represent all the Ultra that was sent to field commands and all that was thought worth sending. The evidence used here is the same as that which was in the hands of the chief intelligence officers on the staffs of Eisenhower, Alexander and Montgomery.

What most of the signals lack, however, is more than a hint of the considerable intelligence servicing which almost every decrypt needed and received. The full meaning of the information conveyed by a message was only rarely self-evident from the translation alone, and it was usually necessary to draw out its significance by providing it with a context and setting it against a background as like as possible to that which would have been in the minds of the German sender and receiver. With the aid of Hut 3's extensive indexes, built up from previous messages, this could nearly always be done in considerable detail, and the teleprint annotated

---

* A larger number of the (far shorter) naval teleprints were also released. These covered rather different dates.

accordingly. An order for a panzer division to move from one part of the front to another, for instance, obviously gained added significance if a note pointed out that we already knew that several others were going in the same direction, or that the new message countermanded previous orders. Little of all this intelligence work appears in the signals, however, partly in order to save scarce signalling time and partly because recipients would draw the same deductions from the same evidence. These annotations – always introduced by the word 'Comment', to distinguish them clearly from the text of the German message – were much scantier in the signals than in the teleprints.

By early in 1941, a convenient flow of work and a suitable division of labour had been discovered by experience; it remained substantially unchanged for the rest of the war.

At whatever hour of the day or night a key was broken by Hut 6, decrypts were immediately passed to the translators in Hut 3. Partly for historical reasons dating back to prewar recruitment, partly by chance, the translators were largely civilians, although almost all the rest of the Hut's personnel were in uniform. From late 1943 onward, an ever-growing number of Americans joined us. So interdependent was every phase of the work and so enthusiastic was everyone to play a part to the best of his or her ability that Hut 3 was from the start, and always remained, a good example of that interservice and inter-Allied co-operation which kept the wheels of the Anglo-American Supreme Command turning smoothly, but which completely eluded the Germans, although they possessed the formal framework for it in the OKW. This spirit of co-operation had to withstand quite severe strains, particularly when an essential expansion of staff brought some overcrowding. On days when several keys were current at once and critical operations were on hand in both theatres, an eight-hour tour of duty could be very tiring, because it required repeated shifts of attention from Normandy to Italy and back again and because it called incessantly for absolute accuracy and continual alertness against errors of judgment while at the same time demanding that everything be done as quickly as possible.

The translators' first duty was to analyse a message possibly corrupted in transmission, suggest emendations where necessary, and expand the many abbreviations used. When they were satisfied that they had produced an English version which fairly represented the sense of the German, the translators handed text and translation to the air and military advisers, service officers who sat opposite each other at the next table in the production line. One or other, as the case required, would use the resources of the huge card indexes maintained by his section to explore the significance of the text before him – for a correct and lucid translation could still present severe intelligence problems. There was also a naval adviser ready to deal with such naval messages as might have wider significance; decrypts from German and Italian naval sources played an extremely important role in guiding British naval and air attacks on the shipping which carried supplies to Rommel across the Mediterranean from Italy and Greece to Libyan ports, and in helping British army headquarters in Cairo to estimate how long the available stocks of food, fuel and ammunition could sustain the successive German offensives. Having solved his problems as best he could, the adviser annotated the translation accordingly, decided whether the item merited a signal to commands abroad, drafted the signal if he so decided, and then handed it over to the Duty Officer for checking and final approval before it passed to the signals officer and his staff of teleprinter operators and coding clerks. Over two hundred such signals were sent on D-day, 6 June 1944, but a rate of a thousand a week had already been common for almost two years. (See Appendix V.)

Duty Officers knew German and the intelligence background well, but their prime function was to be responsible for everything rather than to be as expert as their colleagues in any single field. Theirs was a twofold responsibility. The first was to see that translation and signal both faithfully represented the sense of the original, looking for misconceptions which incautious wording might accidentally convey to recipients of a signal, and ensuring appropriate changes where necessary. A partially corrupt text, a translation unavoidably loose because of the imprecision of the German original, difficulty in drawing confident conclusions from a perhaps incomplete intercept – all these might lead to uncertainties, the exact nature and degree of which it was essential to make clear to recipients, who in some instances might possess evidence capable of resolving them provided they were told exactly what was certain and what doubtful.

As well as overseeing the observance of standard conventions like these, the Duty Officer was responsible for ensuring that strict security was maintained. Nothing must be signalled which openly revealed the source, nothing sent to a recipient which did not directly concern him – the criterion was his 'need to know' its content, which must be of 'value, not interest' to him – and various groups of recipients had to be kept informed on an all-or-none basis lest consultation among them be frustrated.

Behind the sometimes hectic activity of these frontline troops lay several research departments whose specialised knowledge was indispensable.

One of them combined a rigorously academic understanding of grammatical niceties and precise shades of meaning with a knack of divining the correct expansion of novel German abbreviations and a trained mechanic's repertory of technical terms: it invited the Duty Officer to veto inspired guesses at baffling texts if they did not meet its exacting standards, and it knew the meaning of the long German names for the working part of radar sets and rockets, tank tracks and self-propelled guns (without which the significance of repair-shop reports and supply returns could not be grasped). Another section took on longer-term research projects where only the careful sifting of accumulated evidence could solve a problem. Supply returns for both services were normally rendered according to a pro forma, for instance, but the pro forma was unintelligible without a key to the numbered paragraphs. Given enough examples and the dexterous juxtaposition of scraps of information and plausible hypotheses, the key could almost always be found in the end – and commands informed how many tanks and guns a panzer division possessed, or how many serviceable aircraft there were in a bomber squadron and how many under repair in the workshops. When the Enigma used by the German State Railways (first broken in the summer of 1940) was found to contain little more than strings of six-figure consignment numbers, it was this department which painstakingly distilled a meaning from the mass of superficially uninteresting and unrewarding detail, managed to associate some of the consignment numbers with army or air force units, noted how destinations and the timing of movements converged on Germany's eastern frontier in the spring of 1941 – and forecast the invasion of Russia. A third section concentrated on the inscrutable but tremendously important traffic which carried instructions about navigational beams to the long-range bomber Gruppen and (later on) provided valuable clues to the research going on at Peenemuende and to the construction of V-weapon sites for the bombardment of London.* A fourth undertook to assemble and collate German identifications (mainly derived from the German Y Service, which studied the external features of undecrypted wireless traffic and located transmitters by direction-finding techniques) of British and American formations and their ideas about the Allied order of battle. Its studies were of immense value, particularly in the weeks

* Because of the peculiarly complex and technical nature of this material, it was early removed from the normal flow of work and diverted to a special section in Hut 3 which was in direct contact about it with the Air Ministry. The use made of it is fully described in R. V. Jones, *Most Secret War*.

immediately before and after D-day, because they showed the success of the Allied deception plan in creating the impression that the Normandy landings were only secondary and that the main invasion would come in the Calais area.

These research departments had some contact with the world of non-Ultra intelligence outside Bletchley Park and were able to utilise information thus gained to assist and accelerate their work. But they were alone in this. Hut 3 existed to purvey pure Ultra, not to adulterate it with anything else. No teleprint or signal ever bore footnote or comment derived from anything except Hut 3's own card indexes, save that map references were interpolated into frontline reports, etc., as an aid to quick understanding. No hint of forthcoming Allied operations normally reached the Hut, so that we remained 'pure'. This 'purity' was in some respects a hindrance, and no doubt meant that we sometimes sent information needlessly or when it was already out of date, but it ruled out all possibility that we might unconsciously read our evidence in the light of extraneous knowledge, and left it entirely to intelligence staffs in the field to assimilate Ultra to other sources, judge between them if there were discrepancies, and present their commander with a single picture.

This 'purity' had one unforeseen consequence. It meant that we followed the fighting from the German point of view exclusively, and knew much more about most German divisions and some German generals than we did about any on our own side. Rommel, Westphal and Bayerlein were more familiar figures than ever Eisenhower or Montgomery were, the 90th Light Division so daily an acquaintance during the African campaign that there was even a sort of temptation to rejoice when it scored a success. No doubt the mood belonged, as with the general public, to the desert war; it faded soon after Rommel left Africa early in 1943.

Is it possible to discover how much Ultra contributed to the whole intelligence picture? The preceding chapters are an attempt to answer this question, but several points deserve special emphasis.

(i) Because Hut 3 was told little about Allied intentions, nothing in the signals themselves indicates their relative value (save, of course, insofar as the priority given to each is a guide to the opinion of those who drafted it). In order to try to estimate this fairly, I have always compared the signals with the actual course of events as it is now known from official histories and from the memoirs of leading participants, setting what we knew in Hut 3 – and the time at which we knew it – beside what happened (so far as this can be reconstructed) and pointing out the similarities and – where necessary – the contrasts and discrepancies. Essential though it was, in order to ensure a sound frame of reference, this has meant risking unconscious hindsight, and I have tried to be continuously on my guard against it. For Ultra, in common with all other military intelligence, became available piece by piece in no very logical order as a pattern of largely unforeseeable events gradually unfolded itself, while a historian more than forty years later cannot entirely obliterate from his mind an awareness of their outcome.

(ii)   Since every Ultra item carried weight because of its unimpeachable authenticity, however, common sense suggests that a very close estimate of its importance can be obtained through a careful study of the timing of Ultra intelligence. For where an Ultra item can be shown to have arrived in time, it is not likely to have been disregarded. The history of most Enigma messages can still be traced from German time of origin to the moment at which the Ultra signal derived from it was sent off. Reasonable allowance must then be made for transmission time, for decoding upon receipt, and for consideration by the intelligence officer who received it and by the commander who might act upon it. Where this still leaves an interval before the action described in, or consequent upon, the signal, it may be presumed that the Allied commander's measures were taken in the light of the Ultra information. Thus Ultra gave ample warning of Rommel's intentions before Alam Halfa and Medenine, enabling Montgomery to take appropriate measures to frustrate them. Few cases are as simple or as obviously important as these, but I have been at pains to give full evidence about timing so that the probable bearing of information upon decisions may be estimated as exactly as possible.

(iii)   A still more serious danger in this line of thought is the assumption that Ultra's chief value lay in the realm of battlefield tactics. This was almost certainly not the case. Even in the most favourable circumstances, tactical information might arrive too late to be useful. The unspectacular accumulation of evidence about the Germans' supply situation, which Ultra made possible, may in the long run have proved more valuable because it enabled long-term trends to be analysed and pressure to be brought to bear on tender spots. This type of information did not depend for its value on being up to the minute; it could be almost equally useful even when a week old. It first came into prominence in Africa during the summer of 1942, when Ultra enabled a close watch to be kept on Rommel's petrol and ammunition supplies and gave foreknowledge of the restrictions on tank movements and aircraft sorties which the sinking of even a single cargo could bring, as well as providing tactical targets in the shape of convoy movements. Somewhat more intermittent, but of even greater interest, were the long statements of the number of their battleworthy tanks and guns periodically rendered by army corps and divisions, for they permitted the regular monitoring of the enemy's combat readiness in a way no other source could have made possible. The evident importance of Ultra's almost daily advance warnings of GAF operations, even that of rare and outstanding items like the plans for Alam Halfa and Medenine, must not take too much of the limelight away from material of a quite different and less glamorous kind which, recurring at regular intervals, acquired a value all the greater because it was cumulative.

(iv)   Since it was the secret operational communication of one German headquarters with another, every Enigma message was authentic and reliable. There was no need, as with agents, to wonder about the good faith of the source or the soundness of his judgment. But no message had more authority than that of the officer who sent it, nor more reliability as a guide to his superiors' intentions than the extent of the knowledge they allowed him to have or the initiative to which his rank entitled him. It was perhaps easier for the Hut 3 intelligence officers then than it is for the reader of today to keep constantly in mind the caution this imposed. Every Ultra signal had to be suitably attributed (for instance, 'Fliegerkorps II's intentions at 1045 hours ninth were . . .') so that it carried within itself an indication of the credence it deserved as a forewarning of events to come, and it was not uncommon – to take a very simple case – for a signal stating the operations proposed by a Fliegerkorps to be followed within the hour by another announcing that the parent Luftflotte had countermanded them in favour of a different target.

(v)   The scope of the intelligence Ultra could provide was restricted by the natural preference of rearward headquarters and senior commanders for telephone or teleprinter over radio. A large number of very secret and very important messages, the content of which it would have been extremely useful to know, were for this reason never received at all. But as instructions had to be disseminated nearer and nearer to the front, so the chance that all or part of the original order would become accessible through transmission over the ether began to rise. Again, it could be tantalising to intercept the answer to a question which had evidently been asked by landline (destruction of the line by sabotage or bombing could prevent the answer going by the same route), for the one was unlikely to be fully comprehensible without the other, and once more laborious analysis and comparison with parallel evidence was necessary before a plausible conclusion could be drawn and useful intelligence extracted.

For although Ultra was absolutely reliable when it appeared, it could not be relied on always to appear when needed or to answer every question explicitly. Deliberate wireless silence could muffle it completely. A crucial intercept might be missed perhaps because weather conditions or fading temporarily blotted out a radio link while it was carrying an important message. A few hours' delay in breaking a particular key might bring vital information too late for it to be used effectively. The failure of Eisenhower's intelligence staff to foresee Rommel's attack on the Kasserine pass in February 1943 vividly illustrates the difficulties which could arise.

(vi) From a totally different angle, there was the necessary restriction imposed by our own security regulations upon the use of Ultra. The number of those allowed to know about it was strictly limited both at home and in the field. Commanders were strictly forbidden to order any action which might imperil the source by seeming to be ascribable only to the reading of Enigma traffic – thus, for example, ship movements and concentrations of tanks had to be confirmed by aerial reconnaissance, and seen to be observed, before they could be bombed. Ultra was too strong a medicine to be taken neat; unless it was diluted from less secret sources, the consequences might be disastrous – it might be compromised and so lost for the future. For similar reasons, no Ultra signals were sent direct to commands below the level of an army headquarters or the equivalent, and anything passed to corps or division had to be disguised in the form of an operational order. The number of those in the secret was kept to the minimum compatible with effective use. How severe these limitations were in practice, Hut 3 never knew; its duty was done when it had despatched its signal.

(vii) Lastly, it has to be remembered that Ultra was not the only source of military intelligence. It did not replace the traditional sources but was a superb addition to them because it provided what they could not, and because it came straight from the horse's mouth. The traditional sources remained of great value in their own way. Agents might hear things which had not been signalled; low-grade ciphers used in the front line carried tactical details of immediate (if also ephemeral) value if broken at once;

prisoner interrogation and aerial reconnaissance could confirm that the orders conveyed by Ultra were actually being carried out. Thus the old and the new were complementary, each yielding information beyond the reach of the other. To say this is in no way to diminish the importance of Ultra but to see it in its proper light; to recognise that Ultra could not do everything is to appreciate the complexity of the intelligence puzzle as it was painfully put together when there were battles to be fought and a war to be won. The consensus among intelligence officers attached to field commands whose after-action views are known is that blending of all sources was vital, but that Ultra was chief among them. And here again, of course, the question 'How much Ultra, how much the rest?' cannot be answered from Hut 3's signals alone – except by observing how little of what is thought worth recording by the operational histories they failed to reveal.

Ultra's successes were in fact in some respects its own worst enemies at the time, and it is essential that the occasional and temporary mistakes of the past should not be repeated now, or false beliefs become ingrained. Ultra was not omniscient, and could not be, for the reasons already given. But because it was so nearly omniscient so often, there were a few occasions when something like the opinion 'If it's not in Ultra, it can't be true' seems to have prevailed in some quarters. It is not my main purpose to inquire whether this led to errors by Allied commanders, but at the risk of repetition it is worth making two points, both of which are illustrated in the subsequently notorious cases of the surprise the Germans achieved at Kasserine and in the Ardennes. Bletchley's bombes could not decrypt what had never been encrypted in Enigma or sent over the air, and so deliberate wireless silence could make vital information totally inaccessible to Ultra. Because of the consequently unavoidable gaps in the story told by Hut 3's signals, these had to be very carefully interpreted before either being made the basis of command decisions or discarded as unhelpful. The fact that they could occasionally be misinterpreted throws into sharp relief the predicament of generals thrust back upon traditional methods of intelligence-gathering alone, and by contrast highlights the service Ultra was able to render on nearly every other occasion.

To return to the original question: How far can Ultra's contribution be measured? Churchill, Eisenhower, Alexander and others paid such handsome tributes at the end of the war that there is no doubting its incalculable value. It put the Allied general into the position of a chess player whose opponent announces his moves in advance and explains why he makes them. None of the generals, unfortunately, seems to have left a considered account of his opinion of Ultra or to have compiled detailed examples of the use he made of it. But it is a fair presumption that the possession of Ultra did not dispense generals from any of their traditional responsibilities. They still had to plan their attacks and carry them out; Ultra simply helped them to apply force most economically and with maximum effect. Insofar as one of the novelties which distinguished Ultra from older forms of intelligence-gathering was that it was not the monopoly of the battlefield general because it was produced far behind the front, Ultra may indeed have somewhat increased a general's burdens; for he must always have been aware that his political chiefs were in the secret too, saw the same decrypts as he, and were therefore in a good position to breathe down his neck should they choose to do so (as Churchill often did during the desert campaigns of 1941–42).

Sweeping suggestions have been made that the revelation of Ultra would make it necessary to rewrite the history of the war. The evidence presented here does not altogether bear them out. On the other hand, while neither the frequency with which Ultra was able to give Allied commanders forewarning of exceptional strokes planned by their enemies nor the tremendously detailed day-to-day information about the German army and air force it collected (only a comparatively small proportion of which could be included here without overloading the pages) is likely to lead to a wholesale revision of prevailing views about those commanders' actions, Ultra must surely modify them by showing that vital decisions were, or ought to have been, taken against an intelligence background which was sometimes markedly different from what has hitherto been supposed.

Illustrations of Ultra

These extracts from *Ultra and Mediterranean Strategy* and *Ultra in the West* illustrate the detail with which Ultra was capable of revealing the state of German supplies and their military intentions and actions.

A is from *Ultra and Mediterranean Strategy* pp. 79, 95, 102, 134 and covers supply, B from the same and covers Alam Halfa, Alamein and Medenine, C from *Ultra in the West* and illustrates Mortain and Falaise.

A A consistent pattern in shipping and supply information was established in June 1941 and prevailed until the early autumn. At least five or six times a month, the sailing from a Greek or Italian port of a convoy of supply ships or troop transports could be signalled to naval and air headquarters in Egypt (to Malta as well, when a direct link was opened in mid-September) sufficiently far in advance for the convoy to be intercepted somewhere along a route which was usually set out in considerable detail (points at which ships regularly altered course were often disguised under code names, but the disguise was soon penetrated and the points identified). Routine reconnaissance flights by the RAF 201 Group, based on Alexandria, could then be adjusted to ensure that planes were in the right places to spot convoys apparently by chance, after which bombers, submarines, or surface craft, as appropriate, could attack without compromising the source.

Even if attack was impossible or ineffective, the sight of a reconnaissance plane overhead might be enough to scare the convoy into a hasty return to port, thus at any rate delaying the supply programme. On 27 June, for example, air reconnaisance forced a convoy carrying 5,000 men back to Taranto, and the same thing happened again a month later. A series of messages during August and September revealed the tribulations of the tanker *Bellona*, which was too slow to avoid the aircraft and destroyers which relentlessly harried her and was unable to reach Bardia and deliver petrol which was said to be 'of the highest importance' to the Afrika Korps; she had instead to take refuge in Suda Bay before returning to the Piraeus, where she was eventually replaced by a faster vessel.

Among the many cases where it is not now possible to be quite sure that the sinking of a particular Axis transport can be directly ascribed to Ultra, a few stand out as absolute certainties. On the afternoon of 17 August it was learned that a convoy of four large liners escorted by six destroyers would leave Naples at midnight the next day bound for Tripoli, where it was due to arrive early on the 20th; only three of the liners reached their destination, the fourth being sunk on the way by the Malta-based submarine *Unique*. Next month these three were to sail for Tripoli from Taranto, and again we had more than twenty-four hours' notice of their route and timings; this time two more, each of 20,000 tons, were torpedoed and sunk on 18 September by *Unique*'s sister ship, *Upholder*, on the basis of 'special intelligence'. A day or two before this, a cargo of fuel, part consigned to Fliegerfuehrer and part to the Afrika Korps, was sent to the bottom off Trapani four days after its route was signalled to Alexandria and Malta.

Ironically enough, these last events came just after Hitler had ordered Fliegerkorps X to concentrate on convoy protection because of the serious shipping losses which were being suffered! Ultra did not report his decision in so many words but was quick to note action which evidently flowed from it – the planned development of two Sicilian airfields, presumably to house the bomber and fighter Gruppen which it had been proposed to transfer here from Greece in September. The deduction that Fleigerkorps X's move to Greece in June was now being slowed down or reversed was plain.

Force K's first and greatest successes in early and mid-November admirably illustrate the value of Ultra in the logistical war of attrition. CRUSADER began on 18 November between the first and second of them, and their effect on the land campaign can be amply documented from the same source. The mere presence of Force K contributed, within a few days of its arrival in Malta, to the suspension of supply traffic on 1 November, but there was some uncertainty about how long the ban would last because on a previous occasion it had been lifted in twenty-four hours. Thus a signal despatched on the afternoon of 8 November spoke only hesitantly of there being 'some evidence' that in spite of it a convoy had sailed the previous night. The convoy's indubitable existence and its probable ports of departure and destination (Naples and Tripoli) were confirmed the same evening, and the signal was the means of directing first a reconnaissance aircraft and then Force K to the target. In the early hours of 9 November, all seven merchant ships in the convoy, and two out of the four escorting destroyers, were sunk by the gunfire of Force K.* Part of the cargo thus denied to the Germans became known while the action was going on: it included 600 tons of GAF stores and 20,000 rounds of 88mm Flak ammunition. (Rommel, it is now known, immediately reported that all sea transport had been stopped because of this disaster, adding that to date he had received only 8,000 of the 60,000 men he had been promised through Benghazi.) Another and more heavily escorted convoy, first forecast on 15 November, was attacked on the 22nd and driven back to Taranto, where it stayed for a fortnight. Two ships from a third, which Fliegerkorps X had been calling for urgently since the beginning of the month (because threatening British troop concentrations and a serious decline in African fuel stocks made it imperative to accumulate 3,000 tons of aircraft fuel in Cyrenaica at once), was sunk en route to Benghazi on 24 November, by which time a week of the CRUSADER battles had made such inroads into Fliegerfuehrer's stocks that his operations were seriously endangered. Air transport, an extravagant way to move petrol from place to place, had to be hastily improvised.

Even when all proper precautions like preliminary air reconnaissance were taken, such 'close marking' of convoys could hardly fail to arouse suspicions, particularly when it so often proved lethal. Count Ciano, Mussolini's son-in-law and the Italian Foreign Minister, found the annihilation of the seven-ship convoy on 9 November 'inexplicable', for example. Some risk was inseparable from the operational use of Ultra, but it was essential to keep it to the absolute minimum. To preserve the security of the source by restricting the number of those who had access to it (even the commander of Force K was not among them) and to discourage rash actions which might sacrifice it for good in the pursuit of transient advantage were therefore ever-present anxieties. No really serious breach of security seems to have occurred, but Whitehall sent several sharp rebukes to Middle East authorities for carelessly imperilling it.[†] Constant watchfulness was particularly necessary after Ultra showed that the Italians were breaking some British codes and knew, for instance, that Malta had signalled to an aircraft in flight the estimated position of a convoy which Ultra had identified.

* Santoni, 120, mistakenly denies Ultra the credit.
[†] Jealous for the safety of a source which he regarded as peculiarly his own, Churchill himself sent at least two personal reminders about Ultra security that autumn (Gilbert vi. 1233, 1242).

A dozen or more returns of aircraft fuel stocks, rendered at various dates during the summer and early autumn, showed the effects of the British near-blockade in dramatic form. Stocks in Tripolitania – that is to say, reserves already landed and awaiting forwarding to the operational area – stood at 4,000 tons in May but sank to 3,000 in June and to 1,400 at the end of July. By the beginning of September they were down to a little over 400 – just a tenth of the May figure – and remained near that level, with one brief exception, for the next two months. Moreover, the decline in stocks in the rear was not accounted for by a corresponding increase farther forward; on the contrary, figures for the forward area followed the same pattern as those at base. From 2,800 tons in early September, they dropped steadily (again, with one brief exception) to 2,350 tons in October and to only 1,460 tons on 8 November. On the basis of two sets of consumption figures for October, this meant that just before heavy fighting began there was about a month's supply of aircraft fuel near the front and rather less at Tripoli – provided always that the current rate of consumption was unchanged; in fact, of course, it was bound to rise sharply when mobile warfare began again.

As the petrol shortage grew worse with the approach of autumn, so evidence of the anxiety it was causing became more and more striking. As early as July, Fliegerkorps X was being asked to step up its antisubmarine patrols because 'future operations will be imperilled by further shipping losses.' The Fliegerkorps passed this request on to the Italians, referring particularly to British submarine activity off Benghazi, but could do little itself because there was not enough petrol in Africa for it to transfer units even for a short time, since Fliegerfuehrer had only sufficient for two or three days' fighting at the level entailed by the recent battles round Sollum. (It was at this time that Halder contemptuously wrote in his diary, 'Safeguarding transports is an Italian affair. In the present situation ['of aircraft shortage on the Russian front' is presumably to be understood] it would be criminal to allot German aircraft for the purpose,' even though he had recently been told that the 5th Light Division was so short of petrol that it would hardly be able even to get to the battlefield if ordered to attack Sollum.) Fliegerfuehrer was not content that his plight should be known only to his immediate superiors but despatched his complaint direct to Berlin as well. It was because the Afrika Korps was so short of fuel that the tanker *Bellona* was to sail from Italy to Benghazi, with the consequences already noted, and this news was considered so important in Whitehall that the Chief of Air Staff sent a special signal urging that every possible step be taken to sink the *Bellona*. 'All available means' were to be used to move fuel forward from Tripoli at the end of August (the

use. Not content with this, they broke a new army–air co-operation key (christened Scorpion), which proved its worth at once and was to be invaluable before and during the battle of Alamein. The folly of those in control of German signals security magnified this crytographic success beyond all our expectation: a whole month's daily settings of Scorpion could be predicted in advance once the first day was broken, for it was found that a series of settings, already used once and therefore familiar to the cryptanalysts, was being repeated (though in a random order), with the result that each new day's break could be made with much less than the usual expenditure of bombe time. (The machine used to solve Enigma messages was called the bombe.) Thus from shortly after midnight each day, Scorpion transmissions could usually be read soon after they were intercepted, and maximum value extracted from the reports of air liaison officers (*Fliegerverbindungsoffiziere* – 'Flivos' for short) attached to army formations. Before long, the Flivos were among Hut 3's most regular providers of frontline information – not only by announcing when a Flivo (and therefore his division) was about to move from one part of the line to another, or from reserve up to the front, for instance, but by indicating the route to be followed and the speed with which the move was actually being carried out. Orders for tank attacks and requests for air support were also common, but it was seldom possible to go through all the stages (interception, decryption, translation, signal drafting, transmission) in time for these to be tactically useful to commanders in the field. On the other hand, such messages could on occasion prove early indications of a coming shift of the enemy's strategic balance (from one flank to the other, for instance), and in this way they possessed an importance which far exceeded any tactical value they might have. Panzer Army's morning and evening reports, which were often carried on Scorpion wavelengths, conveniently summarised the events of the day, and they too sometimes included items with strategic rather than merely tactical significance.

It followed from all this that a far more complete and accurate picture of Panzer Army's intentions, order of battle, and state of deployment and supply could be painted than had been the case hitherto, when only keys belonging to ancillary arms were being decrypted. Now Panzer Army itself was open to constant inspection. As already described, a small but highly qualified body of men capable of turning this new opportunity to good account was already in post at Eighth Army and GHQ Middle East; from now on, these men had high-quality material to analyse and could rely on daily deliveries instead of only sporadic offerings. Like could now regularly be compared with like, as Flivo reports and Panzer Army appreciations accumulated day after day; deeper insights could be gained into Rommel's mind and actions and into the state of his army. Henceforth there was always a context or background against which a novel or startling item could be set for comparative interpretation: wide-ranging orders like those that Paulus had issued the previous year were less likely to mislead because it was now possible to detect whether they were being implemented or not, and serious miscalculations of the enemy's armoured strength were less likely to occur. From being an occasional blinding flash of light in darkness, Ultra became a standard ingredient of military intelligence. This was a tremendous gain, although for the moment it was obscured by the remorseless march of events which began when the British made mistakes round Tobruk and Rommel was quick to profit from them. By mid-August, the immediate crisis in the desert was past, and in the less anxious weeks which followed the new range of information could be more profitably exploited in what was in some respects Ultra's best period of the whole war. By the early spring of 1943, however, these new qualities had begun to generate a kind of antibody; Ultra's very bulk, reliability and regularity were beginning to lull the critical faculties of less experienced intelligence officers in the Tunisian theatre to sleep, tempting them to regard Ultra as omniscient and as freeing them from the need to consider whether it might not occasionally leave something unsaid.

For the next fortnight, Rommel drove his army forward at breakneck speed, with the object of getting to the Nile before the British could recover from the shock of losing Tobruk and from the ensuing chaos. During the whole of this period, signals could be drafted from decrypts containing frontline information only a few hours old. Most showed where Panzer Army's formations and Fliegerfuehrer's squadrons were, and what they intended to do next; a minority progressively chronicled the Germans' appreciation, from their Y Service (which was replacing the now silenced Fellers as their main source), of the disposition and movements of British troops. The two combined to draw a constantly changing panorama of the fighting which was seldom more than a few hours behind the clock, and in some respects even occasionally ahead of it. Against this background, Auchinleck (who relieved Ritchie and took over direct command of Eighth Army himself on 25 June) could study Rommel's and Kesselring's plans almost as soon as they were formulated, and endeavour to frustrate them.

The Axis infantry was ordered to assemble by 24 June to make a feint attack on the Halfaya-Sollum sector of the frontier while the armour attempted an outflanking movement in the south by night. The purpose was to annihilate what remained after 'the core of 8 Army' (claimed to be

45,000 men, 1,000 tanks and 400 guns) had been taken in Tobruk.* Even when Rommel decided to bring the operation forward by a day, advance warning could still be given. By thus penetrating beyond the Egyptian frontier, Rommel was contravening Mussolini's instructions (and Kesselring's vehemently expressed advice) to halt there by 20 June so that as many aircraft as possible could be concentrated for the final assault on Malta. As soon as he had secured Tobruk as a forward supply port, however, Rommel appealed to Hitler to release him from the obligation to obey this order, and was granted permission to continue his victorious progress. Hitler's 'final decision' to prefer Cairo to Malta – 'the goddess of battles comes to a warrior only once' – gave Rommel freedom to run his head fruitlessly against the slowly consolidating defences of Alamein and has been described as having 'destroyed the Axis' last chance of retaining a position in Africa.'

Although British resistance was stiffer than expected and Kesselring's intelligence staff was crediting the RAF with 2,471 aircraft, of which 761 were believed serviceable,† Rommel determined to launch a major attack on the Alamein position at 1500 hours on 30 June; the signal which betrayed his intention seventeen hours in advance also gave the complete line-up of Panzer Army in preparation for it. After a postponement until 0100/1 July, the revised plan anticipated a quick breakthrough. For a moment, Rommel believed that he had isolated and surrounded the British position, but he had already appreciated that Auchinleck intended to stand his ground, and 1 July – the crucial day for both commanders‡ – passed without the victory he craved. On 2 July, progress was reported difficult and resistance stubborn in face in continuous pressure. Next day, Rommel and Kesselring were back at their old game of blaming each other: Rommel wanted more air support because of 'the condition of the

---

* Only about 32,000 men were in fact taken prisoner in Tobruk. The tanks and guns were less of a prize from the German point of view than the 1,400 tons of petrol, 5,000 tons of provisions (enough for several weeks, and a major relief to their hard-pressed supply lines), and 2,000 vehicles (MME iii.274).
† At the end of May the true figure had been 929, only 190 of which were with the Desert Air Force. Fliegerfuehrer could muster 110 serviceable out of 210 on 22 June (MK 7296). The German total in the Mediterranean theatre as a whole had been something over 400 at the end of May; in addition, there were some 1,200 Italian planes in the Mediterranean (MME iii. 220–1).
‡ Sandstorms in the desert and exceptionally high temperatures added to their own and their tired troops' discomfort.

troops'. Fliegerfuehrer explained that his fighter pilots were strained to their limit and that it was beyond their power to manage more than four sorties a day. He demanded two more fighter Gruppen (officially, 60 aircraft) to ease their burden, but Kesselring's rejoinder claimed that since the army had not kept its promise to lend enough lorries, it was impossible to move men and machines to new landing grounds.

That evening Rommel called a halt, justifying his action by the low fighting strength of the army (only 1,200–1,500 men per division) after its recent exertions, the strained supply position, and the hardening British resistance,* suspended his attack 'temporarily', and ordered Panzer Army over to the defensive. Auchinleck knew of Rommel's decision soon after midnight, and when the next evening's situation report gave notice that the German armour was being disengaged and Italian infantry being brought up to take its place in the front line, he could be certain that, at least for the time being, the German advance had come to a halt.

Evidence to support Rommel's claims about supply and reinforcement problems had been accumulating ever since the fall of Tobruk. Four Italian aircraft were ordered to ferry 70 replacements a day from Lecce, in southern Italy, to Benghazi from 23 June onward, but within a week Panzer Army needed ten times as many every day for a fortnight, and a special transport Gruppe of 43 Ju-52s was commissioned to lift 500 of them; as many as 70 Ju-52s were employed on 5 July. More men were flown from Greece via Crete – 1,500 on 3 July – but this drained Crete of petrol, and arrangements were hastily made to send men by sea until petrol became available again. After this, a remark appended to Berlin's notification of his July quota must have sounded ominous to Kesselring: if there were 'more urgent tactical needs' (the Stalingrad offensive and the drive into the Caucasus had just begun), the amount might have to be reduced. Petrol for the panzer divisions was so urgently needed by 24 June that Hitler himself ordered the tanker *Avionia* from the Piraeus to Tobruk with all speed; its route appeared in Ultra next day, and an exceptionally large number of intercepts enabled its voyage to be followed closely. The ship was set on fire in Heraklion harbour, in Crete, and became a total loss. Hitler also intervened personally to speed up the

---

* Faithful to old habits, Churchill had a fresh translation of this signal sent 'Personal for General Auchinleck by order of the Prime Minister' (MK 8264). Rommel used exactly the same words when he came to write up the story of the campaign later (Rommel, 248–9); he had only 55 tanks and 65 anti-tank guns left (OKW/KTB ii. 107).

despatch of 40 tanks, 49 anti-tank guns, and 30 howitzers on 26 June (20 of them were about to be delivered at Mersa Matruh on 5 July). A list of its requirements put out by Panzer Army four days later appears to take account of them but asks for 40 more tanks in July as well as additional anti-tank guns. A statement by the German quartermaster in Italy on 9 July suggests that not all of them had arrived by then, but shows that he had recently received 60 new tanks from Germany for shipment to Libya.

By the time Rommel halted at Alamein, then, Ultra had taken the measure of the logistical problems his headlong rush had generated for both him and Kesselring, and had sketched the outline of the proposed solution.

B During the bare fortnight which elapsed between the decrypting of Rommel's intentions on 17 August and the start of the battle, Ultra piled up so many confirmatory indications that its ultimate inability to discover the precise moment of the 'off' probably mattered very little. For instance, three senior officers, all of whom had been wounded during the summer, returned from leave on almost the same day – Rommel's Chief of Staff and his operations officer, and the commander of the 15th Panzer Division; Kesselring ordered every available lorry out for 'the short-term supply' of petrol to forward airfields; Italian tanks moved forward by night in conditions of great secrecy and were to be camouflaged; Mussolini approved Rommel's suggested date for 'the offensive' (but did not reveal what it was); two hundred copies of sketches of the Alamein defences and the 'fortifications' of Alexandria were to be flown from Berlin to Tobruk by 27 or 28 August; there would be two conferences on the 25th, one at which Flivos would discuss signals arrangements and another for which Kesselring and five senior GAF officers required maps showing the British defences and the disposition of both air forces; army vehicles were to fetch petrol and ammunition from Benghazi 'for the last time' on 25 August; and, last and most informative of all, Panzer Army told OKH on the 27th that since ships due that day with petrol and ammunition were not now expected for another twenty-four hours, Rommel could not decide about 'the known operation' until 29 August. This signal went out thirty-six hours before the Afrika Korps attacked: all the others had preceded it.

Evidence bearing on Rommel's claim that his strength would grow faster than the Eighth Army's throughout August was inconclusive and contradictory. Three tank returns supported the claim. From 133, on 3 August, the German figure climbed to 185 on 12 August, 216 on the 21st, and 234 on the 28th, and in the last two cases the 'Specials' numbered 90 and 97 respectively, almost half the total. The Italian count was 151, 210, and 243 on the same three dates, and all but a couple of dozen were mediums. Clearly, Panzer Army was being re-equipped with more powerful tanks at a faster rate than ever before, whereas the Eighth Army, far weaker now than at Gazala, could count among its 478 tanks only 71 Grants, which alone were a match for the 'Specials'.

Under several other heads, however, there was more encouraging news for the Eighth Army. First, Rommel was revealed as in scarcely good enough health to command the offensive he had planned. A medical report which he forwarded to Berlin on 21 August (it was decrypted three days later) explained that low blood pressure and stomach trouble, aggravated by the strain of recent weeks, meant that only 'fairly long' specialist treatment in Germany could restore him to duty fully fit. He therefore requested the earliest possible appointment of a successor, and suggested Guderian, the originator of Blitzkrieg tactics. Alleging that there was no suitably qualified panzer general fit for tropical service (Guderian had been dismissed from the command of the Second Panzer Army in front of Moscow in December 1941, after a quarrel with von Kluge, and was now in disgrace), Berlin authorised the temporary promotion of General Nehring from the Afrika Korps to Panzer Army, but under the supreme command of Kesselring, who had never had authority over Rommel. Thereupon Rommel made a sudden recovery, and on 26 August he was declared fit enough to direct the offensive, provided that a doctor was in constant attendance.

Secondly, right up to the end of August, Ultra gave good reason for believing that none of the Eighth Army's preparations to give the attackers a hot reception had been detected, and that British camouflage and deception had fooled the Germans into supposing that no special steps had been taken to strengthen the fixed defences in the south. Neither Fliegerfuehrer's daily air reconnaissance reports nor the frequent Ultra summaries of German Y Service results suggested that anything out of the ordinary had been noticed. A Panzer Army situation report, signalled only a few hours before the tanks moved forward, was almost conclusive proof that the 44th Division had not been spotted manning the Alam Halfa ridge, and that a tentative suggestion on 20 August that 'a new division had arrived' had been discounted (the 44th Division does not seem, in fact, to have been confidently identified until about 8 September), while another showed that no special opposition was expected there.

Only a couple of months earlier, things would have been very different.

But now the Fellers decrypts were gone for good, and Seebohm's successor lacked Seebohm's skill. Instead of knowing all about British preparations – perhaps even enough to suspect why they were so remarkably appropriate – Rommel had no inkling of the reception that awaited the Afrika Korps. His unawareness magnified Montgomery's advantage.

What the official Italian naval history calls 'the hecatomb of the tankers,' which began now and lasted until after Alamein, was the chief consequence of the unprecedented amount of logistical intelligence supplied by Ultra during this period. Although Malta could not yet be relieved, pressure on the island diminished sufficiently after the cancellation of HERKULES to give it 'a new lease of life' (to quote the German quartermaster in Rome), and allowed it to resume its former role of harrying Axis trans-Mediterranean traffic, thus significantly assisting the work of the Royal Navy and the RAF from their Egyptian bases.* A Panzer Army appreciation of 18 August underlines the proviso about fuel deliveries with which Rommel had qualified his statement of intentions by pointing out that at the current rate of consumption, petrol stocks would be exhausted by 26 August – the very day Rommel had chosen for his offensive. Taken together, these two signals put Alexander, Montgomery, Harwood (Naval C-in-C), and Tedder in at least as good a position to estimate the strength of the thread by which Rommel's chances of success hung as the staff at OKW to whom Rommel had addressed his 15 August appreciation, and enabled them to do their utmost to cut that thread. The conclusion was inescapable: unless tankers reached Tobruk regularly (petrol landed at Benghazi could not be brought forward in time), the offensive would wither for lack of nourishment. A comprehensive supply survey which Panzer Army issued on 20 August went even further than that of the 18th by demonstrating that consumption had exceeded reciepts by 4,600 tons since the beginning of August, and that only 3,000 tons (equivalent to ten days' supply at the current relatively low rates) had been received in the same twenty-day period. Inside information of this kind led to a deliberate policy of assaulting Rommel's supply lines on a scale which had not been seen since the previous autumn, and Ultra was at once able to demonstrate the success of a policy which it had itself prompted.†

* Too late, the Italians began to regret their part in the abandonment of the plan to invade Malta. 'Unless we neutralize Malta, all is lost,' said Cavallero on 6 September (OKW/KTB ii.108; GS iv.64).
† The total tonnage of ships sunk in the last three months of 1941 was

A few examples must suffice. The torpedoing and subsequent beaching of the tanker *Pozarica* on 23 August reduced all three Italian army corps to such serious straits that they were compelled to borrow petrol from their allies – who were soon heard complaining that the Italians had had an unfairly large share of fuel deliveries in June, July and August, although the Germans had done most of the fighting – and forced the German supply officer in Rome to publish a revised sailing programme next day. The new programme provided for nearly 5,500 tons of fuel to be delivered by 4 September, but cautiously added that while 'every effort will be made to adhere to this programme, no guarantee can be given.' Rome's caution was soon justified. The route and sailing date of the tanker *Giorgio* (carrying nearly half the 5,500 tons) and orders for it to make all possible haste to Tobruk had already been signalled, together with much information concerning other ships, including the tankers *Picci Fassio* and *San Andrea* and several cargo ships carrying petrol in barrels. *Giorgio* reached Tobruk (where half its load was found to be contaminated), but *San Andrea* (with 3,000 tons of German army petrol), *Picci Fassio* (with 1,150 tons of Italian army petrol), *Istria*, *Dielphi*, and *Camperio* were soon at the bottom. The loss of the three last-named, complained Panzer Army, meant that of 2,400 tons of petrol promised for 28 August, only 100 tons had actually arrived. In consequence of all this, the already much-revised sailing schedule was thrown into complete disarray and the opening of the planned offensive delayed. Complaints flew thick and fast: Panzer Army ended a powerful plea for a special delivery of 3,000 tons of fuel and 2,000 tons of ammunition with the bleak comment that because of the recent poor performance of the supply services, it had now no fuel reserves; Rome countered with a long review which included the unconvincing claim that nearly 4,500 tons of army petrol had crossed the Mediterranean safely in August, and only 550 tons had been lost in transit. The 15th Panzer had to refuel its tanks with aircraft petrol on the first day of the offensive, although Kesselring was complaining at the same time of a severe shortage of aircraft fuel. (Berlin became so confused by

actually 7,000 tons more than in the first *seven* months of 1942. June and July 1942 saw only 22,000 tons of Italian shipping lost, but in August the total rose to some 60,000 tons and remained at that monthly level, or higher, until the surrender in May 1943. German and Italian losses together totalled almost 320,000 tons in the period August–December 1942. (Figures are from Roskill i.537, ii.76, 344, 432. BI ii.728–38 gives details of ships sunk between June and October 1942 as a result of Ultra information.)

events that it first refused Kesselring's plea for special treatment and then withdrew its refusal a couple of days too late to affect the fighting.) Convincing proof of the effect of the fuel interdiction policy came with Rommel's explanation that he was forced to halt the attack on 1 September and go over to the defensive in an exposed position under the Alam Halfa ridge because petrol expected on *San Andrea* (sunk; see above) and *Abruzzi* (bombed and set on fire) had not arrived.[*]

Emphatically as these and other signals underlined the Axis' supply problems, and close as they suggest that the Afrika Korps' tanks came to lasting immobility and Fliegerfuehrer's aircraft to being grounded, it is necessary to repeat the warning already given – that on their own they do not give a true picture of the situation. Improvisation had enabled Rommel to overcome apparently insuperable difficulties in the past, and would do so again. Increasing experience of Ultra was beginning to force the reflection that German quartermasters were no more immune than those of other armies from the temptation to exaggerate their shortages in order to obtain a larger share of the next allocation,[†] so that statements like 'all reserves used up' were not to be taken literally. Postwar analysis has shown that a great deal more petrol and ammunition reached Libya than was sunk on the way. Even in August (the worst month so far from the Axis point of view), only 41 per cent of fuel loaded in Italy or Greece was lost at sea. Ultra could now usually discover that a given tanker had been carrying such-and-such a tonnage of petrol for the German or Italian army or air force, and thus offer precision in place of what would otherwise have been no more than guesswork, but it ought not to have led (and as far as can be seen did not lead – no doubt because of the new care and minuteness with which its much-enlarged logistical component was now studied in Cairo) to over-optimistic conclusions of the kind Sir John Kennedy expressed to Churchill during a conversation on 26 August – that Rommel would not be able to attack because he was too short of supplies.

[*] The safe arrival of *Picci Fassio* and *Abruzzi* had been declared 'of decisive importance for the fighting in Africa' on 31 August (QT 505). Neither reached its destination. Visiting the Afrika Korps next morning, Rommel was bombed six times in two hours, and was nearly hit himself. Fliegerfuehrer's aircraft were outnumbered and outfought by the RAF's new tactics (Rommel, 279–80; Terraine, 378–83).
[†] Rommel discovered the prevalence of this habit as Panzer Army retreated through Cyrenaica after Alamein. He demanded accuracy in future, and threatened offenders with severe penalties (QT 7058, of 25 November).

Apart from revealing, in fairly good time, that it was shortage of petrol which made the Afrika Korps halt 'temporarily' on the morning of 1 September, and from confirming on the 5th that it was returning to its starting line (except that Montgomery controversially allowed Rommel to retain possession of the Himeimat plateau in the south), Ultra contributed nothing of importance to the 'Six Days Race', as the Germans called the battle of Alam Halfa. It had performed a tremendous service by disclosing Rommel's intended strategy in advance and had little to add on the tactics of a battle where all the movement was by one side. As soon as it was over, however, Panzer Army usefully summarised its after-action conclusions: just over 3,000 casualties (including 369 Germans and 167 Italians killed) – due mainly, it had already reported, to continuous day and night attacks by the RAF, the decisive effect of which Rommel later stressed; 36 German tanks destroyed; a present strength of 42,000 Germans and 82,000 Italians (yet the German contingent had received only 8,500 tons of supplies in August and the Italians three times as much); the imminence of a serious supply crisis – only eight days' fuel and fourteen days' ammunition in stock (Panzer Army forbore to remark that this was a great deal better than a week earlier), so that more air transport was essential to make up for the 'uncertainty' of the sea route; and, because the British were reinforcing, the urgent need to transfer the 22nd Division from Greece and Crete* (here Panzer Army forgot that the more men there were to feed and equip, the worse the logistical problem would become, as Rome had explicitly pointed out on 29 August).

An Ultra signal transmitted on 15 September momentarily took some of the gilt off the gingerbread of the Eighth Army's success by suggesting that the enemy might suspect that Enigma was being broken. British prisoners taken during the recent fighting had said that an Italian officer captured by the British had given away Rommel's plan of attack, its place, and its date, so that the British had been ready to meet it. This sounded so alarmingly like a thin and unconvincing disguise for the Ultra signal of 17 August that it awoke doubts about security at Eighth Army headquarters. Whatever the precise origin of the story, the Germans made no damaging inquiries and made no change in Enigma, but measures were at once taken to prevent a recurrence of this sort of anxiety: signals containing particularly sensitive 'hot' news or 'gossipy' items about individuals were henceforth to be given a specially restricted circulation. The system was

---

* It never arrived, but was retained to garrison Crete against an imagined threat. An infantry regiment was sent instead.

cumbersome to operate, but at least it had the merit of appearing to prevent one type of dangerous leak.

His first three weeks with the Eighth Army, even his first few days, were possibly the most influential of Montgomery's whole period of military command; during this short time, the seeds of his reputation for invincibility were sown, not least in his own mind. After thirty years of waiting, his chance had come. The prospect inspired him. He was like a coiled spring when he landed in Cairo: touchdown and the 'meat-safe' released the power compressed in the spring. Before him lay the opportunity to demonstrate his superiority over his predecessors by pulling their chestnuts out of the fire, while all the world watched an almost unknown general take on the world-famous Rommel who had always carried everything before him. He came, he saw, and at once he made the plan for victory which his military training and experience, tempered by the physical geography of the battlefield, dictated to him. This was rational and soldierly. Yet it was done so fast – in no more than twelve hours – that it was almost intuitive.* Only four days later, an intelligence source of which he had no previous experience showed him that his enemy was about to act exactly as he had foreseen. Even the dullest would be lifted by such a discovery; an easily inflatable self-confidence like Montgomery's took it as a sign that the God of battles was with him and that he was destined to triumph. Here was certain proof that he was not like others, but a better, more professional, soldier than they, and that the words he had used in his 13 August address were not only much-needed morale boosting but the very truth. When Rommel's tanks retired defeated a month later, all the world shared his conviction. 'The morale emerging from the promise [made in the address] so positively fulfilled formed the psychological background conditioning the victory which was to follow. Thereafter intelligence came into its own,' wrote Sir Edgar Williams, reflecting on the source of an army's morale in the nature of a man and the fact of a victory: a man with a peculiar and highly individual psychological makeup, and a victory which proved one of the turning points of a war. If, as Sir Edgar insists, intelligence and the attention Montgomery paid to it were the basis of that victory, then may it not be that the strategic confidence – or intolerable arrogance – which

---

* Such speed was uncharacteristic. He was usually much more deliberate – ponderous, his critics said. Only at El Hamma, in all probability, was he as quick and as right in a crucial decision.

sustained Montgomery when he forced through radical revisions of the plans for invading Sicily and Normandy (revisions without which both landings might well have failed) owed much of its strength to Ultra's earlier demonstration that his intuition was correct? The Montgomery legend was born at Alam Halfa; it fed upon itself, and upon the largely Ultra-based successes its hero continued to win, and even its most distasteful aspects cannot hide the immense contribution it made to the eventual Allied victory.

Alamein

Strategy temporarily receded into the background after Alam Halfa, save in the sense that everything hung upon the issue of the decisive battle for which both sides were now preparing. In it, for the first time, the superior weight of British and American matériel, firmly controlled by a newly resolute leadership, would be pitted against the professionalism, the mature experience, and the sheer determination of the German soldier. Rommel called it a battle without hope, but no one in London, Cairo or the Western Desert took the same view or regarded victory as a foregone conclusion. Unable or unwilling to comprehend either why an offensive could not follow hard on the heels of Alam Halfa or why Montgomery had forecast that Alamein would begin with a ten-day 'dogfight', Churchill kept pressing for an earlier date than Alexander and Montgomery proposed, and right up to the last stages of the battle Brooke had to restrain him from sending critical telegrams to the Middle East. Again, because the old desert hands doubted the capacity of their new equipment to beat down the opposition, Montgomery was compelled to modify his original bold plan and to note how the ingrained mutual mistrust of infantry and armour blunted their vigour in action. An earnest faith in victory prevailed everywhere, but no certainty. Alamein can only be understood if this is kept in mind. Could Montgomery stop the swing of the Libyan pendulum at last, or would Eisenhower get to Tripoli first?* This was Churchill's constant worry. If neither moved fast enough, 'God knows how we shall keep Malta alive' when her supplies ran out in October.

The narrow cone of rock and desert in the neck of which the Eighth Army was blocking the Axis advance toward the Delta does not widen out

* The landings in North Africa were to take place at the end of the first week in November.

at its western end until sixty or seventy miles farther from Egypt than Alamein, too far away to influence Montgomery's conduct of the battle until its very last stage. Only tactical manoeuvres and tactical surprise (achieved in the event, remarkably enough) were open to him. The very great number of Ultra signals sent in September and October admirably set out the tactical background to his plans, but only in the field of logistics could anything of wider strategical import be discerned. The Ultra intelligence provided between Alam Halfa and Alamein (that is, between 6 September and 23 October) can therefore be summarised briefly under a few familiar headings.

Rommel's immediate personal future, upon which doubt had suddenly been cast at the end of August, became clear as soon as Berlin decided to appoint a temporary successor. General der Panzertruppe Georg Stumme, who had commanded the 7th Panzer Division before Rommel took it to France in 1940 and had since fought with success in Poland and Russia, was to leave Berlin for Africa on 15 September, it was discovered on the 10th. Ultra followed Stumme to Africa via Rome, and noted that he took over Panzer Army on 22 September and that Rommel immediately flew to Europe. There followed complete silence about his return, but only a few hours before the artillery barrage which ushered in the battle of Alamein began, it became known that he had still been in Austria on the 17th.

Four tank returns (conveniently enough, all of them fell in the three weeks before Alamein) showed the number of German tanks quickly restored to its pre-Alam Halfa level, but the proportion of the powerful 'Specials' increasing by some 20 per cent; Italian numbers rose a little further. The last of the four returns, issued on the morning of Alamein and signalled next day, showed 80 IIIs and 86 III 'Specials', and 8 IVs and 30 IV 'Specials' in the Afrika Korps.* Against them, the Eighth Army could muster 170 Grants, 252 Shermans, 76 Crusaders with 6-pounder guns, and more than 500 tanks of older types – over 1,000 tanks all told.

Other varieties of strength return were plentiful. Two, separated by an

---

* An intention to ship an unspecified number of the new and untried 'Tiger' tanks (Mark VIs) was announced on 23 September (QT 2004). The Tiger's weight in fighting trim was stated as 57 tons (more than twice the weight of a IV 'Special'). An inquiry whether 50-ton tanks could be unloaded at Tobruk went unanswered. OKH planned to send 10 Tigers to Cyrenaica in November and 10 more in December (QTs 3413, 3639), but TORCH resulted in their diversion to Tunisia (QTs 6291, 6452, 6528, 6866, 7537, 7998).

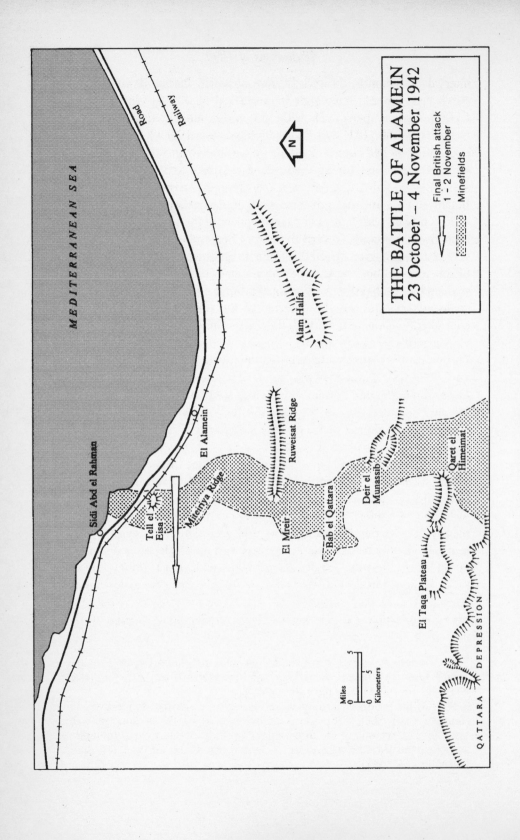

THE BATTLE OF ALAMEIN
23 October – 4 November 1942

Final British attack
1 – 2 November
Minefields

N

MEDITERRANEAN SEA

Road

Railway

Alam Halfa

Sidi Abd el Rahman

El Alamein

Ruweisat Ridge

Tell el Eisa

Miteirya Ridge

El Mreir

Bab el Qattara

Deir el Munassib

Qaret el Himeimat

El Taqa Plateau

QATTARA DEPRESSION

Miles
0   5

0   5
Kilometers

interval of a month, showed the rate at which Panzer Army was being reinforced. On 21 September it numbered 59,000 fighting troops and 15,000 ancillary personnel; with sick and wounded, this made 76,000 Germans in all (GAF and Flak added another 19,000). Just four weeks later, the total had risen to 91,000 – a reinforcement rate of 4,000 a week (too few tank crews among them, Panzer Army complained). There were also 146,000 Italians in Africa, some of whom were under independent Italian control and did not form part of Panzer Army.[*]

Side by side with figures like these appeared the first signs of a German manpower shortage. Toward the end of September, the GAF as a whole was ordered to give up 50,000 men to the army, and in mid-October fifteen-year-old boys were to be recruited as auxiliaries in order to release soldiers for combat duties.[†] The local influence of the manpower shortage could at the same time be detected in the various GAF returns, which continued to come to hand with their accustomed regularity. The number of Fliegerfuehrer's serviceable aircraft was known almost every day. Fliegerkorps II's and X's rather less often, together with the base airfields and temporary locations of most units. Thus in the week before Alamein, Fliegerfuehrer's serviceability rate could be observed fluctuating between 30 and 50 fighters, 10 and 20 ground-attack aircraft, and 40 and 50 dive-bombers – less than a quarter of the total in the Desert Air Force, which supported Eighth Army. This discrepancy in air power was now leading to fatigue and sickness among German bomber crews as they tried to compensate for it by flying extra sorties, as well as to low serviceability rates and serious wastage. For example, Fliegerfuehrer lost 81 aircraft, including 54 fighters, in the first three weeks of October, and attributed it mainly to the pilots' lack of skill and experience. Kesselring bluntly refused to accept this excuse: fighter losses on that scale, he said, could not be replaced, and ways (he did not explain what) must be found to reduce them. The shortage of thirty or more bomber crews in the two Fliegerkorps, he had already ruled, was to be made good by raiding the transport Gruppe – which was itself soon under heavy pressue to fly in

---

[*] The opposing fighting strengths at Alamein are stated by the official British history to have been 195,000 British and 104,000 Axis – 50,000 Germans and 54,000 Italians (GS iv.62).

[†] Thus Ultra produced significant evidence of a German manpower shortage shortly before the general crisis caused by the opening of a third front in Tunisia was made apparent at the highest German command level (see the letter from Fromm, Commander of the Home Army, to Keitel in GS iv.337).

reinforcements for Panzer Army to make up for the unreliability of sea transport!

More striking than any of this, and of greater significance both immediately and in the longer term, were repeated indications of the chaos into which the Axis supply system was falling in the weeks before Alamein. So far as petrol for its tanks and lorried infantry was concerned, Panzer Army could scarcely be described even as living from hand to mouth by the third week in October, so erratic and so subject to last-minute interruptions had the supply become. If British action could create such an extraordinary state of affairs now, what might it not accomplish if, following a victory by the Eighth Army, the RAF could reoccupy the Martuba airfields, which would give its aircraft the range necessary to protect Malta, and then, in company with the navy, make the island once more a base from which both could prey at will upon the Axis supply lines?

For the first week or two after Alam Halfa, a cautiously optimistic tone prevailed in German reviews of the supply situation. Panzer Army* thought that things had improved a little on 12 September, for there was now sufficient petrol for sixteen days at current rates of consumption; a week later, it believed that with strict economy it could manage on the 9,000 cubic metres of fuel it expected to receive each month, in spite of a calculation which showed that consumption had never dropped below 9,500 cubic metres in any of the last four months, and had almost touched 15,000 in June, when the capture of Tobruk and the great advance had consumed vast quantities. Perhaps further reflection brought second thoughts; by 24 September, a monthly intake of 8,000 tons (considerably more than 9,000 cubic metres) was felt to be barely sufficient, and no real improvement was expected until coastal shipping and the railway linking Tobruk with Alamein could eliminate the need for road haulage eastward from Benghazi and concentrate supply traffic on Tobruk, the alleged underuse of which had lately been the cause of several complaints. Another survey the next day still foresaw all needs being satisfied except fuel, of which there was a universal shortage, but the special allocation of 10,000 cubic metres of petrol announced on 29 September would have provided some alleviation had there been any sign of its delivery.

The number of ships sunk on the way to Africa showed no sign of

* Officially renamed German-Italian Panzer Army on 24 September (QT 2112).

diminishing, however – there would be none at all left in another six months, commented Ciano – and Panzer Army began to sound a sourer and more apprehensive note in the first few days of October. Only 54 per cent of its requirements had been met in September, it declared, and 8,000 of the 11,000 tons of petrol received had been used up on unavoidable supply journeys and current needs; at this rate, stocks would be exhausted in three weeks' time even if the British remained quiescent. The comparable figures for rations were far worse: only 1,800 tons were received but almost three times as much was consumed; fresh fruit and vegetables, flour, and soft drinks were particularly short; and severe cuts in daily rations had been necessary. The food shortage was emphasised again in the same week, and was blamed for the prevalence of undernourishment, lessened efficiency, and the high sickness rate. Now that all the British provisions captured in June and July had been eaten up, the situation was intolerable because of consistently inadequate deliveries, ran another complaint from the same source. As soon as he had settled himself into Rommel's seat, Stumme described rations as having reached 'an almost unsurpassably low level' in a forthright statement to Kesselring in which he demanded 30,000 tons of supplies a month as 'an imperative necessity to maintain the African theatre of war,' and pointed to the urgent need to reinforce an army whose numbers were 'daily decreasing through illness'.* Kesselring's answer was to make promises which he probably knew he could not keep. Stumme may now have gone over his head, for Hitler soon took a hand, urging Cavallero to do everything in his power to improve the transport of German supplies, particularly ammunition and food.

The last week before the British offensive saw two important decrypts complete this picture of disarray and unpreparedness. One was the complete tanker programme for 21–29 October, the critical period, which was signalled on the 17th. Only four days later, the devastating consequences of the action taken on this signal were made plain when Panzer Army reported a serious fuel shortage because the tanker *Panuco* (listed in the programme as due to arrive in Tobruk on the 21st with 4,500 tons of petrol) had been torpedoed. Stocks in hand (less than four-fifths of the cargo of *Panuco* alone) would now last eleven days at current rates if all went well; but by 25 October there would only be four days'

---

* Other evidence showed that this was little or no exaggeration. In two successive ten-day periods, 1,500 men reported sick, and in the first of them the men flown in were barely numerous enough to make good the wastage (QTs 3059, 3638).

worth east of Tobruk, with the result that the mobility of the German troops would be seriously impaired if the British attacked. Another signal confirmed, leaving aside new deliveries, that unavoidable current consumption would use up all the petrol in the forward area by 29 October.

In just three weeks, then, air and sea attacks had halved the potential endurance of Panzer Army's tanks and motor transport – from twenty-one days on 1 October to eleven on the 20th – and left its commander to ponder the unpleasant fact that unless fresh supplies of petrol arrived almost daily and were instantly brought up to the front, he would be compelled to stop fighting before the end of the month even if he did not move his tanks from their present positions to meet the needs of battle. It was well for what remained of his peace of mind that he was unaware that his British opposite number knew as much about his difficulties as he did himself.

The grim situation thus displayed presented Alexander and Montgomery with an incomparable opportunity. Nemesis was at long last about to overtake the enemy in retribution for past errors of judgment: Hitler's and Halder's, in not realising that an African commitment could prove as much of a running sore for Nazi Germany as Spain for Napoleonic France, unless designed on a scale large enough to guarantee quick and total victory, and unless an efficient transport system capable of maintaining the large army this made necessary was placed under exclusive German control; Rommel's, in repeatedly insisting that it was the duty of the quartermaster's branch to meet his every operational demand no matter what the practical difficulties. By October, all that was required to set Nemesis to work was a blow heavy enough to make a breach in the strong defences behind which Panzer Army was sheltering, a breach wide enough for the tanks to pour through into the rear areas and, by creating immediate chaos there, prevent an orderly retreat by the fighting troops and expose the shortcomings of a maintenance organisation so starved of resources that it could neither recover from a severe setback nor find the means to establish a second line of defence.

The whole Axis army could then have been wiped out at, or even before, the same Egyptian-Cyrenaican frontier area where long ago O'Connor had discomfited the Italians under Graziani. Montgomery might in that case have reached Tripoli quickly enough to distract the attention of the scratch force hastily assembled against TORCH sufficiently to enable Eisenhower to capture Tunis in December 1942 instead of May 1943,* thus perhaps shortening the war by six months. None of this was achieved. By the middle of October, Ultra was showing the British commanders a vision, but they let it vanish before their eyes like mist in the sun.

A few aspects of Ultra's contribution to victory in the battle deserve mention before this point is pursued further.

An elaborate deception plan was devised to mislead the enemy about the time and place of the coming attack. The Long Range Desert Group raided Benghazi, Barce and other Cyrenaican airfields in mid-September, using an approach route through the oases of Siwa, Kufra and Jalo. Success was only moderate, but the aftermath of the raids was more profitable than the raids themselves. As had been intended, they drew German and Italian attention to the southern end of the front and encouraged just those fears of a southabout 'left hook' by the Eighth Army which 'A' Force was endeavouring to implant in their minds. Documents captured from the LRDG at Jalo showed, according to OKW on 18 September, that the British intended to hold the oasis for three weeks in conjunction with their offensive, which anyhow was expected to open in about that time. Kesselring called for aerial reconnaissance of Kufra, the British garrison which the Italians planned to overwhelm, and from late September until Alamein intercepts steadily showed that the deep margin of the Sahara was being kept under regular surveillance from the air or, in the case of Siwa, on the ground.

Evidence about the success of the rest of the deception plan was mixed. British order of battle and locations were known fairly accurately, but in spite of what has just been said, as well as of sightings of fresh tracks (mostly faked, no doubt) and of tanks and armoured cars on the edge of the Qattara Depression, the likely point of attack was not placed quite as far south as the deception planners hoped. Instead, the main British concentrations were thought to be near the Ruweisat Ridge – some ten miles south of the Miteiriya Ridge, where the blow actually fell – and the attack was expected there and possibly on both sides of the coast road as well. Platitudinous warnings that the attack would come 'soon' were common, but even in the third week in October, Fliegerfuehrer's reconnaissance pilots regularly reported 'quiet day' or 'nothing special' –

---

* Even as things were, the Axis command was anxiously preoccupied with threats to the Gafsa-Gabès sector linking Libya and Tunisia in November.

that is to say, that the various camouflage devices (covers that hid tanks, ammunition dumps disguised as parked lorries, etc.) were deceiving both eye and camera. The evening reconnaissance report for 22 October ran, 'quiet; slight increase in British forces in south' (perhaps a reflection of the MELTINGPOT plan, which sought to suggest that the 10th Armoured Division had moved south), and this was signalled twelve hours before the attack began. Even at last light on the 23rd, just before the guns opened fire, it was still 'Quiet day. No change.' This regular negative evidence put it beyond doubt that Eighth Army was about to secure complete tactical surprise, in spite of the flatness of the ground, the absence of cover, and the familiarity of the tactical options open to it.

Stumme having died of a heart attack while reconnoitring the battlefield on the first morning, Rommel flew back from Austria to resume command of Panzer Army on the evening of 25 October. The news that greeted him was grim. Two tankers, carrying 4,000 tons of petrol between them, had been sunk that afternoon; others followed them to the bottom in the next day or two. ('Now we really are up against it,' he remarked as a third went down.) This precipitated an immediate crisis. With the main attack still to come, it was believed, only two or three days' reserves of petrol were within reach of Panzer Army, as Kesselring ordered planes to operate continuously day and night to fly in emergency supplies from Crete while a hundred or more transport aircraft and gliders, most of them hastily brought in from south Russia, resupplied Crete from Greece. Coming on top of the existing fuel shortage, the tanker disasters meant that a situation which had become 'grave in the extreme' by the evening of the 28th was the more threatening because adequate petrol for the Afrika Korps' remaining 81 tanks was not to be relied on. The same reasoning also made it virtually certain that when Rommel followed his instinct and concentrated the Afrika Korps once again by shifting the 21st Panzer northward from its position opposite the British centre (where it was 'corseted' with the Italian Ariete armoured division) to join the 15th Panzer in confronting the British spearhead, he would not be able to move it back again if Montgomery later chose to switch his main assault elsewhere – an uncomfortable truth which Rommel himself was being forced to recognise. The destruction of the tankers could be signalled almost at once, the move of the 21st Panzer only with a delay which did not in the end matter, since it had been picked up in good time by the Y Service. The same was true when the 90th Light was ordered into battle alongside the Afrika Korps on the afternoon of 29 October: decrypting difficulties held the signal up until early on the 31st. The knowledge that the main German strength was now concentrated within eight or ten miles of the coast was instrumental in leading Montgomery to choose – though after more hesitation than hindsight now finds it easy to understand – a more southerly line for the decisive thrust (Ultra located the 21st Panzer well to the north of it on 31 October), which made the final breakthrough on the night of 2–3 November.

Hitler now did his best to destroy the army whose victorious commander he had in triumph promoted Feldmarschall a mere four months ago. By the end of the summer it had become evident that the grandiose campaign to wipe out the Russian armies in the bend of the river Don, reach the Caspian, and occupy the Caucasus, which he had planned as Commander-in-Chief of the Army (a post he had assumed in December 1941), was flagging badly. Possessed by a new madness as reality refused to dance to the tune played by his fantasies, he became morose and ill-tempered, shunning the company even of sycophants and flatterers. In September he dismissed Halder, the Chief of Staff of the Army, for daring to criticise his amateur strategy, and announced his intention to educate the General Staff in his own brand of fanaticism and bend the whole army to his will. Halder noted in his diary that already 'the correct choice of words was more and more disregarded when orders were given. High-sounding words like "annihilate" or "destroy," phrases like "prevent them from escaping" were used, even when the action they described was impossible, instead of soberer and more precisely calculated instructions.'

Thus Hitler was in no mood to comprehend what was happening at Alamein or to react rationally to two radio messages which Rommel sent him on the evening of 2 November and which Ultra enabled Alexander and Montgomery to read soon after dawn next day. The first reported that the army was exhausted, that a breakthrough could not be prevented, that there was not enough petrol to move more than a short distance, and that 'the possibility of the annihilation of the army must be faced', the second that orders had been issued for a fighting withdrawal to begin at once.* Hitler's reply was the first in a series which was soon to become

---

* The duty officer at the Fuehrerhauptquartier who received the teleprinted copy of the second message in the middle of the night failed to realise that it differed significantly from its predecessor by announcing that the retreat had started, and therefore did not bring it to Hitler's notice immediately. As soon as he discovered this, Hitler reduced him to the ranks and dismissed General Warlimont, the head of his section at OKW. Some time later, he was persuaded to restore them both to their

familiar as the fortune of war turned against him: '. . . hold on, do not yield a step . . . victory or death.' 'This order demanded the impossible,' Rommel wrote later, but for twenty-four hours he loyally tried to carry out his Fuehrer's command. But the situation was already out of control, and putting the withdrawal order into reverse added to the confusion among the broken divisions. On the morning of 4 November he asked permission to retire to a nominally prepared position at Fuka, and in the evening Hitler and Mussolini gave their reluctant consent. But there was no stopping at Fuka or anywhere near it: the long retreat and the lumbering pursuit had begun.

Ultra had discovered in good time the first – and from the intelligence point of view by far the most important – of these telegrams[*] (signs of withdrawal were not observed from the air until later the same morning), and the acceleration of events thereafter would have reduced the operational value of the others considerably even if they had been decrypted sooner. In any case, however, it was not tactical details, even when they were as important as these, but the revelation of Panzer Army's threadbare logistical state which was Ultra's chief contribution to the battle, as it had been to the preparation for it.

Medenine

As if in repentance for letting the new boys down, Ultra now lavished its bounty on the old hands of the Eighth Army, providing daily bulletins about Rommel's next move. It had, of course, long been appreciated that if his Tunisian attack stalled, Rommel might switch his armour back east for a pre-emptive strike at the Eighth Army before it could breach the Mareth Line, but his change of direction came with astonishing speed. Commando Supremo's orders to break off the attack and Rommel's to move across to the other front were issued in quick succession late on 22 February, and both were in Eisenhower's and Montgomery's hands by the following evening.[†] (Fliegerkorps Tunis's version of the plan included

former positions (OKW/KTB ii.894–98).
[*] The texts are printed in full in MME iv.475–77.
[†] On reading these signals, Churchill sent Montgomery a copy of a note he had written in August 1941: 'Renown awaits the commander who first, in this war, restores the artillery to prime importance on the battlefield, from which it has been ousted by heavily armoured tanks,' adding, 'if Rommel tries to chop up your spearheads in the next few days he may easily bring about an encounter battle on terms unexpected

the forecast that after smashing the Eighth Army's spearheads, the German armour would return whence it came to mount another attack on the Fifth Panzer Army's front.) Fashionable Eighth Army jargon arrogantly had it that in rushing back and forth so hastily Rommel was behaving like a 'wet hen' skittering brainlessly across the farmyard. It was in the same spirit of pride that Montgomery told Alexander that he would positively welcome an attack, but in later years he confessed to having felt some anxiety until he had completed regrouping, his force having become unbalanced. He could not know that Axis opinion was still deeply divided about prospects. Keitel now shared Warlimont's pessimism (see Appendix V) and admitted to 'serious misgivings about our whole position in Tunisia', but Kesselring and Ambrosio (Chief of Staff of the Italian Armed Forces since the dismissal of Cavallero earlier in the month) were convinced that the Allies had suffered such heavy losses in the recent fighting that they would be compelled to postpone their next offensive for a month or six weeks, thus giving Rommel his opportunity. Rommel himself, dispirited again after his burst of activity, saw no chance of a more than illusory success, and repeated his recommendation on a retreat to the hills of Enfidaville in northern Tunisia.

It was quickly evident that the whole of the German armour was to be thrown against the Eighth Army, the 10th Panzer again joining the desert veterans 15th and 21st Panzer. The strength – 31,000 men and 135 tanks – the rate of progress eastward, and the plan and date (4 March) of the intended attack at Medenine (which the Eighth Army had occupied on 17 February) were all fully documented by 1 March.

Rommel's chief quartermaster set out his fuel requirements on 1 March in such a way as to imply that the 'intended operation' had been deferred until the 6th or later. The 'known units' were on their way to their jumping-off positions on the 3rd, under orders to follow two thrust lines, both of which pointed at the southern edge of Medenine. By dawn on 6 March it was confirmed that the attack would take place that day, but the warning was not needed.

Not even before Alam Halfa had Ultra so completely foreshadowed the pattern of future events. Thus forearmed, Montgomery prepared an impregnable all-round defence, with 600 anti-tank guns dug into the ground to kill off the tanks before they could get at the infantry, and with 400 of his own tanks ready for a counterattack should one be required. Everywhere the assault recoiled in face of the defenders' fire, and soon the

by him.' (Gilbert vii.358–9.)

ground was littered with burning tanks. Not an inch did the attackers gain, and by evening Rommel called the battle off.

So total a failure – perhaps made all the sourer by the fact that his desert veterans had been humiliated under the command of a mere Italian (General Messe had taken over the renamed 'First Italian Army' when Rommel was given the Army Group) – completed the collapse of Rommel's health. He left Africa for good three days after the battle.

Mortain and Falaise

C Some time on 2 August Hitler telephoned to von Kluge an order to replace armour by infantry in the line and to assemble at least four Panzer divisions for a heavy blow westwards to the coast at Avranches. A confirmatory signal was timed 2315 hours and passed on to Army Group B just after midnight. It was a sudden snap decision, for it had not been mentioned the previous evening when Warlimont (deputy head of the Operations Staff of the OKW) was sent off on a special mission to the western front, and Warlimont only heard of it at Army Group B's headquarters on the 3rd.

As an abstract conception, the idea had something to recommend it. The coastal road had only been in American hands for three days, and all 3 Army's supplies had to pass along it; if it were cut, the spearheads of the incipient American enveloping movement would wither and die (this point was specifically made by XLVII Corps when it attacked). But the practical obstacles were insuperable. The process of disengaging and assembling so much armour was bound to be long and difficult (even Rommel had not managed it under the more favourable conditions of early June), and the weight of Dempsey's and Bradley's blows from opposite directions was already threatening to hammer the life out of 7 Army before so far-reaching a plan to rescue it could be put into operation. Moreover, the shortage of motor transport, upon which the effective use of armour directly depended, had just been highlighted by a circular issued by the Inspector-General of Panzer Troops after consultation with Keitel at OKW. Addressed to all SS and police authorities, it said bluntly: 'Men and tanks are standing ready, but I lack lorries, tractors, passenger cars (particularly Volkswagen), carbines, field kitchens and war equipment of every kind', and appealed for them to be surrendered to the army immediately. Lastly, Hitler's order overlooked the probability that a new drive to the west would increase the likelihood

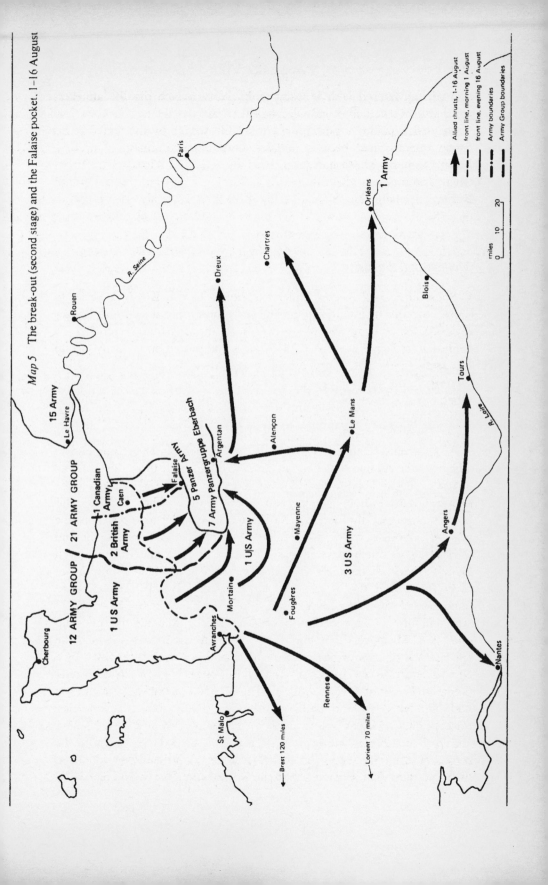

Map 5 The break-out (second stage) and the Falaise pocket. 1–16 August

Cherbourg

Le Havre

15 Army

Rouen

R. Seine

Paris

12 ARMY GROUP   21 ARMY GROUP

1 US Army   1 Canadian Army

2 British Army

Caen

Falaise

5 Panzer Army

7 Army Panzergruppe Eberbach

Argentan

Dreux

Chartres

Alençon

Avranches

Mortain

Fougères

Mayenne

1 US Army

Le Mans

3 US Army

St Malo

Rennes

Brest 120 miles

Lorient 70 miles

Angers

Nantes

Tours

R. Loire

Blois

Orléans

1 Army

Allied thrusts, 1–16 August
front line, morning 1 August
front line, evening 16 August
Army boundaries
Army Group boundaries

miles
0   10   20

(great enough already on 2 August) of 7 Army being surrounded and crushed to death. This possibility was converted into the disaster which soon overtook the whole of Army Group B by one thing above all: Hitler's intention was known to the incredulous Allied commanders in time for them to take steps to counter it and to make Hitler's order the agent of his own army's destruction.

Foreknowledge at this juncture and on this scale made Ultra security more vital than ever. The Allied command had always planned to begin the eastward advance to the Seine from about the line it had now reached; here was Hitler proposing, by a large-scale attack in the opposite direction, to double its effect and to run his head into a noose of his own devising. Hotter news there could hardly be, yet no unwise use of the information was made, and the secret was safely kept. 'How does the enemy learn our thoughts from us?' Hitler had asked a few hours before he issued his order; but, still trembling from the shocks of 20 July, he had ascribed it to the plotters' treason.

Montgomery did not know what Hitler intended when, pursuant to the plan drawn up before D-Day, he issued new instructions on 4 August, directing the Americans to aim for Paris and 1 Canadian Army (which had just become operational) to strike down towards Falaise, but there could not have been a bolder counter-move. If both new drives were successful, 7 Army and Panzergruppe West (renamed 5 Panzer Army on 6 August) would be surrounded unless they extricated themselves by retreating speedily eastwards instead of attacking westwards. Montgomery's directive did not explicitly mention the possibility of an encircle-ment – indeed, he pointed 12 Army Group in too easterly a direction for it, and did not make a junction with the Canadians its main objective – and he seems only to have done so on 8 August, after the German attack had begun. It is more surprising that the fear of being encircled does not seem to have occurred to von Kluge until the previous day, 7 August, just before Hitler ordered him to push on regardless of risks and thereby 'bring about the collapse [!] of the Normandy front'; we intercepted his operations report for the week, which set out his fear of being caught in a trap, and it did not perhaps much matter that we could not decode it until 13 August, when encirclement was already an accomplished fact.

Whatever misgivings he may have had about the wisdom of Hitler's original astonishing order, von Kluge made new dispositions in accord-ance with it on 3 August, arranging for an attack on both sides of Sourdeval (a few miles north of Mortain) by XLVII and LXXXI Corps with 2 Pz, 9 Pz and 116 Pz and elements of 2 SS Pz and 17 SS PzGr.

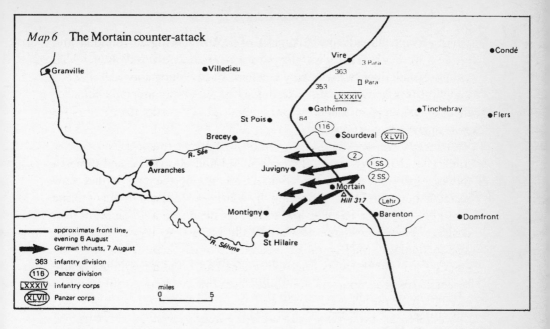

Map 6   The Mortain counter-attack

● Condé
● Granville
● Villedieu
Vire ●
3 Para
363
□ Para
353
LXXXIV
● Gathémo
● Tinchebray
● Flers
St Pois ●
84
116
● Sourdeval   XLVII
Brecey ●
R. Sée
2
1 SS
Avranches ●
Juvigny ●
2 SS
Mortain ●
Hill 317
Lehr
Montigny ●
● Barenton
● Domfront
R. Sélune
St Hilaire

—— approximate front line,
       evening 6 August
➤ German thrusts, 7 August
363 infantry division
116 Panzer division
LXXXIV infantry corps
XLVII Panzer corps

miles
0   5

There was no evidence of this in Ultra, but there were signs of the withdrawal of the front by which he hoped to free the armour and of the impediment to his plans caused by the British attack, which forced him to rush II SS Pz Corps in to plug a dangerous gap at almost the same moment as Hitler was having his 'inspiration' and to hold 21 Pz, 9 SS and 10 SS Pz Divisions in that sector for several days. The formations listed by von Kluge were a shade less well reported, but 2 SS Pz, 2 Pz and 116 Pz were clearly located in the Sourdeval area until 116 Pz was relieved by 84 Division on the night of 5–6 August, while 9 Pz and LXXXI Corps were coming from the south and the Channel coast respectively but had not yet arrived.

News of the German attack came in several signals during the evening of 6 August. The first asked for night-fighter protection for 2 SS Pz in an attack through Mortain (which the Americans had just captured) south-westwards to St Hilaire, another a few moments later said that XLVII Corps would attack with 116 Pz, 2 Pz, 1 SS Pz (which had been assembling far away at Falaise the previous night) and 2 SS Pz. The most explicit of them timed the attack for 1830 hours (only ninety minutes after the German signal was sent; ours went out at midnight), gave its start-line as Sourdeval–Mortain and its first objective as the north–south road from Brécey to Montigny ten miles ahead, and said that it would be conducted by 'strong forces of five Panzer divisions'. The attack did not in fact begin until after midnight – this, like the discrepancy between four and five divisions, no doubt reflects the confusion which prevailed in the German command that day – so that at any rate the first two of our signals had time to arrive before the event.

The Germans did not even reach their first objectives. Plentiful information about the fighting came in throughout the next few days, and a great deal of it could be signalled five or six hours after the German original (sometimes sooner – several of our fastest deliveries belong to early August); it made cheerful reading in Hut 3, deprived as always of news from Allied sources, but probably told Montgomery and Bradley little they had not already learned from their own battle reports. Some elements of 116 Pz were already in retreat at dawn on 7 August, for instance, and at midday 1 SS Pz complained that it had been brought to a standstill by fighter-bombers, while hostile aircraft had prevented the GAF from coming to its rescue, with the result that it decided to withdraw for the night. The sustained, violent and (thanks to Ultra) well-prepared attacks by 83 Group RAF and IX US Air Force were in fact one of the turning points of the battle. Another was the heroic resistance of the American 30 Division, isolated and surrounded on Hill 317 just east of Mortain, but there seems to have been no Ultra information about it beyond the statement that 2 SS Pz, which had recaptured Mortain at dawn, was still trying to take St Hilaire, one of its first objectives, in mid-afternoon. Of more lasting value was confirmation during the evening that, notwithstanding the small advance so far made, the attack would be continued next day: Hausser of 7 Army ordered XLVII Corps to keep at it and to drive on to Avranches, but a return (unfortunately not available for another three days) of its available guns and small arms casts doubt on its capacity to do so: neither 116 Pz nor 2 SS Pz had any 88-mm anti-aircraft/anti-tank guns at all, for example, and although 2 Pz was somewhat better off with eight, it had fewer light and medium howitzers.

With 3 US Army ranging almost at will up the Loire valley next day (8 August), Ultra was able to show how the German command was losing grip of the situation on what was now its southern flank but had so recently been its undefended rear. All road movement was impossible because of enemy fighter-bombers, complained both LXXXIV Corps and 2 SS Pz during the morning, and a regimental commander on II Para's left boundary completely lost control of his men, who were running away under the slightest Allied pressure. By evening, American tanks were in Le Mans and Tours, making the situation as far east as Blois 'obscure', and attempts were already under way to cobble together elements of Pz

Lehr and 9 Pz to block them, as well as to form a new defence line behind Mortain. The situation here was the more acute because of the swift success in the afternoon and evening of 6 August of the British XXX Corps' assault on Mt Pinçon, which might otherwise have anchored the German defence; there was very little news of this, save about some of 10 SS Pz's difficulties, but after it 12 SS Pz, which had been brought across from Caen to strengthen the defence, had only thirty-four serviceable Mark IV tanks out of a total strength of fifty, and only twenty Panthers out of thirty-four.

Measures were already being taken to bring some order out of the chaos which threatened Occupied France and to anticipate and halt a general advance by the Allied armies by constructing a defence-line east of Paris. Ultra quickly got wind of them, but at first only in fragments and often out of time-sequence. The first became known when the Military Commander of north-eastern France reissued an OKW order on 5 August, but the decode was five days late. It provided for the 'immediate development of a rearward position' from Reims to Châlons and the Marne-Saône canal by a special staff empowered to use 'the severest measures' to conscript French civilians between the ages of sixteen and sixty and to commandeer entrenching tools and excavating equipment. Before this could be signalled, we had passed on the news that 1 Army headquarters was moving from Bordeaux to the neighbourhood of Poitiers, closer to the flank of 7 Army, and that on 7 August it had appointed officers to take charge of local operations in Nantes, Angers and Tours. An even woollier Hitler order than usual of the same date for the defence of 'fortresses' (Brest and St Malo were already cut off, and when 1 Army moved out the U-boat bases on the Atlantic coast were soon to suffer the same fate) completed the outline of a pattern that held broadly true for several weeks: speedy evacuation of all France except the north-east, which was to be held as a forward defence of the Reich frontier. The urgent business of controlling Army Group B's operations kept von Kluge near the front, and he left Blumentritt, his Chief of Staff, in charge at OB West. From there Blumentritt sent him a wide-ranging set of proposals on 8 August. These could not be decoded until the 14th, but even then it was still useful to know of his suggestion that 1 Army should be transferred from Army Group G to Army Group B, that LXIV Corps should fill the gap which was beginning to open on the upper Loire at the junction with 19 Army, that 6 Para Division was moving to Chartres and a static division being brought from Germany to Paris, and that Blumentritt considered the situation urgent enough to warrant 15

Army surrendering two divisions from Belgium and Holland without waiting for replacements.

The daylight hours of 9 August saw us continuing to provide news of more emergency measures by the other side. Among a large number of routine Flivo reports of divisional locations, the most striking items were that a new formation, LVIII Corps, was taking over command of 2 SS Pz (and presumably other divisions too), that 9 Pz and 708 Divisions would cover the exposed southern flank around Domfront (708 Division was coming from the south-west, and even 1 Army was not sure how many train-loads of it had started out that morning), and that Army Group B had ordered up 11 Pz from the south to Blois and Chartres.* All this had been passed to SHAEF, the two Army Groups and all others concerned by the late evening.

Excitement at the significance of the intelligence we were providing at a moment which might be decisive for the whole campaign was already intense in Hut 3 at midnight, but it soon rose still higher. Good fortune sent me on duty then, and I can still vividly recall the exhilaration of the next few hours; in recollection they surpass even D-Day for the volume and importance of the information Ultra produced. The size of the net which was being drawn round Army Group B, and the number of divisions which would be caught in it, clearly depended on whether Hitler persisted with his foolhardy attack or whether he ordered a general retreat before the Americans had got far enough east to prevent an escape. 'We checked him hourly at Mortain,' wrote Bradley later, adding that he needed forty-eight hours from 8 August to complete the envelopment. Aerial reconnaissance – to which he was of course referring – could show what the Germans were doing at a given moment, but not what they intended to do an hour or two later. Only Ultra could give warning of their plans in advance, and in the early hours of 10 August it did so superbly.

We intercepted orders issued by von Kluge the previous evening which called for a renewal of the attack 'probably on the 11th' although there might be a postponement. We were able to signal the crucial first part during the night; the second part (listing the troops to be employed) came in later and went out early the next afternoon. This resolved the issue conclusively. Whatever his misgivings, von Kluge had allowed himself to be over-ruled by Hitler. For the next twenty-four hours at least there

---

* Hitler subsequently countermanded von Kluge's order for 11 Pz's move.

would be no retreat; Bradley would have almost as much time as he needed, and the Allies could proceed in the confident expectation that if they acted quickly they would be able to surround most of the German troops in northern France.

The orders were issued by von Kluge in his capacity as commander of Army Group B (he had doubled this with OB West since Rommel was wounded). They called for an attack on the southern wing of 7 Army to be led by General Eberbach (for whom a new staff would be provided under von Kluge's own son) 'after regrouping and the bringing up of decisive offensive arms'. Eberbach's objective was to be 'the sea at Avranches, to which a bold and unhesitating thrust through is to be made'. The assembly area and start-line would be communicated verbally, but Mortain–Domfront was envisaged; the attack was intended to go in on the 11th, but there might be a postponement of twelve or twenty-four hours. Troops engaged would be XLVII Panzer Corps, LVIII Reserve Panzer Corps, 2 Pz and 116 Pz Divisions, 1 SS, 2 SS and 10 SS Panzer Divisions, the main body of 9 Panzer, two rocket brigades and some army artillery (we had already known about the last four for several hours). To ensure the success of the 'decisive thrust', 5 Panzer Army (where Sepp Dietrich was to take over in place of Eberbach) and 7 Army were to hold their lines to the last man and the last round.

Twice in three days Ultra had given information of unsurpassable quality; first, sufficient advance warning of the Mortain attack to nullify it completely and to assist in inaugurating a riposte which was to turn COBRA from victory into triumph and to make an orderly German withdrawal to new defence lines impossible, and now (with at least twenty-four hours in hand) the certainty that the attack would be persisted in long enough to ensure the almost total dissolution of von Kluge's forces.* It might be thought that only anti-climax could follow. The truth was far otherwise. These were some of Ultra's most prolific days of the whole war;

---

* Group Captain Winterbotham gives a rather different account of the first ten days of August in *The Ultra Secret*, 147–54 (Lewin, *Ultra*, 337–9 derives from it). There appears to be no Ultra warrant for a number of his statements, in spite of the circumstantial detail with which he surrounds some of them. Several can, however, be approximately reconciled with the signals by a change in dating. There were three stages in the Mortain attack: (1) Hitler's order of 2 August, of which Ultra knew nothing, (2) the attack order of 6 August and (3) von Kluge's renewal order of 9 August, both of which Ultra reported in time. It seems possible that Group Captain Winterbotham's memory confused stages (2) and (3) with (1).

unprecedented amounts of Enigma traffic were being intercepted, and most of it was decoded with such rapidity that signal after signal could be prepared so close to the German time of origin that each seemed more urgent than the last and the mind could scarcely hold on to a myriad details long enough to comprehend the relation of one to another. Unexpected quantity brought no decline in quality, but was so great that for the period of the Falaise pocket a mere selection from the bewildering riches poured out by the source must serve to show how Ultra depicted the confusion as a swift and terrible fate overtook Hitler's armies in Normandy.

Von Kluge's orders were not the last important item on 9 August. The move back of a number of fighter Gruppen to Germany for rest and refit, and their replacement by others, gave away the whole relief plan and – remarkably enough – showed that a revised version of it put into force

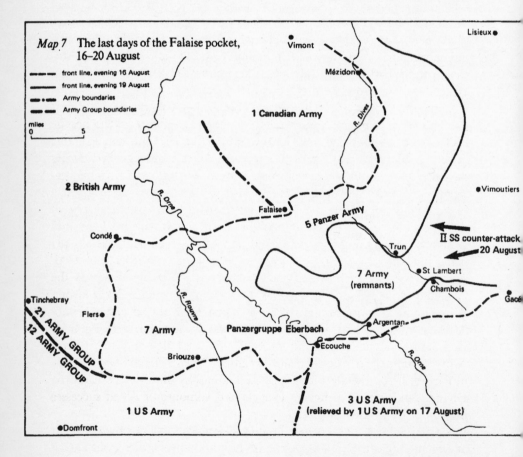

Map 7   The last days of the Falaise pocket, 16–20 August

that day actually reduced the number of fighter Gruppen serving in France from seventeen to thirteen. Two divisions previously reported (6 Para and 49 Divisions) were still on the way to reinforce 7 Army, and by midnight next day we had signalled the positions occupied that morning or afternoon by most of the divisions and corps in the thick of the fighting (in three cases adding that they were short of petrol, ammunition or transport), located Eberbach's headquarters, and discovered that 1 Army was to hand over to LXIV Corps in Bordeaux and move to Fontaine-bleau by rail (its exact time of departure, 0600 hours 12 August, came though a little later).

By way of contrast, the most important 11 August items were not available until late that night or the following morning: the assembly area of 116 Pz Division (which was coming out of the line), the battle headquarters of Army Group B, a list of new army boundaries to come into force as soon as 1 Army arrived, and news of so serious a petrol shortage in XLVII Corps that several Panzer divisions could barely move (thirty of Pz Lehr's tanks were completely immobilised next day). Our first intimation that von Kluge realised he might be surrounded came into this category; he had feared it already, but his repetition of it now, though delayed, was decoded before the earlier message.

The new destination – Alençon – of 116 Pz became apparent the next day as part of a major shift of emphasis to the southern flank whereby LVIII Corps took over from XLVII and the GAF concentrated its efforts in the Le Mans area at the army's request. All this was signalled during daylight. Two useful bits of information were subject to delay: reinforce-ments for 1 Army to help it fill the open spaces south-west of Paris, and a reasoned case by Hausser of 7 Army for giving up the westernmost tip of the pocket in order to strengthen the front round Falaise, Flers and Domfront. Something like the second part of this argument was already being put into practice by 13 August, when it was described in a GAF situation report which was signalled currently. A recognition that the Canadian drive towards Falaise was threatening to strangle Army Group B by closing its only escape route was apparent from an extraordinary Army Group B order that every tank and assault gun arriving from Germany, no matter for whom intended, was to be delivered to 5 Panzer Army. A similar air of emergency breathed through instructions to units in Paris to be on the alert for expected landings by the British 8 Airborne Division and against believing exaggerated rumours of Allied successes put about by French civilians.

This was the moment when Bradley halted Patton's northward thrust at Argentan (lest the violent closing of the trap between there and Falaise

cause the collision of allies as well as the capture of enemies), directing
him forward to the Seine instead, and when Eisenhower broadcast to the
troops to 'go flat out'.

Reference Notes

Introduction

xviii   the Admiralty in 1914; Patrick Beesly, *Room 40* (Hamish Hamilton, 1982), 4–7.

as early as 1916: John Ferris (ed.), *The British Army and Signals Intelligence during the First World War* (Army Records Society, 1992), 21.

xix   '. . . a legion of grandchildren': MME vi/1, 293.

appear to have survived: Aileen Clayton, *The Enemy Is Listening*, covers the RAF in the Battle of Britain and the Mediterranean down to 1943. Hugh Skillen, *Spies of the Airwaves*, deals with the army but leaves a great deal to be desired.

'were extremely small beer': Airey Neave, *Saturday at MI9* (Hodder & Stoughton, 1969), 68. The other classic of the subject is M. R. D. Foot and J. M. Langley, *MI9* (Bodley Head 1979).

xx   '. . . search for the truth': Andrew and Noakes, 226, 230–2.

xxi   '. . . whole truth too late': This wording comes from a private memorandum. Identically the same sense is to be found in WO 208/3075, composed by the same author in October 1945.

'. . . essence of the matter': ibid., 9.

xxii   '. . . the two cardinal virtues': *Leviathan*, part 1, ch. 13.

Colonel Dudley Clarke: No satisfactory account of Clarke and the work of his 'A' Force existed until the publication in 1946 of articles based on Clarke's 'A' Force War Diary by Mr H. O. Dovey in INS 11/4.

the whole Mediterranean theatre: Clarke's relationship with Wavell was completely informal at first. Formalisation came later, with the expansion of 'A' Force's responsibilities, and reached its peak when a special section, an offshoot of Colonel

Bevan's deception HQ in London, was attached to 21 Army
Group in Normandy and worked closely with Montgomery's
Chief Intelligence Officer.

xxiv would have been perpetuated: See Chapter 5.

the strategic air offensive: Webster and Frankland, iii.311.

Chapter 1: 1939: Thick Darkness Brooding

1 'early and good intelligence': Winston Churchill, *Marlborough* (1947
edn, Cassell) Book 2, Vol 4, p. 933. I am indebted to Dr Piers
Brendon, Keeper of the Archives, Churchill College, Cambridge,
for locating this reference for me.

3 capable of carrying them: The intelligence gathered and the
assessments made by all three services in the middle and late
1930s are studied in Wesley Wark, *The Ultimate Enemy*.

4 in the butler's pantry: Colville, 36.

'. . . a world of imagination': Ismay, 87, 84.

5 called the public: Lord Vansittart, *The Mist Procession* (Hutchinson,
1958), 399.

6 '. . . under control at once': E. O'Halpin, *Head of the Civil Service*
(Routledge, 1991), 205. Joad and Haldane quoted in Solly
Zuckerman, *From Apes to Warlords* (Hamish Hamilton, 1978), 114.

8 be ready for war: Fraser, *Shock*, 11.

the time of Munich: Watt, 20; Beesly, *Very Special Admiral*, 76; P.
Hennessy, *Whitehall* (Secker & Warburg, 1989), 92.

to fight against Germany: Watt, *How War Came* (Heinemann,
1989), 454; also Watt, in May.

9 were still going on: Watt, in May, 248. Soviet radio traffic had
remained unreadable since Baldwin let the cat out of the bag in
1927.

10 '. . . and drowned in whey': Jones, *Reflections*, 99.

'. . . what Germans were like': Vansittart, 430.

the Chiefs of Staff: Strong, 24, 36; D. Dilks (ed.), *The Diary of Sir
Alexander Cadogan* (Cassell, 1971), 158; C. M. Andrew, *Secret Service*
(Heinemann, 1985), 421.

12 for war against Germany: Watt, in May, 251.

His reports: FO 371/17695, 18822, 18840. I am much indebted
to Sir Peter Thorne for drawing my attention to them and to
Donald Lindsay's biography of his father, *Forgotten General* (Michael
Russell, 1987). Wark's account (*Ultimate Enemy*, 82–3) is insufficient.

13 of the British army: WO 190/283 and 32/4612. See J. P. Harris in INS 6.395–417.
German Military strength: Strong, 16.
13–14 in 1924, for instance: Bond, 67.
14 '... obstacle to military development': N. Dixon, *On the Psychology of Military Incompetence* (Cape, 1976), 115.
compulsory for many years: Slessor, 82–3; Jacob, 19; Harris, 24; B. Newton-Dunn, *Big Wing* (Airlife, 1992), 56. Lieutenant-General Jacob, who along with Hastings Ismay and Hollis formed Churchill's staff as Minister of Defence, and 'Bomber' Harris both went through Staff College about 1930. Jacob's biographer reports that Jacob thought the drag hunt 'archaic' and remarks, *à propos* the precedence of the horse over mechanisation, that 'for some time yet to come intimate contact with the internal combustion engine, with its association of oily spanners and dirty fingernails, would still be considered beyond the pale in fashionable circles'. Harris is rougher: the army would never take tanks seriously, he wrote, until they could eat hay and make noises like a horse.
brilliant teacher of tactics: M. Carver, *Harding of Petherton* (Weidenfeld & Nicolson, 1978), 39.
he warned me: Letter, 2 December 1985, and subsequent conversation.
land battle was discounted: Strong, 18.
'... pre-war inadequacy of training': ibid., 15.
15 '... army in peace time': Bond, 64; Mockler-Ferryman, 2; Cloake, *Templer*, 66; Strong, 34.
but no more: Scotland, 58.
the summer of 1939: Anthony Clayton: *Forearmed* (Brassey 1993), 65–6).
until spring 1940: Mockler-Ferryman, 104, 179.
16 '... most incompetent of men': Colville, 111.
'... which the post demanded': Fraser, *Shock*, 26.
'... could find no better': Colville, 273; Fraser, *Alanbrooke*, 297.
to their inherited beliefs: Dixon, 67, 152.
as soon as war came: Wark, 124.
17 '... will it be resisted': Dixon, 30.
'... unimaginative, impersonal and over-populated': Ismay, 68.
convoy across the Atlantic: Barnett, 44–6.
18 of German naval strategy: Watt, in May, 260.
of sound strategical appreciations: H. W. Richmond, *Naval Training*

(Oxford University Press, 1933), vi.2–3, 11, 35, 130.

19 expansion of the fleet: Ferris in INS 4.425, Wark, 148–50.

'. . . twenty years of peace': MacLachlan, 339.

20 for the rumour: ibid., 245–6.

had in fact used: BI i.105n.

'. . . from Cinderella into Princess': MacLachlan, 108.

22 200 tons between them: Watt, in May, 259.

'. . . was spent on buildings': Terraine, 91; Harris, *Bomber Offensive*, 46.

23 to collect essential intelligence: Wark, 76–7.

24 '. . . in equal measure': E. O'Halpin, *Head of the Civil Service* (Routledge, 1989), 247.

'. . . nothing of it': Vansittart, 397.

26 '. . . it can wait': Cadogan, 155.

27 '. . . our renowned foreign agents': Colville, 48, 121.

28 in spring 1944: Much of the information in the last three paragraphs supplied from personal knowledge by Sir Alexander Glen, to whom I am grateful. Dunderdale's obituary is in *The Times* of 16 November 1990 and the *Independent* of 28 November 1990. After the war Wolfson became Middle Eastern manager for British European Airways; he was killed in the first crash of a Comet aircraft over Elba in 1954. For Elliot, see his *Never Judge a Man by his Umbrella* (Michael Russell, 1991).

30 '. . . a melodramatic spy story': Admiral B. B. Scholfield, unpublished MS diary, kindly lent me by his daughter, Mrs Victoria Willis.

well aware of this: Robert Cecil, PA to Menzies, 1943–5, interview 19 June 1990.

'. . . intellectuals and university men': Watt, 443.

31 marked by intellectual rigour: Winterbotham, *Secret and Personal, The Ultra Secret* and taped memoirs in the Imperial War Museum.

32 to thoroughly 'amateur' rules: Numerous illustrations in Andrew, ch. 6.

'. . . were still standard issue': Cecil, ' "C's" War', in INS 1.183.

33 Dr Jones himself in 1955: See Jones, *Reflections*, 276–332.

of a German scientist: Jones, *Most Secret War*, 67–71, and *Reflections*, 265–350.

34 before December 1941: Kahn, in May, 476.

'. . . of the manure pile': F. Pogue, *George C. Marshall* (Macgibbon and Kee, 1964), i.133.

'. . . traditional language of regulations': ibid., 110.

35 '. . . without appreciation of significance': Quoted in R. W. Winks, *Cloak and Gown* (Morrow, 1967), 71–2.

in July 1941: Kahn, in May, 482–9.

participation in the Ultra programme: National Archives, Washington SRH 110; Bradley F. Smith, *The Ultra-Magic Deals* (Presidio, 1993); and Howe, 6–7.

Sigint material to field commanders: Strong, 226; Foot and Langley, 46.

36 '. . . occupied by civilian recruits': Parrish, 155.

'. . . to be entirely wrong': Ismay, 84.

Chapter 2: 1940–1941: First Rays of Light

39 '. . . operation of feeble counsel': H. Macmillan, *The Blast of War* (Macmillan, 1967), 59.

with a naval officer: Beesly, *Very Special Admiral*, 154, quoting MacLachlan.

'. . . whole thing is harebrained': Ismay, 119.

British Minister in Copenhagen: BI i.122.

40 to do the same: Horst Boog in INS 5.354.

'. . . the invasion of Norway': INS 1.117. At about the same time, the Admiralty refused to accept air photographs showing a destroyer with one of its four-inch guns mounted between the funnels, on the ground that this arrangement had been tried in the First World War and found unworkable. Officialdom was only convinced when a French photographer managed to photograph the vessel at sea-level.

in Copenhagen and Oslo: Ismay, 118.

46 an increase in traffic: BI i.137.

'. . . as soon as they're laid': Bartlett, 61; cf. 77, 89.

47 records before Dunkirk: Skillen prints some examples.

'. . . from *some* quarter': C. Richardson, *Flashback* (Kimber, 1985), 56–7.

beginning of May 1940: BI i.131.

49 HQs and communications problems: Mockler-Ferryman, 63.

'. . . four bottles of champagne': Entries for 2 and 3 May in Bartlett, 13, 17. On the Battle of France in general, see Haswell,

166–83; Skillen, ch. 3; BI i.143–9. A letter to me from Mr J. Broomfield dated 26 November 1990 added some details.

50 '. . . and modern shells': Churchill College Archives Centre, HNKY 10/9. I am indebted to Dr Eunan O'Halpin for bringing this document to my notice.

51 two years later: Babington-Smith, 21, 145; W. B. Eaton, *APIS: Soldiers with Stereo* (Intelligence Corps, 1978), 11, 14.

52 context of what *was*: Babington-Smith, 45, 56; Beesly; *Very Special Admiral*, 135.

53 part in the war: Babington-Smith, 134–5; MME i.335–8.

54 spring 1942: Babington-Smith, 71, 151; BI ii.34–9; personal knowledge.
in August and September: William Shirer, *Berlin Diary* (Sphere, 1970), 271–2, 363–4, 421, and passim.
'. . . on a Danish island' Powyss-Lybbe, 25–6.
'. . . the visual reports': Quoted Terraine, 272.

55 '. . . accept this report': Babington-Smith, 101.

56 '. . . would have been lost': Basil Collier, *Defence of the UK* (HMSO, 1957), 40.

57 '. . . swear words increased considerably': Clayton, 47, 49.

58 examples to the contrary: BI i.170, 178.
in early August: *The Ultra Secret*, 44, repeated Lewin, 83.
to the Ultra list: Gilbert, vi.849, Sebastian Cox in INS 5.432–3.

61 '. . . a quarter of the picture': BI i.524.
invasion had been lifted: BI i.159–90.

64 to a certainty: *Most Secret War*, 105.
'. . . had been so scathing': ibid., 169.

68 was sunk next day: Beesly, *Very Special Admiral*, 24–87, BI i.337–46; Barnett, 278–316. Estimates of *Bismarck*'s position during her voyage were greatly assisted by knowledge of her speed. This had already been calculated according to a formula originating at Medmenham and depending on theoretical work by Lord Kelvin, the nineteenth-century scientist. The formula used the wave-patterns of a vessel's wake to calculate its speed. Ultra showed when and where *Bismarck* would undertake her speed trials. Medmenham PR'd the trials. *Bismarck*'s speed was 31 knots.

The Admiralty had for some months refused to take any interest in the research which ended by providing this valuable piece of intelligence (Powys-Lybbe, 116–21).

Chapter 3: 1941–1943: A Brighter Prospect in the Mediterranean

72 the enemy's thinking: Dudley Clark's 'A' Force War Diary was
recently put into the PRO. It has been ably edited by H. O.
Dovey in INS 11/1 672–695, 12/2 69–90 and amplifies the
account in Howard, *British Intelligence*, vol 5.

73 would bar its path: BI i.219–21.

76 at odds with itself: Personal knowledge; BI i.271–3.

78 was to be avoided: Skillen, 128–9; Hunt, xv, and INS 6.270. The
Y records did not survive the evacuation.
of Wilson's own staff: KOTs 7, 12, 65, 85, 107, 108, 126; UMS
49–50.

79 fortnight before the event: Freyberg, 268; UMS 54–5. Hunt, *A
Don at War* (2nd ed. 1990).

80 from 17 to 20 May: OLs 267, 302, 334, 341, 370; UMS 55–6.

82 which followed have survived): Clayton, 157–8; OLs 497, 692,
715.

84 usually to be worked out: Skillen, 147–8.
numbers of the RAF: UMS 70–9.

86 they could use them: Clayton, 157.
ran Auchinleck's official *Despatch: London Gazette*, 15 January 1948.
in the wrong places: The German deception measures have only
recently come to light in an article by Dr Horst Boog of the
Militärgeschichtliches Forschungsamt, Freiburg, in INS 5.403.
UMS 98–9 should be amended accordingly.

86–7 meeting them in combat: UMS 97–100.

87 as long ago as 1895: Haswell, 136.

88 Second World War intelligence: MacLachlan, 342–6.
official history of deception: BI vol; v; M. Howard, *Strategic
Deception* (HMSO, 1990), 37. Cf. VMS 83.
only just escaping death: Carver, 74.

90 in quick-moving situations: Skillen, 163–6, is aridly uninformative
on Army Y. Clayton, 160–3, passes over air operations with
scarcely a mention of the ground fighting.
Westphal wrote later: Westphal, *Erinnerungen*, 137.

91 the spring of 1942: Carl Boyd in INS 2.304–5.

92 the end of May 1940: Churchill, *Second World War*, ii.119–20.

93 at all costs: John Erickson, in May, *Knowing One's Enemies*
(Princeton 1994) 419, and *The Road to Stalingrad* (1975), 58–77;
Churchill, iii.320. Barton Whaley, *Codename Barbarossa* (MIT, 1973)
was published four years before the release of Ultra and therefore

could not take account of most of the evidence in the next three paragraphs.

during the war: P. S. Milner-Barry, in INS 3.248–50; C. Andrew and O. Gordievsky. *KGB: The Inside Story* (1990), 249–50. Milner-Barry was a senior Ultra cryptographer at Bletchley Park, Gordievsky a senior serving officer of the KGB until 1985, when he defected to Great Britain.

'or hard to obtain': David Glantz, *Soviet Military Deception in World War II* (1989), xxxix.

94 and Chiefs of Staff: BI i.299.

95 was about to happen: In the absence of first-hand evidence (none of the translated decrypts can be consulted in the Public Record Office), the last few paragraphs draw heavily on BI i.429–86.

excellent service: David Kahn, *The Codebreakers* (London 1967), 473. See also H.-O. Behrendt, *Rommel's Intelligence in the Desert Campaign* (London 1985).

Ultra had shown: BI. ii.389n 233.

98 the end of July: MK 5812; Skillen, 175; UMS 117.

99 his adopted country's enemies: Hunt, 103; Skillen, 314.

was already becoming productive: R. Jenner and D. List, *The Long Range Desert Group* (1983), 5; Eaton, 20.

Alamein line in July: Carver, 125.

100 he himself had sent: Xan Fielding, *Hide and Seek* (1973 edn), 20–1.

101 by 50 per cent: BI v.36–44.

102 in Montgomery's hands: MKA's 2094, 2095; UMS 140–54.

strengthening its garrison: Hamilton, *Monty*, i.634.

103 '. . . going to use it': WO 3575, pp. 3–4.

105 would have to penetrate: Dr James Mark, interview 11 March 1991, and memorandum 'Intelligence at an Army HQ', dated 27 October 1942.

107 '. . . forces in the south': UMS 154–63; BI v.65–7; Skillen, 208–13; information from Sir Edgar Williams.

109 Mussolini accepted the inevitable: QT 5086, despatched at 0555/3; QT 5207, despatched 1111/4; QT 5340, despatched 2215/5.

111 on 5 November: QT 5265.

pass it over in silence: BI ii.435–9; Richardson 125–30; cf. Hamilton, ii.63–95.

117 the convoys had arisen: BI ii.478–9; INS 4.335–56.

118 watchers on neutral territory: BI ii.720–1; Jones, *Most Secret War*, 254–9. Powys-Lybbe, 124–8. Doubts about the practicability of infra-red technology were raised in INS 6.447–52. They were

confuted by Ralph Erskine in INS 12.110–127.

to London via MI6: Jones, *Reflections*, 226–7.

120 Vichy France: M.R.D. Foot: *SOE 1940–46* (London 1984); D. Howarth: *The Shetland Bus* (London 1951); Sir Brooks Richard: *Secret Flotillas. The Clandestine Sea Lines to France and French North Africa 1940–44* (London, HMSO 1996).

K. A. Merrick, *Flights of the Forgotten* (Arms and Armour, 1989) gives statistics of air operations but does not reveal their specific purpose.

supplies to Rommel's army: Rygor Slowikowski, *In the Secret Service: The Lighting of the Torch* (Windrush Press, 1988). See also Brooks Richards 347 sqq and 557–9, which describe Slowikowski's previous history.

122 last days of January: INS 2.274–90. PR does not escape similar strictures: Babington-Smith, 159–60, calls it 'chaotic' in the early days of TORCH.

123 Further similar evidence: UMS 189–91.

124 soon after the war: Papers lent me by Dr Mark; Mockler-Ferryman, 179.

'. . . not to be doing': Hunt, 149.

125 '. . . successfully in the field': INS 2.286.

125 now held the initiative: UMS 193–5.

128 the game of intelligence: Currer-Briggs in INS 2.285–6; Skillen, 282–9. For further Ultra details, see for instance UMS 186–209.

135 value of 'active' intelligence: Papers of Brigadier Maunsell, Head of Security Intelligence Middle East 1940–4, in the library of the Imperial War Museum (Documents section 20/30/1); BI iv.144–57; articles by Mr Hugh Dovey, who served in a Field Security section 1941–5, in INS 4.357–73, 800–12 and INS 6.418–46; also interview 7 November 1990. I am indebted to Mr Dovey for drawing my attention to the Maunsell papers.

Chapter 4: 1939–1945: Ten-Tenths Cloud Cover: Intelligence and Bomber Command

136 '. . . see a way through': Gilbert, vi.665–6.

137 '. . . Air Force can win it': Terraine, 260.

was almost 150,000: Figures from Terraine, 97, 146, 267; Harvey, 192.

139 at this time: However, Beesly (*Very Special Intelligence*, 100) talks

somewhat airily of 'the AOCs of Coastal, Bomber and Fighter Commands and their immediate subordinates' being on the list of those entitled to see Ultra. I have found no evidence to support this.

139–40 the rumours about them: Jones, *Most Secret War*, 332–3.

142 the coast of Normandy: ibid., 233–49; G. Millar, *The Bruneval Raid* (Bodley Head, 1974).

145 '... precision bombing at night': Webster and Frankland, i.208, quoted Terraine, 108.

146 which were their target: Terraine, 268, 274.
the point aimed at: Harris 73; Terraine, 267; Harvey, 67.
of British bombing raids: BI ii.257.

147 military power on land: Gilbert, vi.655–6.
'... is pitifully small': ibid., vi.850, 881.

148 'this method of attack': ibid., vi.1205.
'... an end by itself': Saward, 209, 223.

149 '... to have been achieved': Terraine, 292–3.

150 on the aircraft industry: BI ii.265–6.
month's production was lost: Webster and Frankland i.486; BI ii.265; Harvey, 111.

151 achieved maximum production capacity: Webster and Frankland castigate this unwarranted assumption with great severity at i.476 and iii.302.
and the transportation system: Saward, 141.

152 an army of occupation: Terraine, 290–1.
'... of the industrial workers': ibid., 474.
was 'the only way': Gilbert, vii.179.
'... and paralyse the population': ibid., vii.259.
than to accept defeat: Webster and Frankland, ii.255.

153 paid to the report: Zuckerman, 141–5, 354; Harvey, 133, 143, 162. See also Webster and Frankland, ii.247, 255–7, commenting adversely on JIC reports of 1943.

154 facts were almost irrelevant: BI iii/1.300, 307.
'... opposition to the regime': BI iii, 300, 307.
'... the other two services': Bryant, *Triumph in the West*, 190.

155 not open to inspection: BI iii/2.504n.

156 '... are not really useful': Jones, *Most Secret War*, 169.
'... seen in any photograph': BI iii/1.297.

157 account of the circumstances: Harris, 196–200.
'... lead directly to disaster': Tedder, 504, cf. Harris, 192–3.

158 so much invaluable information: See, for instance, BI ii.308;iii/2.

Appendix 21.

'Soldier at Bomber Command': Charles Carrington, *Soldier at Bomber Command* (Leo Cooper, 1987).

159 '... debate of the war': Barnett, 476.

'... we lose the war': CAB 69/4, quoted in ibid., 440, 458 and BI ii.263.

160 'entrails of his command': Terraine, 470.

161 on 4 July 1944: Jones, *Most Secret War*, 426–7.

163 had given further information: The last two paragraphs draw heavily on relevant chapters in Jones, *Most Secret War*, and BI iii/1 and iii/2.

Bomber Command's cardinal weakness: Hastings, 251.

164 '... information about German industry': Harris, 264.

'... flow of essential supplies': Slessor, 580.

was argued by Harris: Harris, 265–6.

164–5 in September 1943: BI iii/1.295; Albert Speer, *Inside the Third Reich* (Weidenfeld & Nicolson, 1970), 278–9.

165 the entire British army: BI iii/2.515.

86 out of 161: Terraine, 696–700.

the previous five years: VW i.487; cf. Harvey, 192.

'... resistance is fatally weakened': GS iv.263.

166 US Strategic Air Force: BI iii/2.277.

the commander of USSTAF: Diane T. Putney, *Ultra and the Army Air Force in WWII: ... An interview with Col. Lewis F. Powell* (Office of the Air Force History, 1987), 34–41.

167 Bomber Command's actions closely: e.g. KVs 2116, 2131 in late April.

it is said: BI iii/2.782; cf. 977–80.

which could be cited: For instance, fighter moves KVs 6647, 6989, 6997, 7228; raid damage reports KVs 7240, 7473; flak locations KV 7725 – all in the first week after the invasion.

supplies and duty journeys: KV 6673.

168 he recalled later: Putney, 34–41.

'... can destroy with Oboe': BI iii/2. 503.

'... irrefutable evidence of Sigint': BI iii/2.510.

169 '... to render Germany defenceless': Hansard 1945–6, vol. 420, cols 960–6.

170 '... taking this too far': Gilbert, vii.1257.

had so long supported: Gilbert, vii.437.

'... for overseas invasion stand': ibid., 689.

171 '... across the world': Tedder, 516–33.

Chapter 5: 1941–1945: Shadow and Sunlight Over the Atlantic

176 the battleship *Deutschland*: Beesly, *Very Special Intelligence*, 17.
177 were left unsatisfied: Beesly, *Very Special Admiral*, 155; BI ii.137.
No evidence survives to show whether naval information
provided by Yellow was operationally useful.
179 danger to British trade: Barnett, 45.
'. . . crass error of judgement': ibid., 253.
180 thirty there at once: Rohwer, *Convoy Battles*, 24.
200 were regularly operating: Terraine, 236; Barnett, 271, 594.
181–2 merchant ships were lost: BI ii.170–1.
182 '. . . of worry and anxiety': Rohwer in Andrew and Noakes,
283–4.
until spring 1943: Terraine, 442.
in August 1942: Ibid., 433.
187 half of the total: Figures from BI, Barnett and Roskill.
188 '. . . may not be forthcoming': Gilbert vi.936.
'. . . against the stream': ibid., 1091.
is hard to understand: GS iii/1.12.
191 a month's sick leave: Beesly, *Very Special Intelligence*, 153–5.
193 end of the war: BI ii.Appendix 19.
194 do their own 'killing': This seems entirely to have escaped the
notice of U-Boat Command until the middle of 1944, and to
have led to a neglect of counter-measures which might have
prolonged the U-boats' mastery of the Atlantic. The possibility
that Allied ships were equipped with HF/DF was considered as
early as August 1941 but dismissed; not until June 1944 was a
warning that most Allied vessels carried HF/DF issued to U-boat
captains. See the article 'U-Boats, Homing Signals and HFDF' by
Ralph Erskine in INS 2.324–30.
195 Naval Cipher No. 3: BI ii.179.
according to one calculation: Rohwer in Andrew and Noakes, 279.
200 '. . . all points at once': Barnett, 396, quoting ADM 205/10 of 25
August 1941.
203 whole year by extrapolation: Barnett, 597–8.
204 in full spate again: BI ii.750; Rohwer in Andrew and Noakes, 283.
205 never before remotely approached: BI ii.570; Barnett, 605–8; P.
W. Gretton, *Convoy Escort Commander*, Cassell, 1964.
had begun war cruises: BI ii.566.
206 three million in 1943: Roskill, iv.479.
less than six months: Beesly, *Very Special Intelligence*, 203.

209 and been more costly: ibid., 184, 255.
forefront of his mind: Rohwer, *Convoy Battles*, 198.
view on this occasion: Rohwer in Andrew and Noakes, 269, 292.
210 Atlantic conflict: the last three quotations are from BI ii, 549,
Andrew and Noakes 217–8, and Barnett 602 respectively.

Chapter 6: 1943–1945: Clear Skies in Italy, Storm Over the Balkans

211 German Commander-in-Chief: KOs 496, 525; UMS 322.
212 '. . . know it was Sicily': Montagu, *Man Who Never Was*, 24.
'. . . we know it's Greece': INS 2.70. The reference in UMS 227
was incorrectly printed.
213 were being taken: ML 1055; UMS 222–5.
the Balkans via Greece: BI v.33–97.
a new Army Group: UMS 242.
216 rather than by radio: OKW/KTB iii.1449.
219 has since been re-emphasised: UMS 255; BI iii/1.172–4.
enemy was fully accomplished: MME vi/3.334–5, 351–2; CTA
535.
223 but never to SOE: information from the late Colonel Rodney
Dennys, senior SIS officer Cairo, 1942–5, 20 April 1993.
225 was withdrawn from SOE: BI iii/1.141n., 502, v.13–14. Basil
Davidson, *Special Operations Europe* (Gollancz, 1981), 116, says that
the decrypts Keble showed him were of SD traffic. On several
grounds, however, they are more likely to have been ISOS.
'. . . flood of new information': BI v.47.
and the JIC: Letter dated 7 July 1975 from the Hon. Ewen
Montagu, Judge-Advocate-General of the Fleet 1945–73, formerly
of the Naval Intelligence Division, kindly communicated to me
by Sir Alexander Glen, to whom it was addressed. BI ii.668. I
am grateful to Mr Nicholas Elliott for valuable contributory
information. A conversation with Dr Mark Wheeler started a
profitable train of thought on this complicated matter.
the case in Cairo: Information from SOE adviser, FCO, based
on SOE HQ file 'Yugoslavia: Summary of Guerrilla Warfare and
Sabotage'.
226 Early in January: Davidson, 116.
227 collaborating with the Germans: H. Neubacher, *Sonderauftrag Südost
1940–1945* (Munterschmidt Verlag, Göttingen, 2nd edn) 152–3,
165–7). I am indebted to Mr Hilary King for bringing this book

to my attention.

228 '. . . our most dangerous enemy': OKW/KTB iii.1252–5.
same order of magnitude: JP 6919. Frank McLynn, *Fitzroy Maclean* (Murray, 1992), 158. Fitzroy Maclean, *Eastern Approaches* (Cape, 1949) has '150,000 or more'. SOE Cairo estimated 180,000 (McLynn, as above).

229 divisions of poor quality: See, for instance, Gilbert, vi.435; OKW/KTB iii.1161.

231 and 3 Panzer Grenadier: Skillen, 351–2; Howe, 69; BI iii/1.182.

233 abbreviation of *Abteilung*, 'detachment'): Hunt, 246.
at that moment: OKW/KTB iv.124–5. See also Siegfried Westphal, Kesselring's Chief of Staff, *The German Army in the West*, (Cassell, 151).

234 via Alexander's HQ: P. Tompkins, *A Spy in Rome* (New York, 1968); Carlo d'Este, *Fatal Decision: Anzio and the Battle for Rome* (HarperCollins, 1991).

235 the British CIGS, Brooke: Fraser, *Alanbrooke*, 404.
levels of strategic planning: UMS 268–72.

237 this degree of safety: Owen Chadwick, *Britain and the Vatican During the Second World War* (Cambridge, 1986); D. Alvarez, 'Vatican Intelligence Capabilities in the Second World War', in INS 6.593–607.
fortifications to be completed: KV 9843. Hitler's order was intercepted on 17 June but not decrypted until ten days later. It is interesting but fruitless to speculate whether, had it been possible to decrypt it at once, the decision about ANVIL might have gone the other way. The point is briefly discussed in UMS 389–91.

238 '. . . have to be responsible': XLs 6253, 6919; GS v.356.

242 months of the war: This section relies heavily on conversations with Mr Hugh Dovey, formerly of Field Security, on his article 'The Unknown War: Field Security in Italy 1943–45' in INS 3.285–311, and on the unpublished record of his war service by Mr Donald Gurrey, formerly of Counter-Intelligence, 'Across the Lines: German Intelligence and Sabotage Operations in Italy, 1943–1945', a copy of which Mr Gurrey kindly lent me.
by April 1944: Kesselring, *Memoirs*, 245.

243 more quickly available sources: For more detail on this section see, for instance, Charles Macintosh, *From Cloak to Dagger* (Kimber, 1982), Davidson, *Special Operations Europe* and J. G. Beevor, *SOE: Recollections and Reflections, 1940–1945* (Bodley Head,

1981).

244 'Reich fortress' in Austria: UMS 306–23, 385–91.

Chapter 7: 1944–1945: Set Fair in the West, Then Autumn Showers

247 '. . . in any foreseeable future'. Bradley F. Smith: *The Ultra – Magic Deals* (Presidio 1993) 152.
'. . . which have just met': NA SRH.110, pp. 056–7, dated June 1945.

248 had 'come of age': Smith describes the background to the Anglo-American agreement. T. Parrish, *The Ultra Americans* (Stein and Day, New York 1986) is confined to the Americans at Bletchley Park, and is more discursive.

249 arrive at its destination: Westphal, *German Army in the West*, 172.

253 in preparing for OVERLORD: Richard Collier, *Ten Thousand Eyes* (Collins, 1958); Jock Haswell, *The Intelligence and Deception of the D-Day Landings* (Batsford, 1979); Foot, *Resistance*, 24, 242.

257 supplies they would need: KV 3763; UWest 50–51.

258 since January 1941: Jones, *Reflections*, 134.
to the best advantage: Smith, 256.

260 '. . . been stripped of troops'; Speer, *Inside the Third Reich*, 354–5.
for its schemes: See my article 'Ultra and the Need to Know' in INS 4.482–502, which is unfortunately marred by several misprints and by too little consideration (which I now regret) of ISOS and ISK.

262 it has been said: BI v.191. On Josephine, see Horst Boog in INS 4.137–60; and Peter Tennant, *Touchlines of War* (University of Hull Press, 1992), 148.
held at the Führerhauptquartier: OKW/KTB iv.1798.

263 are far from clear: It is notable that Professor Howard's official history (BI v) leaves many questions unanswered.
neither Masterman nor Howard: John Masterman, *The Double Cross System* (Yale University Press, 1972); Howard, *Strategic Deception*.

265 and March 1944: BI v.213–15; Nicholas Elliot, *Never Judge a Man by His Umbrella* (Michael Russell, 1991), 132–9.

267 nervousness were encouragingly numerous: Full references to the part played by Ultra in the western campaign of 1944–5 are given in UWest. It has therefore seemed unnecessary to repeat them here. They are given here only when it seems desirable to

draw attention to particular points, or when they refer to matters outside the scope of UWest. See Appendix VII.

274 end of the year: GS v.401; Gilbert vii.944; BI iii/2.369.
muster for the purpose: WO 219/1933.
afternoon of the 5th: XLs 9819, 9246.
'. . . will collapse before then': GS v.402.

275 directed towards the Ruhr: Hamilton iii.4.

278 was not taken seriously: BI iii/2.384.

281 But which?: In connexion with intelligence before the German Ardennes offensive, it may be of interest to note that BI iii/2 (published 1988), which was written with access to far more sources than were open to me when I was writing *Ultra in the West* (published 1979) arrives at substantially the same conclusions as I but makes no acknowledgement either of my nine-year priority or of the fact that my conclusions were novel when they appeared.

282 as Portal had demanded: There is an ironical element in Strong's involvement with intelligence about the Ardennes offensive. He did not foresee it – though he later implied that he had done so – and he is said to have been severely shaken when it occurred. He had succeeded Mockler-Ferryman when the latter was dismissed after Kasserine, and soon gained influence over Eisenhower. Like his predecessor, he faced an Ultra puzzle. But Strong had one advantage, and failed to use it. The interval of three months between the first report of Sixth Panzer Army in September and the German advance on 16 December gave him time to reflect on the Ultra signals at leisure and seek further evidence, whereas Mockler-Ferryman had only a day or two and no means of securing further enlightenment. Yet Mockler-Ferryman was dismissed, but Strong survived – to make another mistake over the National Redoubt (see p. 283).
the higher command's intentions: BI iii/2.418–19, 429.

285 raids on (unspecified) targets: William Casey, *The Secret War against Hitler* (Simon & Schuster, 1989), 185–7.

286 a wildly incorrect deduction: Casey, 202–5, writes that one of his intelligence teams found no sign of preparations for serious resistance and 'did its best to demolish the myth' but 'found no one who would listen'. A little retrospective credibility was lent to it by at least two later discoveries: 750 bars of Belgian gold, captured in 1940 and since stored in Berlin, were taken to Munich in April 1945 but moved south to the Berchtesgaden

area in early May (Ian Sayer: *Nazi Gold* (1984) and *Times* 28 July 1997); Wing Commander Oscar Oeser of Hut 3 found a command train and a large number of Enigma machines at a deserted railway station in the same area, also in May (Ronald Lewin: *Ultra Goes to War* (Hutchinson 1978) 362–3).

286 '. . . Bavaria, not Norway': Peter Thorne in INS 7.309.

Appendix II: The Controversy Over Crete

294 Admiral Cunningham later wrote: Cunningham, *Sailors Odyssey*, 378.

when the parachutists landed: Gilbert, vi.1086.

'. . . easily than he can': ibid., 1088.

'. . . all aid you can': ibid., 1096; Cunningham, 378.

Appendix III: Harris and Intelligence

297 '. . . mine-laying of this Command': ADM 223/209, quoted in BI iii/1.242–3.

'. . . done to ordinary potential': BI iii/1.547–8 prints the decrypt.

Select Bibliography

Cited by Initials

BI	*British Intelligence in the Second World War*. 6 vols. 1979–90.
GS	*Grand Strategy*. 6 vols. HMSO. 1954–72.
INS	*Intelligence and National Security*, a quarterly historical journal.
MME	*The Mediterranean and Middle East*. 6 vols. 1956–84.
UMS	*Ultra and Mediterranean Strategy, 1941–45*. Ralph Bennett, Hamish Hamilton, 1989.
UWEST	*Ultra in the West*. Ralph Bennett, Hutchinson, 1979.
VW	*Victory in the West*, 2 vols. 1963, 1968.

Other Books

C. Andrew and J. Noakes (eds). *Intelligence and International Relations*. Exeter University Press, 1979.

C. Babington-Smith. *Evidence in Camera*. Chatto & Windus, 1957.

C. Barnett. *Engage the Enemy More Closely*. Hodder & Stoughton, 1991.

P. Beesly. *Very Special Intelligence*. Hamish Hamilton, 1977.

——. *Very Special Admiral*. Hamish Hamilton, 1980.

B. Bond. *British Military Policy Between Two World Wars*. Oxford University Press, 1980.

A. Bryant. *The Turn of the Tide*. Collins, 1957.

——. *Triumph in the West*. Collins, 1957.

A. Clayton. *The Enemy Is Listening*. Hutchinson, 1980.

J. Colville. *The Fringes of Power: Downing Street Diaries 1939–1955*. Hodder & Stoughton, 1985.

I. C. B. Dear and M. R. D Foot (eds). *The Oxford Companion to the Second World War*. Oxford University Press, 1995.

M. R. D. Foot. *Resistance*. Eyre Methuen, 1976.

——. *S.O.E. 1940–1946.* BBC, 1984. (For S.O.E. see also P. Wilkinson and J. B. Astle. *Gubbins and SOE* (Leo Cooper, 1993) and P. Wilkinson *Foreign Fields* (I.B. Tauris 1997).

D. Fraser. *Alanbrooke.* Collins, 1982.

——. *And We Shall Shock Them.* Hodder & Stoughton, 1983.

M. Gilbert. *Winston S. Churchill.* Vols vi, vii. Heinemann, 1983, 1986.

N. Hamilton. *Monty.* 3 vols. Hamish Hamilton, 1981, 1983, 1986.

A. Harris. *Bomber Offensive.* Collins, 1947.

M. Harvey. *The Allied Bomber War.* Spellmount, 1992.

M. Hastings. *Bomber Command.* Michael Joseph, 1979.

J. Haswell. *British Military Intelligence.* Weidenfeld & Nicolson, 1973.

G. E. Howe. *American Signal Intelligence.* US National Security Agency, 1980.

D. Hunt. *A Don at War.* Kimber, 1966.

H. Ismay. *Memoirs.* Heinemann, 1960.

R. V. Jones. *Most Secret War.* Hamish Hamilton, 1978.

——. *Reflections on Intelligence.* Heinemann, 1989.

C. B. MacDonald. *The Battle of the Bulge.* Weidenfeld & Nicolson, 1984.

D. MacLachlan. *Room 39: Naval Intelligence in Action, 1939–1945.* Weidenfeld & Nicolson, 1965.

E. R. May. *Knowing One's Enemies.* Princeton U.P., 1984.

C. E. Mockler-Ferryman. *Military Intelligence Organisation.* 1982.

T. Parrish. *The Ultra Americans.* Stein & Day, 1986.

U. Powys-Lybbe. *The Eye of Intelligence.* Kimber, 1983.

J. Rohwer. *Critical Convoy Battles of March 1943.* 1977.

S. W. Roskill. *The War at Sea,* 4 vols. HMSO, 1954–61.

R. Saundby. *Air Bombardment.* Chatto & Windus, 1961.

D. Saward. *Bomber Harris.* Sphere, 1984.

A. P. Scotland. *The London Cage.* Evans, 1957.

H. Skillen. *Spies of the Airwaves.* Privately printed, 1989.

J. Slessor. *The Central Blue.* Cassell, 1956.

Bradley F. Smith. *The Ultra – Magic Deals.* Presidio, 1993.

D. Stafford, *Churchill and Secret Service.* John Murray, 1997.

K. Strong. *Intelligence at the Top.* Cassell, 1968.

A. Tedder. *With Prejudice.* Cassell, 1966.

J. Terraine. *The Right of the Line: The RAF 1939–1945.* Hodder & Stoughton, 1985.

W. Wark. *The Ultimate Enemy.* Cornell University Press, 1985.

D. Cameron Watt. *How War Came.* Heinemann, 1989.

C. Webster and N. Frankland. *The Strategic Air Offensive Against Germany.* 1961.

Main Events 1939–1945

1939

1 September	Germans invade Poland
3 September	Britain declares war on Germany

1940

10 May	Germans invade France, Belgium and Holland
10 June	Italy declares war on Britain
23 June	Capitulation of France
August–September	Battle of Britain
13 September	Italians invade Egypt
7 December	British advance against Italians begins
Winter 1940–1	Night riads on Britain: the Blitz

1941

21 January	British capture Tobruk
6 February	Italians annihilated at Beda Fomm
12 February	Rommel arrives in Tripoli
7 March	British troops land in Greece
28 March	Battle of Cape Matapan: British defeat Italian fleet
30 March	Rommel attacks in Cyrenaica
6 April	Germans invade Jugoslavia and Greece
12 April	Tobruk invested
29 April	British evacuate Greece
20 May	Germans attack Crete
31 May	British evacuate Crete
8 June	British and Free French invade Syria
22 June	Germans invade Russia

1 July	Auchinleck replaces Wavell as Commander-in-Chief Middle East
11 July	Vichy French surrender in Syria
14 August	Atlantic Charter signed
2 September	Eighth Army established
16 September	British and Russians occupy Persia
18 November	CRUSADER: British offensive in Cyrenaica
26 November	Ritchie replaces Cunningham in command of Eighth Army
7 December	Japanese raid on Pearl Harbor; Germany declares war on United States
8 December	German offensive halted outside Moscow

1942

21 January	Rommel's counter-attack in Cyrenaica begins
15 February	Fall of Singapore
26 May	Rommel's attack at Gazala begins
4 June	Battle of Midway
21 June	Fall of Tobruk
25 June	Auchinleck takes over direct command of Eighth Army
30 June	Rommel halted at Alamein
8 August	Churchill in Cairo; Alexander and Montgomery appointed Commander-in-Chief Middle East and commander of Eighth Army, respectively
19 August	Dieppe raid
31 August	Battle of Alam Halfa
September	Russian offensives at Moscow and Leningrad
25 September	Hitler dismisses Halder as Chief of Staff, OKH
23 October	Battle of Alamein begins
3 November	Rommel's retreat from Alamein begins
8 November	TORCH: Allied landings in North Africa
23 November	Eighth Army reaches Agheila
13 December	Rommel evacuates Agheila

1943

14 January	Casablanca Conference
23 January	Eighth Army captures Tripoli
30 January	Dönitz replaces Raeder as Commander-in-Chief German navy
31 January	German surrender at Stalingrad
19 February	German attack at Kasserine
6 March	Battle of Medenine
20 March	Eighth Army attacks the Mareth Line
6 April	Battle of Wadi Akarit
11 May	Second Washington Conference (Trident)
13 May	German surrender in Tunisia
23 May	First British liaison officer parachuted to Tito; Dönitz withdraws U-boats from the Atlantic
10 July	HUSKY: Allied landing in Sicily
12 July	ZITADELLE: German offensive at Kursk abandoned; Russian offensive at Orel begins
25 July	Mussolini arrested
17 August	Quebec Conference (Quadrant); Axis resistance in Sicily ends
3 September	BAYTOWN: British landing at Reggio
9 September	AVALANCHE: Allied landing at Salerno; surrender of Italy
15 September	British occupy Cos and Leros
25 September	Russians capture Smolensk
1 October	Allies enter Naples
4 October	Germans recapture Cos
6 November	Russians capture Kiev
16 November	Germans recapture Leros
22 November	Cairo Conference, first stage (Sextant)
1 December	Tehran Conference (Eureka)
3 December	Cairo Conference, second stage

1944

22 January	SHINGLE: Allied landing at Anzio
6 March	Russian offensive in Ukraine begins
18 March	Germans occupy Hungary
11 May	DIADEM: Allied offensive in Italy

23 May	Anzio bridgehead and main front join up
25 May	RÖSSELSPRUNG: German raid on Tito's HQ at Drvar
3 June	Tito flown to Vis
4 June	Fall of Rome
6 June	OVERLORD: Allied landing in Normandy
20 July	Attempt on Hitler's life
4 August	Allies enter Florence
5 August	Russians outside Warsaw
13–20 August	Battle of the Falaise pocket
20 August	Paris freed
25 August	OLIVE: Allied assault on the Gothic Line
4 September	Antwerp captured
17 September	MARKET GARDEN: the Arnhem attack
20 October	Russians and Partisans enter Belgrade
16 December	German attack in Ardennes

1945

4 February	Yalta Conference (Argonaut)
13 February	Russians capture Budapest
23 March	Allies cross the Rhine
9 April	Allied offensive in Italy
12 April	Death of Roosevelt
13 April	Russians capture Vienna
25 April	Russians and Americans meet at Torgau
29 April	German surrender in Italy
30 April	Hitler commits suicide
7 May	German surrender in northern Europe
17 July	Potsdam Conference
6 and 9 August	Atomic bombs dropped on Japan
14 August	Surrender of Japan

Abbreviations

AA	Anti Aircraft
Abwehr	German equivalent (approximately) of the British Secret Intelligence Service
ADM	Admiralty
ADGB	Air Defence of Great Britain
AFHQ	Allied Force Headquarters
AOC	Air Officer Commanding
APIS	Army Photographic Interpretation Section
ARP	Air Raid Precautions
BEF	British Expeditionary Force
'C'	Chief of SIS
CAB	Cabinet
CAS	Chief of the Air Staff
CCS	Combined Chiefs of Staff (Anglo-US)
CI	Counter-Intelligence
CIGS	Chief of the Imperial General Staff (in effect, head of the British army)
COS	Chief of Staff
COSSAC	Chief of Staff to the Supreme Commander (Designate)
CSDIC	Combined Services Detailed Interrogation Centre
D/F	Direction-finding (radio)
DMI	Director of Military Intelligence
DNI	Director of Naval Intelligence
DSO	Defence Security Officer
FO	Foreign Office
FUSAG	Notional 1 US Army Group
GAF	German Air Force
GC&CS	Government Code and Cipher School
GCHQ	Government Communications Headquarters

GHQ	General Headquarters
GOC	General Officer Commanding (commanding general)
INS	*Intelligence and National Security*
IO	Intelligence Officer
ISK	Intelligence Service Knox (decrypts of Abwehr Enigma transmissions)
ISOS	Intelligence Service Oliver Strachey (decrypts of Abwehr hand-cipher transmissions)
ISTD	Inter-Services Topographical Department
JIC	Joint Intelligence Committee
LCS	London Controlling Section (deception)
LRDG	Long Range Desert Group
MEIC	Middle East Intelligence Centre
MEW	Ministry of Economic Warfare
MI5	The Counter Intelligence Service
MI6	Another name for SIS (q.v.)
M/T	Motor transport
NA	National Archives, Washington
NID	Naval Intelligence Division
OIC	Operational Intelligence Centre (Admiralty)
OKH	Supreme Command of the Army
OKL	Supreme Command of the Air Force
OKM	Supreme Command of the Navy
OKW	Supreme Command of the Armed Forces
OKW/KTB	OKW War Diary
OSS	Office of Strategic Services (US)
PI	Photographic Interpretation
PR	Photographic Reconnaissance
PRO	Public Record Office, London
PRU	Photographic Reconnaissance Unit
RAF	Royal Air Force
RN	Royal Navy
R/T	Radio Telephony
SD	Sicherheitsdienst
SIME	Security Intelligence Middle East
SHAEF	Supreme Headquarters Allied Expeditionary Force
Sigint	Signals intelligence (the general term for the processes of interception, analysis and decryption and the intelligence they produced)
SIS	Secret Intelligence Service

SOE	Special Operations Executive
USAAF	US Army Air Force
USSTAF	US Strategic Air Force
Wehrmacht	German Armed Forces
WO	War Office
W/T	Wireless telegraphy
Y	The interception, analysis and decryption of wireless traffic in low- and medium-grade codes and ciphers. The term 'low-grade' refers to the degree of security provided by a code or cipher and does not imply that the traffic in it was either unimportant or easy to break and interpret.

Index

Figures in italics refer to maps.